Gender and Education

Gender and Education

An Encyclopedia

Volume II

Edited by
Barbara J. Bank

Sara Delamont and Catherine
Marshall, Associate Editors

Westport, Connecticut
London

Library of Congress Cataloging-in-Publication Data

Gender and education : an encyclopedia / edited by Barbara J. Bank ; associate editors Sara Delamont and
  Catherine Marshall.
     p. cm.
  Includes bibliographical references and index.
  ISBN-13: 978–0–313–33343–9 (set : alk. paper)
  ISBN-13: 978–0–313–33344–6 (vol 1 : alk. paper)
  ISBN-13: 978–0–313–33345–3 (vol 2 : alk. paper)
1. Educational equalization–Encyclopedias. 2. Women–Education–Encyclopedias. 3. Sex discrimination in
education–Encyclopedias. I. Bank, Barbara J. II. Delamont, Sara, 1947- III. Marshall, Catherine, 1946-
LC213.G425 2007
370.8203—dc22   2007023758

British Library Cataloguing in Publication Data is available.

Library of Congress Catalog Card Number: 2007023758
ISBN-13: 978–0–313–33343–9 (set)
ISBN-13: 978–0–313–33344–6 (vol 1)
ISBN-13: 978–0–313–33345–3 (vol 2)

First published in 2007

Praeger Publishers, 88 Post Road West, Westport, CT 06881
An imprint of Greenwood Publishing Group, Inc.
www.praeger.com

Printed in the United States of America

The paper used in this book complies with the
Permanent Paper Standard issued by the National
Information Standards Organization (Z39.48–1984).

10 9 8 7 6 5 4 3 2 1

Contents

Part VI

Gender Constructions and Achievements in the Extracurriculum

Overview

The extracurriculum consists of school-sponsored and school-recognized organizations and activities that are not considered to be part of the official curriculum. As the titles of the essays in this section indicate, in contemporary educational institutions, particularly in the United States, these organizations and activities include academic, arts, and service clubs, sports, cheerleading, fraternities, sororities, service learning programs, student government, and women's centers. Some of these activities and organizations, such as academic clubs, student government, and interschool or intercollegiate athletics, are officially sponsored by schools or by institutions of higher education. Some of these officially sponsored organizations, like women's centers, were initiated primarily by students, but others, like honors societies, were initiated by faculty or administrators. Other activities and organizations are officially recognized and regulated, but not sponsored, by the schools, colleges, and universities in which they exist. Included among these would be fraternities and sororities as well as newer, student-initiated organizations for which gaining official recognition usually means that they can meet in a school or campus building and sometimes also that they receive funding from the student activity fees paid to that educational institution. Organizations of this latter type are often political or religious in nature, and, because they are controversial, educational institutions go to great effort to indicate that they are not "sponsoring" such activities, merely allowing them to exist, meet, and publicize themselves in school or on campus.

There also are activities and organizations that seek official recognition, but have not yet achieved it. Groups advocating on behalf of equal treatment for gays, lesbians, bisexuals, and transgendered people sometimes fall into this category, although in some schools and in many colleges and universities such groups are officially recognized. And, on some campuses and in many secondary schools, either they do not exist at all or they are treated as peer groups and denied any official support.

Outside of the United States, educational institutions are far less likely to sponsor or even give official recognition to a plethora of extracurricular activities and student clubs. At the university level, these activities and clubs are likely to be sponsored by student unions or associations that often own their own buildings in which extracurricular activities and club meetings take place. These student unions or associations generally have their own budgets and considerably more autonomy than student governments in the

United States. Neither universities nor secondary schools have the elaborate, expensive school-sponsored athletic programs common in the United States. Indeed, many of the extracurricular activities common to U.S. schools are either unknown in other countries or are considered leisure-time activities unrelated to schooling. The reasons for many of these international differences can be found in the history of how and why the extracurriculum developed in the United States.

Historically, many of the activities and organizations that are now considered to be part of the official extracurriculum of U.S. universities were initiated by students, often in rebellion against the academic emphases of the faculty. These activities and organizations included athletic programs and contests, "school" newspapers, debating clubs, fraternities, sororities, and other social clubs. They evolved on college campuses, especially at the male-only institutions, throughout the eighteenth and nineteenth centuries as ways for students to gain some control over their own status systems, independent of the faculty. Whereas the faculty considered the status of students to parallel their academic performances, the students judged each other on the basis of other skills, such as the writing and speaking talents, athletic prowess, and social skills they exhibited in the extracurriculum. To many students, the activities and organizations of the extracurriculum were more important than the classes in which they were enrolled, many of which were seen as irrelevant not only to future careers but also to life more generally. Not surprisingly, their differences in emphasis led to many conflicts between students and faculty, some of which resulted in quite violent rebellions of male students against faculty rules and regulations.

In the United States, these rebellions date back to the colonial period and occurred on almost all campuses in the first half of the nineteenth century. Although the reasons for them were often campus specific, underlying all of them was a struggle for power. Many campus riots resulted from an unwillingness of faculty to entertain grievances from students, a refusal the students interpreted as an unjust and unreasonable and authoritarian exercise of power. Faculty efforts to retain their authority and power took different forms. Until the latter part of the nineteenth century, college heads and the faculty they represented were generally determined to keep students in their place, viewing their rebellions largely as results of immaturity and bad judgment.

Some colleges, especially those founded in the early decades of the twentieth century, tried to prevent the extracurriculum from developing on their campuses, stressing the importance of hard work in the academic curriculum and telling potential students not to attend unless they planned to be serious about their studies. Other colleges had been unable to stop the extracurriculum from developing in the nineteenth century, but instead of continuing to fight with the students, they began in the twentieth century to bring the extracurriculum under their own control. This was accomplished, in part, by creating and working with student governments and, in part, by creating new college officials, such as deans of students, whose job it was to help plan and coordinate student activities that were compatible with the goals of the campus administration.

The outcome of these efforts can be seen on contemporary university campuses in the United States where there is likely to be a large office of student affairs or department of student services responsible for supervising student housing, including fraternity and sorority houses, and for working with student government to recognize and regulate a vast array of student clubs and organizations. In addition, there is likely to be a department of athletics. Unlike the departments of physical education that award credits or degrees to students whom they have successfully educated and trained as teachers, coaches, and physical trainers, departments of athletics are the part of the official extracurriculum that is in charge of intercollegiate athletics. So large and dominant have these departments become both on campus and in the nation that they often have budgets in excess of those of even the largest of the academic departments, and it is not unusual for the head football coach at a major university to be paid more than that university's chief academic officer, usually titled the president or chancellor.

The importance of intercollegiate athletics at major U.S. universities is reflected in the importance assigned to school sports beginning in middle schools and junior high schools where interschool sports are often the only or the major extracurricular activity that receives official school sponsorship and funding. The official status and high visibility of interschool sports in these schools create a major competition among students, particularly males. Although participation and interest in sports are requirements for being thought masculine, they are no longer enough for prestige as they were in elementary school. Instead, well-regarded boys become those who are members of school teams that compete with teams from other schools. For many years, athletic success has been the major source of prestige for young men in secondary schools, a finding that has been reported by researchers in Australia as well as in many high schools in the United States.

In *The Adolescent Society,* published in 1961, James Coleman explained the high prestige assigned to athletic success on the grounds that extracurricular activities, such as athletics, are seen by adolescents to be activities in which they can carry out positive actions on their own, in contrast to schoolwork, where they carry out assignments from teachers. Coleman's explanation masks the extent to which interschool sports are—and were at the time he wrote—part of the official school extracurriculum in which the athletes are not only recruited by official school personnel, but are also coached by them and expected to comply with their instructions. It may very well be true, as Coleman and many other researchers since his time have concluded, that the extracurriculum, especially interschool athletics, tends to undermine the academic goals of the school. But, this no longer means, as it did in nineteenth century colleges, that the official school culture, in the form of intellectual endeavors, is at war with the student culture, in the form of sports. Instead, the official school curriculum is often at war with the official school extracurriculum.

It is not only the peer group, but often the schools themselves, that give a highly visible priority to school sports over academe. In the United States, schools that have only one convocation per year to present awards for academic excellence, artistic talent, and student leadership may have a football rally before every varsity game plus additional sports rallies during basketball and baseball seasons. School-sponsored squads of cheerleaders and pompon girls, along with special pep or spirit clubs, are often created to lead the rallies and to ensure an enthusiastic audience for sporting events. This heavy emphasis on athletics has implications for the ways in which students come to be viewed, not only by other students but also by teachers and school administrators who are not above giving favors to star athletes whom they perceive to be valuable assets in their efforts to enhance the reputation of the school in the eyes of parents and the local community.

Within the student culture, male athletes often form peer cultures of their own, sometimes in combination with cheerleaders or, more rarely, with female athletes. For at least three reasons, these peer cultures are usually accorded elite status in the school. The first reason, alluded to above, is the high *visibility* of athletic teams even to students who never attend a game. Not only is school time devoted to sports rallies, but considerable space in the school paper and yearbook are devoted to athletic contests. Rare is the American high school, or junior high school, that does not have a glass-fronted cabinet in the hallway displaying athletic trophies. Also common are banners, posters, and other forms of decoration that publicize forthcoming games and announce support for the school team. Nor is this visibility limited to the school. In small and moderate-sized towns, local papers often cover high school athletics in considerable detail, and high school sporting contests attract sizable numbers of parents and other adults from the community. Even in major metropolitan areas, mass media coverage of citywide high school athletic tournaments is commonplace, especially for football and basketball, and the media are also likely to take a keen interest in regional and statewide tournaments, especially if a local team is participating.

Two other, interrelated reasons why students and school administrators accord elite status to athletes are the high *value* assigned to athletic talent and the *competition* that exists for positions on varsity teams. Undoubtedly, the high value assigned to athletics reflects the emphasis on them not only in the school, but also nationally and internationally. Undoubtedly, also, the value of team membership increases if there is a great deal of competition for positions. And both the value of and competition for positions are likely to increase if the team is winning. Even sports teams that are not usually very visible in schools, such as men's tennis and swimming or most of the women's sports, can become increasingly prestigious and attract increasing numbers of students to "tryouts" if they have recently won a championship. As these comments indicate, the athletic programs of schools, far more than their academic programs, provide ample, public opportunities for male students—and increasingly for female students—to compete for success and to convert their successes into prestigious social standing in their school.

As is true of athletics and cheerleading, the social status accorded to other extracurricular activities and organizations will depend on their visibility, perceived value, and the amount of competition for positions. Although student government tends to be highly visible in most schools and is selected on the basis of competitive elections, it may not be as valued as, for example, a band or chorus that can win competitions and create a positive image for the school. Throughout the world, schools honor certain kinds of student activities and achievements and try to ignore or punish other kinds of activities. The emphasis found in U.S. schools on getting involved in the extracurriculum, having school spirit, and being a winner will not be found in all countries, but most schools will develop a dominant image of what a good student is and does. In some schools this image will be organized around academic achievement. In other schools, particularly in the United Kingdom, the dominant image will be closely tied to social class background, with students from middle-class or elite backgrounds assumed to be "naturally" better students than those from the lower orders. In schools that honor athletics and other types of extracurricular behaviors, students can often gain major status rewards from those activities without having to be interested or committed to the official curriculum of the school. Such students may make some effort to obtain the average or passing grades in their courses necessary for eligibility to continue their participation in the extracurriculum. They will be handicapped, however, if they do not acquire the skills, knowledge, and orientation necessary for educational and occupational success beyond the secondary level. The heavy emphasis on the extracurriculum in many schools, especially in the United States, contributes little to the intellectual mission that is central to the official curriculum, and may even undermine it.

See also "Title IX and School Sports" in Part X.

Academic, Arts, and Service Clubs

Adolescents in the United States spend more than half of their waking hours in leisure activities. These activities may be unstructured, such as playing computer games, talking on the telephone, or hanging out with friends. Alternatively, teens may spend time in more formally structured activities such as academic, arts, or service clubs. Organized extracurricular activities are an integral part of high school for many students. Approximately 60 percent of high school sophomores and 70 percent of high school seniors participate in at least one extracurricular activity. According to a national study of U.S. high school sophomores in 2002 (see Ingels et al., 2005), sports were the most popular activities, with 54.8 percent of sophomores reporting sports involvement. Academic, arts, and service activities also represented an important part of many students' lives. Twenty-one percent of sophomores reported being in a musical group, while 11.2 percent of them were in a service club, and 8.4 percent of them were in an academic club. These participation rates vary considerably by gender and socioeconomic status, with girls and more affluent children more likely to participate in academic, arts, and service clubs.

Aside from the importance indicated by their prevalence, extracurricular activities influence teens' development in a variety of ways. Involvement in extracurricular activities, such as academic, arts, and service clubs, has been associated with academic achievement and other positive outcomes. Those who participate in extracurricular activities are more likely to be satisfied with school than those who do not. They have higher levels of personal empowerment, a greater sense of commitment to the school, and a stronger belief that the school organization is valid. Those who participate in extracurricular activities are less likely to engage in risky behavior, such as using drugs, or to drop out of school than students who do not participate.

Children are not equally likely to succeed in school. Girls are more likely than boys are to complete high school and attend college, while a growing number of adolescent boys say that they do not like school. Meanwhile, boys are more likely than girls are to engage in risky behavior, such as alcohol and drug use, and drop out of school. If academic, arts, and service clubs can help students succeed, such findings suggest the importance of understanding why students choose to participate in clubs and what mechanisms link club membership to other positive outcomes.

WHO PARTICIPATES IN THESE CLUBS?

Girls perform at higher levels than boys do not only in the formal curriculum but also in the extracurriculum. In the national study of sophomores mentioned above, girls were more likely than boys were to participate in arts, academic, and service clubs. Another study of 1,259 sophomores in the small industrial areas surrounding Detroit, Michigan (Eccles & Barber, 1999) also found that more females than males participated in these clubs.

In an analysis of performing arts, the national study of sophomores reported that 27 percent of girls, but only 16 percent of boys, were in a music club such as band, orchestra, or choir. The Michigan study, which examined many types of performing arts activities, found that some activities had more gender parity than did others. Gender differences ranged from less than 1 percent for art clubs (8.6 percent of girls belonged versus 7.7 percent of boys) to almost 10 percent for dance clubs (14.4 percent of girls belonged versus 5.2 percent of boys). The most popular performing arts activity for both sexes was band/orchestra with 19.1 percent of girls and 14.3 percent of boys participating.

Overall, academic clubs are less popular than are performing arts clubs, but gender gaps in participation persisted. Ten percent of girls participated in academic clubs, compared to 7 percent of boys. The Michigan study reported that in a few types of academic clubs, the proportion of boys actually outnumbered the proportion of girls. The debate club had 1.2 percent of girls compared to 1.4 percent of boys, and the math and chess clubs did not have any girls, but 0.5 percent of boys were in math and 0.7 percent of boys were in chess clubs. Foreign language clubs are the most popular academic activity for both boys and girls, but more girls (12.5 percent) than boys (4.5 percent) participate.

For service clubs considered alone, the Michigan study found that about 3.2 percent of girls and 2.4 percent of boys were members. Church clubs were more popular than were secular service clubs, and the gender gap in participation was greater for the church-related activities with 18.2 percent of girls involved compared to 10.8 percent of boys.

In addition to gender, other factors influence student participation decisions. Socioeconomically advantaged students are more likely to participate in extracurricular activities than are their peers. Ingels et al. (2005) report that 13.3 percent of U.S. high school sophomores in the highest quartile of socioeconomic status were in academic clubs and 27.1 percent of them were in music clubs. In contrast, among those in the lowest quartile, only 5.6 percent were in academic clubs and 15.6 percent were in music clubs. Some of this difference across social class reflects the relative affluence of different schools. Those with more affluent students probably have more resources to support extracurricular activities, and more impoverished schools do not provide the same number or range of clubs as their wealthier counterparts. Regardless of the affluence of the school, however, students from more affluent families were more likely to participate in performing arts, academic clubs, honor societies, publications, student government, and service clubs than were students from poor families. Costs for transportation and items such as equipment or uniforms may prevent some students from joining.

WHY DO STUDENTS PARTICIPATE IN CLUBS?

Understanding these participation gaps across gender and socioeconomic status is important because arts, academic, and service clubs help students succeed in high school. In addition, students who participate in these activities have been found to be less likely to engage in risky behaviors such as drug use and more likely to enroll in postsecondary education. Boys and poorer children are more likely than girls and affluent children to be suspended from school, to fail courses or proficiency exams, and to drop out of school. Given that boys and poorer children are less likely to participate in clubs, it may be useful, or even crucial, to discover ways to involve them in more high school clubs.

Investigating why some students decide to participate in clubs may give some insight into why those who might benefit most from joining tend to shy away from these clubs. Some students decide to participate because they believe they have talent and want to challenge themselves and improve their skills. Some join clubs to be with friends in the club or to please others, such as their parents or teachers. Others think that these activities will help them later in life, such as when applying to college. Perhaps boys are more likely than girls to find other ways to improve their talents, spend time with friends, impress adults, and enhance their resumes, or perhaps they do not see the connection between these activities and those outcomes as clearly as girls do.

Students may join clubs to become more popular. In *The Adolescent Society,* Coleman (1961) found that, in some schools, girls from higher-class backgrounds joined and led clubs in order to enhance their social status. For boys, playing sports was a way to gain prestige, but for girls, arts and academic clubs were more important than sports clubs. Forty years after this landmark study, academic and arts clubs, and probably service clubs, continue to be relatively more important avenues for prestige for girls than they are for boys. These different paths to prestige may help explain why boys are less likely than girls to participate in academic, arts, and service clubs. If this explanation is correct, it suggests that teachers and administrators who want to increase the participation of boys in clubs will have to find ways to increase the social status associated with club memberships and activities, especially among boys.

WHY DOES CLUB PARTICIPATION PRODUCE POSITIVE OUTCOMES?

To encourage administrators to recruit underrepresented students into academic, arts, and service clubs, researchers need to do a better job of identifying the mechanisms through which club participation helps boys and girls become better students. Recently enacted federal and state education policies have emphasized school and student accountability measured by performance on standardized tests. As a result of these policies, schools are tending to place more emphasis on core subjects and give less attention to creating learning opportunities in other areas. The combination of accountability policies and state budget shortfalls may mean that schools are less able or willing to sponsor as many arts, academic, and service clubs. Thus, demonstrating the links between such club participation and academic outcomes may give policy makers incentives to promote these activities.

Even without the recent emphases at the national and state levels on high-stakes testing, administrators may feel that their major responsibility is to improve the academic performance of students and reduce the drop-out rate. Thus, to give more support to arts, academic, and service clubs, they need to understand how these activities enhance academic outcomes. Some research suggests that these clubs might help students improve their academic performance and stay in school through the following mechanisms: changes in students' attitudes toward self and school, interaction of students with more prosocial peers, and increased contact of students with teachers and other authority figures.

Participation in clubs may lead to changed attitudes toward self including gains in self-knowledge, enhanced emotional, cognitive, and physical skills, and knowledge about how to take initiative. Additionally, participation may lead to improved attitudes toward school. Existing research suggests that academic, arts, and service clubs have different influences on these forms of personal development. Academic clubs are not associated with self-knowledge or interpersonal development, but performing arts activities have been found to produce higher rates of self-knowledge among those who participate than among those who do not. Compared with academic and arts clubs, service clubs provide the most benefits for personal development. Those in service activities report that these activities give them opportunities for identity reflection and emotional regulation. They are likely to refer to these activities as a "positive turning point." They are also more likely to report having interpersonal development experiences, such as "learning to be supportive of others," and they experience higher self-esteem. These patterns persist whether the service activities in question are faith-based or secular. It is not clear, however, whether psychological or emotional benefits of these service activities are the same for boys and girls. However, students who participate in service clubs are more likely to say they like school than students who do not participate, and this benefit is greater for boys than for girls.

Participation in academic, arts, and service clubs gives students the opportunity to interact with other students during club meetings. These activities may expand a student's peer group, allowing him or her to meet and befriend others from different social classes, neighborhoods, and ethnic groups. Unlike sports, which are typically sex-segregated, arts, academic, and service clubs provide opportunities for boys and girls to explore common interests, working together to achieve a shared goal. Joining clubs based on common interests and shared goals may help teens make friends beyond cliques in their school.

Organized activities such as arts, service, and academic clubs also help adolescents by giving some structure to their discretionary time. Teens spending time in structured activities have less unsupervised time to engage in deviant behavior and more time to interact with motivated and similarly interested peers. Teens who participate in arts, service, and academic clubs have a higher proportion of academically oriented friends than would be expected by chance, and this outcome is true for both boys and girls. If joining clubs gives a student positive peers, then opportunities for such activities may be more important for at-risk students.

Extracurricular activities have different influences on student behavior. Participation in sports has been found to be associated with risky behaviors, particularly alcohol abuse; however, participation in academic, arts, and service clubs is associated with reduced rates of risky behaviors in high school. Perhaps the peer groups formed in these clubs tend to be more prosocial and less rebellious against school authority.

Some research has examined the long-term effects of participation on risky behavior. Those who had joined service clubs in high school were less likely than nonparticipants to engage in risky behaviors such as drinking alcohol or using marijuana both in high school and when they were young adults. In contrast, performing arts clubs produced different effects over time. Like other club members, as high school students, performers were less likely to drink alcohol, less likely to skip school, more likely to like school, and more likely to attend college than those who did not belong. However, later in life, performing arts club membership has a positive association with risky behavior, especially for men. Male performers had a dramatic increase in drinking alcohol from ages 18 to 21. This rate of increase for male performers was greater than for female performers, male nonperformers, and female nonperformers. Similar patterns persist for marijuana use. It would be important to know how peers influence drinking among male performers and whether these drinking rates decline as male performers move into more adult roles.

In addition to opportunities to interact with positive peers, academic, arts, and service clubs facilitate getting to know adults within a nonclassroom, nonfamilial setting. Adolescents interact with the club advisors more informally than they might in class and then potentially have more adults to talk to if they have a problem. In fact, teachers have higher academic expectations of students who participate in academic, arts, and service clubs than they do of students who have jobs or who do not participate in any structured after-school activities. In addition, teachers' beliefs about students' academic potential can influence the students' academic gains during the year. In other words, a teacher directly or indirectly communicates her expectations of the student's potential to the student, and then the student lives up to those positive or negative expectations. If teachers' expectations influence student academic outcomes and teachers have lower expectations of boys in general but higher expectations of club participants, then boys may benefit even more from participating in these types of activities.

Regardless of the mechanism through which participation in academic, arts, and service clubs helps students, it is clear that such clubs do enhance school engagement. Currently, it is difficult to know whether personal growth and changes in attitudes toward school, peer interactions, or contact with adults are equally important mechanisms by which participation in arts, academic, and service clubs affect academic performance. Nor is it clear whether these mechanisms have equally strong effects on boys and girls and on poor and richer students as one moves across different school contexts. And, because almost all research showing the effects of clubs has been done on students who volunteer to participate, little is known about whether the effects of clubs would be the same if school officials required or pressured students to join. More research in these areas could give policy makers incentives to provide more of these activities and make them appealing to greater numbers of students.

REFERENCES AND FURTHER READINGS

Coleman, J.S. (1961). *The adolescent society: The social life of the teenager and its impact on education.* New York: Free Press of Glencoe.

Eccles, J.S., & Barber, B.L. (1999). Student council, volunteering, basketball, or marching band? What kind of extracurricular involvement matters? *Journal of Adolescent Research, 14*(1), 10–43.

Hansen, D.M., Reed, W.L., & Dworkin, J.B. (2003). What adolescents learn in organized youth activities: A survey of self-reported developmental experiences. *Journal of Research on Adolescence, 13*(1), 25–55.

Ingels, S.J., Burns, L.J., Charleston, S., Chen, X., Cataldi, E.F., & Owings, J. (2005). *A profile of the American high school sophomore in 2002: Initial results from the base year of the Education Longitudinal Study of 2002.* Washington, DC: National Center for Education Statistics.

Mahoney, J.L. (2000). School extracurricular activity participation as a moderator in the development of antisocial patterns. *Child Development, 71*(2), 502–506.

Schreiber, J. R., & Chambers, E. A. (2002). After-school pursuits, ethnicity, and achievement for 8th- and 10th-grade students. *The Journal of Education Research, 96*(2), 90–100.

Suiter, J. J., & Reavis, R. (1995). Football, fast cars, and cheerleading: Adolescent gender norms, 1978–1989. *Adolescence, 30*(118), 265–273.

Elizabeth Glennie

Elizabeth Stearns

Femininity, Cheerleading, and Sports

Extracurricular activities are a central component of most middle schools and high schools in the United States. Two of the most visible activities in these schools are sports and cheerleading. Girls are participating in sports in record numbers, and cheerleading continues to be a high status activity for girls. Sports and cheerleading are also two of the most gendered extracurricular activities.

This essay examines the social and historical construction of gender in cheerleading and girls' sports in middle schools and high schools. While the essay focuses on the construction of femininity, it is important to consider the construction of masculinity, as well. Historically, both cheerleading and sports were considered masculine activities in the United States. Today, both activities are surrounded by a complex and often contradictory set of cultural meanings concerning gender. The need for adjectives in the phrases "female athlete" and "athletic cheerleader" symbolizes this complexity. Scholars have analyzed several gendered meanings in cheerleading and girls' sports including appearance, sexuality, physicality, and athleticism. This essay provides a historical overview of each activity, examines the gendered meanings in cheerleading and sports over time, and concludes with a discussion of the "athletic cheerleader" and "female athlete."

CHEERLEADING

Many popular articles and manuals have been written about cheerleading since its emergence in late nineteenth-century collegiate sporting events. Most high schools and the majority of middle schools have cheerleading squads. Yet, cheerleading has received relatively little attention by scholars. One book provides an overview of the historical development of cheerleading and its cultural significance (Hanson, 1995); while another book examines the multifaceted nature of cheerleading using historical sources, popular materials, interviews, and observations (Adams & Bettis, 2003a). There are few empirical articles based on studies of contemporary cheerleading.

Cheerleading emerged as an exclusively male activity in the late 1800s and represented ideal or normative masculinity. Cheerleaders were extroverted, athletic, college students.

Males who cheered and performed athletic stunts were considered manly. Women started participating in cheerleading in small numbers at the collegiate level during the 1920s. However, cheerleading was still considered to be a male activity until the 1930s, and some educators felt that girls would become "mannish" if they performed athletic stunts. Dance became an appropriate activity for female cheerleaders, and girls were encouraged to use their appearance to lead crowds to cheer.

Girls' participation in collegiate and high school cheerleading squads intensified during the 1940s due, in part, to World War II. During the 1950s, cheerleading spread to junior high and elementary schools, and the activity gradually became feminized. By the 1960s, cheerleading was transformed from a male activity to a female activity and represented ideal or normative femininity. Cheerleaders were wholesome and attractive girls who supported male athletes and were popular with their peers. They cheered, chanted, danced, and performed simple stunts such as cartwheels. Cheerleaders were assumed to be heterosexual, and they were expected to adhere to higher moral standards than their peers.

During the 1970s, professional cheerleading squads were introduced, and cheerleading became sexualized. Professional cheerleaders became sexual objects to be displayed for the pleasure of men. Males returned to cheerleading at the collegiate level in the 1970s. However, Davis (1990) found that male cheerleaders avoided activities associated with femininity (e.g., dancing) and embraced activities associated with masculinity (e.g., tumbling and stunts). Thus, a sexual division of labor was constructed within coed squads. The display of physical strength defined male cheerleaders as athletes and men.

The feminist movement of the 1960s and 1970s, the passage of Title IX in 1972 (discussed in the next section), and the introduction of regional, state, and national cheerleading competitions contributed to another transformation in cheerleading. Athleticism was reintroduced and cheerleaders became serious athletes. Contemporary cheerleading includes difficult jumps, pyramid building, tumbling, and complicated cheers and dances. Competitive cheerleading squads were formed in the 1990s. These squads were not affiliated with teams; they only competed against other squads. The reintroduction of athleticism into cheerleading has made it easier for males to participate at the high school level. However, males who participate in cheerleading may have their masculinity and sexual identity questioned.

Two qualitative studies illustrate how gendered meanings are constructed and reproduced in schools. Eder and Parker (1987) examined the effect of extracurricular activities on the peer group culture of early adolescents. Since male athletic events were the main social events of the school, male athletes and female cheerleaders had considerable visibility and status among their peers. Therefore, the activity of cheerleading had the most influence on female peer culture. The values promoted by cheerleading were appearance (neatness), attractiveness (cuteness and thinness), and a bubbly personality expressed through smiling. These values, particularly the focus on appearance and attractiveness, were interpreted and modified in informal peer groups. As girls discussed clothing, hairstyles, weight, and makeup during lunchtime conversations, they developed different behavioral norms across groups. Nevertheless, cheerleaders symbolized the importance of appearance for adolescent girls.

In another study of middle school adolescents, Adams and Bettis (2003b) examined how cheerleaders actively constructed their gendered identity. Cheerleading offered a safe space for girls to take pleasure in the physicality of their bodies. Cheerleaders were expected to discipline their bodies (master movements, techniques, and tumbling, and adopt a stance of invulnerability to pain), control their emotions, and develop an ability to smile at all times. Cheerleading also provided a school-sanctioned space for girls to play with a sexualized identity. Girls experienced a form of power and pleasure that they did not experience in other extracurricular activities, including sports. They enjoyed being the center of attention and the object of others' gazes. Girls thought they had the power to control how the players and crowd responded to sporting events. At the same time, girls took their leadership role in the school seriously. Thus, cheerleading provided an opportunity for a girl to be an athlete, a nice girl, and a "girlie girl."

While cheerleading is primarily a gendered activity, race also interacts with gender (see Adams & Bettis, 2003a; Hanson, 1995). Prior to the *Brown v. Board of Education* decision in 1954, Black students participated in cheerleading at segregated colleges and public schools. The style of cheering that developed on Southern African American squads was influenced by popular music and church hymns. Innovative rhythms and fluid improvisation were important elements of cheers and routines. Representation on squads became an issue in schools during desegregation. African American students were expected to adopt a style of cheering that was associated with White squads. Black students as well as Chicano students were not well represented on squads in the late 1960s and 1970s. Protests erupted at schools across the country. Today, schools have implemented selection processes to promote racial and ethnic representation on squads. Moreover, squads are challenging the perception that cheerleading is for White girls by constructing a different look and a different style of cheering. Nevertheless, cheerleading squads are still disproportionately White in some parts of the United States.

Bettis and Adams (2003) examined how and why a cheerleading equity policy in a middle school failed to achieve more racially, ethnically, and economically diverse squads. The researchers found there were problems with implementing the policy (cost of participating in cheerleading and limited opportunities for girls to learn tumbling skills). Moreover, the board did not consider the peer status system in the school when they created the policy. Cheerleading was associated with membership in the "Preps," the dominant peer group in the school. Prep girls embodied the cheerleader look in the school (pretty, petite, and smiling all the time). Girls defined themselves in relation to this peer group. Some girls simply could not be Preps and other girls had no desire to be Preps. Thus, the cheerleading squad remained predominantly White and middle class, despite the school board's effort to implement an equity policy.

SPORTS

Girls' sport participation in schools has increased considerably since the 1972 enactment of Title IX, the legislation that required all schools receiving federal aid to provide equal opportunity for participation in sports. Data from the National Federation of State High School Associations (2005) indicates that participation increased from 294,015 in 1971 to 1972 to 2,908,390 in 2004 to 2005. However, female sport participation did not begin in 1972. Women have participated in physical activity and struggled for acceptance into the sports world for over a century.

Competitive sports have always been associated with masculinity and physical strength. Biological differences between the sexes have been celebrated in sports and interpreted as evidence for the natural superiority of men. Sociohistorical accounts of women's sport participation have examined the connections between sport, femininity, and sexuality (for example, see Cahn, 1994). As women's access to and participation in sports increased in the early twentieth century, cultural tension between athleticism and femininity and concerns about female sexuality emerged. Female athleticism was associated with "mannishness" between 1890 and World War I. Vigorous physical activity was viewed as harmful to women's health (potential damage to reproductive organs) and morality (uncontrolled heterosexual desire). Consequently, educators promoted a philosophy of athletic moderation for women.

The 1940s were a period of advancement for women due largely to the social and economic impact of World War II. Women's participation in sports became more acceptable. However, as women became more physical, their appearance was emphasized. In subsequent decades, the "mannish" female athlete was depicted as undesirable, and she became explicitly linked with lesbianism. Female athletes felt pressured to prove their heterosexuality and femininity. Consequently, many developed an apologetic stance about their athletic skills. However, some research suggests that Black women did not adopt this stance. They adhered to a more active ideal of femininity than White women.

The feminist movement of the 1960s and 1970s and the fitness boom of the 1970s and 1980s revitalized the national interest in women's sports. Despite the increased acceptance of female athletes, concerns about lesbianism persisted. Femininity and heterosexuality were viewed as incompatible with athletic excellence. Moreover, some sports were viewed as less appropriate for women. The success and coverage of women in the 1996 Olympics games and the 1999 Women's World Cup Victory marked a cultural celebration of female athleticism. Today, women's athletic skills and achievements are emphasized more in the media, and the image of the athletic, muscular woman is more acceptable. However, sexualized images of female athletes have also surfaced, and women have been marketed according to their appearance rather than their athletic performance.

One of the most persistent themes in the literature on girls' sport participation is the connection between athleticism and femininity. Historically, researchers have used two frameworks to analyze this relationship. The role conflict perspective asserts that female athletes perceive and experience a conflict between their role as female and their role as athlete. Yet, research conducted over several decades suggests that female athletes perceive and experience low levels of role conflict.

The second framework, the apologetic defense strategy, argues that girls experience tension between being an athlete and being a female. The apologetic defense is a strategy that allows girls to compensate for the perceived masculinization of sport participation by exaggerating feminine behaviors. In other words, a girl downplays her athleticism and overemphasizes her femininity. Research indicates that girls have used this strategy within the athletic context. Moreover, some research suggests that the strategy has changed over time. In contrast to earlier times, girls today embrace their athleticism. Nevertheless, they still must be appropriately feminine. Thus, they continue to overemphasize feminine behaviors. Other researchers suggest that female athletes may use the apologetic defense strategy to avoid being labeled a lesbian.

Two qualitative studies illustrate the complexity of female athleticism in high schools. One study examined female athleticism within the peer culture of a team, while the second analyzed female athleticism in relation to male athleticism. Enke (2005) analyzed how White girls interpreted and negotiated cultural meanings of athleticism and femininity within the peer culture of a high school varsity basketball team. While there were multiple meanings of athleticism on the team (competitiveness, teamwork, and toughness), physical appearance was the only meaning of femininity. Players grappled with the meanings collectively through the cultural routines of gossip, funny stories, and teasing. In the process, they indirectly discussed their concerns, conveyed information about appropriate behavior, and expressed underlying emotions. Sexuality was not a concern for the

members of this team because they were attractive by heterosexual standards of femininity, and they had a losing record. The players' athleticism may have been interpreted differently if the team had produced a winning record. In sum, the girls' produced an
understanding of female athleticism that included displays of athleticism and femininity.
They did not experience a role conflict or employ the apologetic defense strategy. However, they reproduced the cultural concern with women's appearance within the athletic
context.

Shakib and Dunbar (2002) examined the meanings of athleticism among a diverse sample of male and female basketball players from three different schools. Both sexes viewed
female athleticism as different and subordinate to male athleticism. By emphasizing perceived differences in style of play, girls' performance was viewed as less competitive,
weaker, and less socially valuable than boys' performance of the game. In two of the
schools, the girls' teams were ranked higher than the boys' teams, but this fact did not
challenge the perception of boys' superior athletic performance. Ironically, girls' basketball was viewed as less entertaining because girls' games were less stylized, slower paced,
and more inclusive. Yet, girls were teased for winning or beating boys and labeled
"dykes." Nevertheless, girls negotiated meanings they found empowering. For example,
beating a boy at basketball affirmed female equality.

A recent theme in the literature is the relationship between gender, sport, and physicality. Research conducted in Canada analyzed girls' experiences in ice hockey, a contact
sport in which opponents physically confront one another (Theberge, 2003).

The rules of play are the same for men and women except for one. Body checking, the
intentional effort to hit another player, is prohibited in women's ice hockey. As a result,
the style of play is different. Women's hockey emphasizes speed, finesse, and playmak-
ing; men's hockey emphasizes force, power, and intimidation. The girls in Theberge's
study described games as aggressive and physical. Playing hockey meant taking control,
being powerful, and sometimes acting fearless in the use of their body, even though body
checking was prohibited. Consequently, girls' understanding of hockey and athleticism
was grounded in the physicality of the sport. While the players endorsed the women's
version of the game, they recognized that "real hockey" involved body checking. In other
words, they knew that the men's version of hockey was valued more than the alternative
version of the sport.

GIRLS' ATHLETICISM IN CHEERLEADING AND SPORTS

As scholars have noted, the social construction of gender is a product of discourses, social
practices, and social relations that vary over time and across social locations. Normative
or ideal femininity in the twenty-first century includes displays of behavior that are considered masculine, such as athleticism. Sports and cheerleading provide an opportunity
for girls to experience empowerment (confidence that develops from using one's body
skillfully) and pleasure through physical activity. However, the cultural meanings of athleticism differ in the two activities.

The phrase "athletic cheerleader" highlights the recent transformation in the activity.
The athleticism required in cheerleading takes hours of practice, training, and physical
conditioning. But, the activity is still regarded as a feminine one. The basic function of a
cheerleading program in schools is to support athletic teams and the achievement of
others. Moreover, the femininity of cheerleaders is highlighted through uniforms,
demeanor, and appearance. Hence, contemporary cheerleading affirms heterosexualized
femininity.

Girls' sport participation in schools has become widely accepted in contemporary society. Yet, the framing of an athlete as female and the sexualization of women's sports suggest that competitive sport is perceived as a male domain, which girls and women have entered. Consequently, the rules of play may be modified, girls' athleticism may be subordinated to boys' athleticism, and girls who play sports may have their sexuality or femininity questioned. Thus, girls' display of strength, competency, and skill in sports continues to pose a challenge to the social order. In this post-Title IX era, gender still counts.

REFERENCES AND FURTHER READINGS

Adams, N.G., & Bettis, P.J. (2003a). *Cheerleader! Cheerleader! An American icon.* New York: Palgrave.

Adams, N.G., & Bettis, P.J. (2003b). Commanding the room in short skirts: Cheering as the embodiment of ideal girlhood. *Gender & Society, 17*(1), 73–91.

Bettis, P.J., & Adams, N.G. (2003). The power of the preps and a cheerleading equity policy. *Sociology of Education, 76*(2), 128–142.

Cahn, S.K. (1994). *Coming on strong: Gender and sexuality in twentieth-century women's sport.* New York: Free Press.

Davis, L.R. (1990). Male cheerleaders and the naturalization of gender. In M.A. Messner & D.F. Sabo (Eds.), *Sport, men, and the gender order: Critical feminist perspectives* (pp. 153–161). Champaign, IL: Human Kinetics Books.

Eder, D., & Parker, S. (1987). The cultural production and reproduction of gender: The effect of extracurricular activities on peer-group culture. *Sociology of Education, 60*(3), 200–213.

Enke, J. (2005). Athleticism and femininity on a high school basketball team: An interpretive approach. In D. A. Kinney & K. B. Rosier (Eds.), *Sociological studies of children and youth* (Vol. 11, pp. 115–152). New York: Elsevier.

Hanson, M.E. (1995). *Go! Fight! Win! Cheerleading in American culture.* Bowling Green, OH: Bowling Green State University Popular Press.

National Federation of State High School Associations. (2005). *2004–05 NFHS high school athletics participation survey.* Retrieved November 19, 2005 from www.nfhs.org

Shakib, S., & Dunbar, M.D. (2002). The social construction of female and male high school basketball participation: Reproducing the gender order through a two-tiered sporting institution. *Sociological Perspectives, 45*(4), 353–378.

Theberge, N. (2003). "No fear comes": Adolescent girls, ice hockey, and the embodiment of gender. *Youth & Society, 34*(4), 497–516.

Janet Enke

Fraternities

Fraternities, in North American colleges and universities, are organizations of men who share common ideals and values, enjoy a sense of communal brotherhood and social orientation, and have pledged allegiance to each other and to their particular organization. These groups are often named with Greek letters, frequently express ideals of scholarship, service, and leadership, and have become largely social in nature and purpose. As social organizations, fraternities can be distinguished from other groups that are known by Greek letters. Such groups—literary societies, honorary organizations, and professional organizations—may share similarities with fraternities in basic structure, origin, or purpose, but today's fraternities have become unique as outlets for male students to feel a sense of social belonging and community.

Sharing the values of brotherhood—the quality of support and friendship rooted in kindred minds and spirits—has been an original aim of fraternal life and has been enhanced and passed down through generations of members. Because many fraternities were founded as academic and literary societies, striving toward scholarly achievement in academic life also has been a goal, building on the spirit of mutual challenge and support in bettering oneself academically. In addition, a vast commitment to others—a "love of humankind"—is often demonstrated through philanthropic activities of community service and the benevolent support of charity and those less fortunate.

Along with this rich and positive heritage of brotherhood, academic achievement, and philanthropy, social fraternities also have a tradition of peer rebellion against faculty and administrative authority that began with open and violent student revolts in the late eighteenth and early nineteenth centuries. Although these outbreaks were forcibly and successfully suppressed by leaders of the colleges in which they took place, acts of student rebellion against institutional control—often in the forms of pranks, rowdiness, ritualized violence, insubordination, academic cheating, and what is now called substance abuse—continued to characterize many college and university campuses. Such acts were and are not unique to fraternity members, but fraternities have provided an organizational context and brotherly support for all sorts of activities, legal or not, that have come to be regarded collectively as fun, good fellowship, and bases for social prestige.

In response to the problems created by fraternal crimes and misbehaviors and the other challenges facing fraternal life today, student affairs professionals and some faculty have begun to assess the need for greater attention to undergraduate chapters and intensified training for fraternity leaders. With particular focus on liability issues, the need for leadership, diversity, raising academic and ethical standards, and other strategies for positive membership development, there is a renewed commitment to support fraternities in "returning to their roots" and redefining the fraternal experience in light of each group's founding values. The ability of college men to join together with common interests and shared concerns, to pledge to uphold all that is good in an organization's heritage and subscribe to the positive beliefs handed down through the generations, to wear a member's badge and celebrate an age-old ritual, and to exemplify the best characteristics of educated gentlemen are the renewed goals of fraternal life today. Overcoming the negative stereotypes and destructive behaviors remains a challenge to truly reaching these goals.

HISTORICAL DEVELOPMENT

America's first institutions of higher education were small colleges founded to educate preachers, teachers, and statesmen. Because of the frequent lack of intellectual excitement and social freedom in the formal curriculum, students began to create their own extracurricular activities. They formed debating societies and literary clubs; some colleges witnessed the founding of "secret" societies comprising students who were "pledged" and "initiated" into the traditions of the societies as defined by each group's founders. Often reflecting the aims of the philosophical-scholarly schools of ancient Greece, these groups would take on distinct characteristics—whether as literary societies, debating groups, or other academically focused bodies—that would later distinguish them entirely from each other. Sometimes the groups' motto or guiding values would be named in Greek, and the organizations came to be known by the initial letters of those Greek words. These initials served through the decades as the distinct "nicknames" (and later, the formal names) of the organizations. These groups eventually developed a much more social focus, primarily because they began to offer housing to students. This created the modern prototype of the fraternities of today.

The Phi Beta Kappa honorary fraternity was founded in 1776 at the College of William and Mary and is the forerunner of today's Greek-letter organizations. Phi Beta Kappa established precedents that today's groups still follow, including a name composed of Greek letters; secret rituals and symbols that affirm shared values and beliefs; and a badge that, in general, only initiated members wear. Despite these similarities, it can be argued emphatically that today's Greek organizations lack the scholarly emphasis of Phi Beta Kappa, which now admits its members, including women, solely on the basis of their grades and other academic achievements.

In the past two centuries, student life at American colleges and universities expanded broadly beyond the walls of the classroom. Early leadership in this expansion was often exercised by groups of male students who shared common interests and banded together to discuss not only academic matters but also the affairs of campus and society. These groups developed into friendship networks and became brotherhoods defined by shared values, beliefs, and perspectives. These distinct brotherhoods—these *fraternities*—were a mainstay on the landscape of U.S. higher education for much of its history.

Throughout their rich histories, fraternities have often been the birthplace of leaders who have taken their place on the national and international scene in government, athletics, entertainment, and other public venues. All but two U.S. presidents have been fraternity members, and 16 vice presidents have been members of fraternities. Approximately two-thirds of all who have served in Cabinet-level posts in any administration since 1900 have been fraternity men, and over three-fourths of U.S. Senators and Representatives have been members. Over 85 percent of U.S. Supreme Court Justices have been fraternity members, as have 43 chief executive officers of the nation's 50 largest corporations. Fraternity membership runs wide and deep and is often the birthplace of leadership for many who choose it.

Fraternities have a long history of relationships with sororities, or women's fraternities. These women's organizations were founded almost a century after Phi Beta Kappa first appeared primarily as a way for women to gain male acceptance and to ally themselves with male power on coeducational campuses. Although modeled after the men's fraternities, sororities developed their own character on the landscape of campus life. Both historically and in contemporary times, they have been less likely than fraternities to engage in rebellion against college authority, and they are generally less likely to attract attention because of antisocial or illegal behaviors. Nevertheless, they remain closely associated with fraternities as "siblings" or "partners" in campus Greek communities.

CONTEMPORARY ORGANIZATION, CHARACTERISTICS, AND ACTIVITIES

Today's college fraternities are national or international organizations composed of undergraduate members and large networks of support provided by alumni members. Each group is governed by a national office and organizational structure, and local "chapters" of these groups are installed at individual campuses of colleges and universities. Fraternities that are officially recognized on this "local" level are supported by these national or international structures of government, resources, and leadership and are also hosted and guided by the college or university at which the chapter is located.

Many fraternities have chapters in both the United States and in Canada, making them truly *international* organizations; however, few, if any, have chapters or branches outside North America. Nationally and internationally, and usually on an annual basis, undergraduate and alumni members of fraternities gather for organization-wide events such as conferences, summer institutes, and training sessions to learn more from each other about ritual, values, scholarship, and leadership. This ongoing commitment to membership development is an investment in each organization's future; providing sound training and education for its members beyond the classroom walls helps to develop and prepare future leaders for each group and for greater society. Such activities are reminders of a shared vision of the past and the development of shared perspectives on the future.

Today's college and university campuses feature a wide range of fraternities that vary in size, purpose, mission, involvement level, age, and character. Although there are 66 nationally and internationally recognized fraternal organizations for college men, few campuses host a chapter of each organization. Instead, smaller Greek communities (on the campus level) are composed of chapters that have demonstrated interest and willingness to become an established part of the college or university community in that location. Campuses must recognize a chapter and often declare that a special relationship exists between the college or university and the chapter, outlining the support and contributions that each will provide, before the national organization will grant a charter at that location. Not all fraternities are affiliated with a national or international organization, however; some remain independent or "local," in order to retain more control and reduce organizational costs.

Some colleges and universities in North America do not allow fraternities (or sororities) to organize on their campuses. Among those that do, small to midsized institutions may typically host between 5 and 20 fraternities; some larger universities may feature more than 40 or 50 chapters. These organizations are governed locally by interfraternity councils, composed of chapter members from that campus who volunteer to help regulate and guide the fraternal community through structured governance. The North American Interfraternity Conference is the international body that provides oversight and standards for campus interfraternity councils and men's fraternities in both the United States and Canada.

Individual chapters are traditionally composed of a general membership led by officers and a committee structure. They operate on an annual calendar that features marketing, recruitment, education, social, athletic, and philanthropic events. Recruitment, formerly known as "rush," is the process by which new members are invited to learn more about the organization and affiliate with the chapter; a more intensive education period ("pledging") is the formal education or formation period for new members. Through a series of other programs, events, and activities, each chapter takes on its own "personality" on campus, often raising support for charities, competing against other student organizations in intramural athletics, developing a vibrant social atmosphere for members and other interested students, and otherwise making unique contributions to the campus and Greek community.

In terms of physical environments, Greek housing is often concentrated or grouped together or in close proximity on college campuses. "Greek Rows" of houses—each belonging to a particular chapter—dominate sections of campuses, and the homes of members of fraternities and sororities coexist near each other in a true and tangible, neighborly Greek community. More often than not, the shared experience of "being Greek" encourages friendships and relationships among men's and women's organizations, and chapters often cosponsor events or share responsibility for philanthropy projects. These partnerships continue to grow as today's fraternities and sororities rise to the challenge of portraying positive images for their organizations, and they continue to celebrate their rituals and to role model behaviors for their peers on campus and beyond.

Among members of Greek communities on some campuses there exists a friendly, competitive tension to visibly demonstrate a positive image on college and university campuses. A vibrant spirit of community is demonstrated by interfraternity athletic contests, charity fundraisers, homecoming float decorations, house landscaping, or other types of competition. Such activities express the spirit of "doing good" (philanthropy) through community building that is a foundational value of Greek life. More often than not, campuses benefit from the good that is done by fraternities and their members, but they also suffer from the few (but significant) episodes of unhealthy choices and destructive behavior often associated with fraternity life.

Unfortunately, some unique characteristics of men's fraternal groups—common interests, shared values, distinct housing, and the occasional lack of internal leadership or supervision—often can encourage "group think" and lead to poor choices and unhealthy decision making. In recent decades, the attention of campus administrators and the media has focused on fraternity members' alcohol and drug abuse, hazing, academic cheating, sexual assault, and other acts that either are criminal in nature or violate the values or standards of the organizations they pledged and of the institutions of higher education that host them. Currently, hazing and alcohol abuse lead the list of problems that are making colleges and universities the targets of legal action, followed closely by examples of offensive and insensitive behavior. Forty states have antihazing laws, some nearly 30 years old, but hazing continues. Research shows that members of fraternities are more likely to abuse alcohol than their non-Greek peers. Such forms of crime and misbehavior perpetuate a negative image for these groups, and exemplary chapters are often forced to battle the stereotypes created by other chapters' destructive behaviors. Because of these instances, some campuses have gone so far as to reduce or close the entire Greek community rather than to continually address the problems created by certain behavior. Yet, without proper guidance and support from alumni and institutional staff, fraternity members are left alone to (mis)manage an often dangerous environment.

Some of today's fraternities suffer the stigma of being "party houses" on campus, centers of debauchery and delinquency, and are devoid of any opportunities for positive role modeling. Those who support fraternities argue that these lackluster chapters have nothing in common with their founding organizations or values except the name, and other, values-driven, chapters of the same fraternity on other campuses take great displeasure in sharing their name with what they regard as their less-than-worthy brethren. Thus, there are tensions both within and outside of each group, making it ever more necessary to develop strong internal and external leadership for fraternities on every campus.

DIVERSITY, ACADEMIC, AND ETHICAL CHALLENGES

Fraternities today are being challenged to turn themselves into ethical learning communities that can address not only ways to eliminate or reduce crime and misbehavior but also ways to improve diversity, academic commitments, and ethical standards and expectations. These challenges are broad in scope and very different from those that their founders faced more than two centuries ago, but success in dealing with them is likely to be critical to the survival of fraternities as communities of scholars, friends, learners, and leaders.

A long-standing criticism of fraternities is that they are highly exclusive and lack diversity. Although the United States and Canada have been multicultural societies since their founding, multiculturalism has received increasingly explicit attention in recent years, and colleges and universities in both countries face increasing demands to prepare graduates who can live and work effectively in a multicultural world. Greek leaders assert that the Greek experience helps students appreciate individuals from diverse backgrounds and cultures, but fraternities remain largely homogeneous in their ethnic and racial makeup. Research has shown that undergraduate students who participate in educational activities and programs focusing on diversity displayed greater openness to diversity than their peers who did not. Similarly, workshops and training programs designed to prevent sexual harassment and rape on campus have been found to reduce hostility toward and abuse of women. The challenge remains for fraternities to move closer toward a stronger commitment to—and appreciation of—diversity in the years to come.

Fraternity men are also being challenged to commit to high standards in academic honesty and achievement. Possibly because of a lack of highly regulated housing environments, fraternity house residents may not be held responsible for maintaining study hours, completing homework, or attending classes; other members may suffer from poor time management and the frequent choice to socialize more than study. These choices lead to lower achievement in scholarship, greater temptation to cheat, and lower rates of degree completion for some Greek communities, thereby increasing efforts by national organizations, institutional staff, and faculty to work closely with fraternity men to better strategize and maximize their academic potential. Although there are good examples on many campuses of fraternity scholars and those who achieve highly in academics, there remains a stigma against the efforts of fraternities to encourage their members to truly become "scholars among men."

Nevertheless, fraternities must consider cognitive outcomes (such as critical thinking, reasoning, and understanding) as a priority as they seek to redefine themselves as learning communities of scholars and leaders. Unfortunately, research has shown that early Greek involvement can negatively affect cognitive development, particularly because the first year of college tends to demonstrate lasting implications for a student's college career. Healthy involvement may lead to healthy outcomes; anything less may lead to more negative results.

Not only high academic standards but also clear, high ethical standards and expectations for student behavior are important if fraternities are to become true learning communities shaped by values, friendship, scholarship, and service. Unfortunately, studies show that fraternity membership influences ethical development in a negative way through pledge education and various social events that do not respect other people, values, or cultures. Historically, many fraternities have had codes of behavior and standards that stress moral values and personal integrity to which members commit at initiation. If these standards truly become part of the lives of chapter members, fraternities could indeed become effective and ethical learning communities. There must be a shared expectation and demand that members commit to and live out the positive values that they and their organizations espouse; to miss this goal is to disregard much that is positive in the heritage and the original purpose of their brotherhood.

REFERENCES AND FURTHER READINGS

Anson, J.L., & Marchesani, R.F., Jr. (Eds.). (1991). *Baird's manual of college fraternities.* Indianapolis, IN: Baird's Manual Foundation, Inc.

Horowitz, H.L. (1987). *Campus life: Undergraduate cultures from the end of the eighteenth century to the present.* Chicago: University of Chicago Press.

North American Interfraternity Conference. (n.d.). Retrieved May 22, 2006, from http://www.nicindy.org/

Whipple, E.G. (Ed.). (1998). *New challenges for Greek letter organizations: Transforming fraternities and sororities into learning communities.* San Francisco: Jossey-Bass.

Edward G. Whipple

Keith B. O'Neill

Masculinity and School Sports

Sociologists have conceptualized schooling as a process through which children are exposed to two types of knowledge. The first and most obvious is the formal curriculum in which information is "packaged" into different "subjects" and taught as "facts" that then become the focus of tests to establish a hierarchy of achievement among students. Although these packages change over time as new knowledge is developed and specialization increases, most of these subjects are not generally perceived as socially controversial. Health and religious education are notable exceptions because they include elements of the second type of knowledge that children encounter in schools. This is knowledge about morality and values, knowledge that has come to be labeled the "hidden curriculum" because it is not part of formal education but is developed as students interact with each other and adults during extracurricular activities often sponsored by the school when formal classes are over.

This chapter is about gender identity development, one of the most important and controversial issues of the hidden curriculum, and the role played by school sports (arguably the most important extracurricular activity in our schools) in shaping that identity. As the title implies, the development of a masculine identity is closely tied to school sports and has been seen by many as the reason why school sports have become such a powerful institution. Linkages between masculinity, sports, and "character building" have characterized the entire history of school sports since their origins in the nineteenth century. The contemporary value structure of school sports and the rituals that surround and support it show male (and female) students how boys should "do" masculinity. Given the history of gender stereotyping in which male and female "characteristics" have been defined as opposites, school sports also show females (and males) how not to "do" femininity. The power of school sports to legitimize a limited, hegemonic (or dominant) view of masculinity has received considerable criticism, and suggestions have been offered about how to use school sports to present more variety in gender identity choices.

ORIGINS OF SCHOOL SPORTS

Modern organized sport developed in exclusively male contexts as an archetypal masculinity right. Born out of the fear that Edwardian and Victorian middle- and upper-middle class British schoolboys were becoming "effeminate," team sports (called "games" by the British) were developed as a form of social control in the typically Spartan conditions of private boarding schools. According to contemporary historians, compulsory sports became an integral part of the curriculum and reached almost cultic levels in many schools. These sports "built character." By participating in them, boys learned to accept physical pain and deprivation without complaining, to strive for success for the honor of the school, and to accept victory and defeat with equanimity. In a popular phrase of the time they learned to "play up and play the game." These boys survived sports and demonstrated that they were the fittest examples of gentlemen, ready to fulfill their social Darwinist destinies in service to the British Empire by helping to "civilize" the lesser races of the world. Behavior in school sports defined "manliness" for that age and continues to perform this function even as contemporary definitions of "manliness" differ from the original British version.

The belief that participation in school sport "builds character" was exported to America as elite private schools adopted the curriculum characteristics of their British counterparts during the mid-to-late nineteenth century. A similar definition of manliness was accepted with the exception of the value attached to winning. Whereas the British gentleman was already morally superior by the fact of his birth, in America, moral superiority had to be earned through victory. Only through victory over one's opponents, it was thought, could one demonstrate morality, superiority, and character. The link between masculinity, winning, and elitism was "invented" in emerging American sports such as football. Participation in, or rather winning in, football was seen as exemplifying the best characteristics of American "manhood," and team sports became required activities in schools attended by the future leaders of the country.

The impetus to apply the "sport builds character" belief more widely, and within it the masculinity/winning connection, came from the social reformers of the Playground Movement. These leaders believed that urbanization and immigration were undermining "American" values and saw adult-supervised physical activity in city playgrounds and gymnasiums as a way of countering this threat. Physical activities and sports were believed to reduce juvenile delinquency, give a sense of moral purpose to youth, and allow them to break away from their ethnic roots and become "Americanized." Organizations such as the Young Men's Christian Association and the Public School Athletic League helped to bring organized games and sports to the masses. By the 1920s, Americans were convinced that team sports were essential for promoting ethnic harmony, physical vigor, moral direction, psychological stability, and social skills in urban youth, and interscholastic athletics became institutionalized in virtually every school district in America. Many contemporary coaches and school administrators would endorse this positive view of school sports without questioning the underlying problems that the winning/masculinity construct has for male (and female) athletes and, by association, for gender identity choices and constraints potentially affecting all adolescents.

DECODING SPORTS RITUALS IN HIGH SCHOOLS

Like their Edwardian and Victorian predecessors, contemporary schoolboys play sport in predominately homosocial groups. Their teammates are male, their coaches are male, their behavior defines masculinity for the student body, and their sports choices are often "gendered." The most prestigious sports they play, such as football, ice hockey, and wrestling, utilize the body as a weapon against opponents and are seen as "appropriate" only for boys. Symbolically these "power and performance" sports make violence and aggression legitimate as a male but not a female trait. "Female" sports and physical activities like gymnastics and dance are characterized by beauty of movement and aesthetics. These activities are stereotyped as not "appropriate" for boys. The choices that children (or their parents) make about participation in these sports influence how their masculinity and femininity are defined. Boys and girls who participate in gender "inappropriate" sport risk having their heterosexuality questioned.

Sports performance in contemporary high schools is located within rituals that naturalize the importance of victory and male entitlement. More specifically, although females are part of the picture because schools are usually coed, they tend to play a support role for the male achievement that mirrors traditional gender-based relationships in society. Consider a hypothetical pep rally—that most uniquely American of sport rituals. On one Friday afternoon in fall and spring (or sometimes every Friday afternoon during the high school football season in more traditional communities) classes finish early. The students, teachers, administrators, and sometimes parents and other community members gather in the auditorium to honor the sports teams. With words of praise and encouragement from coaches, the principal, and team captains, the athletes are presented as role models who deserve the students' support in the upcoming season as they put their masculinity on the line for the glory of the school and the community. Students shout and clap and hold up banners exhorting the teams to win (no banners advocating fair play and respect for opponents are ever displayed), the band plays the school "fight" song, and the cheerleaders (predominately physically attractive females) provide symbolic support for male achievement with victory chants and coordinated movements.

Like all public rituals, this one naturalizes relations of power within and between groups, in this case relations within the student body where athletes are exalted as role models, and the superiority of boys over girls. The format of contemporary pep rallies may have changed to reflect the fact that large numbers of high school athletes are now girls, with female teams being honored alongside male teams, but the legacy of male superiority is still evident. In fall pep rallies, the football team is invariably introduced at the end, even though its last season's win/loss record might be inferior to that of the girls soccer team. Also, the content of cheerleading is changing, and it has begun to resemble a "real" sport with difficult (and dangerous) human pyramid formations and gymnastic stunts. However, a closer look reveals that traditional gender stereotyping is retained. The male cheerleaders are doing the heavy lifting, not balancing on top of the pyramid.

In sports rituals such as pep rallies and homecoming, an event that involves former students and other community members supporting the school teams at a special game, the gender stereotyping is more discrete and below the surface. Other sports rituals provide more blatant examples of male superiority. For example, the powder puff football game is a popular end-of-the-season ritual in some schools. In it, high-status girls divide into two football teams coached by two of the football players and play a serious game. However, other high-status male athletes dress up as cheerleaders and mock the girls' efforts, turning a role reversal ritual into a male superiority ritual.

More serious are bullying rituals that are associated with some groups of male athletes and hazing rituals in which athletes are initiated into male (and sometimes female) teams. These rituals reflect and make legitimate what some sociologists refer to as the "sports ethic," a set of norms defining what is expected behavior of an athlete in power and performance sports and, by association, a restricted view of masculinity. These norms are dedication to "the game," striving for distinction, accepting physical risks and playing with pain, and the obligation never to quit in the pursuit of victory (Coakley, 2007). Dedication to "the game" means that a commitment to the sport takes precedence over all other demands on the athletes' time and requires athletes to put the interests of teammates above all others in social and personal relationships. Striving for distinction means that the athlete is continually trying to improve performance and achieve perfection. Accepting physical risks and playing with pain means that athletes should be willing to inflict physical pain on their opponents and themselves in the pursuit of victory. Underlying this ethic is a narrow form of bonding in male sports teams based on intragroup competition, one-upmanship, sexually aggressive trash talking, and self-destructive behavior.

Values such as these become the hallmarks of masculinity in male adolescent groups and wrap athletes in an aura of elitism in their own eyes and in the eyes of their peers. Athletes, particularly male athletes, can sometimes abuse the power that their elite status gives them by bullying members of less popular cliques that they see as having a different or inferior gender identity. This bullying can take the form of verbal insults such as calling a lower status boy a "wimp" or a "fag" or actual physical intimidation. Of course, not all male athletes bully, and bullying is sometimes institutionalized in schools (e.g., Freshman Friday) so that many different groups practice it. However, bullying is another masculinity ritual that can be legitimized in male adolescent groups especially if male athletes use it as a "put-down" or as a masculinity test to see how well other boys cope with physical pain.

The practice of hazing is widespread in male and female high school sports teams. Hazing is a process by which potential members undergo some test or imposition in order to gain access to the group. In athletics, this test can run the gamut from freshmen having to carry sports equipment for seniors to extreme forms of psychological and/or physical (sometimes sexual) abuse. Most athletes (and some coaches) accept hazing as a positive exercise that develops team spirit and see it as a test of their commitment to the sports ethic that they must pass in order to gain the elite status of an athlete. Yet, it performs other functions for the group not usually recognized or acknowledged by its members. These include hazing as a way of controlling new members who might upset the current status hierarchy, as a form of entertainment, and (among male sport teams) as a way to reinforce a restricted view of masculinity. Initiates may be forced to drink to excess or to undergo verbal abuse or physical pain and are expected to take their punishment "like a man." The most extreme sports hazing can involve symbolic and occasionally physical attacks on the presumed heterosexual identity of the hazee, including acts of sodomy and other forms of sexual degradation. On occasions of such extreme hazing, public investigation is sometimes hampered by the athletes' commitment to the sports ethic that causes them to erect a wall of silence about the event to protect guilty teammates. Few athletes, coaches, and administrators make the link between extreme hazing and athletes' masculine identity, preferring to attribute the event exclusively to the deviant behavior of "a few bad apples."

BROADENING MASCULINE IDENTITY IN SPORTS

The information in the previous section is based mainly on qualitative research conducted with small groups of athletes. This research paints a rather negative picture of the contemporary relationship between high school sports and masculinity, one that would probably be contested by most athletes, coaches, and sports administrators who are more likely to accept the "sport builds character" belief that has reached almost mythical levels in our culture. Since believing is seeing, rather than the other way around, and the hidden curriculum is hidden, it is difficult to make simple definitive statements about the relationship between sports and masculinity in schools. The results of quantitative research with large-scale samples have shown both positive and negative effects of sports on character development, as well as no effects at all. One conclusion is that if high school sports involvement can encourage a masculine identity based on aggression violence, elitism, and homophobia, it can also nurture a masculine identity based on acceptance, love, and tolerance. This raises the question of how athletics can help to develop a broader concept of masculine (and feminine identity) than the one described above.

One example of an attempt to change the concept of masculinity reinforced by sports is offered by former professional football player Joe Ehrmann, now an ordained minister and football coach of Gilman High School in the Baltimore area. Ehrmann and head coach Biff Poggi argue that the importance attached to athletic ability, sexual conquest, and victory via violence are components of "false masculinity" that actually sets men up for failure in our society. Instead, they have developed a religious-based program they call "building men for others," which uses football experiences to teach life skills such as respect for opponents, accepting responsibility, empathy, and social responsibility (Marx, 2003).

This program and others that stress values outside the limited masculinity enshrined in the sports ethic are steps in the right direction, but they do not confront the underlying homosocial reality of male sports experiences in schools upon which the myth of masculine superiority is based. Even in the post-Title IX era, where participation in high school athletics has become a reality for three million or so girls, boys' and girls' sports experiences are separate. Women have yet to attain positions of power in coaching and sports administration, even in girls' sports. Traditional ideas of male superiority in sports make acceptable the idea of males coaching girls' sports teams, but it is unlikely that male high school athletes have ever been coached by women. On the extremely infrequent occasions that girls and boys compete against each other in power and performance sports (as sometimes happens in contemporary high school wrestling), it is still a "double jeopardy" situation for the boy. Losing is bad enough, but losing to a girl is unthinkable. However, interaction between male and female athletes on the same team may lead to respect and acceptance and a realization that gender differences between boys and girls (and by association men and women) exist on a continuum rather than as binary opposites. High school sports have the potential to legitimize a broader view of masculinity than has been popular in the past but only if the current model is perceived as problematic.

REFERENCES AND FURTHER READINGS

Coakley, J. (2007). *Sports in society: Issues and controversies* (9th ed.). Boston: McGraw-Hill.

Marx, J. (2003). *"Seasons of life": A football star, a boy, a journey to manhood.* New York: Simon & Schuster.

Messner, M.A. (2002). *Taking the field: Women, men and sports.* Minneapolis: University of Minnesota Press.

Miracle, A., & Rees, C.R. (1994). *Lessons of the locker room. The myth of school sport.* Amherst, NY: Prometheus Books.

C. Roger Rees

Service Learning and Activism

The relationship between service learning and feminism is a complicated one with deep philosophical differences sometimes masked by shifting terminology. Service learning is often used interchangeably with activism and with experiential education, the catchall term that includes any structured learning experience outside the traditional classroom. *Experiential education* might include the experiences of a business major interning in an accounting firm or a women's studies major interning in a radical direct action group. The term *internship* is usually applied to experiential education involving a major time commitment and preparation for a specific career area. It is typically unpaid work. While participating in an internship may enhance a student's future career possibilities, some students may not have the time or cannot afford to give up paid work to engage in this form of experiential learning.

Service learning tends to be the term used for experiential education projects that are short term and not necessarily connected to a career area. Service learning has proven to be a politically useful term for some since there are now national organizations, such as Campus Compact, dedicated to its promotion and funding. Some teachers who use the term focus on traditional service projects such as tutoring and working in homeless shelters, whereas others use the term to include projects that might be characterized as social change or advocacy work.

Because of these different definitions, service learning has proved to be a controversial concept, especially among those feminists who contrast it with activism aimed at challenging gender norms and changing the social structure. Nevertheless, women's studies programs have been particularly receptive to all forms of experiential learning, including service learning, but the possibilities for feminist activism and other forms of experiential learning depend upon the institutional constraints and political climate in which those programs find themselves.

FEMINIST UNEASE WITH SERVICE LEARNING

The term *service learning,* with its connotations of traditional charitable work, has long made many feminists uneasy. Although celebrated by some strands of feminist thought as embodying an ethic of care, charitable work has been regarded with suspicion by feminists who have seen such work as implicated in female subordination or as an attempt to prop up an unjust status quo. At the 1973 convention of the National Organization for Women (NOW), the Task Force on Volunteerism passed a resolution that advocated for political activism as opposed to the "band-aid" approach of service-oriented volunteerism. The resolution stated that NOW believed that service-oriented volunteerism was a hit-or-miss, patchwork approach to solving major social problems, most of which are reflections of an economic system in need of an overhaul. Worse yet, the political energy devoted to service-oriented volunteerism actually provided administrative support for the current system, thereby preventing needed social changes from occurring.

NOW has since changed its bylaws to remove its prohibition against service-oriented volunteerism. Although the 1973 NOW statement may seem somewhat extreme, it does raise some important questions and reflects a legitimate (and prescient) concern that a parsimonious government will abdicate its responsibilities to its citizens and try to substitute "hit-or-miss" volunteer efforts for much needed social programs.

The NOW members who argued for the removal of the prohibition against service-oriented volunteerism thought it missed something extremely important—the mutually reinforcing relationship between direct service and advocacy for social change. The political energy that NOW wanted to encourage is often developed as a consequence of the experience of direct service. Determination to attack a social problem at its roots can be an outgrowth of the experience of direct service.

The ambivalent responses of feminists to volunteerism (and by implication to service learning) is an extremely useful lens for exploring conflicts in contemporary feminist thought. The debate about volunteer work is intimately bound up with the difference/sameness debate that runs throughout the feminist thought of the past 150 years. Traditional service-oriented volunteerism is more likely to be valued by "cultural feminists" or "difference feminists" who value women's different voices and concerns and tend to emphasize women's special attributes. Volunteer work is most likely to be viewed with suspicion by the strand of feminist thought that focuses on the struggle for equality based on the assumption that men and women are fundamentally the same and should be treated the same in the public sphere. Such "equal rights feminists" are more likely to adhere to individualist values; "cultural feminists" are more likely to adhere to communitarian values.

Ironically, at the same time that some feminists were criticizing the volunteer ethic, a new kind of volunteer work—volunteering on the job—was emerging, a kind of volunteer work largely exempt from feminist critique and often encouraged by feminist organizations. This new kind of volunteer work has clear affinities with the kinds of charitable works women have traditionally performed throughout the history of American society. And, as was true in earlier periods, volunteers tend to come from the ranks of relatively affluent women. In contemporary society, volunteering on the job is mainly characteristic of professional women and tends to be most prevalent in the less-prestigious professions such as teaching and social work. For many women in education and human services, their jobs have become their volunteer work as they put in far more time than the hours for which they are paid. Volunteering on the job can become really insidious when a woman's job is also her cause. Some of the most compulsive volunteers on the job are directors of women's studies' programs and directors and staff of women's advocacy groups.

WHAT IS FEMINIST ACTIVISM AND WHAT MAKES IT POSSIBLE?

The debate about activism versus volunteer work has been part of the reflective component of many service learning/experiential education courses. NOW's encouragement of feminist activism (loosely understood as activities that challenge prevailing gender norms) rather than traditional volunteer work has resonated with many feminist educators. However, there is no clear consensus among feminist educators as to what counts as activism or the extent to which it is to be valued over traditional volunteer work. For some, the activist project is intended to help students develop a deeper understanding of feminist issues; for others, it is intended to promote the development of skills necessary for building a powerful feminist movement. Many feminist educators would no doubt lay claim to both goals with the emphasis shifting depending upon the level of the course. A focus on expanding awareness is more likely to be the top priority in the introductory course; an analysis of strategies for advancing the feminist agenda is more likely to be the focus of a senior seminar intended for women's studies majors.

To further complicate matters, projects that meet the usual understanding of activism might be characterized by some feminist educators as service learning. The shifting terminology and the use of the term service learning to characterize what might well be described as activism is apparent in recent collections exploring the relationship between service learning and activism, on the one hand, and the academic field of women studies, on the other. Naples and Bojar (2002) and Balliet and Heffernan (2000) present a wide range of possibilities that have been included under the rubric feminist activism or service learning.

Some feminist educators have found the term "service learning," with its connotations of charity rather than social change, politically useful when they are writing grants to fund an activist project or seeking support from college administrators. Academic administrators (even liberal ones) tend to be reluctant to channel resources to anything that might be considered controversial by their boards of trustees or by local political leaders, in the case of public institutions dependent on state and local funding. The compromises feminist educators make (or choose not to make) depend on institutional constraints, local political climate, and the extent to which feminist educators are in position to take risks.

Institutional constraints shape both the possibilities available to feminist educators and the language used to describe them. In women's studies courses that enroll large numbers of nonmajors, students are often resistant to feminism, in particular, and to activism. Furthermore, possibilities for community partners are very dependent upon location. Options abound in urban areas rich in feminist organizations. Frequently in such urban areas, institutions are managed by liberal administrators who provide support or at least are not actively opposed to efforts of women's studies programs to promote feminist activism. Once one leaves the Boston-Washington megalopolis, the Pacific coast, and a few urban centers in the South and Midwest (Atlanta, Austin, Chicago, and the Twin Cities), the range of potential community partners for feminist projects dwindles more generally.

In addition to institutional constraints such as geographical location and political climate, another powerful constraint is time. Residential campuses provide opportunities for campus-based projects not available at commuter colleges where students rush off to jobs and family responsibilities. Finding time for activist projects is an especially urgent issue for teachers at community colleges desperately trying to pack as much as possible into their introductory women's studies courses, knowing this may be the only women's studies course their students will ever take. The options available to them are worlds apart from those available to teachers of senior seminars for women's studies majors in four-year colleges.

RELATIONSHIPS AMONG ACTIVISM, SERVICE LEARNING, AND WOMEN'S STUDIES

Women's studies as an academic discipline has been particularly receptive to experiential education in its many forms. In the minds of many women's studies practitioners, women's studies and feminist activism are inextricably intertwined. Women's studies as an academic discipline has defined itself in terms of its subject matter, methodology, and pedagogy. A commitment to experiential education has been a major theme of feminist pedagogy, and many women's studies practitioners would argue that it is central to feminist pedagogy. In the early days of women's studies programs, the link between the academic study of women's lives and the feminist movement was, for the most part, unquestioned.

However, as women's studies programs became institutionalized, a note of anxiety about compromising one's scholarship by political engagement was sometimes heard; increasingly, some feminist scholars began to see feminist activism as something of a career risk. Of course, the riskiness of a public commitment to activism varies considerably depending on one's situation. A teacher in a community college might be rewarded for what is seen as laudable civic engagement; a feminist scholar seeking tenure in a traditional academic department at an elite institution might well worry that activism might jeopardize her career. Whether feminist activism is likely to reap rewards or punishment is clearly dependent on the political climate of the institution and its surrounding community.

Some women's studies programs, heavily influenced by postmodernist theory, disengaged from activism. Feminist scholars began to write what were seen by some as unintelligible theoretical articles that sought to "problematize" key concepts and categories—such as the category *woman*. These scholars argued that gender boundaries are permeable, that "woman" is an unstable category, and that ultimately there is no such thing as "woman." This shift to theory coincided with a shift from women's studies to gender studies. It is not surprising that navigating these minefields has led some feminist educators to use more politically acceptable terminology such as service learning or experiential education, rather than activism, to describe activist-oriented pedagogical strategies.

Interestingly, the activist projects (often characterized as service learning) developed by feminist educators usually do not include projects related to electoral politics. The service-learning movement itself is on every level shot through with the notion that politics is dirty business. Tobi Walker (see her chapter in Balliet & Heffernan, 2000), who is one of the few service-learning practitioners to argue for encouraging student involvement in electoral politics, cites numerous examples of leaders of the movement—such as a director of a student-run national service organization and government officials at the Corporation for National Service—who exalt service over politics and reflect what Walker calls "a troubling tendency within the community service movement to conclude that politics is evil." Much of the literature on women's grassroots activism, such as Temma Kaplan's (1997) *Crazy for Democracy* and Nancy Naples's (1997) *Grass Roots Warriors,* report similar distrust of participation in electoral politics on the part of community activists and the widely held belief that "authentic" grassroots activists must stay above the fray of electoral politics.

Whether defined as service learning, experiential education, or activism, there is agreement that these activities represent a labor-intensive approach to education and that the resources available are limited. Women's studies practitioners generally agree that there is a need to build support for their efforts to include experiential/service learning/activist components in their courses. This support could take many forms, such as smaller classes, additional resources such as teaching assistants, additional compensation either in the form of increased pay or released time, and recognition for such work when decisions are made regarding promotion and tenure. This agenda might seem hopelessly utopian to those who teach at financially strapped colleges that would have great difficulty providing additional financial resources or at elite institutions that would be very resistant to considering a commitment to experiential education when awarding promotion and tenure. Yet, there are other feminist goals that seemed hopelessly utopian in earlier times but have been at least partially realized. If feminist educators are committed to an experiential/activist approach, they must also build an institutional commitment to experiential education.

REFERENCES AND FURTHER READINGS

Balliet, B.J., & Heffernan, K. (Eds.). (2000). *The practice of change: Concepts and models for service learning in women's studies.* Washington, DC: American Association of Higher Education.

Kaplan, T. (1997). *Crazy for democracy: Women in grassroots movements.* New York: Routledge.

Naples, N.A. (1997). *Grassroots warriors: Activist mothering, community work and the war on poverty.* New York: Routledge.

Naples, N.A., & Bojar, K. (Eds.). (2002). *Teaching feminist activism: Strategies from the field.* New York: Routledge.

Report of the National Organization for Women Task Force on Volunteerism. (1973). Reprinted in *MS,* February, 1975, p. 73.

Karen Bojar

Sororities

Sororities are Greek-letter voluntary associations for college women and alumnae that aspire to foster a sense of belonging, character development, and cultural awareness through ritual, traditions, and the shared experiences of members. Inspired by secret societies, including the Masonic orders and men's Greek organizations, or fraternities, sororities have existed on American college campuses for over 150 years, functioning within the context of undergraduate student culture. Approximately four million women are affiliated with college sororities today.

Sorority membership first served college women to enrich the formal curriculum of the mid-to-late nineteenth century. As coeducation progressed, sororities conferred prestigious social standing upon members in male-dominant environments and enhanced their participation in student governance. Sororities flourished over time by meeting a range of member needs including providing meals and lodging, introducing suitable associates and good marriage prospects, promoting academic success and persistence among members, providing entrée into alumni-sponsored business and employment networks, and addressing the distinct needs of different racial and ethnic groups as student populations diversified.

While some sororities reside as isolated chapters on individual campuses, sororities also exist apart from colleges and universities as large, multichapter, national or international corporations with executive offices, million dollar budgets, independent philanthropic foundations, and extensive alumnae networks. Sororities, along with fraternities, receive special endorsements such as land and administrative staff support from colleges and universities. However, the nature of the relationship between sororities and academic institutions is best described as symbiotic, meaning sororities and their host colleges and universities exist in a mutually interdependent state but are not necessarily of benefit to each other. Campus prohibitions on Greek housing or policies that delay member recruitment until sophomore year, for example, demonstrate that colleges and universities may curtail sorority growth and operation. Well-documented incidents of hazing, high-risk drinking, and eating disorders among sorority women illustrate that at times members indulge in behaviors that may undermine the academic goals of individuals and the institution.

Despite the pervasiveness of sororities, limited research exists about their short- and long-term membership and community effects as well as their larger consequence to women's and men's education. Proponents claim that sorority membership promotes academic achievement, student involvement, institutional loyalty and pride, overall satisfaction with college student life, and alumni giving. Opponents contend that sorority membership promotes frivolity; detracts from student learning; perpetuates unhealthy behaviors; and accentuates women's appearance, manners, and traditional female roles. Thus, scholars, educational practitioners, students, and even sorority members themselves contest the purpose, value, and customs of sororities, and any conclusions about their contribution to the collegiate extracurriculum are contradictory at best.

HISTORY AND DEVELOPMENT

Although the term "sorority" may denote various civic clubs for women, a Syracuse University Latin professor coined the term "sorority" in 1874 in reference to Gamma Phi Beta, the first women's voluntary association to actively identify as a sorority on a college campus. Prior to that, sororities existed as isolated secret societies without Greek nomenclature or they were known as fraternities. The secret literary societies founded in 1851 and 1852 at Wesleyan Female College in Macon, Georgia, and known, respectively, as the Adelphean and Philomathean societies, are considered the first sororities. Only after the turn of the twentieth century did these two groups come to identify as Alpha Delta Pi and Phi Mu fraternities and expand their membership to other campuses.

I.C. Sorosis is the first sorority founded as a national women's "fraternity" and the first sorority to start chapters in other locations, although its chapters quickly folded. Founded at Monmouth College in Monmouth, Illinois, in 1867, I.C. Sorosis became Pi Beta Phi fraternity 21 years later when members perceived an advantage from the adoption of Greek letters. Founded in 1870, Kappa Kappa Gamma followed I.C. Sorosis at Monmouth by three years; and during that same year, creators established another sorority, Kappa Alpha Theta, at DePauw University. Interestingly, these two women's groups, Kappa Kappa Gamma and Kappa Alpha Theta, intentionally adopted the principles and practices of men's organizations.

Greek-letter sororities proliferated rapidly around the turn of the twentieth century. They arose at various institutional types; operated in concert with societal norms and discriminatory constraints related to race, religion, and ethnicity; and reflected women's opportunity and participation in various fields of study. The pattern of organizational beginnings shows that sororities often began in close proximity to others where an established group sparked competition and gave models to emulate. This happened at Longwood College (then the Virginia State Normal School in Farmville, Virginia) where Kappa Delta (1897), Zeta Tau Alpha (1898), and Sigma Sigma Sigma (1898) originated, and at Stephens College in Columbia, Missouri, then a junior college where three sororities—Kappa Delta Phi, Zeta Mu Epsilon, and Theta Tau Epsilon—began in 1921. Three groups primarily, but not exclusively, for African American women originated at Howard University, a historically Black university in Washington, DC, namely, Alpha Kappa Alpha (1908), Delta Sigma Theta (1913), and Zeta Phi Beta (1920). For Jewish women, three sororities began in New York City: Iota Alpha Pi (1903, Hunter College), Alpha Epsilon Phi (1909, Barnard College), and Delta Phi Epsilon (1917, Washington Square College of New York University). In addition, women created their own professional recognition societies in many academic fields including but not limited to Pi Kappa Sigma

(1894, education), Nu Sigma Phi (1898, medicine), Kappa Beta Phi (1908, law), Phi Upsilon Omicron (1909, home economics), and Gamma Epsilon Pi (1918, commerce).

Particularly among the early social sororities, fierce competition or "rushing" for the "best" women brought about informal agreements among sororities. To promote the extant agreements, curb problems like concurrent membership in different groups, and stave off external regulation by college faculty and deans, representatives from nine sororities came together in 1902 to create what later became the National Panhellenic Conference (NPC). Deriving authority from the unanimous agreements that its autonomous member sororities adopt and observe, the NPC offers advocacy and support for its 26 national and international member sororities and the local Panhellenic associations that oversee Greek women's affairs on the individual campus level. Similarly, the National Panhellenic Council, Inc. (NPHC), established in 1930, acts as an umbrella organization that promotes and supports the distinct mission related to racial uplift of the nine international predominately Black Greek-letter organizations, including the three historically Black sororities, already mentioned, that were founded at Howard University and a fourth historically Black sorority, Sigma Gamma Rho, that was founded in Indianapolis, Indiana, in 1922 and became a collegiate sorority when chartered at Butler University in 1929.

In addition to the long-standing NPC and NHPC affiliated groups, a large number of local sororities emerged along with sororities designed to meet the distinct cultural needs of an increasingly diverse population of college women. Defined as a single chapter on a specific college or university campus, local sororities can be robust and lasting or fragile and fleeting. Sometimes, local sororities occur when universities forbid nationally recognized Greek organizations from colonizing or when existing chapters exclude new members with diverse backgrounds or characteristics. In fact, many of the multicultural or ethnic-interest groups that thrived in the last decades of the twentieth century started and continue as local groups. These emergent sororities include groups in support of Asians (e.g., Sigma Omicron Pi, 1930; Alpha Kappa Delta Pi, 1990), Latinas (e.g., Lambda Theta Alpha, 1975; Chi Upsilon Sigma, 1980), Native Americans (e.g., Alpha Pi Omega, 1994; Sigma Omicron Epsilon, 1997), South Asians (e.g., Sigma Sigma Rho, 1998; Kappa Phi Gamma, 1998), and Muslim women (Gamma Gamma Chi, 2005) as well as lesbians, bisexuals, and transgendered women (e.g., Gamma Rho Lambda, 2003). In addition, over 20 multicultural sororities formed for the purpose of bringing about multiethnic, multiracial organizations to promote multicultural awareness (e.g., Mu Sigma Upsilon, 1981; Lambda Sigma Gamma, 1986; Theta Nu Xi, 1997). Some of these emergent groups also created their own national advocacy and support agencies, including the National Association of Latino Fraternal Organizations and the National Multicultural Greek Council, Inc., both formed in 1998.

CHARACTERISTICS OF AND CONTROVERSIES ABOUT CONTEMPORARY SORORITIES

To the outside world as well as internally, sororities evidence their priorities and shared commitments through mottoes, crests, creeds, badges, songs, colors, flowers, calls or chants, grips, hand signs, member nicknames, and rituals. These representations also reveal the public history and predominantly, though not exclusively, Christian ideals of each group, often nestled in respect and reverence for founding members or "mothers." Because Greek-letter groups often begin in proximity to other social sororities, tremendous similarity exists between organizational symbols and ideals among groups founded in similar eras with similar purposes and with slight variation in the sororities' surface characteristics. For example, many NPC sororities use Greek and Roman mythology, and NPHC sororities draw inspiration from African lore. Emergent groups reflect aspects of popular culture in their public identities, including a few who employ the terms "herstory" and "womyn" to emphasize a woman-centered purpose and knowledge of language as gender constructed among group founders and members. In addition, sororities also subscribe to philanthropy and, on the whole, members contribute thousands of service hours and raise millions of dollars on an annual basis for nonprofit, service-oriented, and community-based organizations.

This focus upon philanthropic work, combined with the various rituals and representations centering on the themes of "sisterhood" and "ideal or true womanhood," make sororities a legacy of the clubwoman era (mid-to-late 1800s through the early 1900s) when civic organizations and culture clubs, as a means to enter public affairs, gave purpose to a burgeoning group of middle-class women liberated from the constraints of the "domestic sphere" by industrialization. Just as rising middle-class clubwomen faced constraints against participation in public affairs, college women, though relatively privileged, faced a number of restrictions upheld by law and policy when they sought and eventually gained access to higher education. Once women gained admission to institutions of higher education, these restrictions included, but were not limited to, admissions quotas, ineligibility for enrollment in classes or majors, and being banned from participation in student government and many extracurricular clubs. In addition, women faced strict behavioral codes that enforced rules about attire, curfews, daily activities, and use of campus spaces. Early on, these affluent but relatively conventional college women embraced sororities as a tool for making inroads into student governance to bring about emancipation from oppressive restrictions.

For young college women establishing independence from their families, sororities serve as an instrument of female agency within historically conservative, competitive, male-regulated or centered educational institutions. At women's colleges, which can be similarly male ordered, sororities provide females a vehicle for working with faculty and administration as they navigate the passage into independent adulthood. Sororities do this at coed institutions, too, but they also ally members with the competitive and relatively privileged fraternity men whose interests and activities (e.g., athletics, drinking) dominate the extracurriculum. In this way, sororities help women date and mate the "best" men on campus.

Within this competitive, heterosexual milieu, sorority membership offers women increased control over their identities and sexualities prior to full adulthood with its requisite sobriety and substantial responsibilities. Hence, sororities offer a cocoon of sorts, permitting privileged members to indulge in lifestyle freedoms semiprivately with reputable and like-minded associates under the public protection of their Greek affiliation within a select or closed system. Within the campus or local context, this competition and exclusion often evolves into a gender-differentiated prestige hierarchy, whereby whole sororities and fraternities informally pair with an opposite gender group having members of equivalent appearance, economic status, and social standing. Because membership signifies status within the bounds of this community, simply stating identity as a member of a particular sorority conveys meaning about that member's place within the community that other community members implicitly recognize and understand. Thus, joining a sorority in general and a "better" sorority in particular provides "better" associates, protects a woman's reputation while engaging in permissive behaviors, and foretells future financial success, as well as membership in prestigious clubs and junior leagues.

On a typical college campus, the Greek system has spaces for all the women who would like to participate. Therefore, the membership recruitment process aligns each prospective new member with a chapter, ideally allowing for each side to have a say in the outcome of the selection, with some variation in the member recruitment or "intake" process for the historically Black, ethnic-interest, and multicultural groups. Often when women fail to attain Greek membership it is because they limit their opportunities, seeking only to join the highest status groups and refusing to take the places offered in groups of lesser standing within the campus Greek prestige hierarchy. On the whole, sororities maintain or attain status within the undergraduate cultural context when they are reputed to be more selective than others and when the majority of members display the desired social characteristics that advance or uphold the group's status within the local system. These implicit rules about maintaining reputation also apply to participating members; for those members who overindulge in lifestyle freedoms or bring disrepute to the group face consequences such as probation, suspension, or expulsion from the group.

From the outside looking in, it troubles some observers that sorority women frequently describe their association as a "sisterhood," and members often refer to each other as "sister" or "soror" in the predominantly Black and some ethnic-interest as well as multicultural sororities. But, sorting out this ideal of sisterhood and the role of sororities among relatively privileged women within the context of higher education requires wrestling with women's history in postsecondary education and the larger effects of socially constructed undergraduate campus cultures. Among participants in women's clubs, the Woman's Suffrage and Women's Rights movements, and, especially, African American women, the term "sisterhood" refers to a shared struggle in the face of oppression and signals women's collective power to bring about social change. Critics of sororities, including many feminists, believe the word "sisterhood" rings hollow for sorority women, especially those in predominantly White sororities, because of their exclusivity and focus on competition for men and social status. As well, these opponents argue that sororities promise little positive social change compared to early clubwomen who were concerned heavily with social welfare activities. Given the term's sociohistorical usage, especially its ties to feminism and to struggles against racial and class oppression, these opponents challenge the appropriateness of the term "sisterhood" as a description of the bonds of association among members of social sororities. Nevertheless, the term remains popular among sorority members themselves, including White members of predominately White organizations, who often use the term as a synonym for "close friendship" and who often cite sisterhood within their sorority as a positive—sometimes the most positive—experience of their undergraduate years.

The desire for and high value assigned to close friendship probably also explain why sororities continue to be popular among many undergraduate women and why women from minority backgrounds, cultures, religions, and ethnic groups that were previously excluded from sororities band together to establish similar associations with similar rituals and activities, rather than other forms of student organizations. For minority women, sororities offer not only close friendships but also kinship-like ties with other members of underrepresented groups in predominantly White college settings. The added dimension of a shared desire among members to sponsor educational, economic, political, and social advancement or "uplift" for other members of their gender, race, ethnicity, and culture fits the individual aspirations of many college-going members of these populations, too. This emphasis on uplift historically separated NPHC from NPC groups and their members. For example, the first public act of Delta Sigma Theta, now a member of NPHC, was to march in a woman's suffrage parade down Pennsylvania Avenue in Washington, DC, on March 13, 1913. The activities of Black sororities, in partnership with Black fraternities, have included providing leadership for the American Council on Human Rights, the United Negro College Fund, the National Urban League, and the National Association for the Advancement of Colored People, to name a few.

In contrast to the NPHC sororities, those in the NPC have continued to place more emphasis on sociability. Their philanthropic work has rarely had the personal relevance or exhibited the intense commitment of the uplift work of NPHC sororities that has been rooted in racial and gender identities. Thus, it is surprising that even now, when women have increased their independence from men, have become more career oriented, and outnumber men in many academic fields and institutions of higher education, NPC sororities remain popular in contrast to fraternities whose numbers and popularity fluctuate. Given the demands of membership, including its financial costs, and the potential negative effects of being perceived as someone who focuses on superficial or status-oriented aspects of life such as appearance, popularity, wealth, and reputation, why would contemporary White women want to participate in them? Their popularity may result not only from the desire for close friendships, mentioned earlier, but also from the fit between organizational ideals and the values of the women they attract. Some studies show, for example, that women in traditionally and still predominantly White sororities are politically conservative, reject feminism, and hold traditional gender attitudes regarding dating and marriage as well as conventional stereotypes about male dominion in interpersonal relationships.

Sororities' popularity also has something to do with the fact that, just as sororities reflected their times, they also changed with them. Certainly, society and sororities, along with the colleges and universities that host them, indulge much more permissive behaviors and attitudes among female students than was true years ago. Not only a relic of the past, today's sororities adapt and meet new member demands for persisting in a male-ordered academy and offer keys to "succeeding" within the bounds of patriarchal society without undoing it or requiring that women give up becoming wives and mothers. Thus, even first-generation college students from diverse backgrounds and groups find sororities useful as a vehicle to support their career aspirations and personal success ideologies. So in addition to activities and practices that focus on appearance and perpetuate traditional notions of womanhood, sororities also strive for high scholastic achievement and leadership development among members. Sororities devote time and resources to member education on issues related to women's health, academic success, and professional networking, and their investment often pays off in members' academic persistence and success. Though much of the research examining the effects of the Greek experience does not separate effects of sorority membership from fraternity membership, researchers have found that Greek affiliation positively promotes greater feelings of belonging, involvement, increased academic effort, as well as higher levels of satisfaction with the college experience.

In a society where women are encouraged to want and have both successful careers and families, sororities have been found to help women achieve their romantic goals by establishing their femininity and value to men through their appearance, reputation, and attractiveness while simultaneously supporting their members' academic and career aspirations. While the advent of multicultural sororities helped to break the mold of sororities as racially and ethnically exclusive organizations, gender constructions among these groups most often fit familiar patterns with sororities claiming association with opposite gender "brother" groups, for example, and some groups participating in new member hazing or high-risk drinking activities. These conflicting tendencies within and among sororities to both promote and impede women's liberation and success contradict simple claims about their benefits and liabilities and also make clear the need for more and better research into their purposes, values, and contributions to the higher education of women in the United States.

REFERENCES AND FURTHER READINGS

Bank, B.J. (with Yelon, H.M.). (2003). *Contradictions in women's education: Traditionalism, careerism, and community at a single-sex college.* New York: Teachers College Press.

Blair, K.J. (1980). *The clubwoman as feminist: True womanhood redefined, 1869–1914.* New York: Holmes & Meier.

Brown, T.L., Parks, G.S., & Phillips, C.M. (Eds.). (2005). *African American fraternities and sororities: The legacy and the vision.* Lexington: University of Kentucky Press.

Holland, D., & Eisenhart, M.A. (1990). *Educated for romance: Women, achievement, and college culture.* Chicago: University of Chicago Press.

Horowitz, H.L. (1987). *Campus life: Undergraduate student cultures from the end of the eighteenth century to the present.* Chicago: University of Chicago Press.

Nuwer, H. (1999). *Wrongs of passage: Fraternities, sororities, hazing and binge drinking.* Bloomington: Indiana University Press.

Amy E. Wells

Deborah Worley

Student Government

In the United States, student government is both an oxymoron and a central feature of the extracurriculum in secondary schools and institutions of higher education. Its seeming self-contradiction arises from the fact that in no educational institution do students have full governmental powers, and in many institutions, the powers of student government are severely constrained. Nevertheless, student government plays a central role in the extracurriculum, one that is rooted in the contradictory educational goals of promoting democracy and controlling student activities. Given this contradiction, it is not surprising that the relationships between student governments and the school or university administrations to which they report are often fraught with tension concerning the extent to which administrators have the power to control the agenda of the student government and to veto student votes and initiatives.

Tensions also exist between student governments and the student body they supposedly represent. Some of these arise when the student government is thought to represent the interests of only a segment of the student body, while ignoring or even working against the interests of other student groups. Other tensions occur when students feel that their government is failing to represent them and is, instead, simply carrying out the dictates of school administrators. Also, because student governments rarely have real power in school or on campus, they are often viewed with disdain or indifference by the student bodies they supposedly represent. Election turnouts tend to be low, and it is often difficult to get students to contribute their time and energy to the many activities for which student governments have come to be responsible.

As a result, campus and school personnel whose task it is to work with student governments often find themselves in the somewhat ironic position of having to figure out ways to make student governments stronger. And, parts of the contemporary literature about student government, and the extracurriculum more generally, read like recruiting brochures with a heavy emphasis on the rewards and benefits that individual students can gain by getting involved. To date, no publications have appeared that analyze student government using a gender lens, although both researchers and the mass media report that, in the United States, females now outnumber males in student government positions at the secondary level and on an increasing number of coeducational college and university campuses.

STUDENT GOVERNMENTS AND CAMPUS OR SCHOOL ADMINISTRATIONS

Many of the student clubs and activities that are now called the extracurriculum were initiated and organized by students seeking some relief from the rigid, narrow academic curricula characteristic of U.S. colleges and universities during the eighteenth and most of the nineteenth centuries in the United States. Because the extracurriculum was outside of the official academic curriculum, it was also outside of the control of faculty and college officials who often found themselves in serious conflicts with students. It was not uncommon for students to use parts of the extracurriculum, such as debating and discussion societies, literary magazines, theatrical events, and "school" newspapers as instruments of criticism and attack on official school policies and practices. And, even more frivolous components of the extracurriculum, such as the football games, homecoming weekends, proms, and "socials," were occasions for student hedonism and acts of rebellion against the academic seriousness and hard work advocated by faculty and campus administrators.

During the Progressive Era of 1890–1920, administrators of most colleges and universities came to an accommodation with the students' extracurricular clubs, activities, and organizations. The mechanism for achieving this accommodation was the creation of student governments. By creating governments run by students who were elected by their peers, institutions of higher education gave official recognition to the students' own status system. Those elected were not necessarily the best students nor the students whom the faculty held in highest regard, but rather those who were most popular among their peers and considered by those peers to be good leaders. From the standpoint of institutions of higher education, the purpose of student government was not to give such students recognition, but rather to establish lines of communication with them and to co-opt them. Student governments rarely had the power to make the policies that governed students' lives on campus, but they could give college administrators advice about those policies and they could run the student courts that enforced them. Progressive Era ideology placed a heavy emphasis on citizenship and service, and colleges became increasingly successful over time in using student government to harness student energies to these progressive values.

In conjunction with the establishment of student government, many colleges and universities, especially those with more than a small number of students, also established a dean's office to supervise the nonacademic life of the students. As increasing numbers of men's and newly established universities became coeducational, most college presidents felt it necessary also to appoint a woman to guide and protect the women students and help them develop suitable activities. On many campuses, the women who did this work were not given the title of dean and were subordinate to a man who was. For example, a campus might have a dean of students who was a man with an associate dean of women students who was a woman. No associate dean of men students would be appointed; however, as it would be assumed that the dean of students was also the dean of men. It was also not unusual on campuses that became coeducational before World War I and the passage of the Nineteenth Amendment to the U.S. Constitution granting women's suffrage for the dean of students/men to work with an all-male student government, while the associate dean of women worked with an association of women students that functioned as a secondary student government concerned with the nonacademic activities of women students. Eventually, these separate women's governing bodies merged with the men's student government although some did not do so until after the rise of second-wave feminism in the 1960s.

At the very time that separate governments for women students were disappearing, separate student governments for graduate and professional students were appearing on many campuses, and a few predominantly White campuses also saw the development of separate governments run by and for Black and minority students. The growth of universities, especially in the period following World War II, also led to a growth in student service personnel and the metamorphosis of the dean of students office into the directorship of a large, multifaceted set of activities known collectively as the office of student affairs or the office of student life or the office of student services. Throughout this evolution, working with the student government(s) has been one of the major duties of such offices.

Not the least of the powers delegated to student governments on many campuses is the power to recognize and to fund student organizations, activities, and programs, thus putting student government at the heart of the campus extracurriculum. On some U.S. campuses today, student governments have oversight of millions of dollars of so-called student activity fees to use for this and other purposes. The other purposes vary from campus to campus, but may include involvement in such issues as student safety on campus, day care for student families, recycling and other environmental activities, campus smoking policies, race relations on campus, tuition increases, organizing state or national lobbies, drug testing, and alcohol use in student housing (see also Cuyjet chapter in Terrell & Cuyjet, 1994).

Although the scope of activities of student governments at the middle and secondary school levels are much more limited than in higher education, these student governments also received their major impetus during the Progressive Era. Many progressives saw education as the key to social reform, and some saw training in student government under the tutelage of teachers and school officials as a way to cure the many corruptions in civic society that the progressive movement was seeking to abolish. In the urban areas in particular, student government was seen as a way to train the children of immigrants for participation in democratic government and as an applied civics lesson for all. Of particular importance in promoting the development of student government nationally was the publication in 1918 by a commission of the National Education Association (NEA) of the now-famous *Cardinal Principles of Secondary Education.* In general, this report advocated comprehensive high schools, but such schools offered very different curricula to the students, such as college preparatory, commercial, vocational, and general. To unite the students across these different curricula, schools were encouraged to develop the extracurriculum including not only a schoolwide student government but also school newspapers, athletic teams and games, and frequent assemblies. One of the cardinal principles advocated by the NEA was worthy leisure time, and many of the extracurricular clubs sponsored or recognized by the student government and school officials were justified on the ground that they helped students to fill their leisure time with constructive activities rather than indolence or deviant behaviors.

Joel Spring (1986) points out that even in the Progressive Era, the purpose of student government was not to run the school, and he quotes school administrators of the period who flatly assert their opposition to any plan that would give students real power. Thus, it is not surprising that studies conducted throughout the twentieth century (e.g., Cusick, 1973; Eckert, 1989; Gordon, 1957; Larkin, 1979) found that school administrators often intervened in the functioning of student governments. Sometimes they tried to determine who got elected. More commonly, they set the agenda for discussion in student councils or assemblies, ignored or resisted student proposals with which they disagreed, and got student leaders to approve actions already planned or taken.

Student members of governing councils and other student leaders have been found to respond to these control tactics by administrators in at least three different ways. First, they may adopt an apathetic, cynical posture toward student government. No attempt is made to challenge school officials in a sustained or serious way, although many complaints and jokes are made about the decisions students are asked to make. This response seems likely to be more common at the middle school or junior high school level than at the high school level and among student leadership groups that are not very cohesive because they represent many different peer cultures in the school.

The second response student leaders may adopt toward administrative controls is to identify with their controllers. An example of this response is described by Larkin (1979) who uses the name "politicos" to identify the distinct group of students at Utopia High School who held the student offices and were prominent in the committees that operated the student government. Unlike their predecessors in the previous decade of 1960s student activism, the politicos could no longer depend on the student body to engage in political action on its own behalf. As a result, the politicos often felt that they were shouldering the responsibilities and work that the rest of the student body was too lazy and apathetic to assume. This disdain for their apolitical peers made the politicos highly likely to accept adult definitions of the situation, thereby becoming agents of adult goals and values.

The third possible response student leaders can make to administrators is resistance or rebellion. Cusick (1973) describes an example of resistance by a committee of the Student Council at Horatio Gates Senior High School against Mr. Rossi, the vice-principal for students. The willingness of these students to confront Mr. Rossi was probably increased by the fact that they all belonged to the same chosen peer group. Because they were friends, they trusted and supported one another more than they probably would have done if they had been only political allies. It also seems likely that sustained acts of resistance by student leaders are more common in senior than junior high schools. Such actions also seem likely to occur when student leaders and their student constituency perceive that they share an identity, values, and interests distinct from those of school staff, as was the case in the 1960s (Larkin, 1979).

The fact that Mr. Rossi was "really shook up" by the students' rebellion probably resulted both from his fear of losing control of the Council, the student body, and the public image of the school and from his surprise that the Student Council would oppose him. Indeed, such opposition is rare in most schools not only because there is little support for student power in the broader culture at the present time but also because student leaders risk losing the privileges that they have gained by being elected to positions in student government. In middle and secondary schools, these privileges include being excused from class to attend meetings of the student governing body, being able to wander around the school building more or less at will, receiving greater leniency from teachers and administrators than other students receive, and having one's way paid to student leadership conferences.

Not only student leaders, but all who participate in extracurricular activities, are likely to gain some privileges like these. Which students teachers come to know well, and to favor, depends partly on teachers' own involvements in the extracurriculum and partly on the visibility of various extracurricular activities and organizations to the teaching staff. Thus, in contemporary schools, it is not always or only the better behaved or highest achieving students who gain favor with teachers and administrators.

STUDENT GOVERNMENTS, PEER CONSTITUENCIES, AND SELF-DEVELOPMENT

Aside from athletics, cheerleading, and the clubs that are organized to promote athletics, the most visible student organization across and within most U.S. schools is student government, sometimes called the student council, student senate, or student assembly. As is true for athletics and cheerleading, there is often intense competition for positions in student government. Thus, it is not surprising that researchers have found that, in some school settings, student government has been highly regarded by students, and election to student government has been a way for individuals to enhance their reputations as "Big Wheels."

In contrast to athletes, however, officers of student government often find it difficult to gain popularity in the school. To be popular, they need to exhibit an ability to get along well with everyone in the school, but the demands of their offices often require them to make choices among their peers. They may, for example, select performers for the annual variety show, choose members of the pompon squad, and allocate funding to competing student clubs and activities. Such choices leave student officers vulnerable to charges of bias and favoritism. In addition, where student government is controlled by only one or a few of the school's peer groups, student leaders are likely to be perceived as an exclusive clique. The popularity of student leaders is further undercut in schools where they are thought to be supportive of administrative efforts to limit student autonomy and to deal harshly with student misbehavior.

If students who participate in student government are unlikely to achieve popularity with their peers and true power over school policies and practices, how might they be motivated to run for office? One answer to this question is reported by Kuh and Lund (see their chapter in Terrell & Cuyjet, 1994) whose analysis of survey data collected from college seniors about the outcomes associated with their on-campus experiences revealed that participation in student government was the single most potent experience associated with the development of practical competence, which they defined as decision-making ability, organizational skills, such as time management, budgeting, and dealing with systems and bureaucracies. In addition, participation in student government made a significantly higher than average contribution to the participants' social competence, including their capacity for intimacy, for working with others, for teamwork and leadership, and for assertiveness, flexibility, public speaking, communication, and patience. In contrast, participation in student government was less important than other kinds of activities, on average, in the development of self-awareness, reflective thought, knowledge acquisition, and aesthetic appreciation. Taken together, these findings suggest that participation in student government may be a particularly good way to develop the job skills most employers indicate are needed for workplace competence.

The consequences of participation in student government in middle and secondary schools are harder to determine. Although the research literature tends to show that participation in the extracurriculum is positively associated with self-esteem, grades, school engagement, and educational aspirations, many of these studies are based on small, nonrepresentative samples and are correlational, which means it is not possible to determine whether participation in student government is the cause or the effect of the characteristics with which it is positively associated. Even longitudinal studies that use larger and more representative samples and can examine the effects of participation in the extracurriculum over time often fail to separate participation in the student government from participation in pep clubs and other kinds of school involvements (see, for example, Eccles & Barber, 1999). It seems likely, however, that students who have successfully participated in student government in secondary school would be more likely than those who have not to continue their participation in college or university with the positive impact on their job skills that were indicated above.

REFERENCES AND FURTHER READINGS

Cusick, P.A. (1973). *Inside high school: The student's world.* New York: Holt, Rinehart, & Winston.

Eccles, J.S., & Barber, B.L. (1999). Student council, volunteering, basketball, or marching band? What kind of extracurricular involvement matters? *Journal of Adolescent Research, 14*(1), 10–43.

Eckert, P. (1989). *Jocks & burnouts: Social categories and identity in the high school.* New York: Teachers College Press.

Gordon, C.W. (1957). *The social system of the high school: A study in the sociology of adolescence.* Glencoe, IL: Free Press.

Larkin, R.W. (1979). *Suburban youth in cultural crisis.* New York: Oxford University Press.

Spring, J. (1986). *The American school, 1642–1985.* New York: Longman.

Terrell, M.C., & Cuyjet, M.J. (Eds.). (1994). *Developing student government leadership* (New Directions for Student Services, No. 66). San Francisco: Jossey-Bass.

Barbara J. Bank

Women's Centers

Women's centers emerged on college and university campuses in the United States in the late 1960s mainly as a response to the large numbers of nontraditional women entering or returning to college. Women's centers initially served as information houses to help these women negotiate their reentry to and progress through higher education. The centers often counseled women about their academic studies, career aspirations, and child-care issues, and helped them develop job skills such as resume preparation and interviewing.

The pressure to establish women's centers and to expand the services they provided increased as the women's movement took hold across the country in the 1970s. Women's centers quickly became locations on the college campus in which to house education programs and support services directed toward women of all ages, including antirape, antiviolence, and sexual assault hot lines and awareness programs. Given their roots in the women's movement, many centers were and remain committed to feminist principles and ideologies, and many have close affiliations with women's studies programs or departments on their campuses.

Today there are over 440 women's centers listed by Davie (2002) and 460 according to Kasper (2004a) providing services to meet a myriad of campus women's needs. New centers are being created even today (see Kunkel chapter in Davie, 2002). These centers take a variety of organizational forms, have many different missions, are relatively more or less successful than other centers, face similar but not identical challenges, and have evolved a variety of survival strategies.

ORGANIZATIONAL FORMS

Collegiate women's centers exist on all types of campuses, both public and private, community colleges, liberal arts colleges, and research universities. Students or a single determined faculty, staff, or community member started many of them, although sometimes the impetus for their founding was completely idiosyncratic as when the administration of a college, within a large university, wanted to retain control of a newly empty building and did so by turning it into a women's center (see Willinger chapter in Davie, 2002).

Women's centers are funded by various means. Some are funded in-house by administrations, through student fees, others from outside grants and through private donations.

Some are student based and student run, while others have full-time professional directors with administrative support. Some have operating budgets of nearly nothing while others have six figure budgets (Kasper, 2004b).

They are also structured in a variety of ways. Many are autonomous units, while others are affiliated with other campus offices or departments (Kasper, 2004b) such as student affairs, support services, a diversity or ethnically affiliated office, an office of women's affairs, or a women's studies department or program. Women's centers have various physical spaces as well. Some claim whole buildings while others are lucky to have their own phone line.

MISSIONS

Despite their variety, most women's centers see their central mission as one of meeting the needs of campus women. Five central needs were identified by Kunkel (1994) and are echoed in the mission statements of women's centers across the country. These needs are *safety, education, support and advocacy, equity,* and *community.*

With regard to *safety,* many women's centers are the central office for reporting sexual assaults and harassment, for counseling survivors, and, thus, for serving as sounding boards for sexual assault and harassment policies. Clothesline projects, Take Back the Night marches, eating disorder awareness projects, and, most recently, performances of the *Vagina Monologues* are common actions or events produced and/or supported by women's centers. Teaching nonviolence to the whole community is a way in which women's centers can promote proactive change instead of healing survivors after the fact (Allen, 2001). Myriad local actions are just the everyday common praxis supported by campus women's centers.

When it comes to *education,* some argue that this activity should no longer be central to the mission of women's centers especially on campuses where women's studies programs are well established. But, such arguments ignore the ways in which women's centers have been directly active in enhancing women's learning by engaging curricular issues. Many women's centers are linked to women's studies programs, and it is quite common for women's centers to sponsor speakers, workshops, conferences, and even scholarships for women that supplement the formal curriculum. Other women's centers have worked directly to change curriculum, for example, through curriculum transformation projects and summer programs training girls in science. Bryne (2000) suggests women's centers are instrumental in creating feminist pedagogy by linking theory to practice. Bryne sees the action programs sponsored by women's centers as prime locations for women's studies and other academic programs to develop internships, offer workshops, and organize conferences. Kasper (2004a) likewise sees the campus women's center as being fertile for the interactions of academic social workers, faculty and students alike. She urges social work faculty and students to get active in campus women's centers to gain experience in service, the community, serving clients, internships, and program evaluation.

Those who argue against women's centers also claim that the time when campus women needed special *support and advocacy* has passed. On most campuses, women constitute the majority of the students, and there are many offices on campus that serve the needs of women students as well as or better than those of men. Such arguments fail to make the important distinction between serving women and serving in women's best interests.

There are still sexist tendencies in the academy, for example, in tracking women out of science and math or into elementary education. There are real discrepancies yet today in both numbers of female faculty and in wages. Recently a woman student visited a professor during office hours. In the course of their conversation, the student told the professor that she was the first female professor the student had ever had. The student was in the spring of her second year, which means she probably had taken nearly 18 courses. Could a student really get through half of her college career and not have a female professor? Some informal investigation discovered there were other students who also had had only one female professor and several others who said they had had only two female professors in their college career. This was in 2006 at a liberal arts college.

At this particular college in that year, the full-time faculty composition was 37 percent female and rose to 43 percent female if part-time faculty were included. Women comprised 33 percent of the tenured faculty, and they numbered only 17, or 31 percent of full professors. The highest administration was 33 percent female (2/6) while department heads numbered just 6 out of 25 or 24 percent female. In contrast, the student body was nearly 60 percent female. These figures are consistent with those reported nationally. The American Association of University Professors reports that in 2003 women comprised only 38 percent of college and university faculty nationally and earned on average only 80 percent of what male faculty earned.

In 2006, the United States had not yet achieved gender equity on college campuses in terms of numbers of faculty or wages. We have not eradicated ideologies of gender inferiority, androcentrism or male bias, or the incidence of sexual harassment and assault on campus. Some suggest college women have a greater risk for sexual assault than their non-college bound peers. It is estimated that nearly 5 percent of college women are assaulted in a given year, although most students do not report their assault. A women's center can be a refuge for women who feel isolated, undervalued, or under siege. It can also be educational, supportive, and celebratory. Women are at the center of a women's center, which is why women's centers are still needed on college and university campuses today.

Women's centers can also give support to and advocate on behalf of women by coordinating services for women across the campus. At many colleges and universities, women's centers serve a vital role in building bridges and centralizing services for women on campus and in the community. Even if there are offices intended for women's special interests such as an Office of Women's Affairs or Committee on Women, Harassment Officers, Displaced Homemaker Programs, or Women's Colleges, these programs are not always coordinating with each other. They may even be duplicating services for women. For example, such offices as student health services, student life, a recreation or sports center, and a diversity center may each address issues of women's sexual health. Women's centers can serve as coordinators of services building bridges among programs and service providers. In fact, women's centers probably work best when they do not try to reproduce or take over these services, but when they are able to provide connections between these offices and to support students' efforts to gain access to existing services.

Support and advocacy for women can also take the form of action programs designed to promote gender *equity* and *community* among women. To achieve these goals, women's centers engage in a broad variety of activities including campus and community service, research, programming, producing publications such as newsletters and working papers, and providing library collections. They have often been instrumental in college policy making about issues important to women, such as racism, homophobia, sexual assault, or academic achievement.

On many campuses, women's centers are often more focused on social action that promotes the equality of women on campus and in society than are women's studies programs/departments. Whereas activism may be welcomed by the campus women's center, its struggling women's studies department may discourage it. Historically, many women's studies programs strategically distanced themselves from activism in order to achieve legitimacy as an academic discipline. Women's centers, thus, became the activist arm of the women's movement on many college campuses. Nevertheless, linking feminist ideologies and knowledge to practice is vital for social change, and Parker and Freedman (1999) have written compellingly about the renewed need for collaborations between women's centers and women's studies.

Celebrations of women's achievements and women's lives are a form of activism that women's centers can engage in to meet several of the central needs of campus women. Celebrating and honoring the women before us, and the women of today, creates community at the same time as it provides education about women's achievements. Celebrating women who are all too often missing from the standard curriculum provides educational enlightenment, promotes greater gender equity, supports women by providing them with role models, and highlights the achievements they have made in society.

EXEMPLARY CAMPUS WOMEN'S CENTERS

The successes of campus women's centers depend largely on knowing their own community, on acquiring broad-based support and funding, and on integrating women and women's needs into campus-wide goals. The most successful centers have a commitment to not marginalizing or ghettoizing the center by making it the only place to serve women. Women's services must be addressed throughout campus, but the successful women's center must gain recognition as an important and necessary provider of some (but not all) of these services.

There are many exceptional college and university campus women's centers. The Women's Resource and Action Center at the University of Iowa, the Women's Research and Resource center at Spelman College, the Women's Resource Center at Washington State University, the Women's Center at Miami University of Ohio, and the Newcomb Center at Tulane University are five that illustrate well how varied women's centers are and the different ways in which they have become successful.

The Women's Resource and Action Center at the University of Iowa is unique in its outright claim to serve not only campus women but women in the community and the state. It has an advisory board of 15 to 18 members drawn from students, faculty, staff, and the local community. The center reports serving over 10,000 clients a year with a very low staff turnover rate. They attribute their success to diversity, cooperation, and open and direct communication.

Spelman College is a historically Black college for women, and it started a women's center in 1981. The Women's Research and Resource Center has a threefold mission: curriculum development in women's studies with a focus on women of African descent, community outreach, and research on Black women (see Guy-Sheftall & Sanders chapter in Davie, 2002). The center at Spelman houses the women's studies program and has an outstanding record of achievements including hosting a journal, holding national conferences, winning grants, and sending delegations to international world conferences. Spelman's women's center is exceptional for both its academic excellence and its overtly political focus on Black women's agency and activism.

The Washington State University Women's Resource Center is exceptional for its very successful transit program, which provides free door-to-door service for women who are walking alone at night. In 2003, three transit vehicles provided 12,000 rides to women on 150 nights. The transit service not only prevents sexual assault but also gives the resource center widespread campus visibility. The service also has provided training and volunteer opportunities as drivers and dispatchers for 274 students (Kasper, 2004a). The program serves as a model for educating and involving students in outreach, service learning, and activism while providing safety for women. It clearly is a college-wide effort.

The center at Miami University (Ohio) is unique because it focuses on student concerns rather than developing and offering its own programming. The director of the women's center reports to each of the four university divisions and procures funding from each. This funding is awarded to students and groups who come to the center with problems or requests. The center aids these students and groups in creating solutions and implementing them. In other words, the activities of the center are truly student driven.

The Newcomb Center at Tulane University is notable in that it exemplifies the successful transition from what was primarily a resource center with a mission to provide "opportunities and programs focusing on personal growth, professional awareness, and educational planning" to a research center that aims to "produce and promote research for women and foster curriculum development in women studies." This transition was indicated by the change of names from the Newcomb Women's Center, at its founding in 1975, to the Newcomb College Center for Research on Women in 1985. The center today is thriving as a research center with actively involved faculty who are interested in the study of gender (see Willinger chapter in Davie, 2002).

CHALLENGES AND SURVIVAL STRATEGIES

Despite some notable successes, women's centers across the country are still struggling to be all that they can and to act in the best interest of campus women. Insufficient funding is most often cited as the number one obstacle inhibiting a center's mission because staffing and programming are most often contingent on funding. In times of education budget cuts, the women's center is often on the chopping block. The threat is real. Some centers have histories that include closing one year only to open a year or two later.

Visibility, factionalization, and prioritizing are a few more of the challenges women's centers face. Visibility is vital to women's center's success. Publicity is one way for centers to be known—make the news. Being seen is another. Sometimes women's centers are tucked away in an off-the-beaten path location, but a central location is key to visibility. The perception of the center is also important. Being known around campus is one thing. Being seen as open and welcoming to all women is even more vital to a center's success. For example, if the active voices are all perceived to be White or middle class, the center may struggle with serving women of color and working-class women. If the center takes an anti-Greek stance on some issues, it may alienate sorority women.

The center works best by diversifying staff and building alliances between groups of women. These alliances can be strengthened through broad programming and outreach programs to various campus women's groups. Even the perception of a center as "feminist" is sometimes perceived as negative. Center visibility and publicity emphasizing access and relevance to all women can combat these stereotypes.

Other challenges women's centers might face are those of factionalization. When centers are student run, faculty and staff may believe they are less welcome or not intended recipients of services. When centers are closely affiliated with women's studies or have a research focus, women staff and community members may not see the center as applicable to them. Including staff women in women's center programming is often challenging. Various centers have encountered challenges concerning racism and homophobia just as the women's movement in the United States has historically struggled with its own racism and homophobia. Women's centers must be careful not to reproduce these inequalities but rather to use their politics and location directly to challenge the matrix of dominations of sexism, racism, homophobia, and classism. Today there is also much more awareness of the power of involving men in eradicating inequality, and yet getting men involved is a particular challenge to women's centers.

Prioritizing goals and resources, including time, are also issues for many women's centers. This is especially true for those with perceived competing interests, multiple interest groups, and/or limited resources and staff. In addition, Kasper (2004a) identifies attitudes toward feminism, apathy, lack of administrative support, and territorialism as reported problems of women's centers. Many campus-based women's centers report negative perceptions of feminism, antifeminist sentiment, and just basic student indifference as challenges they face. Young women may not be aware of challenges that many women face and think the "women's movement" of their mother's generation solved all those problems.

REFERENCES AND FURTHER READINGS

Allen, S.L. (2001). Activist anthropology in a women's center. *Voices—A publication of the Association for Feminist Anthropology, 5*(1), 11–15.

Bryne, K.Z. (2000). The role of campus-based women's centers. *Feminist Teacher, 13*(1), 48–60.

Davie, S.L. (2002). *University and college women's centers.* Westport, CT: Greenwood Press.

Kasper, B. (2004a). Campus-based women's centers: A review of problems and practices. *Affilia, 19*(2), 185–198.

Kasper, B. (2004b). Campus-based women's centers: Administration, structure, and resources. *NASPA Journal, 41*(3), 487–499.

Kunkel, C.A. (1994). Women's needs on campus: How universities meet them. *Initiatives, 56*(2), 15–28.

Parker, J., & Freedman, J. (1999). Women's centers/women's studies programs: Collaborating for feminist activism. *Women's Studies Quarterly, 27*(3-4), 114–121.

Charlotte A. Kunkel

Part VII

Gender Constructions in the Hidden Curriculum

Overview

In the overview to Part VI, it was noted that the official school curriculum with its emphasis on the accredited courses necessary to achieve educational credentials, such as diplomas or degrees, is often in conflict with the values and demands of the extracurriculum. The official school curriculum is also sometimes in conflict with the hidden curriculum that is described and analyzed by the essays in this section of the encyclopedia. Although he was not the first educational researcher to use the concept, Philip Jackson is regarded as the first to use the term *hidden curriculum,* which he introduced in his 1968 book, *Life in Classrooms,* to refer to the institutional expectations and implicit rules that are used to evaluate students regardless of their academic performance. Thus, Jackson considered it useful to think of there being two curricula in the classroom, the official one focused on students' intellectual achievement and mastery of the subject matter, and the hidden one focused on students' conformity to institutional expectations about matters other than intellectual mastery. For students to be successful in school, they not only must learn the subject matter but also must "learn how to learn," by which Jackson meant learning to acquiesce to the network of rules, regulations, and routines characteristic of schools and classrooms.

Both in Jackson's book and in the large literature about education that has appeared since its publication, the concept of a hidden curriculum is extremely broad, referring to almost all the socializing influences and processes that occur in schools other than the highly focused effort to impart subject-matter learning. And, even that effort is often argued to be part of the hidden curriculum because, as the essays in Part IV and several in Part V make clear, what the teachers, textbooks, and other course materials say about the subject matter often contains implicit messages about topics, such as gender and race, that are not the overt focus of the official curriculum. Unlike the previous essays, however, the essays in this section do not focus on messages about gender that are embedded in specific lessons or courses in the official curriculum. Instead, these essays concern themselves with the ways in which messages about gender are conveyed without reference to either the specific lessons and courses that constitute the official curriculum, described in Parts IV and V, or the specific organizations and activities of the extracurriculum, described in Part VI.

What kinds of gendered messages are these, and how are they conveyed? Many of these messages concern the kinds of appearances and behaviors characteristic of "good" students versus "bad" students. Research in the United States, and some from other countries, finds that teachers consider good students to be those who work hard and are attentive, helpful, cooperative, considerate, polite, articulate, well groomed, and reasonably self-confident. As Barbara Morrow Williams points out in her essay on "Managing 'Problem' Boys and Girls," these also are characteristics consistent with the middle-class ethos of the United States. And, several researchers have noted that these also are characteristics more consistent with notions of ideal femininity than with ideal masculinity. Thus, even if teachers are sincere in their claims that they have no biases against students of a particular social class, racial-ethnic group, or gender, those biases may be built into the expectations that teachers have for appropriate and desirable student behaviors. As a result, as Morrow Williams points out, students are often rewarded for their "fit" with the dominant culture and their ability to blend into it. And, because students from White, middle-class backgrounds—especially girls—are more likely to fit the mold of the good student, they may be treated differently than their male counterparts and students from poorer, minority backgrounds.

Several of these differences in treatment are documented by Linda Grant and Kimberly Kelly in their review of "Teacher-Student Interactions." Among the many interesting points made in this essay is the observation that, although gender biases in achievement-related interactions, or what might be called interactions in the official curriculum, are decreasing, gender biases in control-related interactions, are not. These control-related matters are often parts of the hidden curriculum in that they have more to do with getting students to be "good" than with improving students' intellectual performance. And, Grant and Kelly, like Morrow Williams, suggest that boys are more frequently the targets of teachers' efforts at discipline and control than girls are. Partly as a result of these efforts, boys are more likely to receive punishments, such as detention, and are more likely to become disaffected and to drop out of school.

Teachers are not the only educators who have been found to bring gender biases to their interactions with male and female students. In the section of their essay about "School Counseling" that is devoted to "Career Development Programs and Gender," Daniel T. Sciarra, Kerri Keegan, and Bridget Sledz discuss the kinds of gender biases that may affect school counselors, and they make suggestions about ways in which these biases can be overcome. The notion that counselors or teachers can be made aware of gender biases embedded in their treatment of students and can be persuaded or trained to overcome those biases is common in writings about the hidden curriculum. In fact, a major purpose of much of that writing is to reveal the hidden curriculum by making educators aware of their differential treatment of boys and girls and of students from different economic, racial, and cultural backgrounds. Often educators will deny that their behaviors evidence gender, racial, or social class biases, but some researchers have been successful in convincing them of the biases in their behaviors by showing them videotapes of their classroom interactions with students of different backgrounds.

An assumption is often made that once counselors or teachers see their biases, they will want to eliminate them. This assumption is based on the notions that most teachers share values of equity and fairness; they not only do not want to appear biased but also do not want to be biased. Even those few who cling to their prejudices are assumed to know that discrimination is forbidden by school rules and by the legal system and that they had better comply or face negative consequences. From this perspective, revealing the hidden curriculum is a very big step on the way to revising it.

Such assumptions have been challenged, however, by research showing that the hidden curriculum is not just a set of behaviors that counselors, teachers, and administrators perform inadvertently because they fail to recognize the biased expectations and evaluative procedures they direct toward students. Instead, these expectations and evaluations about gender, race-ethnicity, and social class are deeply embedded not only in the structure and culture of the school, with its emphasis on what it means to be a good student, but also in the structure and culture of the broader society. Calling these culturally embedded expectations about gender *stereotypes,* the authors of "Expectations of Teachers for Boys and Girls" summarize research evidence showing that stereotypes have more powerful effects on student performance than the expectations of individual teachers, whose assumptions about gender have not been found to be strongly biased. It is because of these widely held and deeply seated stereotypes that teachers often find themselves in situations, described by Grant and Kelly, in which their silent failure to respond when sexism and racism are expressed by students is interpreted as support for gender and racial bias, rather than as disapproval or neutrality.

Silence is also the key to understanding the ways in which the official and hidden curricula (fail to) deal with sexuality. As the authors of "Heterosexism and Homophobia in the Hidden Curriculum" indicate, one of the more deeply held assumptions embedded in the hidden curriculum, as well as the official curriculum and the peer culture, is *heteronormativity,* a term that is used to refer to beliefs and behaviors premised on the assumption that heterosexuality is normal, natural, and universal. The fact that the official curriculum is silent about the homosexuality of some important literary and historical figures reinforces the notion that homosexuality is something to be embarrassed about or hidden rather than something that is normal, natural, or widespread. Along with homosexuality, the positive aspects of all forms of sexuality and sexual desire tend to be excluded from the curriculum. Even the depiction of the "good" student that is central to the hidden curriculum is a sexless portrait. Although it could be argued that there is an unspoken assumption that the good student is heterosexual in orientation, there seems also to be an unspoken assumption that this orientation is not too strong or too central. Good students have their sexual impulses under control, and they do not embarrass their teachers with overt displays of sexiness.

The dangers of being silent about sexuality are apparent when one reads Charol Shakeshaft's essay about "Educator Sexual Misconduct." One way to make sexual abuse in schools less common, she suggests, is to make expectations about sexual conduct explicit and public. Although her suggestion is focused primarily on the sexual conduct of educators, it seems likely that frank acknowledgment and open discussion of students' sexual curiosity, fantasies, and desires might also help students overcome the fear and guilt that so often prevents them from reporting sexual abuse by teachers, students, and other school personnel.

See also essays on "Attrition From Schools" in Part V; "Heterosexism and Homophobia in the Peer Group" in Part VIII; and "Pregnant and Parenting Teens" in Part X.

Educator Sexual Misconduct

Educator sexual misconduct is behavior by an educator that is directed at a student and intended to sexually arouse or titillate the educator or the child. These behaviors are physical, verbal, or visual. Examples include touching breasts or genitals of students; oral, anal, and vaginal penetration; showing students pictures of a sexual nature; sexually related conversations, jokes, or questions directed at students.

Surveys conducted in the United States in recent years reveal that most students experience harassment at the hands of other students. Of those students who report being sexually harassed in school—whether physical, verbal, or visual—21 percent were targeted by an adult employed in the school. Of all students, 9.6 percent in grades 8 to 11 report experiencing unwanted educator sexual misconduct at least once during their school career; 8.7 percent report verbal or visual sexual abuse; and 6.7 percent experienced physical sexual abuse.

While a higher proportion of females than males report being the target of an adult employed in a school, the difference is less than commonly believed. Of those students who report having experienced educator sexual misconduct, 57 percent are female and 43 percent are male. The proportions are similar across all types of sexual misconduct. Students of color (African descent, American Indian, and Latina/o) are overrepresented as targets of educator sexual misconduct in comparison to their relative numbers, while White and Asian students are underrepresented. Females, and particularly females of color, are overrepresented as targets of educator sexual misconduct in relation to their proportion of the population.

There are scant U.S. data on any type of sexual abuse of students with disabilities and none on educator sexual abuse of students with disability. However, studies of sexual abuse without regard to context indicate that children with disabilities are three times more likely to be sexually abused than those without disabilities.

Teachers who sexually abuse belie the stereotype of an abuser as an easily identifiable danger to children. Many are those most celebrated in their profession. Although we do not know how many or what percent of school employees are offenders, we do know that many are chronic predators; thus, the number of teachers who abuse is fewer than the number of students who are abused. Abusers are more likely to be male than female, but how much more likely is unclear. The most reliable data estimate that about two-thirds of abusers are male and one-third are female. The most common pattern is male abuser and female target, followed by female abuser and male target. Of those school employees who sexually abuse students, teachers are reported most often, followed by coaches. Teachers whose job description includes time with individual students, such as music teachers or coaches, are more likely to sexually abuse than other teachers.

Sexual abuse of students occurs within the context of schools, where students are taught to trust teachers. It is also a place where teachers are more often believed than are students and in which there is a power and status differential that privileges teachers and other educators. Sexual abusers in schools use various strategies to trap students. They lie to them, isolate them, make them feel complicit, and manipulate them into sexual contact. Often teachers target vulnerable or marginal students who are grateful for the attention. Moreover, students whom adults regard as marginal are unlikely to be accepted as credible complainants against a well-regarded educator.

In elementary schools, the abuser is often one of the people whom students most like and parents most trust. The abusers of children younger than seventh grade have different patterns than those who abuse older children. The educators who target elementary school children are often professionally accomplished and even celebrated. Particularly compared to their nonabusing counterparts, they hold a disproportionate number of awards. It is common to find that educators who have been sexually abusing children are also the same educators who display on their walls a community "Excellence in Teaching" award or a "Teacher of the Year" certificate. This popularity confounds district officials and community members and prompts them to ignore allegations in the belief that "outstanding teachers" cannot be guilty of such repugnant behaviors.

Many educators who abuse students work at being recognized as good professionals in order to be trusted by colleagues, parents, and students. For them, especially those who abuse elementary and younger middle school students, being a good educator is the path to children. At the late middle and high school level, educator abusers may or may not be outstanding practitioners. At this level, the initial acts are somewhat less premeditated and planned and more often opportunistic, a result of bad judgment or a misplaced sense of privilege. Whether premeditated or opportunistic, selection is influenced by the likelihood of compliance and secrecy. Because most educator abusers seek to conceal their sexual contact with students, offenders often target students whom they can control. In some cases, control is characterized by force. However, most abuse occurs within the much subtler framework of grooming and enticement.

During grooming, the abuser selects a student, gives the student attention and rewards, provides the student with support and understanding, all the while slowly increasing the amount of touch or other sexual behavior. The purpose of grooming is to test the child's ability to maintain secrecy, to desensitize the child through progressive sexual behaviors, to provide the child with experiences that are valuable and that the child will not want to lose, to learn information that will discredit the child, and to gain approval from parents. Grooming allows the abuser to test the student's silence at each step. It also serves to implicate the student, resulting in children believing that they are responsible for their own abuse because, "I never said stop."

Grooming often takes place in the context of providing a child with extras like additional help learning a musical instrument, advisement on a science project, and opportunities for camping and outdoor activity. These opportunities not only create a special relationship with students, they are also ones for which parents are usually appreciative. Although not every instance of educator sexual misconduct includes a grooming phase, because grooming precedes sexual engagement, grooming has the added benefit to the abuser of being able to test a child's compliance. Any complaint can be discredited because it does not yet constitute identifiable sexual misconduct.

Some of the children who are sexually abused by educators do not characterize what is happening as abuse. That is not to say they do not identify what is happening as shameful, unwanted, wrong, or frightening. In many cases, they are told that what is happening is love. Many abusers of children of all ages couch what they are doing to the children as love, both romantic and parental.

Offenders work hard to keep children from telling. Almost always they persuade students to keep silent by intimidation and threats (if you tell, I'll fail you), by exploiting the power structure (if you tell, no one will believe you), or by manipulating the child's affections (if you tell, I'll get in trouble; if you tell, I won't be able to be your friend anymore). Thus, childish or adolescent naiveté is taken advantage of to keep children silent. Because many children who are targeted have previously been abused by others, the legacy of abuse increases the likelihood of silence. Fear of discovery and punishment or shame for doing something forbidden also keep children from speaking. Boys abused by men often do not tell because of homophobia.

Because children often get something positive in the transaction, such as attention, gifts, physical pleasure, and feelings of belonging or attractiveness, they can be made to feel responsible. Offenders use this to their advantage.

Finally, abuse is allowed to continue because even when children report abuse, they are not believed. Because of the power differential, the reputation difference between the educator and the child, or the mind-set that children are untruthful, many reports by children are ignored or given minimal attention.

An analysis of documentation from legal proceedings and from interviews with school officials and student targets indicates that sexual misconduct by educators occurs in the school, in classrooms (empty or not), in hallways, in offices, on buses, in cars, in the educator's home, and in outdoor secluded areas. Sometimes the abuse happens right in front of other students.

Notice of educator sexual misconduct comes to the attention of school officials in five ways: formal complaints, informal complaints, observed abuse, observed suspicious behaviors, or rumors and/or anonymous reports. Many students do not tell anyone about the abuse. Of those who do, most tell a friend and swear the friend to secrecy. The most common reason that students do not report educator sexual misconduct is fear that they will not be believed.

When students do report, they almost always report incidents of contact sexual abuse— touching, kissing, hugging, or forced intercourse. Verbal and visual abuse are rarely reported to school officials. Few students, families, or school districts report incidents to the police or other law enforcement agencies. When criminal justice officials are alerted, it is almost always because parents have made the contact. Thus, most abusers are not entered into criminal justice information systems.

Targets of educator sexual misconduct report that they suffer emotional, educational, and developmental or health effects. Student behaviors in response to educator sexual misconduct that negatively affect academic achievement include avoiding the teacher or other educator, failing to go to school, not talking in class, not paying attention, cutting class, and having difficulty studying. Students who are targets of educator sexual misconduct report academic or discipline repercussions that they attribute to the incident. They think about changing schools or do change schools, receive lower grades in assignments or classes, get in trouble with school authorities, and believe they are less likely to get a good grade.

Health effects such as sleep disorder and appetite loss are also experienced by targets of educator sexual misconduct. Students report negative feelings of self-worth such as embarrassment, self-consciousness, lack of security, and decreased self-confidence. These students also feel afraid, are confused about their identity, and report wondering whether they will ever be able to have a happy, romantic relationship.

The school or district rarely prescribes a therapeutic and healing intervention for targets of educator sexual misconduct or for others in the school. Policies and procedures that debrief other students or their parents are not available, nor are guidelines for the type of support a targeted student should receive from the school.

Where educator sexual misconduct is not adequately addressed, the negative effects spread to other staff and students. Studies of sexual harassment in the workplace indicate that the climate and culture changes when sexualization and abuse are not addressed. Studies also indicate that most abusers do not lose their jobs. Even when the abuser leaves a school district, the person rarely loses her or his license and can, therefore, move to another school.

The primary federal legal remedy for sexual misconduct in schools is Title IX of the Education Amendments of 1972. The language of Title IX does not mention sexual harassment but, rather, is a statute that prohibits discrimination on the basis of sex in any educational organization that receives federal funds. Title IX provides for federal enforcement of the prohibition on sexual discrimination and the possibility of loss of federal funds for any educational institution in violation of Title IX or its regulations.

The Office for Civil Rights (OCR) enforces Title IX and its regulations and publishes guidelines to help schools recognize and effectively respond to sexual harassment of students in educational programs as a condition of receiving federal financial assistance. OCR provides technical assistance to schools in developing sexual harassment policies to clarify the responsibilities of school personnel. Schools are responsible for prohibiting and responding effectively to sexual harassment, and there are potential legal consequences for ignoring sexual harassment of students by staff or students.

Depending upon a number of factors (age of student, age of educator, type of sexual misconduct, etc.), educators who sexually abuse might be prosecuted under a variety of statutes. Criminal codes are not uniform across the states. While all states have laws that prohibit adults from having sex with children, each state defines that crime differently. Child sexual abuse, sexual assault, antistalking, and lewdness with a minor are legal categories under which state laws might exist. State laws regarding "consensual sex" (referred to generally as statutory rape laws) prohibit adult-child relationships but define childhood differently, depending upon the state. In addition to general sexual assault laws and criminal statutes prohibiting adult sexual contact with children, some states have adopted laws that specifically prohibit sexual abuse by educators or people in a position of trust.

Besides federal, civil, and criminal approaches to identifying and stopping educator predators, legally enforceable codes of professional conduct, generally in connection with state licensure, exist in most states. In addition, most states require criminal background checks that use FBI and state records in addition to fingerprinting, although these precautions generally do not identify educators who are sexually abusing since these predators are not entered into the criminal justice system.

Educator sexual misconduct has not been systematically addressed in schools. While the advent of awarding monetary damages to targets of sexual harassment, a result of Title IX legislation and newspaper and other media coverage, has prodded some school district officials to acknowledge educator sexual misconduct, educator sexual misconduct is still occurring.

All school districts need written policies prohibiting educator sexual misconduct and inappropriate educator-student relationships to include consensual relationships between staff and students. The behaviors prohibited should be described in the policy so that there is no ambiguity about what types of actions are unacceptable. In addition to making clear the prohibitions against adult-to-student sex, policies should include descriptions of educationally appropriate touching; limitations on closed-door and after-hours activities with only one student; investigatory rights without formal complaint; required reporting by other teachers and employees; required reports of any criminal investigation or conviction during period of employment; required chaperones, at least one male and one female, for off-site trips; deadlines for reporting allegations with the option for waiving the time limit.

A common form should be used for all employment applications that includes questions on work history, identification that will facilitate background checks, and all information on criminal history. The form should include a statement that incomplete or false information can result in termination. Interviewers should be trained to identify red flags in applicant backgrounds. Screening applicants requires multiple methods that include references, background checks, license information, and application information. Prior to making an employment offer, personnel information from the current employer should be reviewed.

Background checks with fingerprint screens should be completed for all current and new employees. Where collective bargaining agreements prohibit screening of current employees, steps should be taken to change these restrictions. While screening will not identify the majority of educators who have or will sexually abuse, it signals seriousness on the part of the district. To make background screens more effective, those who hire should check for gaps in employment, inquire into reasons for movement between schools or districts, contact school personnel in previous sites reaching beyond those listed as references, ask direct questions, and search DWI offenses. The social security numbers of new hires need to be verified. Finally, all offers of employment should include a probationary period.

One reason that educator sexual misconduct continues is that in most schools and school districts there is no one person to whom all rumors, allegations, or complaints are channeled. As a result, patterns of behavior are often not detected. Selecting one person to whom all school personnel must report any rumor, allegation, complaint, or suspicion is helpful in ensuring that no student falls through the crack and patterns of misconduct are quickly and effectively identified. Each school receiving federal financial assistance must designate at least one employee to coordinate its Title IX obligations. Schools also are required by the Title IX regulations to publish a policy that prohibits sex discrimination and outlines grievance procedures providing for prompt and equitable resolution of sex discrimination complaints. Districts must record all allegations and outcomes in employee personnel files and agree not to expunge molestation findings.

While investigations are best done by those outside the school who are trained in sexual abuse crimes, if districts choose to do in-house investigations, the investigators must be trained appropriately. Ensuring that investigations are completed within 48 hours and reports are presented to school authorities, students, and parents will protect both students and adults. It is important not to terminate the investigation even if the employee who is under investigation resigns since complete investigation reports are required

With rare exceptions, the abuse prevention training that is required in most states for educators and school staff—whether preprofessional or while on the job—does not include educator sexual misconduct. These programs focus on what to do when sexual or any other kind of abuse or maltreatment is suspected from a source outside the school. Therefore, additional training for educators and other staff about educator sexual misconduct is important. Training outlines the behaviors that are not acceptable so that everyone —both those who abuse and those who do not abuse—are working from the same set of expectations. By making expectations explicit and public, school decision makers are also helping educators understand their own responsibility in reporting behavior that does not conform to those expectations. Thus, the training will educate employees about unacceptable behavior and remind them of their responsibility to report abuse.

Like staff, students need to understand the boundaries that educators should not cross. This is important both for students who might be targeted and for students who observe such behaviors. Both sets of students need to know that such behavior is prohibited and that there is a person to whom they can and should report such incidents. Materials and programs that have been developed to protect students from sexual abuse rarely include examples of predators who are educators. Students need to know that educators might cross boundaries and what to do if this happens.

To increase the possibilities for identification of educator sexual misconduct, educators, parents, and students need to know that: Any employee, including volunteers, might molest; educator sexual predators are often well liked and considered excellent teachers; special education students or other vulnerable students are often targets of sexual predators; adults who have access to students before or after school or in private situations are more likely to sexually abuse students than those who do not (coaches, music teachers, etc.); behavior indicators in students might include age inappropriate sexual behavior, late arrivals to class, changes in personality, and increased time at school with one adult; rumors are an important source of information on educator sexual misconduct; behaviors of adults who molest include close personal relationships with students, time alone with students, time before or after school with students, time in private spaces with students, flirtatious behavior with students, and off-color remarks in class.

In addition to district and school policies and practices, state and federal authorities need to develop systematic reporting and screening practices. The U.S. public and criminal justice systems have developed mechanisms for protecting children. For instance, millions of dollars in federal funding, scores of milk cartons, and episodes on television are devoted to preventing kidnapping and child abduction. Without diminishing the tragedy of abduction and kidnapping, it is worth noting that 4.5 million students in the United States experience educator sexual misconduct with 3.5 million reporting physical educator sexual abuse, nearly 150 times the number of U.S. children who are kidnapped or abducted by a nonfamily member. The numbers do not argue against the prevention of kidnappings, but they do argue for more attention to the prevention of educator sexual abuse.

REFERENCES AND FURTHER READINGS

American Association of University Women. (2001). *Hostile hallways.* Washington, DC: AAUW Educational Foundation.

Shakeshaft, C. (2004). *Educator sexual misconduct with students: A synthesis of existing literature on prevalence, planning and evaluation service.* Washington, DC: Office of the Undersecretary, U.S. Department of Education.

Shoop, R.J. (2004). *Sexual exploitation in schools: How to spot it and stop it.* Thousand Oaks, CA: Corwin Press.

Charol Shakeshaft

Expectations of Teachers for Boys and Girls

Do the expectations of teachers shape different aspirations, self-perceptions, and achievement trajectories for boys and girls? That is, can the predictions made by others actually cause outcomes that confirm the original prophecy? Despite a large literature on teacher expectancy effects, most studies have investigated teacher beliefs about individual students—those believed to be more or less capable of learning. Far fewer studies have investigated student gender in interpersonal self-fulfilling prophecies or pursued, in systematic ways, linkages between teachers' gendered expectations, teachers' differential treatment based on their expectations, and the differential achievement of boys and girls. Thus, firm conclusions about gendered expectancy effects, as they have been studied, prove difficult to make. This topic, however, is worth pursuing in more nuanced ways.

Gender disparities in access to schooling and in educational and occupational attainment (especially in math and science) persist. Girls are generally at a disadvantage, especially evident at puberty and in higher levels of schooling. Despite performance differences between boys and girls, no consistent difference in aptitude or intelligence has been found, suggesting the workings of social forces. There exists strong evidence that parents socialize boys and girls differently with regard to achievement and along gender role lines. Thus, children enter school with gender-stereotyped preferences as well as behavioral patterns. Experimental and naturalistic research studies on teacher expectancy effects provide clear support that teachers' expectations about the capability of individual students *can* shape student achievement. The mechanisms underlying such effects include the allocation of differential opportunities to learn and differential reinforcements, supports, or messages of capability, about which even young children are aware. These expectancy effects can be magnified or diminished, dependent upon the characteristics of both individual and social setting.

When applied to student gender, most expectancy studies have looked at such effects on average. What can be concluded thus far is that teacher expectations are not consistently differentiated by gender. Teachers do treat boys and girls differently in the classroom, but student behavioral patterns drive some of these differences. A small number of studies have found that girls may be more susceptible than boys to confirming teacher expectations that are biased in negative directions. Stronger support from experimental studies of stereotype threat exists for the influence of societal gender stereotypes (rather than teachers' expectations) on girls' underperformance relative to males. These gender stereotypes are evoked in math test situations that are described as diagnostic of ability. Priming Asian American identity (a positive stereotype) rather than gender identity (a negative stereotype) was found to protect Asian American girls from underperforming in math tests.

Future research needs to invest in longitudinal studies (to control for student initial differences) in order to address linkages between gendered teacher expectations, differential treatment by teachers, and different achievement trajectories for boys and girls. Gendered interpersonal expectancy effects are likely complex and nuanced, conditional on contextual factors as well as student age and stage of schooling. Perhaps, such effects are heightened with teachers who are more susceptible to holding gender stereotypes, in classroom or school cultures that make ability difference salient and highly differentiate the teaching of boys and girls, and in contexts where parental, teacher, and societal views are aligned around the belief that girls have lesser abilities in math and science. It is also important to acknowledge that the gender disadvantage is not only about girls. Boys are placed at risk in early elementary schooling. Ethnicity and socioeconomic class intersect with gender, such that certain groups of ethnic minority boys may also be disadvantaged by negative stereotypes about inferior ability. Finally, research about the effectiveness of interventions to promote gender equity in the development of talent across disciplinary domains is vital.

GENDER DIFFERENCES AND/OR GENDER INEQUITIES

Gender is a key organizing principle in society. Real and/or imagined biological differences between the sexes are given meaning by cultures, institutions, and historical time, and gender roles are constructed. Historically, schooling has always been differentiated by gender, either with regard to differential access to education or to placement in separate forms of education, such as single-sex schools, or to different tracks and experiences within schools and classrooms. Further, when coeducation does occur, it is far from a simple phenomenon.

Worldwide, there exists gender disparity in access to schooling even at the primary level. In 2005, approximately 135 million children have not received any education at all, and of these, 60 percent are girls (UNICEF, 2005). World regions that continue to lag behind are the Middle East/North Africa, South Asia, and West/Central Africa. In contrast, however, in most Latin American/Caribbean regions, the gender disparity is reversed with more girls attending primary and especially secondary schools. More typically, girls face additional barriers that exclude them from school, such as cultural values, stereotyped gender roles, low social status, family need for economic support, and vulnerability to sexual assault. Thus, girls in developing countries are frequently not enrolled in school, the last to be enrolled, and, during hardships, the first to be pulled out of school. Being a girl and living in poverty pose a double disadvantage.

Even when many barriers of access to higher levels of education are lifted, such as in the United States, women's test performance, choice of careers, ultimate attainment, occupational rise, and earnings continue to reflect gender disparities. Career choices remain sex-typed, and higher levels of attainment and earnings generally favor males. At issue are the underlying determinants for these gender gaps—either nature (inborn) versus nurture (environment) or the possibility that nature may be potentiated by nurture.

One continuing arena of gender disparity is the predominance of males in the domain of mathematics, engineering, and science as represented by faculty in U.S. universities. It has been shown that girls outperform boys in grades in all major subject areas throughout elementary, middle, and high school. Yet, girls do not necessarily perform higher than boys on achievement or IQ tests. Are there sex differences in cognitive abilities? Despite some evidence of test performance differences that may be lessening (for example, men outperform women on math tests and women outperform men on tests of verbal ability), research over four decades has failed to support consistent sex differences in intrinsic aptitude for mathematics and science or in general intelligence. These findings underscore the importance of looking to social causes for the gender disparity in achievement—to gender stereotypes, family socialization practices, school experiences, and institutional support.

Do parents socialize girls and boys differently for achievement? Beginning at birth, children are provided steady signals about gender. Studies suggest that parents provide their sons and daughters with different learning environments through selection of gender-stereotyped toys and activities and through advice about gender-appropriate careers and aspirations. For example, in comparison to girls, boys are often given toys that can be manipulated and their play activities are set in large spaces, which can promote spatial abilities. Parents' gender role stereotypes about math and science have been linked with parents' perceptions of their own children's abilities in math and science as well as with children's beliefs about themselves. In addition, parents have been found to make causal attributions that are gender stereotyped when they attributed success in mathematics to natural talent for their boys and to effort for their girls. Longitudinal studies show that parental expectancies, attributions, and gendered socialization practices may differentially affect the cognitive development, competences, self-perceptions, interests, and aspirations of boys and girls. Such parent differences are not consistently demonstrated across studies. Among the reasons for the inconsistent findings are the differing ages and historical time at which children have been studied, a reciprocal chain of events whereby both child differences and parent responses mutually drive the interaction, and the possibility that these gendered messages and opportunities may be more subtly communicated than are typically measured.

The gender disparity in achievement is also reversed in the earlier grades where boys are more likely to read and mature later than girls. They are also more likely to be held back a grade and referred for special education services. But importantly, individuals are defined by more than their gender. Thus, we must consider gender as it is represented in the intersection between racial/cultural groups as well as socioeconomic class, especially at a time of increasing ethnic diversity and income disparity in the population. Much of the research on teacher expectancy effects is not as fine-tuned. Research at the intersection of gender and culture has found that ethnic minority boys are overrepresented in the discipline system (especially African Americans) and as school dropouts. Thus, in general, gender disadvantages boys in the early grades and girls in the later grades, but certain groups of ethnic minority boys continue to be disadvantaged at every stage of schooling.

LINKING TEACHER EXPECTATIONS AND GENDER

The expectancy construct and its potential for confirmation has had a long history in literature as well as in the social sciences. An early literary example of positive expectancy effects can be found in the ancient Greco-Roman myth about the sculptor Pygmalion where his love for the statue Galatea brought her to life. In 1948, based on his observations of bank failures during the depression, the sociologist Robert K. Merton coined the term "self-fulfilling prophecy," which he described as a false belief about a situation, which, when acted upon, makes the original conception become true. In the classic *Pygmalion in the Classroom* (1968), psychologist Robert Rosenthal and school principal Lenore Jacobson conducted the first empirical test of interpersonal self-fulfilling prophecies. In this experiment, teachers were provided false and positive test information about randomly selected children who were described as intellectual bloomers, expected to show great growth in their achievement. At year end, as seen in the early elementary grades, children who had been identified as bloomers performed higher than other children on intelligence tests. This single study cemented for the public the view that teacher beliefs about student capability created the achievement gap, particularly with regard to Black-White differences, and then extended to the underperformance of girls relative to boys. This study fueled a storm of controversy and thousands of replications, both experimental as well as naturalistic studies.

Overall, the research evidence supports a causal connection between teacher expectations and student achievement, but the debate still rages over the magnitude of effects. Shifting from behavioral to social-cognitive to ecological theory, the causal model has become more complex as qualities of both person (the susceptibility of both perceiver and target) and situation (the salience of expectancy cues) have been found to magnify or diminish the power of expectancy effects.

Research has addressed the formation of expectancy beliefs (including the role of stereotypes), differential treatment or the mechanisms by which expectations exert their effects on student achievement (directly through differential opportunity to learn and indirectly through messages about capability understood by students that come to shape self-perceptions, motivation, and behavior), and moderating factors that amplify such effects. Thus, individuals may differ in their susceptibility to such effects (for example, high-bias teachers and highly susceptible younger and stigmatized students). There also exists potential for teacher perceptual confirmation, even when student behavioral confirmation has not occurred, and for student disconfirmation of negative and even positive teacher expectations. Finally, while most of the studies have addressed interpersonal expectancy effects, these effects can occur at multiple and intersecting levels of systems, such as groups, classes, and schools. Small effects can have implications for subsequent years and accumulate over time.

Turning to studies of gender, how do teacher beliefs about boys and girls differ, how do these beliefs shape practices and policies in schools, and are there demonstrated links between gender-stereotyped beliefs, practices, and achievement?

While young children develop beliefs that boys are better than girls in mathematics, the support for gender-based teacher expectations is slim. A meta-analytic review of research studies on the bases of teacher expectations found little overall evidence that teacher academic expectations differed for boys and girls, but teacher expectancies about social/personality development were weakly related to gender. Girls were expected to get along better, have more self-control, and be neater and more helpful than boys. Given what we know about differential maturation and achievement, it is possible that girls are favored with higher teacher expectations in reading in the early grades and boys are favored with regard to math and sciences in the middle and secondary school grades. One well designed study at the first-grade level distinguished between teachers who thought that boys could learn to read as successfully as girls and teachers who believed that girls would outperform boys. With controls for entering reading readiness, the boys in classes where teachers believed in equitable outcomes outperformed the boys in classes where teachers expected differential outcomes. At the middle and secondary level, there is some evidence that teachers hold different expectations for girls and boys in math and science (favoring boys), but studies also suggest that these differences in expectations are more likely based on student personal characteristics such as performance and are thus accurate, not stereotyped.

The research on sex-differentiated expectations by teachers remains too sparse to draw firm conclusions. Promising directions for research appear to lie in distinguishing between teachers, classroom contexts, and levels of education that hold and, importantly, communicate differential beliefs about competence by gender. For example, researchers have labeled higher education as colder by degrees for females (Sadker & Sadker, 1994). Ethnographic studies also point to single incidents of expressed gender-biased beliefs that appear more powerful than quantitative measures of expected performance.

There exists a large body of evidence that teachers treat boys and girls differently in the classroom. However, interpretations conflict regarding which sex is favored and the reasons behind the differential treatment (whether teacher or student driven). Because of sex differences in behavior, especially in the early grades, boys have been described as more salient in classrooms and thereby more likely to drive the attention of teachers in both academic and nonacademic activities. Boys have been found to have more interactions of all types with teachers including being called on, receiving more complex questions, and accorded more and different criticism, whereas girls are more often rewarded for quiet and obedient behavior. Some evidence, not always replicated, suggests that the criticism directed toward girls is focused on lack of ability and toward boys on lack of effort or poor behavior. These patterns of differential treatment as well as attribution (similar to what has been found with parents) could encourage the achievement of boys and discourage the achievement of girls. However, important for future research, the links between differential treatment and differential achievement have not been documented. Some argue that elementary classrooms are often unfriendly to boys and attempt to feminize them. In the early grades, female teachers require boys to suppress their activity level and behave in more compliant, self-controlled, and verbally interactive ways, like girls. Others argue that the rewarding of compliance in girls does not prepare them well for intellectual risk taking and higher levels of achievement, especially in math and science.

Other potential mediators of expectancy effects lie in differential opportunities to learn accorded by teachers. This might include the identification of reading as feminine and math and science as masculine, and the relative absence of influential females (and ethnic minorities) in the curriculum. This might affect student interest and different patterns of course taking, paving the way for sex-typed careers—a pattern that is lessening in secondary schools but not in universities. When gender and ethnicity are considered together, differential treatment has been documented toward African American and Latino males, who are more often assigned to remedial and lower-level educational tracks, and with regard to African American males, to the disciplinary system.

Longitudinal research linking differential teacher expectations for boys and girls (with prior achievement differences controlled) to differential performance is far too sparse for firm conclusions. However, several studies have found that the predictive relationship between teacher expectations in math and student performance in math (after controlling for prior math achievement) is stronger for girls than for boys. Also, children, who are members of academically stigmatized groups (in this case, girls with regard to math), were also found more likely than nonstigmatized children to confirm teacher underestimates of ability and less likely to benefit from teacher overestimates of ability. Thus, girls may be more susceptible to biased teacher expectations, especially when they are negative.

While links have not been made to teacher expectations or differential treatment, a vast research literature has documented gender differences in beliefs about competence and control, interest in subject matter, self-concept, and career aspirations. These beliefs and attitudes have been shown to predict performance and course taking. Girls are more likely than boys to have lower competence beliefs in math and sports (but not reading), take more internal responsibility for failure, have less interest in science and technical fields, and have more negative self-evaluations and increasing interest in sex-appropriate behavior as they approach adolescence. Researchers argue that these differences undercut the interest and motivation of girls in achieving, especially in math and sciences. While these self-views may result from gender stereotypes, research has not yet linked teacher transmission of stereotypes in the classroom to student attitudes. Again, when gender and ethnicity are examined together, it is ethnic minority boys whose attitude toward and investment in school are more negative.

Beyond teacher expectations and interpersonal expectancy effects, a growing body of work has focused on societal stereotypes that when experimentally primed in social situations create self-fulfilling prophecies. This phenomenon has been called *stereotype threat* by psychologist Claude Steele (1997), a concept that refers to the mechanism by which negative stereotypes about a group triggers beliefs and anxieties that adversely affect the performance of those who identify with that group. This threat can explain gender differences in performance. Many studies, most with college students with a few exceptions, have shown that students with stigmatized identities (such as African Americans with regard to intellectual ability and girls with regard to math ability) who are randomly assigned to a test situation that is described as diagnostic of ability underperform relative to the nonstigmatized students (Caucasians and males). In contrast, in a test situation that is characterized as nondiagnostic of ability, performance differences are not found. To the extent that teacher expectations may represent a form of evaluation, among members of stigmatized groups, low expectations may similarly invoke the threat of confirming a negative achievement stereotype.

Of interest, as gender is only one part of identity, experimental studies with Asian American women have shown that their performance was higher on a math test when their Asian identity was triggered than when their female identity was triggered. The cultural stereotype of Asians as excelling in math acted as a protective factor for these Asian American women while the stereotype of women as poor in math evoked a stereotype threat response. A similar pattern was found in experiments with Asian American women on a verbal test. Consistent with the societal stereotype that women excel in verbal ability, women performed higher on the verbal test when their female identity was triggered than when their Asian identity was evoked. This is promising evidence of a causal link between stereotype and performance, reflecting both enhancing (with positive stereotypes) and undermining (with negative stereotypes) effects.

REFERENCES AND FURTHER READINGS

Good, T.L., & Findley, M.J. (1985). Sex role expectations and achievement. In J.B. Dusek (Ed.), *Teacher expectancies* (pp. 271–300). Hillsdale, NJ: Erlbaum.

Lippa, R.A. (2005). *Gender, nature, and nurture.* Mahwah, NJ: Erlbaum.

Merton, R.K. (1948). The self-fulfilling prophecy. *Antioch Review, 8,* 193–210.

Rosenthal, R., & Jacobson, L. (1968). *Pygmalion in the classroom: Teacher expectation and pupils' intellectual development.* New York: Holt, Rinehart, & Winston.

Sadker, M., & Sadker, D. (1994). *Failing at fairness: How America's schools cheat girls.* New York: Scribners.

Steele, C.M. (1997). A threat in the air: How stereotypes shape intellectual identity and performance. *American Psychologist, 52*(6), 613–629.

UNICEF. (2005, April). *Progress for children: A report card on gender parity and primary education.* Retrieved February, 27, 2006, from http://www.unicef.org/publications/index_25937.html

Weinstein, R.S. (2002). *Reaching higher: The power of expectations in schooling.* Boston: Harvard University Press.

Wigfield, A., Battle, A., Keller, L.B., & Eccles, J.S. (2002). Sex differences in motivation, self-concept, career aspiration, and career choice: Implications for cognitive development. In A. McGillicuddy-De Lisi & R. De Lisi (Eds.), *Biology, society, and behavior: The development of sex differences in cognition* (Vol. 21, pp. 93–124). Westport, CT: Ablex.

Rhona S. Weinstein

Miriam Hernandez Dimmler

Nilofar Sami

Heterosexism and Homophobia in the Hidden Curriculum

During the 1960s and 1970s, across Western societies, feminist, gay, and lesbian activists began to develop a vocabulary that identified the systematic discrimination experienced by women, gays, and lesbians. A number of key terms emerged that have provided the latter with a language to move beyond description of individual prejudice to that of explanations of collective discrimination. These terms included patriarchy, homophobia, and heterosexism. *Patriarchy* means that relations between men and women need to be understood in terms of living in a male-dominated society. Homophobia and heterosexism are closely related and sometimes interchangeably used. *Homophobia* refers to systematic discrimination against lesbians and gays. The term points to a sense of panic, suggesting an association with psychic or unconscious motives. *Heterosexism* refers to a predominant belief in a society or a presumption that male-female sexuality (that is, heterosexuality) is the only natural way of living your life.

In order to fully understand these concepts, it is necessary to place them in relation to similar terms that have been coined to capture a range of other significant forms of social discrimination. Two of them are of specific importance to making sense of both the history and the contemporary understandings of gender and sexual relations. First, *social class* has been identified by social scientists as a major influence in dividing up the population in terms of life chances within the workplace, education, and family life. Early feminists adopted some of the ideas of class analysts in trying to develop understandings of gender relations. For example, they spoke of women as occupying a different class from that of men in order to highlight that dominant institutional patterns of discrimination were operating against women. Equally significant historically has been the relationship between the development of gender/sexual terminology and Black theorizing about race-ethnicity. Some people maintain that the major cultural influence in producing the Western vocabulary of equal rights, social justice, and emancipatory politics has been the impact of Black power and the civil rights movement within the United States during the 1960s. The formation of heterosexual masculinities and femininities are produced at a dynamic interface between the immediate social environment (for example, that of the school), culturally available discourses of sexuality and masculinity/femininity, wider social relations, and the endless unfinished business of the unconscious.

The development of this vocabulary, identifying these diverse experiences of discrimination, enabled the emergence of general theoretical frameworks. At the same time, early theorists of gender and sexuality further developed a more nuanced language to capture the playing out of institutional discrimination within specific arenas. For example, schooling was identified as a key site for the making of particular gender and (hetero) sexual identities. In other words, institutional arenas, such as schools, did not simply reflect or reproduce wider social relations of gender and sexuality. Rather, they were active in producing local meanings that were central to the formation of a younger generation's sexual/gender formation. In order to make sense of this, theorists critically examined all aspects of schooling life. Of central importance was the *official* curriculum, which explicitly transmitted knowledge and skills in reproducing the dominant culture. Alongside this, theorists explored what educational theorists called the *hidden curriculum* consisting of specific institutional implicit or hidden values, meanings, attitudes, predispositions, and social skills. The hidden curriculum has been defined as a central mechanism that shapes how students experience the curriculum, their teachers, and each other; it informs their understanding of what school life means on a day-to-day basis. The concept of the hidden curriculum has been of major importance in exploring heterosexism and homophobia that emerged through critical educational studies. These concepts capture the shaping of schools as a cultural space in which sexualities and sexual relations of power are produced, reproduced, and negotiated.

EARLY FEMINIST AND SEXUALITY RESEARCH IN SCHOOLS

Earlier feminist work on the interplay between gender and the hidden curriculum built on class-based studies that illustrated the exclusionary effects of the social construction of knowledge on working-class students. This feminist work argued that the hidden curriculum was a major mechanism of socialization that served to reproduce sex roles within the arena of education. In other words, they argued that, through socialization, the biological basis of male and female becomes linked to social norms and expectations that are circulating through masculinity and femininity. This work was immensely important theoretically in identifying a wide range of ways in which the hidden curriculum operated to make female students and teachers "invisible." It was argued that a male-centered set of values underpinned all areas of school life, serving to reinforce a hierarchically ordered oppositional structure between boys and girls. This was manifest, for example, in relation to the allocation of subjects, with male students encouraged to take the high-status science subjects. Furthermore, exploring curriculum texts, research revealed a limiting range of female images in which women were linguistically erased or misrepresented. Politically, this work was a major educational intervention in challenging sexist stereotypes in the search for "girl-friendly" schooling. Interestingly, from an early 2000s perspective, the success of the latter has been cited as partly responsible for the crisis of masculinity that some theorists claim is currently occurring.

Similarly, earlier sexuality research in schools identified the pervasiveness of stereotypes, informed by homophobia and heterosexism. Importantly, they reported how students have grown up in a society in which there are no positive images of gay or lesbian people. There is no acknowledgement of gay and lesbian history, sensibility, life-style, or community. There is no recognition of gay or lesbian achievement. For example, the research showed that when texts written by gays or lesbians were read in class, no reference was made to the authors' sexual orientation. In fact, homosexuality and lesbianism were rarely discussed in lessons, and on the few occasions when they were introduced, they were presented in a negative way—for example, in relation to AIDS/HIV. For gay students, this silence—reflecting that in the wider society—pervaded the whole of the formal curriculum, serving to reproduce and legitimate dominant heterosexual hierarchies. From this perspective, heterosexuality was presented as natural, normal, and universal, simply because there are no alternative ways of being. Students emphasized the personal isolation, confusion, marginalization, and alienation that this engendered. Most significantly, without a positive reference group, some tended to internalize ambivalent negative messages about themselves as gays and lesbians.

Later feminists, alongside gay and lesbian scholars and queer theorists, addressed the limitations of this earlier approach. These limitations included fixed notions of gender (one way of being a girl or boy student), an underdevelopment of youth identity formation, and a failure to accommodate explanations of school life that made sense of the interconnections of diverse categories. Of particular significance here, in relation to heterosexism and homophobia, was the complex relationship between gender and sexuality. The conventional approach within sex-role theory serves to shape much sex education, erasing issues of sexuality by subsuming it within a broader discourse of gender. In contrast, Butler (1990, p. 238) suggests that gender is often spoken through a "heterosexual matrix" in which heterosexuality is presupposed in the expression "real forms of masculinity and femininity." This provides a useful framework within which to explore the interconnectedness between gender and sexuality as it is lived out in schools. In structuring the attributes of being a "real boy"/"real girl," the various forms of masculinity/femininity that are hegemonic in schools are crucially involved in policing the boundaries of heterosexuality, alongside the boundaries of "proper" masculinity/femininity. More specifically, for example, to be a "real boy" is often to publicly be in opposition to and distance oneself from the feminine and the "feminized" versions of masculinity.

THE HIDDEN CURRICULUM AND THE INSTITUTION

At an institutional level, student identities are formed in relation to the formal curriculum —and what in the United States is called the extracurriculum—and the categories they make available, including the academic/vocational divide and those between arts and sciences and study and sport. These categories are highly gendered, with the "soft feminine" academic and arts subjects juxtaposed to the "hard masculine" vocational, scientific, and sporting options. Similarly, involvement in sport can be read as a cultural index of what it means to be a "real boy," while not to be involved in sport and its associated "lad" subculture is to be a "bit of a poof." At the same time, it is important to stress here the complex interconnections of class, ethnic, and age variations in these identifications. In particular, to be a "real" boy in school is to be in opposition to the feminine and to "feminized" versions of masculinity. This is illustrated in Redman and Mac an Ghaill's (1996) article "Schooling Sexualities: Heterosexual Schooling and the Unconscious" in which they discuss an English student's (Peter's) experiences of "becoming heterosexual" in an all-boys grammar school in the late 1970s and early 1980s. Using an auto/biographical methodology, they explore the meaning of Peter's investment in a particular form of heterosexual masculinity, what they called "muscular intellectualness." They argue that Peter's fascination with the muscular intellectualness he identified in his teacher,

Mr. Lefevre, could be understood in terms of the access it promised to give him to the entitlements of conventional masculinity. The world of ideas and knowledge that Mr. Lefevre seemed to inhabit no longer seemed effeminately middle class and, thus, the object of ridicule or embarrassment but powerfully middle class, a source of personal strength, and a means to exercise control over others. Thus, as a source of "real" masculinity, muscular intellectualness "defeminized" academic work in the humanities and refused the label "bit of a poof."

An area where teacher relations also reinforce "normal" masculinity is through the legitimation of different teaching styles. Masculinities have to operate or be competent at operating with some degree of power and authority. An inability to be powerful and authoritative is a code for an inability to be a "proper man." Signs of "weakness" in many public arenas are associated with femininity. Masculinities in the workplace have competence as an essential feature, while incompetence is deemed as failure, weakness, or "womanly." Often in school, a competent teacher is one who is able to keep a class quiet regardless of the learning process. A quiet class is deemed a class that can be managed, therefore learning can be achieved. The most common way of keeping a class quiet is to use discipline and force. Often in schools, it is assumed that male teachers are able to use discipline. For example, although violence in many schools is illegal, other forms of physical force are often used to control students.

Research has highlighted that teachers often shake, push, and shove students in the classroom during the course of their everyday teaching. In some single-sexed schools, this corresponds with an ethos of schools for boys and men. The hidden curriculum does not simply target students, as teachers are often subject to implicit control and regulation. Teachers' awareness of other teachers' pedagogical styles—informed by notions of gender—judges whether teachers are "good" or "bad." As a result, "good teachers" are "real men" and "bad teachers" have "problems." There are pressing implications about the use of violence. First, there is the pressure on the teacher that, in order to be competent, violence has to be issued. Second, if a competent teacher is a male who can display violence, what part do women play in the school? Third, if violence is appropriate for teaching, what does this mean for child-centeredness and the ability to create positive working relations?

RECENT FEMINIST AND SEXUALITY RESEARCH IN SCHOOLS

Recent work, including that of queer theorists, have provided sophisticated theoretical frameworks to explore issues of more complex formations of sexual and gender formations among young people, marked by pluralism, fluidity, and contradiction. An important move in exploring the hidden curriculum and the accompanying implicit transmission of schools' values is to shift from a focus on sexual minorities, such as gay and lesbian students and teachers, to critically examine the concept of heterosexuality. A key issue that emerges is the question of what constitutes male and female heterosexuality? In response, it is argued that heterosexuality is a highly fragile, socially constructed phenomenon. The question that emerges here is, how does it become fixed as an apparently, stable, unitary category? Queer theorists suggest that schools, alongside other institutions, attempt to administer, regulate, and reify unstable sex/gender categories. More particularly, this administration, regulation, and reification of sex/gender boundaries is institutionalized through the interrelated social and discursive practices of management, staff room, classroom, and playground microcultures. One way in which theorists have explored this is through investigations of different sexual subjectivities within schools.

In our own studies, we have examined the constitutive cultural elements of heterosexual male students' subjectivity. We see these elements, which consist of contradictory forms of compulsory heterosexuality, misogyny, and homophobia, as being marked by contextual ambivalence and contingency. Our focus was the complex interplay of these cultural elements as specific institutional forms of gendered and sexual power. More particularly, we sought to explore how they were operationalized as key defining processes in sexual boundary maintenance, policing and legitimization of male and female heterosexual identities. In order to understand how students attempted to learn the sex/gender codes that conferred hegemonic (or dominant) masculinity, it was necessary to bring together social and psychic (unconscious) structures. As Butler (1993) points out, heterosexuality does not gain its form by virtue of its internal qualities but rather defines itself against abjected sexualities, in particular, homosexuality. For example, what emerged as of particular importance was the way in which heterosexual male students were involved in a double relationship, of traducing the "other," including women and gays (external relations), at the same time as expelling femininity and homosexuality from within themselves (internal relations). We have explored a wide range of student cultures, exploring the complex identity work that actively produces specific heterosexual dynamics within which young people live their school lives. In one situation, the rejection by a group of dominant heterosexually orientated males reinterpreted the identity of those males who concentrated on their schoolwork as being gay and "poncy." It was the disidentification with the other students that enabled the heterosexually orientated males to produce their own identities. These are the complex and contradictory processes in which heterosexual male student apprenticeships were developed within secondary school contexts.

As young people in recent studies show, they have diverse values, understandings, and feelings as well as local cultural knowledges that they bring with them into the classroom. These young people are active makers of sexual-gender identities. A major flaw in many progressive curriculum policies, exemplified in the "positive images" approach, has been a failure to conceptualize the complexity of student identity formation. We need to focus on the discursively produced subject positions of students and the power relations between students and teachers as well as those among students. As indicated above, in this process, schools can be seen as crucial cultural sites in which material, ideological, and discursive resources serve to affirm hegemonic masculinity while making available a range of masculinities and femininities that young people come to inhabit. At the same time, students illustrate that misogyny, homophobia, heterosexism (and racism) are not pervasively inherited in a unitary or total way. Located within local sexual peer group cultures, they actively select from a range of socially oppressive constructs and, in this process, make their own individual and collective meanings. For example, male heterosexuality can be seen as a highly fragile and fractured construction resulting in the contradictory social and discursive practices within which male students are positioned and, in turn, position others.

Institutional authoritarianism often prevents the development of formal mechanisms that would operate to democratize teacher-student relations and provide student representation and emancipation. For example, often there is no formal acknowledgment of students' perspective of how to manage curriculum policy development as a legitimate view. Through the framework of existing power relations, teacher responses are ideologically presented and represented as legitimate educational strategies, while student responses are juxtaposed as illegitimate. Earlier representations of working-class males and females within educational research have reinforced this dominant perception, with its overemphasis on the negative elements of their contestation of schooling. In such accounts, there is little acknowledgment of the participants' creative construction of "really useful knowledge" that combines rigor and relevance, academic success, and personal and collective empowerment. More specifically here, there is a concern with a search for "really useful sex/sexuality knowledge."

More specifically, gay and lesbian students have outlined an approach that includes a student-centered pedagogy with a focus upon the development of adolescent sexuality, an understanding of power relations that exist between and within social groups, and a discussion-based program that would include such items as feelings and emotional growth. As Fine (1988) points out, a discourse that highlights the positive aspects of sexual desire has traditionally been excluded from the curriculum. Most importantly, young gay men have pointed to the precariousness of all sexualities, suggesting that gays are a vital part of straight culture, with homosexuality always present in heterosexuality. James Baldwin (in Troupe, 1989), describing more graphically the dependence of straight culture on gays, points to the political significance of the male body, implying the Freudian insight that extreme personal and cultural antipathy is premised contradictorily on desire and need.

As this discussion has indicated, the links between gender and sexuality and the hidden curriculum have been a key theme of recent educational research. Much of this work has attempted to clarify some of the connections between schooling and "proper" gender and sexual designations. This work has also mapped out how the hidden curriculum needs to be historically and socially located within the power relations of existing society. Furthermore, much of this work tends to be qualitatively driven. One of the reasons for this is that the focus on the hidden curriculum tends to consider the structural rules of engagement alongside particular situational factors. An underlying philosophical position is that gender and sexuality are something to be achieved and that meaning making is central to explaining what is going on. More specifically, there is a need for more research that continues to prioritize the implicit forms of meaning making in the cultural arena of schooling.

REFERENCES AND FURTHER READINGS

Butler, J. (1990). *Gender trouble: Feminism and the subversion of identity.* London: Routledge.

Butler, J. (1993). *Bodies that matter: On the discursive limits of "sex."* London: Routledge.

Fine, M. (1988). Sexuality, schooling and adolescent females: The missing discourse. *Harvard Educational Review, 5*(1), 29–53.

Redman, P., & Mac an Ghaill, M. (1996). Schooling sexualities: Heterosexual masculinities, schooling, and the unconscious, *Discourse, 17*(2), 243–256.

Troupe, Q. (1989). *James Baldwin: The legacy.* New York: Simon and Schuster/Touchstone.

Mairtin Mac an Ghaill

Chris Haywood

Liviu Popoviciu

Managing "Problem" Boys and Girls

School culture sends powerful messages to students and their families about appropriate ways of behaving and being. "Problem behaviors" are a reflection of the individual child's inability to interact productively with school culture. At the heart of most definitions and examples of problem behavior in the schools is the tendency of that behavior to disrupt the learning process. Whether students perform "problem behaviors" and subsequently come to be regarded as "problem boys or girls" depends on the kinds of cultural capital those students bring to school. Cultural capital—in the forms of knowledge, skills, and ways of being and acting—determine a student's ability or inability to achieve a connection to the broader human community that is represented by the school community.

Because the "fit" between the cultural capital students bring to school and the school culture is affected by dominant cultural assumptions about gender, race, and social class, it is more likely that boys and minority students, rather than girls and majority students, will be considered "problems" and will become the targets of disciplinary actions designed to manage them and their behaviors. The ability of school leaders to understand the impact of gender, race, and class determines if teachers have training and support necessary to manage their classrooms fairly and effectively. Good management also can be enhanced by demonstrating to all parents strong concern for their children and by the improved, meaningful involvement of those parents, especially poor and working-class parents, in the schools in ways that enhance the welfare of their children.

SCHOOL CULTURE AND STUDENTS' CULTURAL CAPITAL

The overall structure of schooling reproduces the dominant culture through its curriculum, its activities (after school, extracurricular, and sports), teachers, and administrators. Schools often have an implicit middle-class *ethos,* one that requires students to be self-confident and attentive (or at least quiet) and to have good social skills such as being helpful, cooperative with the teacher and classmates, and considerate of the feelings of others. Those students whose families and neighborhoods provide them with the cultural background expected and represented by the school are better prepared and more likely to be successful rather than a problem. These children have the social interest, the "tools for living" that enable them to make the transition to the broader community.

French sociologist Pierre Bourdieu (2000) conceived of such tools as forms of *capital.* He defined *cultural capital* as resources of value, or *legitimate* in certain fields or markets, that are distributed among classes of people. For example, cultural capital would include a person's knowledge, skills, or ways of being or acting that are more or less valued by others who are in relationships with that person. Individuals or groups all possess some type of cultural capital; but the value or worth of their capital depends on the reactions of others, such as teachers or fellow students with whom they may have some type of relationship.

The public expects the structure of schooling to act as a "leveler" enabling any child to gain the skills and knowledge to be successful in the broader world. In an ironic twist, students cannot gain from structures of schooling unless their own cultural capital is recognized as legitimate by the school; but the school will not recognize their capital as legitimate unless it is reflective of the dominant culture. At the same time, for students to be able to use the cultural capital they find at school, they must have the means to learn how to appropriate it; yet school does not prepare students to obtain those means and make that gain unless the students' knowledge, skills, or ways of being or acting are valued by the school and other students. When the school affirms the usefulness and the connection of students' cultural capital to the school, these students develop social interest and see themselves as a part of humanity. But when students see that they are not a part but instead they are actually the "Other," wholly foreign and disconnected from the mainstream, they feel useless, anxious, and not safe, and they will engage in problem behaviors that further isolate them.

PROBLEM BEHAVIORS IN SCHOOL

Teachers and administrators identify problem behaviors as those that interfere with the business of learning, or the very structure of schooling, and occur anywhere in the school building or on the school grounds at anytime during the day or during after-school events. Certain areas stand out as particularly troublesome for schools, depending upon the grade levels assigned to the school building and the geographic location of the school in the community.

High on the list of unwanted behaviors at all grade levels is classroom disruption. In the referral slips used to report unruly behavior to the principal's office or other disciplinarian in the building, teachers usually characterize "disrupting the classroom" as follows: not following the teacher's directions for assignments; talking while the teacher speaks to the class or interrupting other children when it is their turn to speak ("talking out of turn"); disturbing other children who are working quietly; getting out of the assigned seating area or seat without permission; not having the appropriate materials for school assignments (such as pencil, paper, or assigned textbook); completely destroying or losing texts or library books; vandalizing school property; not completing homework, or not turning it in to the teacher; and, perhaps the most serious, fighting.

School personnel, parents, and even students cite passing time in the hallways and in stairwells as particularly stressful and threatening to safety and order in schools. School administrators encourage teachers and aides to go on "high alert" during passing time when students, particularly middle and high school students, change classes and engage in a volatile mix of adolescent angst and raging hormones. Some schools, particularly large high schools in suburban and urban communities (and increasingly rural union high school districts, which tend to be very large and take in students from many different communities) place security personnel or devices in the hallways to discourage behaviors that escalate into fighting between groups or individuals. Female students are particularly at risk for sexual harassment and even sexual assault during passing time; the inevitable crowding and chaos in the hallway creates the illusion of anonymity for the assailant or assailants who think they can be invisible.

Many urban and suburban school districts collaborate with the local city police departments who specially train and assign officers to the district as part of their Officer Friendly programs or as Community Service Officers; these officers become a part of the daily routine in the school building, and they help to minimize or eliminate the potential for various kinds of school violence and general bad behavior. For elementary schools, food fights or "unnecessary" loudness or roughness in the school cafeteria during lunchtime and on the playground during recess has prompted many schools to place additional adult aides or parent volunteers on site to ensure the safety of all children—and teachers.

Safety on the way to and from school has become another arena of frustration and alarm for schools and parents alike. Children who walk to school often get into skirmishes with other students or even neighborhood adults and otherwise act out improperly; but fights or acting out in the close, confined area of a school bus moving through heavy morning or afternoon traffic usually adds an extra element of danger not found walking to and from school. To ensure the safe arrival of everyone, district administrators develop elaborate safety rules and etiquette for the bus ride that parents and children must agree to follow each school year. In some districts, the bus ride to school has become so risky that adult monitors or video cameras are used to maintain order or to at least capture rowdy students on videotape for later identification and disciplinary action. School bus drivers usually report student misbehavior on the bus to the principal; and, depending upon the seriousness of the rule violation, students as young as eight or nine may be barred from riding the school bus or even suspended from school for a period of time.

School leaders and parents are generally in agreement that unwanted behavior is disruptive to the orderly conduct of school business—learning. However, studies show that children from families that are more in tune with the school culture will have more successful school experiences that are free of disciplinary actions and punishments, and those children are considerably less likely to be labeled "problem" boys and girls.

DISCIPLINING PROBLEM STUDENTS

Students who are perceived as "problems" are dealt with through an array of disciplinary measures that have become more punitive with each new school year. School officials (sometimes with the outright assistance of or at least the implied concurrence of major parent groups) have enacted "zero tolerance" policies with punishment (some of it draconian) frequently meted out to teens and to younger students alike as the concern for safe schools that are free of violence escalates. The nationally publicized tragedies of school shootings, schools' fears of the spread of drug use among preteens and teenagers, and school officials' desire to avoid legal liability for sexual harassment and other assaults on students advance strong and often questionable disciplinary polices in schools. In one example, a six-year-old African American boy who had been admiring a six-year-old White girl in his class was suspended immediately from school for sexual harassment when he placed his fingers under the waistband of her skirt. Although the school eventually reinstated him and apologized, his parents moved him to another school—after his mother tried to explain *sexual harassment* to the six-year-old child.

The gender of this child certainly affected the disciplinary response to his behavior, and it seems likely that racial identities also came into play. Walking through the average elementary or middle school, observers will see a disproportionate number of males, especially minority males, receiving disciplinary attention in the principal's office, in special rooms set aside for punishment, or sometimes at the back of the classroom or at the front of the classroom under the watchful eye of the teacher or an aide. Similarly, minority males, especially Black and language minority males (i.e., those for whom English is a second language), are disproportionately represented in classes for the low-functioning or educable mentally retarded students. At the same time, however, relatively low percentages of minority males, especially Blacks, are enrolled in talented and gifted classes.

As these observations indicate, schools apply disciplinary actions and academic judgments unevenly across students who have different racial, social class, and gender identities. When teachers and students are not culturally synchronized, the resulting conflict results in educational and social consequences for the students, increasing their sense of uselessness and disconnection. Students who are disconnected from the dominant culture of the structures of schooling lack a strong social interest in school. Disconnected and unsuccessful in school, they are more likely to act out behaviors that are considered disruptive to learning because they have not mastered the tools of living. As a result of their behaviors, they, and sometimes even their parents, are at odds with the school.

Minority students often bring to school cultural capital from families and neighborhoods that struggle with power relationships in the broader community; racism, sexism, poverty, unemployment, or lack of health care puts the entire community at a power disadvantage. Racial or language minority students and immigrant students each bring culturally distinct styles of speaking, knowing, and learning to the classroom and to the school building. In an American cultural climate that is increasingly stratified along wealth and class, race and language have specific implications for perceptions of social class and interactions with school structures.

The students who are most at risk for school failure are males, in contrast to females, and children of color of both genders, particularly African American, Hispanic, Native American, and South East Asian boys and girls. Although schools do convey messages about culture through teachers, administrators, and building environments or climates, as the number of male and minority teachers decreases across the nation, schools are dominated increasingly by females in charge, many of them White.

When White teachers are out of sync with African American students, studies show that they view their students' behavior negatively. A middle-class, White female teacher, for example, may see an urban, Black male student's behavior as boisterous and disruptive, and she may order him to leave the room. Male teachers, especially those from minority backgrounds, who tend to be more tolerant of the high levels of activity of young males, may see the same behavior and think of the student as energetic and intellectually curious. When cultural differences lead teachers to view student behaviors as problems, however, the teachers' disciplinary behaviors may result in the child failing and dropping out, usually preceded by perceptions of the child as "a problem." School drop-out rates of males continue to rise in the United States, and they are dropping out at an earlier age; as a result, fewer are attending college. Thus, it is no surprise that statistics show that American women are attending postsecondary education in higher numbers than American men.

When cultural values weighted heavily toward middle-class constructs of gender, race, and class dominate the school environment, children and young adults who do not bring that cultural capital cannot connect to the school. For example, the school culture regarding appropriate femininity may be channeled through the teacher who rewards girls for being nice and quiet in the classroom and in the hallways, producing neatly completed school assignments and turning them in on time, and generally being "good citizens" in the context of the school community. In subtle and unsubtle ways (think of the selection of cheerleaders, for example), the school community also may reward girls for being pretty or cute, for not being fat or large, or for meeting some other dominant cultural ideal of feminine beauty. In contrast, the school culture rewards boys for behaviors that lead to achievement in the classroom, particularly in math and the sciences, or achievement in sports.

Teachers' direct feedback serves to reaffirm the differentiated messages that boys and girls receive in the school community according to their gender. For example, researchers exploring the evaluative feedback given to fourth- and fifth-grade girls and boys have found gender differences in both negative and positive feedback. When girls failed, they were encouraged to blame their personal lack of ability, while boys were encouraged to blame their own lack of effort, or they were encouraged to blame a source external to them, like a challenging situation or a person.

Positive feedback given to girls encouraged them to give credit to trying hard or being nice or to credit reasons that were external to the girls' self-control. In each case of negative and positive feedback given to boys and to girls by the teachers in the study, girls were encouraged subtly to internalize failure and externalize success, while boys were encouraged to internalize success and externalize failure to be considered successful in that school situation.

Further, schools often discriminate against female students by forcing roles on them that fail to enhance their self-esteem and narrow their options for success in later life—for example, disparaging their answers in science and math classes and excluding them from class participation by not recognizing them when they raise their hands to speak. Similarly, gay and lesbian adolescents heighten the contradictions of gender identity and sexual identity in an environment with strong heterosexual cultural norms. Increasingly, these students are organizing, particularly at the high school level and above, to resist and challenge the discrimination, misunderstanding, and neglect they experience in school. The resistant and challenging behavior in these "Other" students is a result of their exclusion from the mainstream structures of schooling.

Students who do not "fit" into subtly or overtly applied and narrowly constructed roles that schools establish for girls and for boys become the "Other," and they generally are unsuccessful in the environment of the school. These students very likely become the "problem" boys and girls. They are considered problems because they do not act in ways that make positive impressions on the adult gatekeepers in the school. Black girls, for example, who are loud talking, tough, aggressive, and large in stature, or who otherwise do not fit the local Euro-cultural norm for feminine beauty, often find themselves punished for their ways of being (i.e., "attitude" and other behaviors that annoy adult gatekeepers who are culturally out of sync with the girls).

Similarly, South East Asian boys who are quiet-spoken, slender, and short in stature may be ignored by teachers or, in the alternative, they may be singled out by other students or teachers because their behaviors and appearances do not fit in to the cultural norm for boys in that school. In both examples, these students become the racialized, gendered "Other." In sharp contrast to the girls and boys who are rewarded by their "fit" with the dominant culture and their ability to blend into it, the "Other" students earn the disapproval of adult gatekeepers at the school. It is easy to single them out for disciplinary action because of their cultural discontinuity with the school.

TOWARD FAIRER MANAGEMENT

The school's ability to understand and manage the impact of gender, race, and class divisions on relationships in the building and in the district determines if some families feel that the school has a strong interest in their children's best welfare or if they feel that they will be perpetually at odds with the school over everything involving their children. The strategies schools use to address the unwanted behaviors in students can heal or it can create a breach between the school and the diverse communities it serves. School districts, as a general rule, should find creative ways to regularly acknowledge and highlight the value of the cultural diversity of district families and neighborhoods.

Successful school reform has occurred when efforts have focused on organizing poor and working-class parents to recognize the value of identifying and forming their own network resources so that they can influence and improve outcomes for their students. These successes suggest that school leaders should advocate publicly for parent involvement that improves the school's academic performance and lowers its behavioral problems. Effective school leadership can mediate between the structures of schooling and the community by opening the doors to make parents an active, meaningful part of teaching and learning in the school.

Better management also requires that education programs continue to improve teacher preparation and in-service training, including the ability to teach in culturally diverse communities. Helping teaching candidates and professional teachers to reflect on their own ideas about race, gender, and class and how they interact in the classroom is critical to creating positive learning and teaching environments that do not incite resisting behavior from students. The importance of male teachers and minority teachers to schools and ultimately helping problem boys and girls connect to the school must not be overlooked. Students spend their entire days in interaction with teachers and other school personnel, and they need someone in the classroom to whom they can connect and who will connect to them culturally. To this end, all teachers need to be given positive encouragement and support to struggle with cultural discontinuity in the classroom and to make school a place where children feel safe, connected, and useful to the human community.

REFERENCES AND FURTHER READINGS

Bourdieu, P. (2000). Cultural reproduction and social reproduction. In R. Arum & I.R. Beattie (Eds.), *The structure of schooling: Readings in the sociology of education* (pp. 56–69). Mountain View, CA: Mayfield.

Carter, P.L. (2003). "Black" cultural capital, status positioning, and school conflicts for low-income African-American youth. *Social Problems, 50*(1), 136–155.

Delpit, L. (1995). *Other people's children: Cultural conflict in the classroom.* New York: New Press.

Graybill, S.W. (1997). Questions of race and culture: How they relate to the classroom for African-American students. *Clearinghouse, 70*(6), 311–319.

Jackson, D.B. (2003). Education reform as if student agency mattered: Academic micro cultures and student identity. *Phi Delta Kappan, 84*(8), 579–585.

Lareau, A., & Horvat, E.M. (1999). Moments of social inclusion and exclusion: Race, class, and cultural capital in family school relationships. *Sociology of Education, 72*(1), 37–53.

Lei, J.L. (2003). (Un)necessary toughness?: Those "loud Black girls" and those "quiet Asian boys." *Anthropology & Education Quarterly, 34*(2), 158–181.

Sergiovanni, T.J. (1996). *Leadership for the schoolhouse: How is it different? Why is it important?* San Francisco: Jossey-Bass.

Slate, J.R., & Jones, C.H. (2003). Helping behaviorally at-risk middle school students with the No Bad Actions Program: Winning with the N.B.A. *Journal of Education for Students Placed At Risk, 8*(3), 351–362.

Barbara Morrow Williams

School Counseling

There are over 80,000 licensed professional counselors within 48 states, in addition to the District of Columbia. (Two states, Nevada and California, do not currently license master's level counselors.) In states without licensure or certification laws, professional counselors are certified by the National Board for Certified Counselors (NBCC). In 2005, the NBCC had on its active members list 39,176 National Certified Counselors, 2,092 National Certified Gerontological Counselors, 1,192 Certified Clinical Mental Health Counselors, 668 National Certified School Counselors, 617 Master Addictions Counselors, and 165 National Certified Career Counselors. The role of a counselor is to assist people with a wide variety of problems related, but not limited to, relationships (intimate/ family/friends), academic, psychological, career decisions, and substance abuse. The responsibilities and duties of a counselor vary depending both on the population they are working with and on the settings in which they work.

In order to become a *school* counselor, all states require an individual to complete at least some graduate coursework, although most states typically require individuals to complete a master's degree. Most public school systems require advanced degree courses that include the following topics: Human Growth and Development, Theories, Individual Counseling, Group Counseling, Social and Cultural Foundations, Testing/Appraisal, Research and Program Evaluation, Professional Orientation, Career Development, Supervised Practicum, and a Supervised Internship (American Counseling Association, 2006). Although many school counseling programs follow this outline, no mandated training outline currently exists for school counselors.

In addition to graduate coursework, school counselors must also receive state certification. Some states also require public school counselors to have teaching certificates and some teaching experience prior to receiving certification as a school counselor. It is extremely important for aspiring counselors to familiarize themselves with the educational and training requirements, in addition to local and state certification requirements, they must meet in order to become certified school counselors. Requirements tend to differ from state to state and from one school district to another.

The lack of a system for training and certifying school counselors dates back to the early years of school counseling when counselors were simply selected from the teachers in a given school, a practice that may have favored the appointment of women rather than men. Even today, women continue to outnumber men among school counselors although their reasons for doing so may differ from those in the past.

In addition to the lack of uniform training and certification, the American School Counselor Association has identified major problems that plague counseling programs in schools and has developed a model school counseling program that schools can follow. Central to this model and the cornerstone for the role of the professional school counselor is the focus on students' academic, personal/social, and career development. School counselors are in a position to influence students' development and choices, but gender biases on the part of the counselor, while not always conscious, can undermine student development in a variety of ways.

WOMEN IN COUNSELING

The school counseling profession, historically, has been predominantly made up of White females. According to information recently gathered by the American School Counselor Association (ASCA), the predominance of White women still holds true today. Currently, females make up close to 80.3 percent of all certified school counselors, while males make up only 19.7 percent. Racial representation within the field of school counseling includes Whites (89.5 percent), African Americans (5.5 percent), Hispanic/Latino (3.5 percent), Asians (0.7 percent), other (0.9 percent).

Years ago, when there were no set requirements for becoming a school counselor, it was common for teachers within a school to be approached by administrators and be recommended to become the school counselor. Although there is no systematic evidence concerning how and why certain teachers were chosen to be counselors, it seems likely that, compared to their male colleagues, women teachers were perceived by school administrators to have more of the people-oriented interests and skills that counseling requires. Much has changed since those days. The field of school counseling is continuing to grow, with more and more graduate programs being created in universities across the United States. Although they vary in content, specific criteria have been implemented by each state that one must meet in order to become a school counselor, and these state criteria have significantly reduced the number of certified teachers simply being placed in the role of a school counselor.

Although this reduction might also have reduced the preponderance of women in school counseling, other social trends have served to sustain or increase the desirability of school counseling for women. One of these trends is the large increase over time in the number of working mothers. Even though gender roles have evolved significantly, it is still more likely for mothers to be the primary caretaker of children. Since this is the case, the hours worked by a school counselor can be accommodating as they allow women to work during the day, while their children are in school, and end early enough to enable those women to spend quality time with their children. Lastly, the same perceptions that may have led to women teachers, rather than men teachers, being chosen for those positions by school administrators probably continue to affect those administrators and the women who become counselors. If school counseling is perceived as a job that requires a person to possess certain characteristics, such as empathy, compassion, and nurturance that are assumed to be associated with women, these beliefs would make the field of school counseling appear to be a nicer fit for women than for men.

STANDARDS FOR SCHOOL COUNSELORS AND COUNSELING PROGRAMS

Counseling in schools dates back to the early nineteenth century. Since that time, the role of the school counselor has been and continues to be debated. To impose some uniform standards on the role of the school counselor, the American School Counselor Association (2004) recently adopted a new description of the role of the school counselor that stresses the need for counselors to have certification, good training, qualifications, and skills to assess students' developmental needs. In addition, professional school counselors were charged with the duty of implementing a comprehensive school counseling program that pays attention to developmental stages of student growth and promotes and enhances student achievement.

The role of the school counselor, however, varies greatly from state to state and even from school district to school district. Although some state education departments—Missouri, Tennessee, and Texas, to name a few—have adopted standards and guidelines for school counseling programs, more often than not the school counselor's role is defined by the building's lead administrator. As a result, counselors do everything from leading drug and violence prevention programs to sharpening pencils for standardized tests.

Like the counselors, school counseling programs have been the focus of considerable scrutiny. In recent years, six fundamental problems in those programs have been identified (Hart & Jacobi, 1992): (a) lack of a basic philosophy; (b) poor integration of the school counseling program in the overall mission of the school; (c) insufficient student access; (d) inadequate guidance for some students (especially minority students); (e) lack of counselor accountability; and (f) the failure to utilize other resources.

To overcome these problems, the ASCA (2003) developed a national model for school counseling programs. The four basic elements of this National Model are *foundation, delivery system, management system,* and *accountability.* Goals and standards are set for each element. *Foundation* goals, for example, are that every school counseling program should be based on a set of beliefs, a philosophy, the three developmental domains (academic, career, personal-social), and the national standards for school counseling programs.

Delivery systems should consist of the guidance curriculum, individual planning, response services, and system support. The *management system* coordinates the delivery system by specifying the counselor's responsibilities, collecting and analyzing data for monitoring students and closing the achievement gap between White students and students of color, defining action plans to achieve wanted outcomes, and allocating time to be spent on each area of the delivery system.

To meet the goal of *accountability,* every school counseling program should report the results of projects carried out, evaluate the school counselor's performance, have an advisory council to review results and make recommendations, and conduct a program audit to ensure that the program is aligned with the national model.

CAREER DEVELOPMENT PROGRAMS AND GENDER

The focus on student development (academic, personal/social, and career) is the cornerstone for the role of the professional school counselor. While separated in the National Model, these three developmental domains are intricately intertwined. Career development, for example, cannot take place without consideration of a student's personal/social and academic development, and career development is an integral part of a school counselor's job. This development takes place through programmed activities such as *computer searches, career days, field visits, vocational programs, course selection, and work with parents.* Each of these activities can be affected by gender biases. Because they occupy a position that influences the career decisions of young people, school counselors need an awareness of these biases and how they can be overcome.

The purpose of *career searches using computer based programs* is to allow students to explore their interests and give them a general starting point. For example, either Web-based programs such as Guidance Direct (2006) or computer programs such as Choices (1997) allow students to take interest inventories. Students are asked to respond to how interested they would be in doing particular activities. For example, Guidance Direct asks students to respond to questions such as "How would you like to build kitchen cabinets" with "Like," "Dislike," or "Unsure." Based on their responses to 180 questions, results are produced indicating which of six areas of interest—social, investigative, artistic, conventional, enterprising, and realistic—are the strongest for the student. Based on these interest areas, students are able to see what occupations or careers best match what they are interested in. This list of careers is a starting point for students to begin exploring possible avenues for them to pursue in the future.

Gender may play a role in these computer searches for several reasons. First, the questions that are asked in these interest inventories are supposed to be gender neutral. However, some of the questions that are asked during the inventories seem to favor one sex over another. For example, the first question on Guidance Direct's interest inventory ("How would you like to build kitchen cabinets?") is a question about carpentry or construction, typically male-dominated occupations. Second, more often than not students take these interest inventories in a classroom with their peers. The chances of them selecting interests that would stereotypically be considered outside their gender are highly unlikely. Surrounded by their peers who are giggling at questions and asking one another how they responded, students are not likely to answer with responses that go against the norm.

In order to avoid reinforcing the gender stereotypes during these computer search activities, counselors can encourage students to do several things. First, suggesting that students take more than just one type of interest inventory can ensure that students are getting information from several different sources, a procedure that will reduce biases based on test-specific stereotypes. Second, having students take these inventories alone in school is ideal but not realistic given the busy schedules of both counselors and students. Counselors, however, can have students take these inventories and use these computer searches at home. This is more ideal compared to the classroom setting, since there are fewer distractions and less pressure to answer in a way that is desirable to one's peers.

Career days are another guidance activity that many schools organize for their students. Individuals from the community come to the school and either speak to students in the classroom setting or set up tables for a fair-like setting. Both scenarios allow students to obtain information from professionals in the field and ask questions about careers they are considering. Having the opportunity to ask real people questions and get facts and opinions gives students information that is invaluable. Even though both scenarios have their positives and negatives, the fair setting allows students to specifically spend more time on careers that interest them.

The issue of gender arises at these career days as well. First, the professionals who come into the schools must be considered. More than likely, their gender reinforces the gender stereotypes that already exist in the field. For example, having a female come to represent the field of nursing may reinforce to male students that nurses are females. Second, because a career fair usually allows students to visit "booths" with their friends and peers, some students may hesitate to explore some of their interests that defy the gender stereotypes due to fear of ridicule from their friends.

At these career days, counselors can invite professionals who actually break the gender stereotypes in a particular field. For example, inviting a male nurse or a female lawyer would encourage students who may have avoided these tables in other circumstances to approach these individuals and ask questions. Another idea would be to have both a male and a female come in to represent every occupation. In this case, students see that both males and females are capable of pursuing whatever career they choose.

Field days are similar to career days in that students are given the opportunity to visit with professionals in various fields at the work site of the professionals. For example, one may go visit a law firm, observe the day-to-day activities, and speak to a multitude of people who work in a particular field. Some schools may even require that students do an "internship" of sorts in a field that interests them, requiring a certain number of hours be spent at a certain placement. Students have been known to do these mini internships at places such as banks, hospitals, animal hospitals, and law firms. These types of field days or internships are beneficial in that they give a student a comprehensive view of a particular occupation, not just one person's opinion. They provide students with somewhat of a hands-on experience.

The gender-related problem that may arise during these field visits is that students may encounter gender division that already exists within certain occupations. During their site visits, they may have negative experiences or attitudes expressed toward them if they are trying to break through an existing barrier. Considering that students very often make field visits after school, teachers or school counselors are not able to soften the blow of how a student is received. These negative experiences may discourage students from pursuing particular careers if they are given the impression that they are not welcome or will not be successful. Another possible discouraging aspect of internships is that very often students may experience discrimination based on their gender. Possible internship sites may turn away an applicant for an internship because that person is not of the "appropriate" gender. Places of business may not explicitly state their gender preference, but often times there is one.

Counselors do not have the power to change the attitudes of the people their students may encounter in the world. However, they do have the opportunity to educate and discuss with students their present and future encounters in the workplace. These types of discussions in the classroom prepare students to handle potential discrimination/negative attitudes experienced in the workplace and allows them to vent any frustrations they may have.

Vocational programs in schools are another piece of the career development program. Very often schools provide students with the opportunity to explore their interests in vocational programs such as automotive repair, carpentry, or cosmetology during their junior and senior years of high school. Sometimes these programs are based within the school so they are easy to attend, or sometimes students attend alternative programs during the school day. Students who believe college may not be the path they will choose to pursue can begin to explore a vocation and learn the skills needed to obtain a position within that field.

Very often these vocational programs are divided by gender, although perhaps not intentionally. The students who take automotive courses are generally male, while cosmetology's roster is primarily female. To overcome these stereotypic choices, the vocational programs that are offered in schools should be advertised equitably to male and female students. Vocational program choices should be offered to students with explanations and descriptions that are unbiased and have no opinions about gender attached to them. Counselors should also be careful not to judge negatively or react with surprise to a request made by a student if it breaks traditional stereotypes. Counselors should support any choice or interest a student may be interested in pursuing.

The *course selections* students make are influenced by the school counselor. It is the school counselor's job to make sure that students are signed up for the correct classes, in the right placement area (level of difficulty), and are on a path toward successfully completing high school. Aside from ensuring that students are taking the correct number of credits of math, English, social studies, science, and other graduation requirements, the school counselor also assists in helping students decide what electives they are going to take. The course booklet that students are provided with oftentimes can be overwhelming for students—the differences between classes, what interests them, and what is going to allow them to have the most options in the future. This is when students turn to their counselors, having faith that the counselor will guide them in the right direction. The level of work that students pursue during high school also affects their performance and preparedness for college.

Very often, however, gender can have an influence in what classes students are directed to take. The suggestions a female is given versus what a male is given can reinforce the gender stereotypes that have existed for years. For example, a female would probably be given the options of an art class or a cooking class to fill in her open elective; while a male would be given the option of a business class or a computer class. In addition, the level of classes or types of classes may also be influenced by gender. Male students are sometimes pushed to take math and science classes more than are females. This undoubtedly affects the number of females who pursue careers in math and science.

In order to ensure that gender does not play a role in what classes a student takes, a counselor should set a goal to urge every student to take the most rigorous course of study of which she or he is capable. Many school counselors have set unofficial rules that every student has to take a math course of some sort in order to continue practicing math skills. Research has shown that there is a strong correlation between success in college and number of advanced math and science courses taken in high school. Counselors are urging their students to continue to take math and science courses in high school so that they will be better prepared when they get to college. Many colleges require new students to take placement tests with math components; students who continue taking math through their senior year of high school may be at an advantage to place out of certain undergraduate classes. Also, in taking these math and science courses, students provide themselves with more options in regard to what courses of study or majors they will be able to pursue in college. Very often colleges will look at a student's high school course of study to determine whether he or she can be admitted to a particular program. Especially in the science and medical fields, math and science are important for admissions.

Parents also have an influence on their child's education and very often are a force in deciding what a student's educational program looks like. A school counselor should always make an effort to *work with parents,* keeping them involved and informed of what is going on in their student's life at school. However, this may become a problem when families have certain stereotypical ideas about gender. Depending on the cultural background of families, some may value education for males or females more than others. This can potentially pose a problem for a school counselor. One example may be that the parents of a male student insist that he is going to be a doctor or lawyer, but it is clear that this student is not interested in doing so. Instead, he wants to pursue a career as a nurse or hairdresser. Some families may not be open to these types of decisions, and it is the counselor's job to assist the student in dealing with the gender stereotypes his family values. Another example may be of a female student who intends to pursue a rigorous course of study and wants to attend college. Her family does not support her decision because it feels her education is not as important as education for the males in the family and that her role is to get married. Cultural values may become a barrier for some students depending on their gender.

In dealing with parents and gender issues, counselors must be sensitive to the cultural values and backgrounds of students. It is imperative to try and understand where a family is coming from and be empathic to such issues. At the same time, however, it is important to be a child advocate and present the child's point of view as important as well. Counselors should be sure to develop a realistic plan for the student when working with parents and be firm when plans are unrealistic. The goal is to help the student and family reach a decision that is both in the best interest of the student and acceptable to, even if not preferred by, the family.

REFERENCES AND FURTHER READINGS

American Counseling Association. (2006). *Answers to common questions about counseling. Frequently asked questions.* Retrieved March 21, 2006 from http://www.counseling.org/Home/Faq.aspx?

American School Counselor Association. (2003). *The ASCA national model: A framework for school counseling programs.* Alexandria, VA: Author.

American School Counselor Association. (2004). *ASCA role statement: The role of the professional school counselor.* Alexandria, VA: Author.

Choices (USA Version). (1997). [Computer software]. Ottawa, Ontario, Canada: Careerware: ISM Corporation.

Guidance Direct. (2006). [Computer Program]. Rockville Centre, NY: Centris Partners.

Hart, P.J., & Jacobi, M. (1992). *From gatekeeper to advocate: Transforming the role of the school counselor.* New York: College Board.

National Board for Certified Counselors and Affiliates. (2005). *Statistics.* Retrieved March 21, 2006, from http://www.nbcc.org/stats

U.S. Department of Labor, Bureau of Labor Statistics, Department of Labor. (2006). *Counselors. Occupational outlook handbook.* Retrieved March 21, 2006, from http://www.bls.gov/oco/ocos067.htm

Daniel T. Sciarra

Kerri Keegan

Bridget Sledz

Teacher-Student Interactions

Teacher interactions with students are at the heart of the hidden curriculum and are important means by which informal lessons about gender are transmitted in schools. Teacher-student interactions function in part to reproduce and occasionally challenge and transform traditional gender roles in school settings. However, they do not operate in isolation from other dimensions of schools that meaningfully affect gender relations. They are interconnected in complex ways with peer interactions, curriculum, administrative and counseling practices, gender practices originating outside of school, and structural constraints on the roles of teachers and students.

Teacher-student interactions may be initiated by either party, although teacher behaviors directed toward students have been studied far more than the reverse. The nature of interactions are influenced not simply by gender but also by other socially meaningful characteristics such as race/ethnicity, social class, nativity, disabilities, and sexual orientation. Teacher-student interactions embody messages about gender, but these can be strengthened, modified, or contradicted by other influences in schools. Thus, understanding the impact of teacher-student interactions is more complex than it may initially appear.

Two types of encounters initiated by K–12 teachers or by their students have frequently been studied: students' academic work and behavioral and social control. Of these two, academic-related interactions have shown more movement, albeit slow movement, toward gender equality than control-related interactions. Not only can teachers' equitable or inequitable treatment affect student outcomes for boys and girls, but so also can teacher *inaction:* What teachers do *not* do in relation to gendered encounters has consequences for students' informal learning about gender.

HISTORICAL TRENDS IN THE STUDY OF TEACHER-STUDENT INTERACTIONS

Concern about the influence of teacher-student interactions on gender dates back to popular writings of the 1960s suggesting that routine interactions between women teachers and young boys contributed to the poorer performance of boys compared to girls in reading. With the rise of feminism and feminist scholarship, attention shifted to the ways in which girls were disadvantaged in teacher-student interactions. This research often concentrated on mathematics and science, areas where girls' educational attainment lagged behind boys'.

A series of reports sponsored by the Association of American University Women (AAUW) appeared in the 1990s that analyzed the multiple ways in which schools "short-change" girls, including girls' interactions with teachers. In that same decade, as girls' educational attainments improved but boys' underattainment in schools persisted, attention shifted back once again to the schooling experiences of boys.

The current consensus views boys—especially minority boys—as disadvantaged in schooling. Nevertheless, White boys from affluent families are still the most advantaged group educationally. It is now recognized that strategies that have proved successful in raising girls' achievement are not always successful with boys. Hence, researchers are now seeking ways to improve boys' attainment without sacrificing gains made by girls.

The renewed concern about the educational experiences of boys also presents challenges to teachers who are expected to find new ways to interact with diverse groups of boys to improve their schooling experiences and attainment but without undermining the stronger performances of girls. In an era of greater government scrutiny of teacher work and conservative backlash against progress toward gender equity, progressive work on the part of teachers may be undermined.

INTERACTIONS FOCUSED ON ACHIEVEMENT

Substantial research has documented boys' academic work receiving the majority of teacher attention. Summaries of research in several academic fields report that girls experience less overall teacher attention in classrooms, less complicated and challenging interactions with teachers, less constructive feedback on academic work, and less encouragement in failure situations than do boys.

Although some studies in the United States and some parts of Europe and Australia suggest movement toward greater equity in patterns of teacher attention in recent years, others find substantial persistence of earlier-reported patterns. One implication of these latter findings may be that the behaviors teachers regard as girls' classroom strengths—good conduct, a desire to please teachers, and diligence in completing tasks—could actually be detrimental to their academic achievement. Boys' supposed weaknesses as students—poor behavior and frequent off-task activity—may actually benefit them academically by bringing them more teacher attention. In contrast, teachers may sometimes avoid giving girls detailed critiques of their academic work for fear of hurting their feelings.

Patterns of differential teacher attention to boys and girls in K–12 schools are fairly consistent throughout private, public, and parochial schools, and they appear in both coeducational and single-sex classrooms. They also remain steady across subject areas. In nearly all contexts, teachers still give more attention to the academic behaviors of boys. Patterns are particularly skewed in favor of boys in classes focused on mathematics, natural science, and computer science, and girls still lag behind boys in these areas. The introduction of computer-assisted, technology-based instruction does not eliminate and, in fact, often intensifies gendered patterns of teacher-student interactions.

The AAUW's most recent report (2000) indicates that established patterns of interaction are hard to break. For example, teachers are generally tolerant of established achievement behaviors of boys and girls and accept, rather than attempt to modify, the reluctance of Asian American and Native American girls to participate in class unless specifically called upon. Teachers allow boys to dominate class discussion in computer and hands-on science lessons. As a result, the gender gap in technology use widens between grades

K–12. Patterns of male dominance may emanate from peer interchanges and teachers may not be wholly responsible for gender gaps, but they rarely intervene successfully to disrupt them.

Teachers are more apt to call on boys than girls for responses in classrooms and to accept unsolicited responses from boys. In Japan, research suggests that men teachers foster sexism in classrooms by imposing higher academic standards for boys and giving preference to boys in class discussions. In the United States and much of Western Europe, both women and men teachers pay more attention to boys' academic work (Good & Brophy, 2003). Teachers overselect boys for special learning opportunities, leadership roles, and academic awards, especially in mathematics and science.

When students experience academic difficulty, teachers differentially evaluate the source of academic difficulty based on gender. Boys receive far more referrals for remedial reading and other academic interventions. This appears to be the result of disruptive behavior on the part of boys with reading difficulties while girls with the same difficulties exhibit fewer undesirable behaviors, receive less teacher attention, and get less remediation (Shaywitz et al., 1990). The effects of teacher interventions in addressing the academic needs of boys remain a matter of debate. While some have seen the greater tendency to evaluate and assign boys to special classrooms as stigmatizing, others have argued that the educational deficiencies of boys, more so than girls, are apt to come to the attention of teachers at a point when they stand the best chance of effective remedy. In contrast, studies link the relative inattention to girls' academic work to slides in their self-esteem and diminished aspirations for higher-level study in mathematics and science. To further complicate this issue, the differential attention to the academic work of boys and girls is largely unintentional on the part of teachers, who believe they provide similar amounts and quality of academic feedback to boys and girls. Only with videotaping and systematic analysis do teachers become aware of their bias toward greater attention to boys (Sadker & Sadker, 1994).

Despite the institutional limitations on teachers' roles, some teachers, especially women, do take on care work or change their interactions with students in an effort to address gender inequality in their classrooms. Extensive debate surrounds the definition of teachers' appropriate roles vis-à-vis students. An idealization of teachers as the maternal figures of schools influences teacher-student interactions. They sometimes are expected to provide for the general well-being of students in ways that go far beyond the duties involved in academic instruction. Teachers frequently accept this caregiving role, especially when it is not met by family or other social institutions, and they use their effectiveness in providing emotional labor as a measure of success in the profession. Stronger teacher-student bonds can result in higher achievement and lower likelihood of disciplinary problems, especially among Latina and Caucasian girls, and may even compensate when parental involvement is lacking (Crosnoe & Elder, 2004).

Students pick up important, if unintentional, lessons from the gendered division of labor of school staff. Additionally, differential assignment of women and men teachers to certain subject areas may reinforce students' perceptions that certain subjects are masculine or feminine domains. Girls' and boys' varying achievement patterns across subjects reflect the dominance of men teachers in math and science and women teachers in language arts and the perceived appropriateness of each subject for a given gender.

Not all boys are advantaged in classrooms, and studies suggest that teacher relationships with minority boys are more hostile than those with White boys. Although minority boys get substantial attention from teachers, much more of it is focused on behavioral control than on academic work. Boys from some minority groups show considerable estrangement from teachers and are among the least likely to initiate interactions with teachers around academic issues or other matters. Higher rates of dropping out, suspension, and expulsion for boys may be attributable, at least in part, to strained relationships between teachers and minority boys (Riordan, 2003).

Other research shows that teachers pay less attention to the academic work of Latina, Asian American, and Native American girls in comparison to White girls and that teachers may be reluctant to encourage more active classroom roles for these girls. Thus, patterns of teacher-student interactions may vary not only by gender but also by racial and ethnic group, and these patterns rely upon actions of both teachers and students.

The marginalization of girls in teacher-student interactions leads some commentators to call for the establishment of all-girl schools or classrooms. Proponents claim teachers in single-sex schools or classrooms focus exclusively on girls, who do not have to compete with boys for teacher attention. However, studies of single-sex education rarely show appreciable benefits for boys, and the impact on girls is unclear. While studies of postsecondary education show that women benefit in certain ways from attending single-sex institutions, studies of K–12 schools reveal few differences between patterns of teacher interaction in coeducational and single-sex educational environments in the United States. Research in Britain also fails to uncover consistent differences in girls' achievement levels across single- and mixed-sex classrooms. The results are mixed, and, although single-sex educational settings are occasionally associated with benefits for students, other factors beyond patterns of teacher-student interactions may be at play.

INTERACTIONS AROUND BEHAVIOR AND SOCIAL CONTROL

Unlike patterns of academic-related teacher-student interactions, where some studies show movement toward greater equity by gender, patterns of interaction concerning discipline and social-control-related interactions show little change over time. Boys undoubtedly receive the bulk of teacher attention aimed at discipline and social control in classrooms, with minority boys particularly likely to be heavily monitored by teachers. Such monitoring can have both positive and negative effects. It can keep boys on task and ensure that they complete academic work, but intense scrutiny and public criticism of behavior by teachers can make classrooms more hostile and alienating environments for boys. Girls of working-class and certain minority statuses also can be subjected to exaggerated teacher social control, especially if their actions defy expectations of the behaviors of "good girls" or evoke images of explicit sexuality.

Teachers frequently misinterpret the resistance of students of subordinated racial and/or class status to schooling and control as further misconduct and resort to heavier monitoring, especially of African American boys. These complex interchanges between students and teachers ultimately exacerbate the alienation of youth, which may be implicated in patterns of educational failure of boys.

In most schools, boys make more discipline-related visits to principals, spend more hours in detention halls, receive more suspensions and expulsions, and drop out of school more readily than do girls (Riordan, 2003). It is worth noting the messages about gender and authority that disciplinary measures send to students. Principals and other administrative staff are more likely to be men, and classroom teachers are overwhelmingly women who serve as the first corrective measure if a student misbehaves. If the student cannot be made to conform to classroom rules by the teacher, she/he is sent to a masculine authority figure for further punishment. This may send a signal that women and girls need not be taken as seriously as men and boys or that women's authority is less legitimate relative to men's.

Messages about the relative importance of masculinity and femininity can also be conveyed through *shaming,* a method of social control (used by students and teachers) wherein some characteristic of a student is used to place that student outside of peer norms, thus humiliating him/her and providing deterrence to future improper behaviors. Teachers use femininity as a shaming device geared toward controlling the behavior of boys telling a boy he is "acting like a girl" in order to embarrass him in front of his peers. To reestablish their masculinity with other students, a shamed boy will accept physical pain administered by other boys without complaint or insult girls in front of these other boys. Thus, teachers may be reinforcing a form of masculinity that is consistent neither with academic achievement nor behavioral standards in schools.

Shaming does not run along parallel lines for girls. Reprimands for behaving in ways thought appropriate to the other gender are not universal; girls are not reprimanded for "boyish" behavior, although they may be criticized for being unfeminine or unladylike. By stigmatizing boys with a feminine label, but not viewing masculine labels as insulting to girls, teachers may participate in the devaluation of feminine-linked attributes.

TEACHER INACTION

Gender is influenced by what teachers do *not* do as much as what they do. Teachers' inaction is often in response to institutional rules more so than personal preferences or professional training. For example, school rules can require teachers to enforce gender-linked dress codes for students, and teachers might be prohibited from discussing certain topics in the classroom. Such restrictions forbid teachers from challenging gender norms they might otherwise find undesirable. In addition, teachers may inadvertently perpetuate gender inequality by tolerating peer-initiated sexist behavior in classrooms. British studies indicate teachers frequently see students commit homophobic acts, yet do not interfere, feeling that any intervention they offer will have little effect. Misogynist bullying of girls often goes unacknowledged as well, and some teachers who do intervene do so by labeling the girls as promiscuous rather than the boys as bullies and intercede accordingly. The silences that many schools observe around these controversial issues make it difficult for teachers and students to have meaningful interchanges about important gender-related topics (Smith, 2000).

Although silences are sometimes due to institutional rules, teachers still bear some responsibility for these omissions. A desire to avoid classroom disruptions might lead teachers to "undereducate" girls by steering discussion away from controversial topics of particular relevance in the lives of girls, for example, workplace gender discrimination, sexual desire, sexual orientation, contraception, sexually transmitted diseases, or sexual harassment. Teachers, thus, are complicit in the perpetuation of normative teacher-student interactions that can disadvantage girls, lower their self-esteem, and lead them to restricted visions of career options. Teachers also rarely confront bullying by boys or girls, nor critique dysfunctional forms of masculinity prevalent in schools, thus failing to intervene in behaviors that can harm girls and boys. Students are not oblivious to teacher inaction and such omissions in teacher-student discourse define teachers as less trustworthy in the eyes of some students.

As these students realize, teachers do have the power to influence the perpetuation, or the disruption, of gender inequalities and, as such, teacher-student interactions remain an important focus of sociological and educational research. Among the more pressing questions to be addressed over the next several years include the following: How do race, social class, sexuality, and nativity status affect the analysis of gender and teacher-student interactions in the United States and in other countries? How do lesser-studied topics such as role modeling or mentoring shape gender roles? How might the needs of boys in schools be successfully addressed, without eliminating gains or creating new disadvantages for girls? Finally, how can progress toward gender equity in teacher-student interactions stay at the forefront of agendas for schooling in the face of multiple new challenges facing teachers and schools?

REFERENCES AND FURTHER READINGS

American Association of University Women. (2000). *A license for bias: Sex discrimination, schools, and Title IX.* Washington DC: American Association of University Women Legal Advocacy Fund.

Crosnoe, R., & Elder, G., Jr. (2004). Family dynamics, supportive relationships, and educational resilience during adolescence. *Journal of Family Issues, 25*(5), 571–602.

Fordham, S., & Ogbu, J. (1986). Black students' school success: Coping with the burden of "acting white." *Urban Review, 18*(3), 176–206.

Good, T.L., & Brophy, J.E. (2003). *Looking into classrooms.* Boston: Allyn and Bacon.

Riordan, C. (2003). Failing at school, yes; Victims of war, no. *Sociology of Education, 76*(4), 369–373.

Sadker, M., & Sadker, D. (1994). *Failing at fairness: How our schools cheat girls.* New York: Simon and Schuster.

Smith, D. (2000). Schooling for inequality. *Signs, 25*(4), 1147–1151.

Shaywitz, S.A., Shaywitz, B.E., Fletcher, J., & Escobar, M. (1990). Prevalence of reading disability in boys and girls. *Journal of American Medical Association, 264*(88), 998–1002.

Linda Grant

Kimberly Kelly

Part VIII

Gender Constructions in the Peer Group

Overview

The term *peers* is generally used to refer to persons who occupy equivalent positions in an organization or social network. These positions are usually designated by identity labels, and those with legitimate claims to the same label are said to be peers. Thus, students in a school are peers, as are teachers in a school, but students and teachers hold different positions and are not peers. Students in different schools may also be regarded as peers, especially when the students are at the same grade level. Students may also be regarded as the peers of those who drop out of school, but in such cases, a label other than student, such as adolescents, gang members, or 16 year olds, will be used to identify the basis of their peer status. Although teachers or principals or school bus drivers or academics who judge one another's scholarship meet the definition of peers just as much as students do, the term is used in Part VIII to refer to young people, especially children and adolescents.

Peer groups consist of two or more peers who are linked together by more than their common identity label. These linkages usually include contact, interaction, and positive, sociometric choices, such as putting a person's name on a list of friends or naming that person when asked to list classmates whom you like. Peer groups vary in size and in closeness. Closeness is difficult to define precisely because it is based on multiple linkages, but increases in number of contacts, duration and variety of interactions, and reciprocated sociometric choices should all be indicators of increased closeness in peer groups. Network theorists have also stressed the importance of density by which they mean the extent to which the members of a group are interconnected. The more of a person's friends who are friends of one another, the more dense his or her friendship network is said to be. Similarly, the higher the proportion of peers who identify themselves and one another as members of the same group, the more dense that group. Dense peer groups are likely to be perceived as not only closer but also more exclusive than peer groups that are less dense.

Peer groups may be important to their members even when the groups are not dense or particularly close. Peer groups may also serve as positive reference groups for people who do not belong to them. In such cases, people may identify with a group, seek to emulate it, and wish to join it, but they may have little, if any, contact and interaction with group members. Nor would such people be the target of positive, sociometric choices by group members. Indeed, group members may not even be aware of the people who use them as a positive reference group, although researchers have found that some peer groups work very hard to become the most popular or leading crowd in their school.

Some of the research on peer groups has focused on their internal dynamics, and this section contains essays that look at the ways in which children and adolescents construct peer cultures for themselves, the "insiders," and contrasting group identities for those they reject, the "outsiders." Gender and sexuality are often used for these constructions, and large literatures have emerged documenting the ways in which young people develop boundaries between the sexes and contrasts between acceptable and unacceptable forms of masculinity and femininity.

Although these boundaries and contrasts may be somewhat different as one moves across age groups, schools, and national contexts, there seems to be a cross-contextual tendency for young people (and many older ones) to engage in heterosexism, behaviors premised on the assumption that male-female sexuality is the normal, natural way of living one's life. Major corollaries of this assumption are homophobia and beliefs in gender inequality. As part of heterosexism, beliefs in gender inequality take the form of convictions that the best kinds of male-female relationships and sexuality are those in which men are dominant and women are more subservient. Thus, it is not enough for a woman to choose a man for her sex partner; she should also be willing to defer to the wishes and desires of that man with regard to the kind of sex acts they will practice and with what frequency. Homophobia refers to words and actions that express fear and loathing of same-sex sexuality and of those who practice or advocate it. Most studies suggest that, compared to girls and women, boys and men are more likely, on average, to endorse heterosexism, gender inequality, and homophobia, and this difference is thought to be a reason for the higher rates of aggression, violence, and rebellious behaviors among boys and men. There also is a growing body of evidence from research done in the United States suggesting that expressions of heterosexism and homophobia seem to reach their peak among students enrolled in middle schools or junior high schools, but more research in other countries is needed to determine if this finding is truly age-related or if it is a consequence of the structure of schooling and national culture in which U.S. youngsters are embedded.

Considerable evidence exists showing that teachers and school administrators sometimes foster the heterosexism of their students. When teachers create student groupings for learning or disciplinary purposes, gender is often an easy way to separate students. In elementary schools, for example, there probably still are geography or spelling bees that heighten gender identities and differences by pitting the boys against the girls. Even among the teachers who carefully avoid creating gender-based groupings, there are many who allow the students to create such groupings for themselves. When students are asked or allowed to choose teammates or workmates, it is highly likely they will choose their own friends. At some age levels, these are highly likely to be same-sex choices. And, at all age levels, it is likely that boys deemed to be unmasculine and girls thought unattractive will be chosen last or will remain unchosen. Once having given the students their choice, most teachers would be reluctant to challenge them even if they privately disapprove.

Usually, heterosexism, gender discrimination, and homophobia among students have to become highly public and fairly violent before school authorities are willing—or are forced—to take action against the offenders. The same is true of students' disaffection with school, which is often tolerated as long as it does not take the form of overt rebellion. Even when students act out, the focus of disciplinary action by the school is usually directed at a specific, misbehaving student with little attention given to the peer groups or "gangs" that often support the misbehavior and are likely to promote its reoccurrence.

This lack of attention to the peer group reflects a general tendency among educators and educational researchers to adopt an individualistic approach toward students. As part of this approach, it is assumed that the focus of education should be on learning and that the teacher should help each of her or his students to attain the highest level of achievement of which that student is capable. Thus, the most important relationships in the classroom are between the teacher and each of the students. Relationships among the students themselves are seen as secondary and usually become important to the teacher only when they hinder the learning process. When that happens, the tendency of the teacher is to identify one or a few "troublemakers," to subject them to discipline, and to restore classroom order so that learning continues to happen.

There are, however, a variety of teaching-learning strategies, known as cooperative learning, that recognize that there are important ways in which group processes and relationships can interfere with or aid classroom learning. Some forms of cooperative learning were designed specifically to break down prejudices and discrimination among students and to improve their social relationships, especially relationships among students of different race-ethnicities and social classes. The starting point for cooperative learning is the construction of a variety of dyadic and small-group instructional formats that bring together students of different social and economic backgrounds. Contact alone is rarely enough to reduce prejudices, however. To the contrary, some studies have shown that increased contact across racial lines is more likely to increase than to decrease both perceptions of racial dissimilarity and interracial antipathy. To prevent such outcomes, student dyads and small groups have been designed to foster not only contact among heterogeneous students but also interdependence and cooperation. According to a growing body of research, more positive interpersonal relationships, including improved race-ethnic and social-class relations, can be achieved in classrooms if students participate in instructional groupings that are deliberately and carefully structured to meet these goals. What is less certain are the effects that interdependent, cooperative peer groups initiated in school settings will have on prejudices concerning gender and sexual orientation and on the peer groups students choose for themselves both in and out of the classroom.

See also "Fraternities" and "Sororities" in Part VI, and "Heterosexism and Homophobia in the Hidden Curriculum" in Part VII.

Bullying, Harassment, and Violence Among Students

Our nation's elementary and secondary schools are filled with abundant examples of student-to-student gender-based harassment and violence. Despite requirements for compliance and monitoring articulated in state and federal laws and continuing guidance issued by federal agencies and the federal courts on Title IX of the Education Amendments that were passed by the U.S. Congress in 1972 to eliminate sex discrimination in educational institutions that receive federal financial assistance (meaning just about all public K–12 schools), results from surveys attest to the ugly entrenchment of sexual and gender harassment in our schools. Yet, sexual or gender-based harassment rarely shows up in any of the standard analyses of school violence—gender is missing.

Not only is gender missing, but many of these analyses also suffer from a failure to distinguish between acts that meet legal standards for violence and harassment and acts of noncriminal misbehavior. While the latter may require that students be subject to limit setting, retraining, or even discipline of some kind, they do not rise to the standard of criminality implicit in the "zero tolerance" policies now being imposed by many U.S. schools. These policies often fail to distinguish between crimes and minor infractions of school rules with the result that they pose a threat to civil rights and liberties in the schools. Masking the failure to distinguish illegal violence and harassment from bad deportment is the increasing use of the term "bullying" to refer to a broad range of student behaviors considered unacceptable by school authorities. This term not only hides the gendered and sexualized nature of a great many acts of violence and harassment among students but also shifts the responsibility for those acts to the students who perform them and away from the schools that are legally required to provide an environment free from gender-based harassment and violence.

ZERO TOLERANCE POLICIES

The nation was horrified by the April 1999 shootings at Columbine High School in Littleton, Colorado. Overnight, reports appeared on the topic of "school violence" with many urging measures that would allegedly make a school safer than before by suspending and/or expelling more students under the "one-strike, you are out" framework of zero tolerance.

Within this framework, schools have been quick to suspend students for anything that could be deemed a weapon, a drug, or a threat, and the result is that students are being controlled in ways that shred their Constitutional rights. Students have been suspended for papers they have written, thoughts they have had, and drawings they have created (*Commonwealth v. Milo, M.,* 433 Mass. 149 [2001]). Elementary school children have been suspended for comments made in the heat of a touch football game or in response to a teacher denying permission to go to the bathroom, comments that schools characterized as "death threats." In a case from Jonesboro, Arkansas, an eight-year-old boy was suspended for pointing a chicken nugget toward a teacher and saying "Pow, pow."

Zero tolerance is a deeply flawed approach, leaving no room for teachable moments, graduated interventions, or progressive discipline. It is a policy that insults teachers and violates the civil rights of students. The judgment of educators is discounted, and one punishment is meted out for a dizzyingly broad range of acts. Standards are subjective, but sentences are uniformly severe. Not surprisingly, zero tolerance has racial implications —disproportionate numbers of students of color have been suspended and expelled under policies (The Civil Rights Project, 2000; Skiba, 2000).

Zero tolerance mania in schools is part of the pervasive punitive ideology and social policy that also includes trying minors as adults (California's Proposition 21 passed in March 2000), deterrence theories, and mandatory sentencing. Educators are now including bullying behaviors under the ever-broadening umbrella of zero tolerance. Schools proudly state that they will not tolerate bullies; there are bully buster posters around school buildings, and new rules to cover bullying and eradicating bullies are all the rage with state legislators, school officials, and consultants.

The zero tolerance approach has taken over the good senses of the educational and legislative establishments. What has gotten lost in this surge of reports and frenzy to reduce a rather expansive notion of bullying in schools are the rights of students to go to school in an environment that is gender-safe, free from gender-based harassment and violence.

HARASSMENT OR BULLYING?

The extremely popular framework of bullying represents a problematic formulation of violence as it both degenders harassment and removes it from the discourse of rights by placing it into a more psychological, pathologizing realm. Objections to these anti-bullying efforts embodied both in the new laws and the training efforts that have accompanied them are multiple: (a) The laws largely do not hold school administrators liable in the same ways to resolve the problems that Title IX requires but instead put the responsibility for solving the problem on the victim; (b) most of these anti-bullying laws are overly broad and arbitrary with the result that students are suspended or expelled from schools for a variety of minor infractions; and yet (c) sometimes egregious behaviors are framed as bullying when, in fact, they may constitute illegal sexual or gender harassment or even criminal hazing or assault (Stein, 2003, 2005).

In the United States, the discourse around bullying is a relatively new phenomenon, in large part imported from the Europeans and the research conducted there since the 1970s (e.g. Ahmad & Smith, 1994; Olweus, 1993). Prior to the emphasis on bullying as a new trend for U.S. educators and researchers, redress of injustices and wrongs were addressed through civil and Constitutional rights. However, those linkages and legacies are now in jeopardy: The discourse of bullying may ellipse the rights discourse (Stein, 2003).

Consider the case *Davis v. Monroe County Board of Education* heard in the U.S. Supreme Court in 1999, the details of which demonstrate the implications of the bully versus harassment distinction. LaShonda Davis was repeatedly touched, grabbed, and verbally harassed by a male classmate in her fifth-grade class. The boy, who is known only by his initials, G.F., repeatedly attempted to touch LaShonda's breasts and genital area, rubbed against her in a sexual manner, constantly asked her for sex, and, in one instance, put a plastic doorstop in his pants to simulate an erection and then came at her in a sexually suggestive manner. By no stretch of the imagination was this boy subtle or was his behavior ambiguous; rather, it was persistent and unrelenting. Should these behaviors have been called bullying or sexual harassment? The answer to this question has vitally important consequences for LaShonda, for her assailant, and for the teachers and school administrators.

LaShonda did not respond passively to the boy's behavior. Besides telling G.F. to stop, she also told her teachers. Her parents also complained to her teachers and asked to have LaShonda's seat moved. But, her teachers and school officials did nothing, not even to separate the two students who sat next to each other. G.F.'s behavior was clearly affecting LaShonda both psychologically and academically. After several months of this harassment, LaShonda's grades fell and she wrote a suicide note. Her parents filed a criminal complaint against the boy and also a federal civil rights lawsuit against the school district for permitting a sexually hostile environment to exist. In the criminal action, the boy pled guilty to sexual battery. And, after five years of legal battles and appeals, their case was heard in the U.S. Supreme Court. In a five-to-four decision, the Court ruled that schools are liable for student-to-student sexual harassment if the school officials knew about the sexual harassment and failed to take action.

It is highly unlikely that if these behaviors had been framed as bullying that LaShonda's case would have ever been heard in a federal court, let alone in the U.S. Supreme Court. As it was, the conduct that was inflicted upon her, by both the male classmate and the treatment that she received from the school personnel, were framed as civil rights violations. To have viewed this conduct as bullying would have relegated her case to the principals' office, a place where she had not received justice or redress prior to filing a federal lawsuit or a criminal complaint. Moreover, the context and timing of the *Davis* decision proved to be crucial. It came one month after the shootings at Columbine High School (April 1999) putting the subject of sexual harassment in schools into the midst of the national conversation about school safety.

A typical example of the problems associated with the conflation of bullying and harassment can be found in the April 24, 2001, issue of the *Journal of the American Medical Association* (JAMA). This study of nearly 16,000 sixth to tenth graders from public and private schools came from a larger sample of those who had filled out a World Health Organization (WHO) instrument administered in 1998 in 30 countries. To be applicable, the original instrument had to use questions, definitions, and terms that would make sense in all of the 30 participating countries, from France to Indonesia. Thus, behaviors that legally could be sexual harassment or assault in the United States were framed as bullying for purposes of this survey—for example, being hit, slapped, or pushed, spreading rumors, or making sexual comments.

In the United States, the results showed that nearly 30 percent of the sample reported moderate or frequent involvement in bullying, either as the bully (13 percent), one who was bullied (10.6 percent), or both (6.3 percent). Males were more likely than females to be both perpetrators and targets of bullying. But, the term "sexual harassment" was never raised—not by the researchers nor in the accompanying article in JAMA written by two public health researchers. To engage sixth through tenth graders in this discourse of bullying without acknowledging the realities of sexual or racial harassment is to infantilize and mislead them because some of the behaviors described as bullying are, in fact, criminal conduct or could be covered by sexual harassment or other civil rights in education laws.

There is a striking contrast between the research findings reported in JAMA and the findings of two other studies released two months later, both of which received scant publicity. In *Hatred in the Hallways,* Human Rights Watch considered the harassment of lesbian, gay, bisexual, and transgender students in U.S. schools. In *Hostile Hallways II,* the American Association of University Women (AAUW) Foundation and the Harris poll reported the results of a study of students of the same ages as those studied in the JAMA article who were surveyed about their experiences with sexual harassment and gender harassment.

In these two studies, the euphemism of bullying was not used as it was in the two JAMA articles when describing behaviors that constitute sexual and gender-based harassment. In the AAUW study, sexual harassment was found to be widespread in schools with 83 percent of the girls and 79 percent of the boys indicating that they had ever been sexually harassed. Thirty percent of the girls and 24 percent of the boys reported that they were sexually harassed often. Nearly half of all students who experience sexual harassment felt very or somewhat upset afterwards, a finding that points to the negative impact that sexual harassment has on the emotional and educational lives of students. In the Human Rights Watch study, 140 gay, lesbian, bisexual, and transgender students along with 130 school and youth service personnel in seven states were interviewed. The results showed an alarming portrait of daily human rights abuses of the students by their peers and, in some cases, by some of their teachers and administrators.

Rather than suggesting that the word "bullying" be purged from the language entirely, it might be used more appropriately only with young children. Young children, unlike teenagers, might be hard pressed to understand the concepts of sexual harassment or sexual violence. But, even if the term "bullying" is used instead of "harassment" with young children, school officials cannot dismiss their legal liability to abide by sexual harassment laws and to ensure that schools do not discriminate on the basis of sex. Moreover, to use the word "bullying" to cover some behaviors that may constitute criminal or civil violations is to perform a great disservice to young people; the word "bullying" may infantilize them but the law will not.

OMISSIONS AND DENIALS OF GENDER

Psychologists seem to dominate the field of bullying research and largely seem unfamiliar with nearly 30 years of research from the fields of education, sociology, anthropology, and feminist legal scholarship—fields that might instead frame the bullying behaviors as gendered violence or sexual harassment. While the bullying researchers may acknowledge the existence of sexual harassment in schools, they generally cite only surveys or court decisions from the U.S. Supreme Court and largely have ignored a wealth of studies and articles from researchers who have employed widely different methodologies and have long argued for a gendered critique of children's behaviors. In addition, the omission or denial of gender from the dominant construction of school safety and violence contributes to the disproportionate focus on the most extreme, rare forms of violence while the more insidious threats to safety are largely ignored (Lesko, 2000; Stein, 1995; Stein, Tolman,

Porche, & Spencer, 2002). An example of this failure to factor in the saliency of gender in school violence is reflected in the many reports and analyses of the spate of school shootings—the form of school violence that has attracted the most national attention and incited the most panic. In general, the school shootings were widely reported in a gender-neutral way, when, in fact, the majority of these tragedies were perpetrated by White middle-class boys who were upset about either a breakup or a rejection by a girl (e.g., Jonesboro, Arkansas; Pearl, Mississippi) or who did not meet traditional expectations and norms of masculinity (e.g., Columbine, Colorado) and were thus persecuted by their peers.

This failure to consider the role of gender is also endemic to much of the bullying research. Researchers of bullying, for the most part, have unfortunately failed to consider the ways in which adolescent boys (and adult men) unmercifully police each other with rigid and conventional notions of masculinity and the imposition of compulsive heterosexuality. Not to factor in or even recognize these potent elements is to deny a central and operating feature in boy culture, namely the maniacally driven, tireless efforts to define oneself as "not gay." Researchers such as Joe Pleck, R. W. Connell, Michael Kimmel, and Michael Messner have written about this phenomenon and its consequences for several decades, yet most bullying researchers have failed to draw upon their findings.

Teen dating violence is also on the increase. There are two questions on the Youth Risk Behavior Survey (YRBS), a comprehensive survey about general behavior of teens from the U.S. Department of Health and Human Services, the Centers for Disease Control and Prevention, that ask about violence in teen dating relationships. The first question inquires about physical violence in a dating relationship, and the second question asks about sexual violence in a dating relationship (www.cdc.gov/HealthyYouth/yrbs).

Data from both versions of the YRBS (the state-by-state versions and the national version, with its sample of 13,000 students between the ages of 14 and 18 years old) show that in some states, up to 20 percent of girls experience violence from a dating partner—some of that as physical violence and some as sexual violence. Moreover, a recent analysis of the national 2001 data from 6,864 female students in grades 9 through 12 found that 17.7 percent of the girls reported being intentionally physically hurt by a date in the previous year (Silverman, Raj, & Clements, 2004).

However, prevalence data on sexual violence in elementary and middle schools has not been consistently collected, disaggregated, or reported. Researchers lack a complete picture about the violence that children younger than 12 years old experience, whether that violence happens at home, in the streets, in public spaces, or at school. This lack of information may lie largely with the resistance of the parents who will not permit researchers to ask these sorts of questions to children younger than 12 years old.

CONSEQUENCES OF ANTI-BULLYING POLICIES

"Bullying" has become the stand-in term for other behaviors that school and public health officials as well as scholars, legislators, and researchers do not want to name, like racism, homophobia, sexism, or hate crimes. It is an expression that makes adults feel more comfortable but it does not do anything to stop gender harassment and sexual violence. This loose and liberal use of the term "bullying" may be part of a general trend to label children, particularly in a culture that tends to psychopathologize behaviors.

Unfortunately, the new anti-bullying laws may serve to dilute the discourse of rights by minimizing or obscuring harassment and violence. When schools put the new anti-bullying laws and policies into practice, the policies are often overly broad and arbitrary, resulting in students being suspended or expelled from schools for a variety of minor infractions (Stein, 2001). In an era when school administrators are afraid of being sued for civil rights/harassment violations—as a consequence of the May 1999 decision of the Supreme Court in the *Davis* case—naming the illegal behaviors as "bullying" serves to deflect the school's legal responsibility for the creation of a safe and equitable learning environment onto an individual or group of individuals as the culprit(s) liable for the illegal conduct. Under the prevailing definition of bullying, almost anything has the potential to be called bullying, from raising one's eyebrow, giving "the evil eye," making faces (all very culturally constructed activities), to verbal expressions of preference toward particular classmates over others. There may be a tyranny of sameness that is implicitly being proposed in this pursuit to eradicate bullying behaviors.

Why have school administrators been so quick to embrace the anti-bullying movement and to abandon the anti-harassment focus? If behaviors are labeled "bullying," administrators and their school districts cannot be sued in federal court. Harassment and discrimination based on race, disability, gender, or national origin are civil rights violations and rigorous standards of proof must be met. Bullying is not against any federal law, and it is not tied to civil rights. Subsuming serious violations under the bullying umbrella means schools avoid the liability they would face if sued successfully in federal court for a civil rights violation. It may also mean that students who have been bullied lose their rights to redress.

Approaching the subject of bullying without also talking about harassment and hazing leads us in the wrong direction. Rather than assuring civil rights and equal educational opportunities for all students, there will be more suspensions and expulsions under zero tolerance for bullying. Before long, we will be suspending students for all sorts of "discomfort" that they may have caused. Bullying is too arbitrary, subjective, and all encompassing a concept to be the basis for a sound disciplinary approach. Because there is no threshold for bullying, its use as a criterion is rife with opportunities for abuse of power. The broad sweep of the anti-bullying movement and zero tolerance laws are very troubling and need to be challenged at every turn and ultimately dismantled.

REFERENCES AND FURTHER READINGS

Ahmad, Y., & Smith, P.K. (1994). Bullying in schools and the issue of sex differences. In J. Archer (Ed.), *Male violence* (pp. 70–83). New York: Routledge.

American Association of University Women Foundation and Harris Interactive. (2001, June). *Hostile hallways II: Bullying, teasing and sexual harassment in school.* Washington, DC: Author.

Brown, L.M., Chesney-Lind, M., & Stein, N. (2004). *Patriarchy matters: Toward a gendered theory of teen violence and victimization.* (Working Paper No. 417). Wellesley, MA: Wellesley College Center for Research on Women.

Human Rights Watch. (2001, June). *Hatred in the hallways: Violence and discrimination against lesbian, gay, bisexual, and transgender students in U.S. schools.* New York: Author.

Lesko, N. (2000). *Masculinities at school.* Thousand Oaks, CA: Sage.

Olweus, D. (1993). *Bullying at school.* Cambridge, MA: Blackwell.

Silverman, J.G., Raj, A., & Clements, K. (2004). Dating violence and associated sexual risk and pregnancy among adolescent girls in the United States. *Pediatrics, 114*(2), 220–225.

Skiba, R. (2000, August). *Zero tolerance, zero evidence: An analysis of school disciplinary practice* (Policy Research Report #SRS2). Bloomington: Indiana University, Indiana Education Policy Center.

Stein, N. (1995). Sexual harassment in K–12 schools: The public performance of gendered violence [Special issue]. *Harvard Educational Review, 65*(2), 145–162.

Stein, N. (2001). Sexual harassment meets zero tolerance: Life in K–12 schools. In W. Ayers, B. Dohrn, & R. Ayers (Eds.), *Zero tolerance: Resisting the drive for punishment in our schools* (pp. 130–137). New York: New Press.

Stein, N. (2003). Bullying or sexual harassment? The missing discourse of rights in an era of zero tolerance. *Arizona Law Review, 45*(3), 783–799.

Stein, N. (2005). Bullying and harassment in a post-Columbine world. In K. Kendall-Tackett & S. Giacomoni (Eds.), *Child victimization* (pp. 16-1–16-11). Kingston, NJ: Civic Research Institute.

Stein, N., Tolman, D., Porche, M., & Spencer, R. (2002). Gender safety: A new concept for safer and more equitable schools. *Journal of School Safety, 1*(2), 35–50.

The Civil Rights Project. (2000, June). *Opportunities suspended: The devastating consequences of zero tolerance and school discipline.* (Report from A National Summit on Zero Tolerance, Washington, DC). Cambridge, MA: Harvard University, The Civil Rights Project.

Nan Stein

Gangs and Schools

The subject of gangs has become a hot issue over the past couple of decades. Since the majority of those who belong to youth gangs or have friends who are in gangs are attending school, at least for part of the year, it should come as little surprise to find surveys documenting the existence of gangs on school campuses. Most of the research on gangs has focused on *males,* largely ignoring the role of *females.* A special section devoted to girls and gangs is included in this essay.

WHAT IS A GANG?

The terms *gang* and *gang member* can have many different definitions and be subject to gross misinterpretation. Criminologist Gil Geis of the University of California–Irving has provided one of the *more* interesting comments about the etymology of the term, noting that the early English usage of *gang* was "a going, a walking, or a journey." The definition given by the *Random House College Dictionary* provides similar meanings of a positive or neutral nature, such as "a group or band," "a group of persons who gather together for social reasons," "a group of persons working together; squad; shift; *a gang of laborers,*" along with the more negative meanings. The thesaurus of the word processing program used to type these words gives such synonyms as "pack," "group," "company," and "team."

Not surprisingly, there has existed little consensus among social scientists and law-enforcement personnel as to what these terms mean. One writer defined gangs as groups whose members meet together with some regularity, over time, on the basis of group-defined criteria of membership and group-defined organization. In many studies, researchers have often used whatever definition was used by the police. Many researchers have apparently confused the term *group* with the term *gang* and have proceeded to expand the definition in such a way as to include every group of youths who commit offenses together.

Adding to the ambiguity of the term "gang" is a recent "National Youth Gang Survey" sponsored by the U.S. Office of Juvenile Justice and Delinquency Prevention. In this survey of about 5,000 agencies, a "youth gang" was defined as a group of youths or young adults in your jurisdiction that you or other responsible persons in your agency or community are willing to identify or classify as a "gang." Omitted from this definition were such groups as motorcycle gangs, hate/ideology groups, prison gangs, or other exclusively adult gangs. In other words, a "gang" is whatever an agency says it is.

Two noted researchers, David Curry and Irving Spergel (see Spergel, 1995), define *gang* as a group or collectivity of people with a common identity who interact on a fairly regular basis. The community may view the activities of the gang as legitimate, illegitimate, criminal, or some combination of these. Gangs are distinguished from other groups by their communal or fraternal, different, or special interstitial character. Curry and Spergel define *street gang* as a group or collectivity of persons engaged in significant illegitimate or criminal activities, mainly threatening and violent. The emphasis is placed on the location of the gang and their gang-related activities. Finally, they define the *traditional youth gang* as a group that is concerned primarily with issues of status, prestige, and turf protection. Such gangs may have a name and a location, be relatively well organized, and persist over time. They often have implicit or explicit leadership structures, codes of conduct, colors, special dress, signs, symbols, and the like. They also may vary across time in such characteristics as age, gender, community, race/ethnicity, or generation, as well as in scope and nature of their delinquent or criminal activities.

Another noted gang researcher, Ron Huff (2002), alerts us to a distinction that has gained more significance in recent years, namely, that existing between gangs and organized crime. As he notes, *youth gangs* historically were largely groups of adolescents (mostly male) who engaged in a variety of deviant activities, especially turf battles and gang fights. Now they are increasingly involved in major crimes, especially those that are violent or drug related. *Organized crime* has traditionally meant *adult* criminal enterprises operating businesses. Today such organized activities characterize many youth gangs. As a result, Huff's definition of a *youth gang* includes their frequent and deliberate involvement in illegal activities as well as their tendency to express their collective identity by claiming control over certain "turf" (persons, places, things, and/or economic markets). Youth gangs differ from organized crime groups, according to Huff, because the latter consist primarily of adults who are frequently and deliberately involved in illegal activities directed toward economic gain, primarily through the provision of illegal goods and services. Like participants in youth gangs, those in organized crime groups interact with one another frequently, but organized crime groups generally have better defined leadership and organizational structures than do youth gangs.

A BRIEF HISTORY

Gangs—or groups that have been labeled as such—have been in existence in America since the early nineteenth century. A study of a Philadelphia newspaper covering the years 1836 to 1878 found 52 different gangs identified. The report noted that in the pre-Civil War era Philadelphia was "plagued" by gangs. A report by the *New York Tribune* stated that the northern suburbs of Philadelphia during the years 1849 and 1850 were crawling with "loafers who brave only gangs, herd together in squads" and mark their names on the walls. In New York City in 1855, there were an estimated 30,000 men who owed allegiance to gang leaders and through them to the political leaders of Tammany Hall and the Know Nothings or Native American Party, according to one contemporary account. While public concern about gangs arose again briefly in the 1940s and 1950s, it was during the 1980s when the issue became headline news; and it has remained so into the twenty-first century. The rediscovery of gangs has been augmented by an escalation of media presentations about youth gang activities—particularly those gangs located within America's inner cities.

CONNECTIONS BETWEEN GANGS AND SCHOOLS

Not surprisingly, gangs are more likely to be found within urban than suburban or rural schools. In many parts of the country, the development of gangs can be traced directly to various conflicts in or near public schools. Los Angeles is a case in point. One of the earliest references to a "gang problem" in Los Angeles appeared in African American newspapers during the late 1940s. This was in reference, ironically, to *White* youths ("gangs?") who attacked Black people. There were reported "racial wars" in several Los Angeles area high schools during the late 1940s and early 1950s. Much like the groups of Hispanic youths who were called "gangs" by the White-dominated press when they sought retaliation against White sailors who had attacked Hispanic youths in the "Zoot Suit" riots of 1942, African American gangs emerged as a defensive response. These African American gangs defined themselves mostly in terms of school-based turfs. Some of the earliest of these gangs went by such names as the Slausons, Gladiators, Watts, Flips, Rebel Rousers, Businessmen, and the like. Some of them modeled themselves after the White "car clubs" so common throughout Southern California (e.g., the Slausons and the Flips). Some of these groups divided themselves into two factions, one group on the "Westside" (usually with more money and more sophistication) and the other on the "Eastside" (less money and less sophistication). Some of these "gangs" were merely the extension of intramural athletic rivalries, common in those days.

During the mid to late 1960s, a transformation began with the emergence of groups that called themselves Crips. There is some debate as to the exact origin of this term; some say it came from a movie starring Vincent Price, *Tales from the Crypt,* while others say it came from the word cripple because the original gangs crippled their enemies or suffered a similar fate. Another story was that it referred to a style of walking (i.e., walking as if one were crippled in some way). The most popular story was that the Crips were founded by a group of youths from Fremont High School (a youth named Raymond Washington is generally credited as the founder) that had one member who walked with the aid of a stick and who was referred to as a "crip," short for cripple. Some have suggested that the original gang used walking sticks as a sort of symbol and that the police and the media began to apply the name and so eventually the gang did, too. Several imitators came from the city of Compton. One group called themselves the Westside Crips, founded by a student from Washington High School known as Tookie Williams (whose execution in California in December 2005 caused much controversy nationally and internationally). They borrowed one of the cholo traditions of wearing railroad bandannas, and they added to this the color of blue. Other Crip sets soon began to imitate them by wearing blue bandannas and other blue clothing, a color that set them apart from others. (Some of these sets currently wear the colors brown, purple, and black.) Thus, during the early formation of Los Angeles gangs, schools played a key role. As several researchers have noted, school desegregation ironically contributed to the growth of the gang problem by placing rival gang members in the same schools and, in the process, destroying some of the turf connections of these gangs (more detail is given in Shelden, Tracy, & Brown, 2004).

Today gangs are found within practically every major urban high school in the country. In a study conducted in the early 1990s, Spergel (1995) provided the following percentages of those within the Chicago school system who reportedly were in gangs: 5 percent of the elementary school youths, 10 percent of all high school youths, 20 percent of those in special school programs, and, more alarmingly perhaps, 35 percent of those between 16 and 19 years of age who had dropped out of school. It is normal to find more than one gang within the same school, often resulting in conflicts taking place. This may, of course, result from a certain gang seeking to expand its "turf" or just plain ordinary conflicts over minor matters (e.g., someone "dissed" someone else, fights over girlfriends, etc.). Also common are fights between rival gangs from different schools, such as during athletic events. Although rare, some of these disputes result in a youth being killed, whereupon gang members seek revenge by engaging in a "drive-by shooting," either before, after, or even during school hours.

On some school campuses, certain gang members engage in drug dealing. Studies have shown that the school grounds may be ideal places to engage in such activity. Some gang members have devised rather sophisticated techniques for getting the drugs onto the campus and distributing them, not unlike regular business enterprises. Despite the media attention devoted to the connection between drugs and gangs, the illegal drug market is not dominated by street gangs. To be sure, there is a small number of what are called "drug gangs" who engage in drug dealing, but the evidence is overwhelming that most of the serious illegal drug dealing is done by people who are not involved in such famous street gangs as the "Crips" and the "Bloods."

As almost every study of gangs has found, one very important key to understanding why kids join gangs is the school experience. A close look at the development of Latino gangs in Southern California is a case in point, as school became a serious problem for many second-generation Latinos in this area. This applies equally to other gangs in other cities, as one of the key characteristics distinguishing gang members from other youths from similar backgrounds is that of school failure. A high incidence of dropping out and/or exclusion or expulsion from school resulted in what Latino gang expert James Diego Vigil (1998) called a situation in which significant numbers of barrio youngsters are socialized to a considerable degree in the streets. The majority of the gang youths Vigil studied began to withdraw from school life by the third or fourth grade. For many, their school careers began with skepticism, limited parental encouragement, and early exposure to street experiences that did little to promote self-discipline. Long before they officially dropped out (usually around age 16), they had been turned off by school. Some began to have problems as early as kindergarten, with the language barrier being the predominant cause. Many had experienced a great deal of prejudice and discrimination. Most of the problems at school began long before any involvement with a gang.

A typical experience in school is related by Felix Padilla (1992) in his study of a Chicago gang. He describes the gang members he studied as being labeled deviants and troublemakers by school officials, usually during their elementary school years (some as early as the fourth grade), long before they joined the gang. These youths responded as if their labels were a self-fulfilling prophecy: They joined with others so labeled and engaged in corresponding behavior. These youngsters began to develop various forms of oppositional behavior such as fighting, cutting classes, and not doing homework. Many began to develop a distinctive subculture within which they could examine and interpret what was going on in their lives and in school. In short, very early in their lives these youths began to respond in ways that were almost identical to gang behavior. In effect, says Padilla, they were undergoing early preparation for a later stage in their teenage years (during high school) when they would finally join the gang.

It is important to note that these particular youths experienced a form of public humiliation from some of their teachers and some of their own peers. This humiliation often took the form of negative evaluations of their own Puerto Rican culture. Such experiences were quite painful, and the youths quickly sought out others who were similarly branded and, therefore, perceived to share a common fate. With support from these others, these youths reported that they sometimes talked back to or laughed at the teacher and hit other students, trying by such actions to be as bad as the teacher thought they were.

Another response to the school-based problems faced by the Puerto Rican youth whom Padilla (1992) studied was that most concluded that it was better to simply stay out of school than be victimized by the constant verbal assaults by their teachers. So, they began skipping school, most as early as elementary school. This became a regular experience, one in which they found pleasure. Instead of being facilitators of the goals of these youngsters, the institution of education and its agents—the administrators and teachers—were experienced as antagonistic elements in their socialization.

Like the Puerto Rican youths Padilla studied in Chicago, the Latino youths Vigil (1998) studied in California often experienced marginalization as a result of conflicts between the Latino and White cultures. This conflict has created problems for Latino families, which in turn has meant that these families have lost some of their effectiveness as a social-control institution. As a result, schools and the police have taken over this function.

For gang members, a lack of strong attachment to the home and to the school has created an environment in which the gang provides answers. It is here, in the gang, where they associate and identify with similarly marginalized youths. Vigil noted that the gang has served to "resocialize" members of a group by teaching them alternative norms and behaviors. In this way, gangs help troubled youth feel a sense of importance, self-esteem, and self-identity.

Padilla's Chicago gang members indicated that one of the turning points in their lives came during high school. Prior to this time most of these youths were marginal members of the gang, engaged mostly in hanging out on the street corners or at school; "turning" (becoming regular and committed gang members) came during their early high school years. Throughout their elementary school years, most of the gang members referred to themselves as "neutrons"—that is, those with no affiliation to any of the many gangs within their neighborhood. However, this status was constantly being challenged by members of the various competing gangs. The punishment that they received from these gangs was aimed not so much to pressure them to turn but rather to ensure that they would remember the importance of remaining neutrons. Among gangs there is constant fear that these neutrons might become informants for another gang or, even worse, be informants for the police. The decision to turn came rather informally without much thought.

Over time, youngsters become embedded in the street subculture, which has become institutionalized—that is, a permanent fixture in poor communities. The streets provide these kids with a network of support that is available in neither their families nor their schools. In short, the gang subculture takes the place of the family and the school.

GIRLS, SCHOOLS, AND GANGS

Girls' involvement in gangs has never been as frequent as that of their male counterparts. When they have been involved, it has usually been as so-called auxiliaries to male gangs. However, the extent to which girls have been involved in gang life may be understated because of the vague definitions of gang, gang member, and even gang involvement. Because most male gang members have relationships with females, such females are, almost by definition, at least associate gang members.

There is a general consensus in the research literature that girls become involved in gang life for generally the same reasons as their male counterparts, namely, to meet basic human needs such as belonging, self-esteem, protection, and a feeling of being a member of a family. The backgrounds of these young women—poverty, single-parent families, minority status, and so on—are about the same as those of male gang members.

The case studies of girl gang members in many different parts of the country reveal the common circumstances in their lives. The crimes that they commit are, for the most part, attempts to survive in an environment that has never given them much of a chance in life. Most face the hardships that correspond to three major barriers—being a member of the underclass, being a woman, and being a minority. The gang, while not a total solution, seems to them a reasonable solution to their collective problems (Chesney-Lind & Shelden, 2004).

Not surprisingly, school problems figure prominently in the lives of girl gang members. Most girl gang members are, like their male counterparts, highly likely to drop out of school. For instance, a study of San Francisco gangs found that the median number of years of education was 10, and only about one-third were actually in school at the time of the interviews. These researchers concluded that the prospects for these young women—unmarried, with children, less than a high school education, and few job skills —can only be considered bleak. A study of the Vice Queens in Chicago found that most attended school only sporadically because they experienced much conflict with school officials (for more details about these studies, see Chesney-Lind & Shelden, 2004).

Many analysts have noted that school is often deemed totally irrelevant to the lives of gang members, and this perception motivates them to drop out and become part of a gang. For most girl gang members, success is elusive, as avenues of opportunity for girls living in poverty are blocked in several different ways. These include lack of education, training, access to meaningful employment, and few, if any, career possibilities.

REFERENCES AND FURTHER READINGS

Chesney-Lind, M., & Shelden, R.G. (2004). *Girls, delinquency and juvenile justice* (3rd ed.). Belmont, CA: Wadsworth.

Huff, C.R. (Ed.). (2002). *Gangs in America* (3rd ed.). Thousand Oaks, CA: Sage.

Padilla, F. (1992). *The gang as an American enterprise.* New Brunswick, NJ: Rutgers University Press.

Shelden, R.G., Tracy, S.K., & Brown, W.B. (2004). *Youth gangs in American society* (3rd ed.). Belmont, CA: Wadsworth.

Spergel, I. (1995). *The youth gang problem: A community approach.* New York: Oxford University Press.

Vigil, J.D. (1998). *Barrio gangs.* Austin: University of Texas Press.

Randall G. Shelden

Heterosexism and Homophobia in the Peer Group

Comments hurled at one another in the hallways, on the field, in the locker room, in the classroom, in the cafeteria, on the bus, and virtually everywhere on school grounds, such as "That's so gay," "Stop being so gay," "You throw like a girl," "Dyke," "Bitch," "Ho," "Be a man," "Slut," have become common epithets in the relational culture among students. Kids put each other down as routinely as they comb their hair, often without regard to the impact of their words. Students admittedly *do not mean* anything bad about gay people when they say, "That's so gay!" (object-directed) and "You're so gay" (person-directed), and yet the implications are blatantly negative—"nasty," "disgusting," "stupid," "gross," "weird," or "idiotic." Never would a student go up to his friend and say, "Wow, I love your sneakers! They're so gay!"

Such terminology serves to put each other down while, at the same time, it keeps both girls and boys inside narrowly defined gender scripts. For those who do not conform to these scripts, this language is the genesis of fear and power in the peer culture. The pressures, especially in middle schools, are daunting, and students quickly become aware of what is and is not acceptable. Homophobia and heterosexism permeate the peer culture and affect *all* students (heterosexual, as well as gay, lesbian, bisexual, transgendered, and questioning students). Inherent in the complex nature of peer socialization are both subtle and overt homophobic and heterosexist language by means of which students police each other's behaviors and identities. Thus, whether a student is gay or lesbian is not the focus but rather how students police each other's identities and behaviors through the subtle yet overt use of homophobic and heterosexist language and behaviors.

GENDER AND SEXUALITY MESSAGES IN THE HIDDEN CURRICULUM AND PEER GROUP

Heterosexism—the belief that heterosexuality is normal or homosexuality is abnormal—is ingrained and so powerful. Heterosexist ideology in schools lies behind the message to students, still, that they must display heterosexual behaviors and largely remains an overt yet unspoken requirement in developing an appropriate gender identity in middle school (Mandel & Shakeshaft, 2000).

Homophobic and heterosexist social messages are learned very early in school in a hidden curriculum that has no book and no tests, the implications of which are powerfully clear. For example, heterosexist messaging is inherent in an elementary teacher's comment such as "Isn't that cute—Melanie and Zachary are holding hands. What a cute couple they make!" This type of statement affirms the heterosexual behavior displayed by Melanie and Zachary. But, if Zachary wanted to hold his best friend's hand, regardless if he was gay or not, the heterosexist response would be different: "You know boys aren't supposed to hold other boys' hands, don't you?"

When a girl and boy go to the school Valentine dance together as a "couple," their heterosexuality is not questioned. It is not only a given, it is understood. In fact, most people think it is cute or sweet or romantic. Conversely, this same type of affirmation is not extended to homosexual youth or questioning youth. Teachers and other adults say such things as, "You must just really like him as a friend," "You haven't dated enough girls," "You just haven't met the right girl." Often, gay and lesbian students are told, "It's just a phase" or "You must be misinterpreting your feelings." Even though homophobia and sexism are not in the lesson plan, the attitudes are still taught, and still learned.

Peers do the same to each other. For example, a heterosexual seventh-grade boy who does not show interest in girls is subject to his friend's comments such as, "You don't like a girl? What are you, gay?" It is not at all only gay students who are at risk. Appearing less than masculine or being perceived as gay or lesbian is just as harmful. The Safe Schools Coalition of Washington released research findings in 1999 showing that heterosexual students who had been harassed because someone believed they were gay were three times as likely as nonharassed heterosexual peers to report having missed school out of fear for their safety.

The peer culture has its own curriculum. Homer Simpson echoes the power of the peer culture in an episode of the popular U.S. TV show *The Simpsons* when Marge came home with a new shirt for Homer. He looks at the shirt and says, "I can't wear this pink shirt to work. Everyone will make fun of me! I'm not popular enough to be different." A boy who does not dare wear (or own) a pink shirt consciously, or perhaps unconsciously, fears the (homophobic) implications—"If I wear a pink shirt, does that mean I'm gay? Will others think I'm gay?" or "If I wear a pink shirt, I'll make sure I hang out with a girl so no one will bother me." Fitting in is key, and boys learn early on that not adhering to gender role expectations invites homophobic-driven mockery, laughter, ostracism, ridicule, and isolation.

As Homer Simpson's remark indicates, popularity is a social currency that allows students to transcend homophobic and heterosexist barriers. Boys with social status, for example, those who tend to be athletes, popular, attractive, etc., carry a social currency that allows them to step outside the gender box largely without threat to their image and identity.

MIDDLE SCHOOL EXPECTATIONS

As gender and sex-role expectations become more pronounced in middle school, so do heterosexist and homophobic messages. For example, boys who step outside of traditional cultural gender role expectations or who display traits that are perceived as less than stereotypically masculine, a misogynist component of homophobia, are often subject to ridicule, teasing, and harassment by peers. Boys know and internalize the message that being a sensitive male or a gay male in middle or junior high school is the worst possible thing to be.

Compulsory heterosexuality, especially for boys in middle or junior high school, is essential; the peer culture is often hostile and unwelcoming otherwise. Boys police their own and each other's masculinity. Explicit homophobia and implicit heterosexism found within schools derives from and feeds macho and misogynistic versions of masculinity (Epstein, 1997). Further, being a "proper" boy involves investing in a heterosexual identity within which girls are central to the formation of boys' gender cultures and identities (Renold, 2005). Feelings of homophobia reinforce one's heterosexuality through hypermasculinity. Males who commit date rape or other sexual assaults often adhere to stereotypes about gender and sex roles that view feminine attributes as inferior and, therefore, unacceptable for men, creating a misogynistic mentality and a need to prove their masculinity.

Heterosexism plays a part in the peer socialization and development of gender identity for girls as well, though it may appear to have a more acceptable presence than the ubiquity of homophobia in male peer socialization. It is largely the case that girls buy into and exploit their femininity and sexuality largely to attract attention from boys. The fashion and media moguls marketing to teenagers and tweens are potentially undoing years of great advancements among the work of feminists and gender pioneers. According to a report published in 2004 by the National Campaign to Prevent Teen Pregnancy, 65 percent of girls and boys ages 12 to 19 agreed that teen girls often receive the message that attracting boys and looking sexy is one of the most important things they can do. Girls feel that they are not looked at by boys unless they are perfect (i.e., having a decent body). In a culture where stores are cropping up everywhere enticing young girls to have glamorous makeup parties in dress-me-up clothes, beauty blast accessories, and, of course, Hollywood starlet mood mist and a never-leave-home-without-your-tiara attitude, the messages girls receive blatantly reinforce traditionally stereotypic gender and sex roles now more than ever. Add to this the fact that teen girls are now being given gift certificates for plastic surgery for their 16th birthdays and high school graduation presents.

With growing rates of depression and pressure to be attractive and sexually active at younger ages, heterosexism inherent in this ideology is rarely named or called what it is, especially in schools. We question girls' resistance and resilience to these pervasive images and messages in which females are valued solely by their appearance and their attractiveness to males. Although girls can and do have more leeway than boys to develop a wide range of feminine and masculine attributes, many girls put tremendous emphasis on and energy into their popularity, appearance, and relationships with boys, overemphasizing appearance over intelligence and aspirations.

Another notable disparity that exists in the peer culture is with regard to antigay harassment against lesbian and bisexual girls, which often goes unnamed and unchallenged. For example, boys who stare and make gestures about a girl's body or behavior, refer to girls as "bitches," or ask a girl if they can party with her and her girl friend are engaging in sexual harassment layered with homophobic violence (Goldstein, 2001). These actions are just as antigay as the more familiar type of name-calling and schoolyard bullying. Yet, too often the behaviors boys exhibit toward girls or the statements about wanting to "watch" or "join" the girl and her girlfriend are not perceived by girls (or adults) as an invasion with an implicit threat of sexual violence because of the mixed gender script of the expectation and the girls' conditioning to attract male attention. Despite an expanded role for girls in developing gender identities, girls continue to experience sexual harassment by the simple act of being female. Additionally, girls who question their sexuality are often viewed as doubly enticing to males, further bolstering their masculinity while, in a real sense, invalidating female sexuality.

GAY, LESBIAN, BISEXUAL, AND TRANSGENDERED YOUTH

A decade ago, the *Harvard Educational Review* (1996) was the first of three education journals to publish a special issue on gay, lesbian, bisexual, and transgendered (GLBT) people and education, a chapter of which was dedicated to writings by high school and college students offering their firsthand accounts of the world of pain and alienation they and other young people face when forced to live a secret life. Ten years later, gay and lesbian characters on MTV, in magazines, and on television shows are more visible; high schools are more welcoming to gay and lesbian students; and kids are disclosing their homosexuality with unprecedented regularity and at much younger ages. Nevertheless, the battle for equity is far from over.

Many of the advances just mentioned have not been enjoyed at the middle school level. Violence, bias, and harassment of GLBT students continue to be the rules, not the exceptions, in America's schools. According to a 2004 report by the Gay, Lesbian, and Straight Education Network (GLSEN), 84 percent of GLBT students report being verbally harassed because of their sexual orientation and between 92 percent and 97 percent of students report hearing remarks, such as "Faggot", "Dyke" or "That's so gay" from peers in school. Additionally, 45 percent of GLBT youth of color report being verbally harassed because of both their sexual orientation and race/ethnicity.

Adults are often desensitized to the negative, derogatory impact of such language and kids excel at not getting caught. GLSEN reported in 1999 that 76 percent of the largest school districts in the United States provided no training for staff on issues facing gay youth. The acceptance of derogatory comments by school staff—part of the "hidden curriculum"—continues at unacceptable levels and is too often ignored. Perhaps this is not so surprising given that 41 states have no laws or educational policies that explicitly protect GLBT students. Only eight states legally protect students on the basis of sexual orientation and/or gender identity: California, Connecticut, Massachusetts, Minnesota, New Jersey, Vermont, Washington, and Wisconsin; and these states enroll only 25 percent of the country's schoolchildren.

Further research indicates that GLBT high school students have reported being subjected to either verbal or physical harassment, including genital groping, sexually offensive labeling, shoving, spitting, bra snapping, underwear stealing, being stripped, being tied up, and being mock raped. GLBT students try to make themselves invisible so their sexual orientation and gender identity or expression will not be detected and, as a result, limit their learning experiences. In the peer culture, too often students who are—or who are perceived to be GLBT—are threatened with physical violence as well: "You faggot —I'm gonna kick your ass on the way home from school." "What a dyke—be careful in the locker room, lezzy!" The fear instilled by such threats begins to dictate their actions and even their thought patterns.

GAY-STRAIGHT ALLIANCES IN SCHOOL

One approach to addressing homophobia and heterosexism in adolescent peer groups is by means of gay-straight alliance clubs (GSAs). GSAs are school-based student clubs that provide a safe space for students and staff to advocate for the needs of

GLBTQ(uestioning) students and to promote social justice with students who want to make a difference. GSAs are school-sanctioned clubs that highlight the need for GLBT and heterosexual student allies to come together to promote safety, respect, understanding, and support. According to GLSEN, the number of GSAs has increased during the past 10 years from 100 clubs on U.S. high school campuses to nearly 3,000 clubs today—nearly 1 in 10 high schools has one.

Students who have started gay-straight alliances in their high schools are making notable strides in changing school peer cultures largely because they believe that antigay language and sentiments are actually uncool and, moreover, politically incorrect. Heterosexual students contribute greatly to these inroads by outwardly expressing support for their peers and by responding to offensive homophobic slurs—whether or not a student is homosexual.

In middle schools, far fewer GSAs exist, only 290 nationally. Yet, there are at least three important reasons why addressing homophobic language and sexuality in middle school/junior high school is extremely important. First, the age of sexuality awareness has dropped. The issue of sexuality in general peaks in seventh and eighth grades, and many kids are questioning their sexuality at this age. Although the average age a gay person comes out is around 17 to 18 years old, individuals develop attractions to each other much earlier. Between the 1960s and 1990s, studies indicate that the age of the first same-sex attraction dropped from age 14 to 10 for males, and from 17 to 12 for females —that is, fourth through seventh grades. And, many sense something different about themselves as early as age four or five.

A second reason to address sexuality and homophobia in middle school is that these schools tend to have very homophobic peer cultures that need change. Fortunately, there are many students at this age who sense the injustice of heterosexist and homophobic language and want to make things better. These students want to make a difference, and GSAs are a way to do this. Thus, support for students' good impulses provides a third reason for addressing issues of homophobia in middle schools.

Yet, comments from students in a middle school who joined a GSA reveal that doing so was very difficult. Students who walked through the door of the after-school club meetings had to face their peers who made comments to them such as "There's the GSA kid" when they saw them in the hallway. They even got spit on in the cafeteria, and, during meetings, notes would often be slipped under the classroom door that read, "Look at those fags" or "You're queer!" Non-GSA students would huddle outside the door waiting for the meeting to be over just to see who had attended. Several students shared how they were judged by kids in school and even how some students stopped being friends with them because they were attending GSA meetings.

Addressing gay issues at the middle/junior high school level is difficult and controversial not only for the peer group but also for parents who often fear that mentioning the topic is an invitation for their son or daughter to be gay. Though this homophobic fear is not accurate, it can seem very real. Many parents and adults believe that kids do not really know or understand their sexuality until high school or college and that introducing any discussion in middle school threatens their belief system. In the middle school where the students talked about their GSA-related difficulties, a parent of an eighth-grade student wrote a letter to the principal that stated: "I request that you notify me prior to any classroom discussion of any issues of sexuality, including any discussions of homosexuality or alternative lifestyles in school or in any after school activity so that I may have my child opt out of such discussions."

Even those parents who truly embrace their children expressed their difficulty in accepting or understanding their 13- or 14-year-olds' interest in being in the GSA. These students who believe that speaking out for acceptance and respect is important in middle school express that they do not feel supported by their parents largely, perhaps, because they do not understand that a GSA is a gay-*straight* alliance, not just a gay alliance. Said one youngster, "My dad doesn't understand why I'd be in this club since I'm not gay. He doesn't get it." And, another who reported that her mother did not want her to participate in GSA said in a tearful voice, "I think this is such important work—we're about tolerance. So what if people are gay, or lesbian, or whatever?"

TEACHERS CAN MAKE A DIFFERENCE

Although it is encouraging to witness students working to change the peer culture in their schools by joining GSA clubs that oppose antigay language and educate about antigay language and heterosexist attitudes, these students, especially younger ones, cannot, nor should they be expected to, lead this effort alone. Administration, faculty, and other adults are key in this effort. The importance of a teacher's intervention is nicely illustrated by the case of Jared.

"Try to get 'em now, you fag!" a middle school classmate shouted after kicking Jared's keys down the hallway as they fell out of his backpack. Walking into English class, boys on the lacrosse team whispered, "So who do you like Jared, huh? We know you like him!" They cracked up just as the bell rang for class. These seemingly subtle incidents, along with being shoved in the hallway, spit on in the cafeteria, and finding "Go home you faggot" written in red marker on his locker are only some examples of the taunting Jared endured on a daily basis in eighth grade.

Several months into the school year, Jared's art teacher began a visual communication project in class in which she facilitated a discussion about social issues that they wanted to communicate a message about in their art projects. Students shared about how kids label each other, how peer pressure is difficult, how the media influences kids, etc. Jared raised his hand and said, "I want to do something about sexual harassment." "Why would you want to do it on that?" asked a student. "There's this kid in math and every day—I'm not kidding—he sexually harasses me." One girl immediately shouted, "Ewe!" Another said, "He can't be sexually harassing you!" And a boy snapped, "Uh, I don't think so!" The teacher replied, "Well, wait a minute, what is he doing or saying to you?" "Everyday he blows me kisses and says, 'Hiiiiiii Jarrrrrrred!' I tell him to stop and he doesn't," Jared said. A student said, "Well then he's telling you you're gay!" Another said, "He's putting you down." And, a third said, "That's not sexual harassment, Jared!"

The teacher asked the class, "If a boy blew kisses to a girl everyday, and she didn't like it or didn't like him, but he did it everyday even after she told him to stop, would that be considered sexual harassment?" There was silence. The teacher applauded his courage and affirmed that what Jared described *is* a form of sexual harassment.

The peer culture at the middle school level is fraught with adolescents trying on new roles and identities while at the same time vying for peer acceptance, approval, and belonging. Jared is an example of how heterosexism and homophobia impact all students, not just gay, lesbian, and bisexual students. Though a heterosexual male, Jared has been ostracized, made fun of, sexually harassed, and verbally threatened because he engenders cultural traits deemed by students as less than masculine.

Administration, faculty, and staff are key in addressing, and helping students address, homophobic and heterosexist language, behaviors, attitudes, and assumptions. But, too often schools treat violence not as a problem engendered by the climate of the school but as an individual's problem. It is as if they were saying, "See—if you didn't act that way, or if you weren't gay or lesbian, then people wouldn't treat you differently," instead of identifying heterosexism as the problem.

REFERENCES AND FURTHER READINGS

California Safe Schools Coalition and 4-H Center for Youth Development. (2004). *Consequences of harassment based on actual or perceived sexual orientation and gender non-conformity and steps for making schools safer.* Davis: University of California. Available at http:// www.nclrights.org/publications/pubs/SafePlacetoLearnLow.pdf

Cianciotto, J., & Cahill, S. (2003). *Education policy: Issues affecting lesbian, gay, bisexual and transgender youth.* New York: The National Gay and Lesbian Task Force Policy Institute.

Epstein, D. (1997). Boys' own stories: Masculinities and sexualities in schools. *Gender and Education, 9*(1), 105–116.

Gay, Lesbian, and Bisexual People and Education. (1996). [Special issue]. *Harvard Educational Review, 66*(2).

Goldstein, N. (2001, September 12). *Invisible women: A closer look at anti-gay harassment shows many have yet to see what young women face daily in school.* Available as an independent source from GLSEN Education department www.glsen.org

Lee, C. (2002). The impact of belonging to a high school gay/straight alliance. *High School Journal, 85*(3), 13–26.

Mandel, L., & Shakeshaft, C. (2000). Heterosexism in middle schools. In N. Lesko (Ed.), *Masculinities at school* (pp. 75–103). Thousand Oaks, CA: Sage.

Renold, E. (2005). *Girls, boys and junior sexualities: Exploring children's gender and sexual relationships in the primary school.* London: Routledge Falmer.

Laurie Mandel

Robert Vitelli

Peer Cultures and Friendships in School

Peer cultures consist of descriptive and evaluative meanings that peer groups assign to behaviors and relationships, and the interactions among peer group members consist of talk and behaviors that construct, maintain, consolidate, challenge, or change these meanings. The interpretations peer group members construct for themselves and their own experiences are usually part of a broader process in which meanings are also assigned to other groups and individuals. This seems to be particularly true in school settings where peer groups often construct their identities in contrast to those of "outsiders." A classic example of this process is provided by "the lads," the group of rebellious, English, working-class students studied by Willis (1977), whose conversations make abundantly clear that they defined themselves and their experiences in opposition to attitudes and behaviors attributed to the conformist students they called "the ear'oles." The lads also constructed their own efficacy and superiority through processes of interaction in which limited, sexualized identities were assigned to girls, and ethnic minorities were labeled "wogs" and "bastard Pakis" and treated as "smelly" interlopers.

"The lads" and "the ear'oles" are examples of two kinds of peer cultures: a *chosen peer culture* that is constructed by friends within a given peer group, and a *labeled peer culture* that is constructed by those outside that culture to refer to people different from themselves. Both chosen and labeled peer cultures are often based upon demographic characteristics such as age ("tweens"), social class ("yuppies"), race-ethnicity ("wogs," "brothers," or "bros"), and gender ("lads," "debs"). An extensive research literature has appeared detailing ways in which demographic similarities and differences affect the social construction of peer cultures, with the more consistent findings being reported for social class and gender differences across chosen peer cultures.

A central concern among those who study peer cultures in schools has been the extent to which such cultures support or undermine the official school culture's emphasis on academic achievement. Much concern, even hysteria, has been expressed about the conflicts between adolescent peers and adults both in and out of schools. Criticisms of specific peer cultures and of students, more generally, are often premised on the notion that schools are focused principally, or even entirely, on important academic endeavors that the students fail to understand and respect. Although this notion is fallacious, there is evidence that high academic demands and fair treatment of students may encourage peer cultures to become more positive toward and involved in their schooling.

CHOSEN VERSUS LABELED PEER CULTURES

The literature on peer cultures in schools has yielded a colorful array of identity labels. In addition to the lads, ear'oles, bros, and debs mentioned above, there are normals, freaks, politicos, rads, greasers, rah-rahs, crispies, grits, brains, trendies, grinds, hoods, populars, dweebs, workers, nerds, geeks, outcasts, preppies or preps, debaters, executioners, the power clique, cool kids, and the leading crowd. This list does not exhaust all the names that appear in the existing literature nor would an exhaustive list necessarily be a useful basis on which to construct a systematic typology of peer cultures. Some of the identity labels appear in only one study, and others take on different meanings as one moves from school to school. In addition, many of the labels reflect the national context in which the research was done. It would be most surprising to find North American students calling one another ear'oles, and the lack of cheerleaders in British schools makes it unlikely that students in that country would form rah-rah cultures.

What seems more likely to be comparable across national and school contexts is the fact that names given to groups of children, adolescents, or young adults may be either the accepted names of chosen peer cultures or the names that others give to labeled peer cultures. Cultures based on peer choice are those in which participants choose one another to be friends and construct their own culture out of their interactions. In research, such cultures are often identified by using ethnographic techniques, but some researchers use formal sociometric techniques that ask students to nominate their friends or to list those classmates they associate with most and least. Instead of being free and unbounded, however, both the choices students make and the cultural possibilities available to chosen peer groups are constrained by the contexts in which peers find themselves.

Despite these constraints, members of chosen peer cultures will see themselves and one another as members of the same group who choose to be with one another. Sometimes the group will be given a name like those listed above, but sometimes the identity of the group will not be linked to a specific name ("They're my friends." "They're the guys I run around with."). Personal claims to group membership will be validated by other members of the group and by the interaction patterns that exist among members.

In contrast to chosen peer cultures, labeled peer cultures are identified and defined by outsiders. These outsiders may be other students, parents, teachers, school administrators, researchers, or the mass media. Sometimes the peer cultures identified by outsiders actually exist as the cultural constructions of chosen peer groups, but this is not always true.

Labeled peer cultures serve two major purposes. One is to establish and elaborate the cultural identities of those who construct and label the peer culture. A good example of a peer culture constructed for this purpose is the ear'oles whose passivity and conformity were emphasized by Willis's (1977) lads as a means of asserting their own superior ability to create fun and excitement. Similarly, the students whom Eder (1995) observed at Woodview Middle School bolstered their own social standing by constructing a peer culture known as the grits whom they regarded as losers in the struggle for social status. A second purpose of labeled peer cultures is that they help to shape interaction and relationships. Once people can label one another, they become more certain about the ways in which they can and should behave toward one another. So, even if the students at

Woodview School could not agree on a precise definition of grits, they all knew that students who were grits were not desirable friends or associates.

When researchers construct peer cultures to which they do not belong, their purpose is to advance their analytic and theoretical arguments about adolescent or child cultures in school, national, or international contexts. A classic example can be found in the study of ten high schools by Coleman (1961). Although Coleman presents considerable information about the peer groups that were chosen by the students he studied, the primary argument of his work is that an adolescent culture is emerging in industrial societies. Adolescents are becoming increasingly peer oriented, and they share values, such as prizing athletics above scholarship, that are contrary to the values of their parents and teachers. These trends are particularly evident in large urban schools (vs. smaller rural schools) and among the students who are reputed by their peers to be in "the leading crowd" (vs. nonelite students). To support his arguments, Coleman (1961) presented a large amount of survey data.

Coleman's arguments were paralleled by many of the arguments about the youth culture that were advanced in the decade following the publication of his book. When social constructions such as youth culture and adolescent culture become known to their supposed constituents, they can have important effects on peer cultures in many parts of the world. Connell, Ashenden, Kessler, and Dowsett (1982) observed that the Australian students whom they studied were able to sustain conflict with their parents' views on schooling and other matters because they now had a strong group identity independent of their families, namely, the large complex of peer networks known as the youth culture that is largely outside of adult control. Like the labeled peer cultures identified by adolescents, those that are "discovered" by researchers and popularized by journalists both affect and are affected by the interaction patterns and cultures adolescents choose to construct for themselves.

SIMILARITY AND DIFFERENCES WITHIN PEER CULTURES

Chosen peer cultures are far more likely to consist of students who have the same background characteristics than of students with heterogeneous backgrounds. The reasons for this homogeneity are both structural and social psychological. *Structural reasons* include any features of school organization that promote segregation of students from different backgrounds. Age-grading has become an almost universal feature of schools worldwide. Also common are the tendencies to send students to schools in their own neighborhoods or communities, which are often homogeneous in social class and race-ethnic composition. Where they exist, private and parochial schools deliberately recruit students of particular social backgrounds. In addition, researchers have identified a broad range of school characteristics that affect proximities among students and, therefore, possibilities for friendship formation. These school characteristics include architectural features of the school building and grounds, school size, equipment and supplies, the organization of extracurricular activities, the authority structures of the classroom and school, and instructional groupings, such as curricular tracking or streaming.

Even when structural limits are taken into account, students still tend to choose friends who are similar to themselves. Two *social psychological reasons* seem to account for these tendencies. One is social pressure, which has been found to inhibit the development of friendships that cross age, gender, social class, or racial-ethnic lines. Adults often intervene to make certain that children select "appropriate" friends, and peers frequently do likewise. A second reason is the set of assumptions people tend to make about those who are similar to them. Social psychologists have found that most people make the assumption that similar others will like them more than dissimilar others. This assumption, coupled with the well-documented tendency of people to like those who like them, produces more reciprocal liking among those who are similar than among those who are not. Both assumed and actual reciprocity of liking, in turn, have been found by researchers to be strong predictors of friendship selection and stability.

If peer groups were less homogeneous internally, their cultures would probably become more similar to one another. Instead, research completed in the past half century suggests that the differences across peer cultures in background characteristics continue to be large and socially significant, and there is no indication that these differences are declining in size or importance. The sharpest and best substantiated of these differences are those produced by social class and by gender. The differences produced by age are more debatable, despite the large literature concerned with peer relations among children of various ages (see Bank, 1997, for a review). Surprisingly little research has appeared that directly contrasts the peer cultures of different racial and ethnic groups, and the research that has been done on the nature of minority peer cultures in schools tends to parallel the arguments about working-class cultures, but with less convincing evidence.

The major dimension for characterizing middle-class versus working- or lower-class peer cultures is orientation toward schooling, and a large literature contrasts the more positive orientation of middle-class groups with the negative orientation of those who come from working-class homes. Most of the researchers who have produced this literature agree that working-class and poor adolescents experience fewer successes and more failures in school than their middle- and upper-class counterparts. As a result, participation in peer cultures that rebel against schooling give working-class and poor adolescents (and unsuccessful middle-class students) an opportunity to gain the social support and status that they cannot gain in the official school culture. Although most researchers see these peer cultures as social problems, some argue that the major problem lies in the schools that fail to interest disadvantaged students, denigrate them, and treat them more harshly than students from more privileged backgrounds.

In the United States, researchers have argued that African American adolescents also participate in peer cultures that rebel against schooling. To do well in school is dismissed by these adolescents as "acting White," a sign of betrayal not only of their peer culture but also of their entire race-ethnic community. Evidence to support this argument is mixed, with many studies showing that African Americans value schooling and high achievement in school as much as or more than White Americans, but other studies showing that doing poorly in school is explained by African American students as part of their rebellion against racism. And, as is true of arguments about working-class peer cultures, some researchers see rebellious African American peer cultures as a social problem, whereas others see the problem as one that is created by a racially inequitable educational system. Still others assert that the underlying problem is social class, which is highly correlated with race, and that the same differences in attitudes toward schooling that have been found between White peer cultures of predominantly working- and middle-class students also can be found between Black peer cultures of different social classes.

Unlike working-class peer cultures, middle-class peer cultures (of all race-ethnicities) help to perpetuate the educational system by embracing its central tenets, particularly competitive achievement. Students from middle-class backgrounds, and especially those who are members of elite groups within their schools, tend to value social and academic competition and are more likely to base their friendships on interests and activities, often switching friends as their interests change. In contrast, working-class students have been found to exhibit more support and loyalty to their friends, often to the point of avoiding those activities in which their friends are uninvolved. This has led some researchers to argue that working-class adolescents are more likely than their middle-class counterparts to view their personal networks, including their chosen peer cultures, as the most self-affirming element in their lives.

Although the findings about social class differences in competition versus loyalty to friends have been reported for both males and females, the literature concerned with peer cultures and resistance has tended to focus on boys rather than girls. In addition to being more likely to resist the official school culture, boys' cultures have been found likely to stress a form of masculinity based on toughness and sexual domination, and boys whose behaviors fail to be "masculine" enough are often declared to be homosexuals. Given the centrality of "masculine" aggression in the peer cultures of boys, it is hardly surprising that they tend to view girls as sexual objects and treat them accordingly. Because many of the sexual comments and behaviors boys direct toward girls are unwelcome, they meet the standard definition of sexual harassment, and a large number of studies have documented widespread sexual harassment in elementary and secondary schools.

It is often difficult for girls to resist these forms of harassment effectively. Ignoring them or countering them with sexual comments or behaviors directed at their male harassers may only serve to intensify the attacks directed at the girls. It is also difficult for girls (and boys) to know how to interpret some of the sexual comments and behaviors of their peers. Are these acts of unwanted sexual harassment or tokens of sexual and romantic interest? Popular cultural milieux that put so much emphasis on sex appeal and romantic relationships as the keys to self-fulfillment and happiness create contexts in which most girls would not want to ignore sexual and romantic overtures. In addition, the peer cultures girls construct for themselves often place a high value on attractiveness to the opposite sex.

The emphasis on sex appeal, romance, and boyfriends that is so often characteristic of the girl's peer cultures greatly strengthens the power that boys have over girls. Femininity comes to be defined as attractiveness to boys. Sexually aggressive behaviors by boys come to be seen as normal, even admirable. Similar behaviors among girls are deemed unacceptable and are likely to be sanctioned with derogatory terms, such as "slut," "slag," and "ho" or "whore." These terms do not reference only sexual behaviors. They also function to denounce and control behaviors by girls that are deemed too independent, assertive, or challenging. Not only boys, but girls themselves use these terms against one another. Acceptable girls come to be seen as those who are agreeable and passive.

Not all peer cultures are constructed around these styles of femininity and masculinity, but considerable research has now emerged suggesting that these are dominant cultural constructions in male and female peer cultures, at least in the United States, United Kingdom, and Australia. Although these cultural constructions are undoubtedly more common among middle school and high school students than among younger students, Thorne (1993) reports that the elementary school boys whom she observed used sexual insults and approached relations with girls in a daring, aggressive manner. Generally, however, research on children younger than middle-school age reveals gender differences that are less sexualized. This research has found that friendships of girls are intensively focused on one or a few friends and exhibit high levels of expressive intimacy, but boys both report and are observed to have more extensive friendship networks focused on activities, rather than "just talking."

As these findings suggest, researchers have also found a substantial amount of gender segregation in the peer cultures of children. This segregation is substantial even in preschools, and it tends to increase during the elementary and middle school years. High school peer cultures seem to be somewhat less segregated by gender, but the data to support this claim are often sociometric choices that are subject to alternative interpretations. It is possible, for example, that when asked to list their best friends, high school students include dating partners even though they and their partners are members of different, gender-homogenous peer cultures. Conversely, it is possible that high rates of dating across certain groups in a school may lead to a merger of those groups as when male athletes and female cheerleaders join to become "rah-rahs" or "the leading crowd."

CONFLICTS BETWEEN OFFICIAL SCHOOL CULTURE AND PEER CULTURES

Official school cultures include elements of an individualistic, competitive ideology that is particularly characteristic of the United States. In schools, the purpose of this individualistic competition is presumed to be high achievement, particularly in academic work but also in the nonacademic activities sponsored by the school. Although school staff assume that not all students can achieve at the highest levels, all are expected to take achievement goals seriously. Seriousness can best be demonstrated by working hard, respecting school staff, and obeying school rules. This portrait of official school culture is not unique to the United States, and it seems reasonable to assume that most schools throughout the world expect students to make serious efforts to perform well.

One of the more surprising findings to emerge from ethnographic studies of peer cultures in schools is the relatively low emphasis those cultures give to anything associated with the academic life of the school. This finding gains further support from studies using surveys and other research methods that have also found little emphasis within peer groups on academic matters. Studies in which students were asked to describe and evaluate chosen or labeled peer cultures in their schools report negative associations with being in an academically oriented peer culture (usually called by such names as "the brains" or "scholars"), and none reports that such peer cultures received the highest evaluation given to various peer cultures. The negative associations with being "a brain" include being "a grind," lacking social skills and dating partners, being a teacher's pet, and being "a nerd."

Although the finding that peer cultures ignore academic matters or are hostile to high levels of academic achievement is a common finding, it is also contradicted by a substantial amount of research. Studies have found that many students of all races and social classes admire academic achievement; that less popular and more rejected students are judged to be less able academically; that popularity is positively associated with scores on measures of achievement; that students who struggle scholastically or have to be placed in remedial classrooms lose peer recognition; that high-ability peers are given more positive or neutral ("neither like nor dislike") ratings than negative ratings; and that most students believe that their friends encourage academic achievement, at least to a moderate degree.

How can such findings be reconciled with findings that peer cultures devalue academic achievement? Some answers seem to lie in the age of students, the gender of students (and their friends), and the nature of the official school culture. With regard to age, it is noteworthy that peer support for academic achievement is more likely to be reported by students in elementary schools than in middle schools or high schools. In contrast, for nonacademic behaviors, especially "deviance," most studies report that peer influence increases with age up to mid-adolescence (15–16 years of age) and then begins to decline.

With regard to gender, Riegle-Crumb, Farkas, and Muller (2006) have recently found that same-sex peer influence on academic striving of high school students is greater for girls than for boys. Specifically, they found that for girls, having female friends with higher subject-specific grades increases the probability that those girls will take advanced courses in all subjects the researchers considered: physics, precalculus/calculus, and honors English. For science and math, but not English, they also found that the effects of same-sex friends' grades on advanced course taking were stronger for girls who were in a predominantly female friendship group compared to girls who were not. In contrast to the girls, the effects of same-sex friends' grades on boys' subsequent advanced course-work was not significant. Interestingly, Riegle-Crumb and her colleagues suggest that this finding may result from a tendency among boys, in contrast to girls, to see their high-performing same-sex friends as competitors rather than as peers who can support, encourage, assist, and validate their own academic pursuits.

A third way of reconciling contradictory findings about the academic orientation of peer cultures is to look at the official school cultures in which different peer cultures exist. Many studies support the conclusion that undemanding official school cultures are likely to be found in the same schools as peer cultures that are unconcerned about or hostile toward getting knowledge, and there also are studies suggesting that high academic demands may be a necessary, albeit not a sufficient, condition for producing peer cultures that respect intellectualism. More research is needed to clarify the interaction processes by means of which a positive correlation is produced between the academic values (or lack thereof) of an official school culture and the values and behaviors of the peer cultures in that school. What is already clear from existing research is that many schools violate the popular image that they are places where an official culture that is focused on academic matters and is characterized by high achievement standards clashes with peer cultures that have failed to internalize the academic values of their schools. Instead, official school cultures often fail to develop themselves as contexts in which academic striving is expected, commonplace, and prized and in which all students—even those in "difficult" peer cultures that teachers do not like—are treated fairly and with respect.

REFERENCES AND FURTHER READINGS

Bank, B.J. (1997). Peer cultures and their challenge for teaching. In B.J. Biddle, T.L. Good, & I.F. Goodson (Eds.), *International handbook of teachers and teaching, Part Two* (pp. 879–937). Dordrecht, Boston, & London: Kluwer.

Coleman, J.S. (1961). *The adolescent society: The social life of the teenager and its impact on education.* New York: The Free Press of Glencoe.

Connell, R.W., Ashenden, D.J., Kessler, S., & Dowsett, G.W. (1982). *Making the difference: Schools, families, and social division.* Sydney, Australia: George Allen & Unwin.

Eder, D. (with Evans, C.C., & Parker, S.). (1995). *School talk: Gender and adolescent culture.* New Brunswick, NJ: Rutgers University Press.

Riegle-Crumb, C., Farkas, G., & Muller, C. (2006). The role of gender and friendship in advanced course taking. *Sociology of Education, 79,* 206–228.

Thorne, B. (1993). *Gender play: Boys and girls in school.* New Brunswick, NJ: Rutgers University Press.

Willis, P. (1977). *Learning to labor: How working class kids get working class jobs.* New York: Columbia University Press.

Barbara J. Bank

Playgrounds and Recreational Activities

Gender equity plays an important role in children's education. Children whose educational experiences provide information about the varied roles of men and women and equal learning opportunities for boys and girls are better prepared for adulthood. Thus, it is not surprising that increased focus has been placed on the importance of gender equity in educational settings. Less attention, however, has been given to playgrounds and recreational activities as a stage for gender equity. Nevertheless, playgrounds are important settings for children's interactions with one another and can serve as platforms on which children act out and experiment with social roles both in the preschool years and in the elementary school years.

Before children reach elementary school, they have formed a cognitive foundation concerned with what it means to be a boy or a girl. This formation can be thought of as a process of self-socialization in which children begin to link their growing awareness of gender constancy to their own behavior and interactions with others. Young children actively engage in gendered behavior throughout the day. Through social interaction with others, children extract meaning, assign interpretations, and infer intentions that form the basis of gender construction. Thus, parents and teachers as well as other children contribute to what a child understands about gender and what she/he thinks about the social world.

The playground is an important forum for children to experiment with social roles and activities as well as to receive reinforcement for engaging in certain activities. Cues from such interactions help shape children's cognitive gender schemes and subsequently drive future behaviors and activity choices. Teachers need to be aware of the importance of gender equity on the playground and promote equal access of space for boys and girls as well as engagement in diverse activities. Through modeling, promoting mixed-gendered play, and emphasizing a multitude of activities for all children, teachers can help enhance children's experiences and expand their understanding of gender. To promote gender equity, this work needs to begin when children are young, and it needs to be continued throughout children's school years.

SELF-SOCIALIZATION OF GENDER

In their early years, children develop ideas of gender-appropriate behavior as a function of (a) their categorization of the self and others in the world; (b) the development of individual schemas, consisting of organized patterns of actions and thoughts assumed to be gender appropriate, that cognitively guide each of them in processing new information about gender; and (c) the social learning and behavior of gender-specific behavior. The development of gender concepts is sometimes referred to as self-socialization.

Through the process of self-socialization, children begin to connect their understanding and development of gender constancy to their social behavior choices and interactions with the social environment. When children understand what it means to be a boy or girl, then the environment plays a significant role in cuing what is appropriate behavior across multiple settings such as in the classroom or on the playground.

Children receive valuable information through reinforcement and punishment regarding what is gender appropriate. Reinforcement and punishment may come from multiple social partners. As a result, children's past and current experiences and interactions with others are critical to their construction of social roles.

Through processing environmental and social cues, children revise their gender schemas through self-socialization. These revised schemas, in turn, drive children's behavior and interactions, which then leads to further self-socialization and additional gender schema revisions. This cycle of interactions, schematic modification, and self-socialization is constantly taking place in young children. Therefore, how a child interprets certain activities and interactions in regards to gender will change with cognitive growth, time, and experience. Moreover, children's ideas about gender-appropriate behavior also change. Self-socialization connects the children's understanding of gender constancy, gender roles, and gender-appropriate behavior to the social behavior choices they believe (rightly or wrongly so) are available.

Children's complete understanding of what it means to be a boy or girl typically develops between the ages of two and seven years. Also during this period, masculine or feminine values develop from the child's understanding of what it means to be a boy or a girl as well as his/her ideas about sex roles. In turn, a boy (or girl) will come to value what is perceived as most like the self. These values lead to behaviors the child perceives as appropriate. As with children's knowledge and understanding of gender, what is considered to be appropriately masculine or feminine behavior changes over time.

The primary gender identity achievement of toddlerhood is the ability to label oneself accurately as either a boy or a girl. A simple and fun test of this is asking a child, "Are you a boy or girl?" and then, "Are you a girl or a boy?" Very young children have no understanding what the terms boy and girl mean and will answer the above questions by choosing the last label given. Children who correctly answer both questions may have a better understanding as to their own gender. Two year olds often cannot label other children as boys or girls. They may know the names of their friends, but gender is typically not a factor of consideration when toddlers play together. This is largely due to the type of play that children engage in at this age. Toddlers often engage in solitary play or parallel play on the playground with boys and girls intermingled together. It is not until around three years of age that children know their own gender as well the gender of others based on physical characteristics and appearances.

Next, children will come to believe that gender is stable and unchangeable. Between the ages of four and five years, children categorize the gender of a person based on rigid gender distinctions. Much to adults' disappointment, this is the age when teachers and parents will hear children say that women can be nurses, but not doctors, and only men can be mechanics. This can happen even when a child's own mother is a physician or a mechanic. This rigidity can lead to rigid rules to distinguish between the two genders. This can also lead to overgeneralization in order to cognitively categorize gender. For example, a male came to a child-care center to complete a carpentry project. He dressed and looked like a man and even had a mustache. But, his long hair tied back in a ponytail confused the children and led to a long child-led discussion as to his gender. Some children pointed to his activity and his mustache and said he was a man, while others pointed out his long hair and said he was a girl. In the end, the children asked the teacher, and his gender was established (no child would talk to the carpenter and just ask).

Once children understand gender constancy, they begin to identify strongly with their own gender and show a preference for same-gender playmates as well as same-gender toys and activities. Same-gender peers will positively reinforce gender-appropriate behaviors. This reinforcement will encourage and lengthen the time spent at gender-appropriate activities. Over time, children will learn what members of his/her in-group (same gender) do and do not do and will learn what is considered as gender-appropriate and gender-inappropriate behavior and activities.

At approximately six or seven years of age, children begin to understand that gender is constant despite changes to appearance. In addition, it is not until six or seven that children realize that genitals are the central basis of gender categorization. As children become more cognitively mature, they are flexible in gender typing due to their increased involvement and experiences with diverse groups of people. They will also feel less uncomfortable about occasional deviations from their gender roles and less rigid about gender-role behavior.

INFLUENCES OF PEERS, ADULTS, AND THE ENVIRONMENT

The environment, including the toys and activities, is crucial in the preschool years because with same-gender identification same-gender behaviors and values grow. Hence, if the child's environment offers or indicates gender roles that are narrowly defined, his or her gender schema will limit the choice of behaviors considered to be gender appropriate. As a result, the child can be limited in his/her choice of behaviors, activities, and toys.

On the preschool playground, young children will perceive the best choice as the one that goes along with what the in-group perceives as gender appropriate and then will engage in perceived gender-appropriate behaviors. Often what happens inside the classroom translates to what happens outside on the playground. For example, if the housekeeping area inside the classroom is a magnet for girls and not boys, then a small house-like structure on the playground will, even if it is not called a house, attract preschool girls who may call it a house. If boys do not see other boys or male teachers in the structure, then they will likely find other activities to participate in on the playground. The choosing of what is believed to be gender appropriate becomes a form of self-reinforcement. Such reinforcement leads to positive feelings about the behaviors and activities selected. Likewise, gender-inappropriate behaviors will be thought of negatively and will tend to be avoided.

The peer group is important to children of all ages. In the preschool years, as has been mentioned, young children often play with same-gender children and they reinforce each other's gender-typed behaviors. It is not uncommon to see separate groups of preschool girls and preschool boys at play on the playground.

Often, preschool-age boys engaging in what is considered to be gender-inappropriate behavior will receive greater criticism in comparison to girls. Preschool girls who engage in perceived gender-inappropriate activities may be ignored by same-gender peers and teachers. However, preschool boys who engage in female-preferred activities may receive both negative reinforcement and criticism from both same-gender peers as well as from teachers and parents. They may also receive criticism from members of the other gender. For example, doll play brought out to the playground by boys may be frowned upon by peers, teachers, and parents. Instead of valuing the nurturing aspects found in doll play, some adults fear that boys will lose their masculinity by engaging in such activities and will try to put a stop to such behavior.

Parents and teachers of young children can do much to promote gender equity in recreational activities both on and off the playground. Adults need to consider the kinds of toys they give their children of all ages. Often parents choose toys based on what they feel are appropriate interests for either a boy or a girl. As has been noted, parental treatment is very influential in the process of self-socialization and the development of gender concepts. Children use the information gained from parents and teachers about gender roles and gender-appropriate behavior when forming their own ideas about gender-appropriate behavior as well as their values. They also use such information in their development of gender constancy.

If parents and teachers teach the strong points of both genders, then the information children receive to process may be less gender stereotyped and rigid. The values a child then associates with his or her own gender may be less gender stereotyped as well. Children will probably still pass through the same stages and will process information based on gender, but the values, ideas, and schemas the children develop about gender, gender roles, and gender-appropriate behavior will be more flexible, and the behavior choices the child perceives as open will probably be wider and more varied.

The promotion of mixed-gender play broadens a young child's choices for activities and play. The more diverse children's experiences are, the more opportunities children have to learn a variety of skills. When adults and teachers support a child's gender schemas to be more varied, flexible, and broad and when their behaviors are likewise associated with both genders, then children have the opportunity to observe, practice, and learn skills needed with respect to school readiness as well as for later in life.

On the playground, teachers and other adults need to promote a set of shared goals in fostering each child's development of a positive gender identity without promoting only gender-typed behavior. Adults need to provide activities for both boys and girls that will lead to skills needed for school and life. These activities should include a variety of games and materials for both boys and girls that have traditionally been thought of as gendered. Teachers also need to promote both same-gender and mixed-gender play. It is important that teachers be aware of the negative reinforcement of children engaged in other-gender activity and to be aware of criticism, teasing, or exclusion based on a child's gender or choice of activity coming from other children as well as adults. Teachers must notice children who may feel excluded from an activity due to their gender, such as a girl who sits on the edge of the sand-building area showing interest but not joining the activity. Teachers need to watch for such children and invite them to join in with the other children and the teacher.

In addition, teachers need to make sure that the classroom and outdoor space facilitate children's involvement in a range of activities. For example, outside on the playground there may be dramatic play materials placed on top of the climbing structure, thus allowing boys and girls to engage in gross-motor play as well as dramatic play. Or, dramatic play materials, including dolls, toy people, and cars, as well as shovels and sand toys, can be added to the sand area. If there is a house-like structure on the playground, then woodworking and other tools could be added to it. This would promote mixed-gender play.

Teachers should involve themselves in activities in all areas. Women teachers should play on the climbing structures and men teachers should participate in outdoor art activities and doll play. In addition, teachers need to spend time in areas that are traditionally gender specific. Adults and teachers who keep the goal of gender equity in mind during the early years must continue to be vigilant in the elementary years because children will continue to separate themselves according to their gender. In fact, the highest degree of gender separation may occur among preteens on the playground. At this point in time, children are still actively constructing their social worlds and developing social skills. Through play and other activities, elementary school children actively shape their understanding of gender through social interactions.

On the elementary school playground, children explore and experiment with what they consider to be the norms about friendship, leadership, appearance, and competition through their social interactions. Many elementary schools have a time on the playground, also known as recess, which often occurs after lunch. What goes on during recess is not what one would always consider to be play. During a 20- or 30-minute recess, one may see aggression, romance, anger, embarrassment, humiliation, joy, and fear all mixed together along with play. Gender plays a role throughout all these interactions.

Gender-stereotyped clothing is also a common element seen on elementary school playgrounds. Elementary school children try to follow what they consider to be social rules and wear what they perceive as gender-approved clothing. The addition of coats on the playground is also gendered, and children are very aware of what colors are appropriate as well as what styles are acceptable.

Girls on the playground have many choices during recess. Girls group as dyads, socialize in small groups, participate in all-girl sports or mostly all-boy sports, join skill-building groups, socialize or hang with the adults present (usually monitors), or stand or sit alone. Girls may engage in sport or physical activities, social relationships, or creative arts such as singing or drawing. Boys on the playground have choices, too, but most become involved in sports. A few other boys not interested in sports tend to stick together as small groups. There are also some boys who stand and watch others. Overall, gender is reinforced in that, in almost all choices, children choose and interact with same-gender playmates.

Oftentimes, monitors, usually mothers, stand and watch children as they play but do little else. Girls are more likely than boys to spend time engaging them in conversation. Conversely, boys often try to stay away from monitors, especially when boys are more often than girls the ones that monitors admonish for incorrect behavior.

Most preteens do gender-specific work on the playground by playing in same-gender groups, playing gender-specific games, and conforming to the stereotypic dress. During the recess of preteen children, one will find a variety of team sports such as soccer or kickball. Most of these games are dominated by boys, which reinforces their competency on teams as well their competitive tendencies. The girls who do participate in these sports are often very good and highly skilled. Many girls will walk and talk on the playground and increase their social-relational skills. Girls who are more athletic can choose between walking and talking or joining a sports team with any choice acceptable by the larger groups of boys and girls.

Preteen boys and girls often exhibit border work on the playground. Border work is a term coined by Barrie Thorne (1993). On the playground, border work is behavior that reinforces the boundaries between the genders. Often one can see border work by observing girl versus boy contests on the playground, including team sports with all girls on one team and all boys on the other. Another example of border work is gendered chasing involving boys chasing girls or girls chasing boys. Invading one gender's space or game is done by both genders, but observational research indicates that it is more commonly done by boys. Sometimes the main purpose of invading is to join the game while at other times the invasion itself is the main purpose.

Excluding on the basis of gender is also done on the playground, and boys have been observed to practice more gender exclusion than girls and to be more likely to ignore girls who wish to join in their game. In contrast, one may also see troupes of girls who spend their recess time seeking out boys to talk with even if for a brief time. These troupes' main purpose is to talk with boys and get their attention.

The intent of border work can be just for fun. Other times, the intent appears to be a bit aggressive or it can include a romantic or sexual edge. Overall, boys tend to control the power by using more of the playground space, by being more aggressive, and by dominating mixed-gender play. Teachers need to be aware of these tendencies and work to promote equitable use of space and mix-gendered play that is productive rather than invasive in nature, such as establishing mixed-gendered teams of play. Teachers also need to facilitate and be involved with a diverse range of activities on the playground to promote activities as appropriate for both genders.

Teachers and adults need to do so much more than monitoring on the playground in order to promote children's sense of gender equity. Sometimes a male teacher or monitor will engage the children in a soccer game or other team sport on the playground. However, boys are often the children primarily drawn to such an activity. If the teacher would invite girls to join in and if female teachers or monitors would also take a more active role on the playground, team sports may become something both genders can choose to take part in. This may result in both boys and girls actively engaged in team sports on the playground, and the children might even participate as mixed-gender teams.

The layout of the playground should be considered so that boys do not dominate the area and take up a majority of the space with team sports. Teachers, other adults, and the children could work together to plan how the space of a playground can be equitably used by all the children. If there is room for only one team sport at a time, perhaps mixed-gendered games could be encouraged or a schedule could be implemented.

Gender equity is an important construct throughout children's education and should be considered across multiple settings, including the playground. Through social interactions and environmental cues, children interpret and assign meaning to experiences. These experiences form the basis for children's development of self-socialization and schemas about gender. The playground is an important forum for children to experiment with social roles and activities as well as to receive reinforcement for engaging in certain activities. Cues from such interactions help shape children's cognitive gender schemas and subsequently drive future behaviors and activity choices.

Teachers need to be aware of the importance of gender equity on the playground and promote equal access of space for boys and girls and engagement in diverse activities. Through modeling, promoting mixed-gendered play, and emphasizing a multitude of activities for all children, teachers can help enhance children's experiences and expand their understanding of gender. To promote gender equity, this work needs to begin when children are young, and it needs to be continued throughout children's school years.

REFERENCES AND FURTHER READINGS

Marshall, N.L. (Ed.). (2003). The social construction of gender in childhood and adolescence. [Special issue.] *American Behavioral Scientist, 46*(10).

Thorne, B. (1993). *Gender play: Girls and boys in schools.* New Brunswick, NJ: Rutgers University Press.

Wendy Wagner Robeson

Joanne Roberts

Part IX

Gendered Teaching and Administration

Overview

Both in the United States and in many other countries, educational institutions are characterized by a labor force that contains unequal numbers of men and women. The size and nature of this gender inequality varies considerably as one moves across job types and educational levels. Essays in this section of the encyclopedia focus primarily on teaching and administrative jobs, but even in only these two occupational categories, the distribution of men and women varies considerably across educational contexts. In general, it seems fair to say that men tend to outnumber women in the teaching and administrative jobs that command the highest salaries and give their incumbents the most autonomy, power, and prestige. In contrast, women tend to outnumber men in lower paying jobs. In addition, the jobs in which women predominate are often seen as being more "feminine" than the jobs held primarily by men.

At the present time in the United States and most other countries, the overwhelming majority of teachers at the elementary, middle, and secondary school levels are women. That this was not always the case is documented and explained in "Feminization of Teaching." For more than a hundred years, however, the cultural images of teachers, particularly elementary school teachers, have been dominated by nineteenth-century idealized assumptions about the nature of women and, especially, of mothers. Included among these assumptions are notions that women have maternal tendencies that attract them to infants and young children, that women are naturally more nurturant and caring than men, that women are more interested than men in building relationships with children, that women find mothering to be their primary source of self-fulfillment, and that mothers are willing to sacrifice for their children.

These notions have negative consequences for teachers of both sexes. The assumption that dealing with children is easy and natural for women hides the hard and stressful nature of the work done by women teachers and tends to keep their salaries at a low level. For men, one consequence is that those who choose teaching jobs are seen as making an unnatural, unmanly choice—unless, of course, they are using it as a stepping stone into educational administration. And, if supportive interaction with young children is seen as less natural for men than for women, it may also be assumed that men who teach in the primary grades must work harder to be as successful as women. This might discourage men from becoming elementary school teachers, but it could also have the ironic consequence of allowing them to earn more credit than their female counterparts for being nurturant, caring, and dedicated to their students.

This latter possibility gains some support from Gary Dworkin's extensive research, summarized in "Teacher Burnout," which shows that male teachers at the elementary levels where they have only token, or minority, representation were less likely to experience burnout or alienation from teaching than their female counterparts until educational reforms came along that changed the conditions of their work and caused the burnout rates of these male tokens to rise along with the rates of all the other teachers. Changing work conditions can affect not only the burnout rates of teachers but also the ways in which gender is constructed in schools. The essay on "Masculinity, Homophobia, and Teaching," for example, suggests that the restructuring of state schooling in England in the 1990s has remasculinized teaching with the greatest status accorded to those who have technical bureaucratic knowledge and a commitment to managerial efficiency and economic rationality. Although this change favors men over women, it also favors certain kinds of men over others.

Despite their large numerical majority, women teachers have not been able to control either the images people have of their work or the conditions of the work itself. As Marilyn Tallerico demonstrates in "Career Patterns in Schools," one reason for this lack of power is that women, as well as racial-ethnic minorities, are underrepresented in positions of authority, especially at the highest levels of school administration. Although it is true that teachers have some individual control over their classrooms and their pupils and that they have sometimes engaged in collective action to improve their working conditions, it is also true that their behaviors and outlook are crucially affected by the actions of administrators. Given current efforts on the part of many (male) school administrators to implement the kinds of "reform" efforts by government, described by Dworkin, that are aimed at controlling the day-to-day work of (women) teachers and holding them accountable for student outcomes, it does not seem too farfetched to suggest that some schools are becoming battlegrounds in a war between the sexes.

Would the battle be less intense and the power of women teachers greater if there were more women in school administration? Margaret Madden tackles this question in "Leadership Styles." By the definitions she provides, it is true that female administrators who engage in communal leadership will be more relationship-oriented, more supportive of teachers, and more willing to listen to them than male administrators who adopt an agentic style of leadership that is task oriented and assertive. Even though women may be more comfortable than men with communal styles of leadership, Madden discusses several reasons why it may not be possible for women administrators to behave in a supportive and collaborative manner.

One obvious reason is the fact that women are still far less likely than men to find themselves in leadership positions. Although optimists point out that women are more likely to hold positions in educational administration than they did 30 years ago, realists like Tallerico point out that this is not, in itself, a reason to assume that the proportions of women in educational administration will continue to increase. Reasons to be less optimistic can be found in the essay on "Work-Family Conflicts of Educators," which explains the ways and the reasons why women's teaching and academic careers are more likely to be negatively affected by their family responsibilities than the careers of men.

Not that men have it so easy either. In "Faculty Workloads in Higher Education," Sarah Winslow-Bowe and Jerry Jacobs provide substantial evidence to support the argument that men and women in academic positions are working harder than ever. The heavy demands that must be met to gain tenure and promotions make it increasingly unlikely that men who hold academic jobs will be willing to spend more time helping out at home. Thus, the burdens of home and family life will continue to fall more heavily on women. Even in the academic workplace, where women faculty are expected to meet the same heavy demands as men faculty, those women are often subject to additional job-related demands that their male colleagues can avoid. These demands and the stresses that accompany them are described in "Advising and Mentoring in Graduate Education" and in "Career Patterns in Higher Education."

Despite their extra burdens, women faculty in the United States continue to be paid less, on average, than male faculty. One big reason for this difference is that women are proportionately more likely than men to hold part-time and adjunct positions, rather than tenure-track or tenured positions. Another reason is the fact that women are more heavily concentrated in lower status colleges and universities where salaries are also lower than in higher status, higher paying institutions. Even when men and women are employed at the same college or university, a third reason for women's lower salaries is the fact that they are concentrated in fields of study, such as the humanities or home economics, that pay their faculty less than male-dominated fields such as the sciences or engineering. A fourth reason, central to the discussion of "Salaries of Academics" by Debra Barbezat, is the fact that salaries increase with rank, and women are less likely to be promoted up the ranks in the same proportion or at the same pace as their male counterparts. When women are compared to men who hold the same tenured or tenure-track rank in the same departmental and institutional context, and the women also have the same educational background, years of job experience, and research output as the men, the studies Barbezat reviews show that the gendered salary gap was greatly reduced during the last 30 years of the twentieth century. This is good news for women in academe and for everyone who favors gender equity, but the remaining question is how to eliminate all of the other gender gaps and occupational disadvantages that are documented in the essays contained in this section.

See also "School Counseling" in Part VII; "Evaluation Policies for Academics," "Feminist Pedagogy," and "Work-Family Reconciliation Policies" in Part X.

Advising and Mentoring in Graduate Education

The terms "advising" and "mentoring" are used in different ways within and across countries by those involved in graduate education. In this essay, "advising" and "supervising" are used as synonyms that refer to the assignment of a relatively experienced academic with responsibility for the research work (thesis or dissertation) of an associated student. Although "mentoring" is sometimes used as another synonym, it usually refers to a more intense, extended, and idealized relationship than advising. Both advisory and mentoring relationships are shaped by elements of power and control, positionality, diversity, and contextualization.

Advising is only one aspect—albeit an important one—of the graduate experience. Depending on the national, institutional, departmental, and disciplinary context, students may enjoy more or less funding, fulfill various course and examination requirements, and work alone or with a research team. Sometimes the metaphor of the "journey" is used, especially for doctoral studies, to signify the attainment of a distant goal, reached by traveling across difficult and unknown terrain. Advising falls awkwardly between the more well-known academic functions of teaching and research and, perhaps as a result, has received less scholarly attention. Although there is a widespread belief that it makes a critical difference within the "journey," there is not much consensus over exactly what difference it makes or how it should be done. Similarly, only a small fraction of writing on gender and education takes as its subject this aspect of educational studies.

WHAT IS THE ADVISORY ROLE?

This question is one that is surprisingly difficult to answer. Although the advisor is similar to a teacher, instructors do not usually have a long-term relationship with a student based on a piece of work that extends over a number of years and is examined by other academics. Graduate students (also called postgraduates or research students in some countries) have as their main goal the production of a book-like piece of work called a thesis or dissertation based on original research. The supervisor, who normally has some expertise and authority in the area of the student's research, is charged with the responsibility of assisting the student to conceptualize, plan, carry out, and write up the results of the research. Beyond the student-teacher depiction, the relationship has been expressed in more colorful terms such as master-servant, guru-disciple, parent-child, and so forth. Supervisors have been characterized by analogies as diverse as midwife and business manager. All such depictions imply that an advisor will facilitate the production of the thesis and initiate the student into the secrets of academe. The midwife advisor might help the student give birth to the knowledge already inside; the business manager advisor might make sure the student has dates, goals, objectives, and the means of accomplishing them.

Some writers believe that the process of thesis production and the associated supervisor/ student relationship can be made subject to control and prediction. The model could be called the "technical-rational" approach to supervision and finds its place in many policy documents and how-to textbooks for students and supervisors. The ultimate goal is to improve the chances that a student will finish the journey. Others prefer a "negotiated order" model that stresses the mutual negotiation and interaction between the participants. Any advice that can be given about best practice, this model says, will have to be modified by what happens in real life as well as by the expectations and understandings each person brings to the table. For example, not all students intend a career in academe, while supervisors generally think that is the desirable goal, at least for the superior scholars. Or, if a student desires nurturing and warmth from the supervisor but the supervisor prefers a strictly professional approach prizing student independence, either the parameters will need to be negotiated in some way or the relationship may end in tears.

Some literature about women's preferred styles of learning suggests many women students would prefer a nurturing supervisory style. A Canadian study found women academics in faculties of education struggling to meet the expectations of the many women students who wanted to work with women supervisors and expected a high level of interest and mentoring (Acker & Feuerverger, 1996). Whatever these patterns, studies also show that the majority of students are satisfied with the advising they receive (although a small minority are very dissatisfied) if only because they do not have many other experiences with which to compare their situation.

KNOWLEDGE AND CONTROL

One way to think about the supervisory process is as a site for expression of power or control. As a "deeply uncertain practice" (Grant, 2005), supervision contains elements of power and knowledge that are shifting rather than constant. Supervisors have the most obvious access to resources that produce power. They have the disciplinary knowledge, the academic position, and the gatekeeping role. Many aspects of academic life are tacit or unspoken, part of a "hidden curriculum" (Acker, 2001). First, there is a proliferation of what the French theorist Michel Foucault would see as "disciplinary technologies"— deadlines, rules, forms, timetables, reports, examinations—the cumulative effect of which is to produce docility or conformity. Second, there are many specific subject-area conventions that make up a kind of culture or what Pierre Bourdieu, another French sociologist, called a "habitus." For example, in English or political science, the production of a published book is an expected early career achievement, while in economics or accounting, junior faculty rarely write books but instead devote their energies to accumulating publications in "top tier" high-status journals. Graduate school is a time for learning at least some of these conventions. Departments may provide various ways for students to become informed such as orientations, workshops, and seminars, but advisors are in a key position to communicate the rules of the game to their students, both directly and by example.

Other features of the supervisory dyad relate to shifting power relationships. Generally, there is a generation gap with the supervisor being older, although in some professional fields, students may not be chronologically "young," having already accumulated work experience outside the ivory tower. Gender also invokes power. Given the numerical dominance of men in the academy, especially in higher ranks and in scientific specialties, we are more likely to find men supervising women than the reverse. The supervisor may control financial resources that impact upon the student.

Nevertheless, some writers believe that students have more power than they normally realize. If the pairing does not match the expected power dynamics, for example, if the supervisor is female and the student is male, or the student is older than the supervisor, or the supervisor but not the student is from a minority ethno cultural group, some readjustment—and possibly even some conflict—is likely to take place (see Acker, 2001). Some students with clear goals find themselves taking the lead in advisory sessions. As the research progresses, the student will come to know more about the specific topic area than the supervisor does. In some cases, the advisor relies on the student to do an important part of the work of a research team. More generally, students' success brings credit to their supervisor; conversely, poor completion rates or rumors of inadequate supervision will do some harm to the supervisor's reputation and equanimity.

The power of the supervisor may also be mitigated where it is conventional to have supervisory committees or co-supervision. It may also be reduced intentionally, as in efforts to develop *feminist* mentoring (Humble, Solomon, Allen, Blaisure, & Johnson, 2006) analogous to feminist pedagogy, one of the critical or liberatory pedagogies that attempts to work "against the grain" of teacher authority normally found in classrooms and in hierarchical relationships between faculty and students. Humble and her colleagues point out that conventional mentoring is not very compatible with radical pedagogies because it aims to socialize individuals into an existing environment rather than to create conditions for change. The concept of feminist supervising or mentoring is almost unknown and could bear further development.

IS IT MENTORING?

The title of this essay suggests that advising and mentoring go together. In common usage, mentoring would be the stronger concept, evoking a long-term investment in the welfare and future of a protégé(e), going well beyond the specific goal of producing a thesis or completing a doctorate. Mentoring has also been a popular innovation in efforts to assist women and minority members of organizations or to support persons from disadvantaged communities in an effort to improve their life chances. Graduate students—again, especially women and/or minority students—are sometimes encouraged to find mentors who will help them achieve career success.

However, as Helen Colley (2003) shows, the idea of mentoring is suffused with romantic myths and gendered paradigms. Although the original paradigm for mentoring may have been males helping males, the dominant model is now one where the female-associated virtues of endless caring and self-sacrifice are incorporated into the mentor persona. In her study of mentoring in a program for disadvantaged youth, Colley describes a dysfunctional pairing of two young women who become trapped within a perpetual cycle of accepting and caring from the mentor and indifference from the mentee.

Studies of women and minority academics suggest a parallel downside to mentoring, namely the extra layer of work expected by students, other faculty, the academic herself, and even the wider community, quite possibly occurring at the same time that junior faculty members need to put extensive efforts into research production to secure their own positions. Problems are exacerbated in situations where the representation of women or minorities among the faculty is less than among the student body, for example, in a field like education. In Canadian faculties of education, for example, women are about 43 percent of tenured faculty (i.e., those with permanent positions and likely to be allowed to supervise theses) but 70 percent of doctoral students. If we assume students try to affiliate with supervisors in the same gender and/or ethnic group, then we have a numerical pressure point and a predictable overload for women and minority faculty such as the one reported by Romero (1997), whose interviews with Chicana faculty (women in the United States of Mexican descent) revealed that they were highly isolated, inundated with students and other workload responsibilities, and conscious of a class, race, and gender disparity between themselves and majority faculty.

An extended one-to-one relationship may easily become intense and emotional and present uncomfortable aspects of dependence or desire. At the very least, there are boundary issues that must be negotiated. Not all boundary problems lie in the sexual realm. For example, questions sometimes arise about who should lay claim to the intellectual property generated by the student.

In considering mentoring, we should also beware of too-easy generalizations, such as assuming that same-sex advisor-student pairings are always better. In contrast, there are some hints in the literature that women supervisors (in part, because they may be more junior in the academy) have fewer resources to put at the disposal of their students. A study by Kurtz-Costes, Helmke, and Ülkü-Steiner (2006) found that women students in predominantly male departments like chemistry did not want to work with the women faculty in their field because they found them too "driven" and unlikely to be role models for combining family and work. These researchers suggest that the gender balance of the faculty is probably more important than the gender of a mentor in influencing the climate.

In practice, mentoring in its sense of an intense and extended relationship is probably hit or miss. Few academics can take on a protégé(e) for life. There are too many students, and some will inevitably be disappointed.

POSITIONALITY, DIVERSITY, AND CONTEXTUALIZATION

"Positionality" is important: The group someone belongs to and where they are located in the institution (and society) influences both opportunities and perceptions. A problem with much of the writing on graduate students is that they have been written about as if they are all interchangeable: "the" graduate student (Acker, 2001; Leonard, 2001). Yet the graduate student population is increasingly diverse. Forty or more years ago, the situation was different: Most students were male, White, middle-class, young, living on campus, and studying full time. Many social trends have changed this picture. In some places, numbers have risen steeply while the composition of the student cohorts has changed. For example, in Britain, the number of full-time postgraduates more than quadrupled in 30 years from 1970 to 2000, while the international student proportion rose from 13.7 percent to 41.1 percent (Chiang, 2003, pp. 9–10). Students now have a variety of backgrounds and characteristics, although some marginalized and minoritized categories of the population (e.g., Aboriginal students, those from working-class backgrounds, disabled students) are still greatly underrepresented.

Women remain concentrated in certain fields such as education, health, and social work and scarce in others such as engineering and computer sciences; but overall they are found in much greater numbers than in the past. In many countries, they are now a small majority among master's degree recipients and approaching parity at doctoral level. For example, in the United States in 2002 to 2003, women earned 47 percent of doctorates. The figure was 43 percent in both Canada (2003) and the United Kingdom (2004 to 2005).

Different disciplines require and permit different modes of study. Students who work in laboratory environments are likely to see their supervisors regularly and may well be working on a joint project, while the library (or increasingly home) based student or part-time student may have relatively little such contact. Chiang (2003) refers to the main models as "teamwork" and "individualist" research training structures and uses chemistry and education, respectively, as illustrations. Regardless of the structure, some students may be better positioned than others for excelling and networking. It is likely that academics are most comfortable with others like themselves, a practice that has in the past ensured the continuity of male domination in universities through same-gender patronage. An extension of the same point may account for cases where academics show discomfort with international students and adhere to some cultural stereotypes. However, there is little likelihood that instructors and students can be matched with any precision: Gender alone does not address the myriad of other characteristics (age, class background, religion, race, sexual orientation, etc.) that make up someone's identity. There are also preferences regarding style and closeness/distance of supervision and reasons for undertaking further study and research, all of which vary idiosyncratically.

Students who work on professors' research projects or who can afford to "hang around" a department may be first in line for the important socialization and mentoring experiences. Conversely, those who are working outside the academy to make ends meet, looking after children as a single parent, responsible for caring for an elderly dependent, or commuting several hours to the university may not have the same advantages. Studies of women academics suggest that they are often working against the biological clock to establish their careers; those with children get little sleep as they struggle to keep up with expectations still based on a family-free male model. Although there are not many similar studies of graduate student women, it is likely that many of the same problems exist. Gender, class, race, ethnicity, dis/ability, and other attributes all singly and together influence the experiences of graduate students.

We need to remember that the supervisor-student dyad is not located in a vacuum—far from it. The impact of particular disciplinary cultures and structures has already been mentioned. Many institutional features are relevant. Institutional and departmental status, resources, size, location, cultures, and policies influence the opportunities graduate students have. For example, some universities provide training and/or workload credit for supervisors, while many do not. It is likely that students, especially early in their programs, do not have a full appreciation of most of these contextual factors that impinge on their experience.

Funding policies, both internal and external to the university, are especially important in shaping the graduate environment. In Britain, changes in the social science funding council's practices in the 1980s led to universities providing more research training, keeping better track of students, and putting pressures on students to complete their research more quickly (Leonard, 2001). Funding policies may have gender-differentiating effects. In the United States in the 1960s, there were prestigious foundations—and, indeed, universities—that routinely excluded women from their lists of scholarship recipients. In Australia, a funding formula that emphasized a university's record of dissertation completions as a determinant of its funding for graduate research has been thought to encourage some universities to shift graduate student places into fast-completion fields like physical science and engineering and away from part-time study. Both practices could work to the detriment of women, who are more likely to be in slow-completion fields in social sciences and humanities and more likely to study part time.

A myriad of other policies and practices also impact on graduate students and sometimes women in particular. Again, in the United States in the 1960s, child-care facilities were practically unknown and hiring policies openly discriminated against academic couples. Although there is now child-care provision in many universities, it may be difficult to access, and student parents may lose their university funding while on a maternity or parenting leave. Overt discrimination against couples (which mainly impacted on the women) has declined, yet accommodating partners is still a "problem" for universities. On the surface, we have "come a long way," and the barriers are now more subtle, located in disciplinary cultural traditions, women's competing external responsibilities, and a residue of bias.

Contextual influences go beyond individual institutions to labor market conditions, state policies, and even international events. At the same time as apparently more enlightened policies like maternity leave and child-care provision spread, academic work—and by extension graduate study—has been altered by global trends. Academics do more work in the same or less time, often with fewer resources. Their output is also repeatedly audited, not only by the traditional peer-review procedures assessing the suitability of research for publication but by new modes of what some call performativity: reaching a level of accomplishment *and* showing publicly that the level has been reached, for example, by reports to external assessors or annual reviews. Universities are thought to have become more like businesses and are managed by "executives" who put the emphasis on the bottom line and market-driven priorities.

Although this level of analysis may at first seem remote from the experiences of graduate students and their supervisors, it has important shaping effects. International students may be recruited for the money and contacts they bring with them; in some countries faculty are expected to teach offshore or to find other ways of initiating entrepreneurial activity. Successful graduate student degree completions may be one of the ways in which departments can demonstrate value for money and thus receive further funding. More insidiously, academics are so stretched that they have less and less time to look after their students. Increased reliance on temporary and part-time faculty means that students have fewer individuals available for supervision. And finally, students look at these harried and distracted academics and wonder what attractions are left in academe. We may be heading for an ironic outcome: students—including women—look at their mentors and decide *not* to be like them.

REFERENCES AND FURTHER READINGS

Acker, S. (2001). The hidden curriculum of dissertation advising. In E. Margolis (Ed.), *The hidden curriculum in higher education* (pp. 61–77). New York: Routledge.

Acker, S., & Feuerverger, G. (1996). Doing good and feeling bad: The work of women university teachers. *Cambridge Journal of Education, 26*(3), 401–422.

Chiang, K.-H. (2003). Learning experiences of doctoral students in U.K. universities. *International Journal of Sociology and Social Policy, 23*(1/2), 4–32.

Colley, H. (2003). *Mentoring for social inclusion: A critical approach to nurturing successful mentoring relations.* London: RoutledgeFalmer.

Grant, B. (2005). Fighting for space in supervision: Fantasies, fairytales, fictions and fallacies. *International Journal of Qualitative Studies in Education, 18*(3), 337–354.

Humble, A., Solomon, C., Allen, K., Blaisure, K., & Johnson, M.P. (2006). Feminism and mentoring of graduate students. *Family Relations, 55*(1), 2–15.

Kurtz-Costes, B., Helmke, L., & Ülkü-Steiner, B. (2006). Gender and doctoral studies: The perceptions of PhD students in an American university. *Gender and Education, 18*(2), 137–155.

Leonard, D. (2001). *A woman's guide to doctoral studies.* Buckingham, England: Open University
Press.

Romero, M. (1997). Class-based, gendered and racialized institutions of higher education: Everyday
life of academia from the view of Chicana faculty. *Race, Gender & Class, 4*(2), 151–173.

Sandra Acker

Career Patterns in Higher Education

During the past 30 years, women have increased their presence among faculty members in the United States. According to the National Center for Education Statistics (NCES), women now are 40 percent of the 816,000 faculty in four-year colleges and universities. However, their careers and the positions they ultimately hold differ from those of men. They are more likely to be employed in offtrack positions that do not lead to tenure where they hold 46 percent of the part-time positions but only 23 percent of the full-time faculty positions. As a group, women are more likely than men to be in part-time positions (42 percent compared to 34 percent, respectively) and less likely than men to be in full-time positions (58 percent compared to 66 percent). The significance of full-time tenure-line faculty appointments is considerable. Incumbents receive higher wages and employment benefits; they influence research agenda and the allocation of university resources, shape the direction of a field, and mentor graduate students.

Preparation for a faculty career takes place through graduate education in departments of research-oriented universities. Doctoral students' experiences induct them into the discipline or field by developing skills, influencing their research productivity, and shaping their first networks—which become a foundation for a career of research and teaching. Progress in an academic career principally occurs by successfully negotiating three gatekeeping processes—hiring, tenure review, and promotion—in order to arrive at the visible and valued achievement of a tenured, senior position, the institutionalized optimum faculty employment standard (see chapter by Glazer-Raymo in Sagaria, 2007).

In contrast to faculty careers, which succeed by moving step-by-step up a well-defined ladder of positions, administrative careers in higher education are less well defined. Recent years have seen an increase in middle managerial positions, but the relationships between such positions, faculty positions, and higher level administrative positions are poorly defined. Although recent years have seen an increase in the proportion of women in the higher levels of university administration, they remain a relatively small minority of college and university presidents nationwide and worldwide. In contrast, there has been a striking feminization of lower levels of campus administration, especially in those positions concerned with the provision of external services to client groups.

SEX DIFFERENCES IN FACULTY CAREERS

Despite the increasing proportions of degrees awarded to women, their employment differs across fields. NCES data show that women are most underrepresented among academic employees in engineering (10 percent), natural sciences (23 percent), and business (27 percent). They tend to be better represented in agriculture/home economics (36 percent), social sciences (36 percent), fine arts (37 percent), and humanities (41 percent). In the health sciences, they are close to parity with men (48 percent), and in education the majority of faculty are women (58 percent). Gender representation within a field has a profound influence on women's careers.

A successful faculty career begins with passing through the formal gate of hiring into a tenure-track position, usually directly after a doctoral program or, as in the life and physical sciences, after a postdoctoral appointment. The appointment is likely to begin at the rank of assistant professor for a maximum probation period of seven years. In many fields, qualified female candidates are not being recruited or hired into tenure-track positions proportionate to their presence in the PhD pool. Nelson's (2005) study of faculty representation in the top 50 ranked departments in 14 disciplines showed that women were underrepresented even in fields such as biology, where women earn more PhDs than men. The percentage of women in those departments ranged from a high of 45 percent (in sociology) to a low of 17 percent (in chemistry). Nelson's study further corroborated previous research showing that lack of representation is particularly acute for women of color who may be subject to tokenism, a process whereby they are treated as representatives or symbols of their group and not as individuals as was considered to be the case in leading departments in economics, political science, and sociology (Beutel & Nelson, 2006).

The second gatekeeping process is the tenure review. Promotion and tenure review is conducted in accordance with institutional policies that vary by institutional mission. Nevertheless, there is usually a peer review process in which research, teaching, and service are evaluated, placing most weight on the activity considered central to the institution's mission. Thus, in a research university a faculty member is evaluated principally for the quality and quantity of her or his research and grants. An individual is either tenured and promoted to associate professor or her or his contract is not continued.

Women in the social sciences, sciences, and engineering are less likely to receive tenure than male colleagues. Among women tenure-track faculty who were employed in Research I universities (those that award 50 or more doctoral degrees per year in at least 15 disciplines) in both 1995 and 2001, 54.5 percent of the women received tenure, compared to 59.2 percent of the men. Of individuals not tenured in a Research I university, women (8.5 percent) are half as likely as men (15.3 percent) to move to jobs outside the academy, but women are more likely to be unemployed (2.5 percent) than men (0.6 percent) (National Academy of Sciences, 2006). Moreover, women are more likely to leave a tenure-track position for an adjunct appointment than men.

Across Research I universities, tenure rates are roughly 50 percent or more. Although rates vary by institution, they also vary by field. Field-specific analyses show that women are 1–3 percent less likely than men to receive tenure in physical sciences, 2–4 percent more likely than men to receive tenure in the natural sciences and engineering, and 8 percent less likely than men to earn tenure in the social sciences (Ginther & Kahn, 2006).

Career progression and the tenure review process are likely to differ for men and women in some fields. In the aggregate, women are promoted more slowly than men.

The difference begins early with men being promoted and tenured earlier in their career than women. After tenure, men are also promoted more quickly to full professor than women. These patterns were discerned principally from institutional studies, such as those at the University of California, Berkeley, MIT, and Duke University. These differences become even greater by race. According to the National Academy of Sciences (2006), within 15 years of earning the PhD, African American women were almost 10 percent less likely than men to be promoted to full professor. Possible explanations are that women are expected to meet higher standards for promotion, and they may feel less ready to apply for promotion to full professor.

The gatekeeping process to the rank of full professor is more unyielding for women so that they are less likely than their male counterparts to be promoted to the senior rank. Although sex discrimination has been illegal in academe since 1972, there continue to be fewer women at each career step. According to the NCES, women account for 35.9 percent of assistant professors, 30.2 percent of associate professors, and 15.8 percent of full professors in research universities. This pattern represents different career progressions and experiences for men and women resulting in terrible losses, both in terms of opportunities for individual women and in institutional potential for solving problems and increasing economic performance (Sagaria & Agans, 2006).

When tenure-track faculty change jobs, they are likely to do so for multiple reasons—most importantly, salary and promotion, regardless of field. Yet, women leave tenure-track positions for reasons different from men. Rosser's (2004) study, using a national data set of faculty across four-year colleges and universities, showed that female faculty members are less satisfied than their male counterparts with advising, course workload, the quality of their benefits, job security, and salary levels, and that this affects their intent to leave—a good indicator of actually leaving. A national study of actual job changers among tenure-track faculty members in engineering and the life, physical, and social sciences corroborated the Rosser study regarding the importance of pay and promotion for women and men. Across fields, however, female academics consistently rated working conditions, family, and job location higher than males among reasons for changing jobs (National Academy of Sciences, 2006).

THE CONTEXT OF FACULTY CAREERS

Changing political and economic forces are shifting the orientation of universities from serving the public good to entrepreneurial efforts. Within the current competitive context, universities are striving to increase their economic strength by preparing individuals for the labor market and contributing to profitable research (see chapter by Sagaria & Agans in Sagaria, 2007). In the competitive market context, the higher the prestige or reputation of an institution, the greater its competitive advantage.

For universities, increasing economic strength can mean increasing cost efficiency and strategic reallocation of funds. Some universities have restructured by reducing or not increasing funding for tenure-track, full-time faculty lines, opting instead for adjunct, part-time faculty. In universities that have reallocated funds, the recipient departments have most often been those that are expected to contribute to the institution's competitive advantage by way of external research funding and prestige. Consequently, retrenchment and selective investment strategies tend to redirect funds from the humanities, social sciences, and education, where the majority of women faculty members are found, toward life and physical sciences and engineering, which have a small percentage of women faculty. Thus, strategic redirection of funds has had disproportionately adverse consequences, reducing the number of tenure lines and the amount of resources in disciplines and fields where the largest concentrations of women faculty work (see chapter by Sagaria & Van Horn in Sagaria, 2007). The importance of a department to an institution (and the department's resources) influences a faculty member's work, which may have career consequences that can differ for men and women. In a study of highly valued (core) departments and less valued (periphery) departments in a public research university, Volk, Slaughter, and Thomas (2001) found that departments powerfully influence faculty members' access to institutional resources. They report that funding for departments characterized by male, full-time faculty, graduate degrees, grants, and contracts tend to be more highly resourced than departments characterized by female faculty, high use of female adjuncts, undergraduate teaching, and degree granting.

In addition to education and position, an academic career depends on productivity and recognition. For purposes of hiring and advancement in rank, research productivity, usually in the form of peer-reviewed publications and significant books, is weighted most heavily in universities. This is the case regardless of whether a faculty member's responsibilities also include substantial teaching and administration or service. Moreover, advancement involves judgment and recommendations of academic referees. Yet, a substantial body of research shows that these judgments can be arbitrary and linked to sponsorship and networks that may disadvantage women in fields where they are in the minority. Although women's productivity in many fields is now equal to men's (National Academy of Sciences, 2006), women continue to experience subtle, often unexamined gender bias by both men and women, which is even more oppressive with the interlacing of racism that women of color in predominately White institutions confront.

In many fields and disciplines, women are the leaders and most distinguished scholars regardless of whether they are a part of a numerical majority or minority. Even more women will be able to thrive as colleagues and institutions continue to chip away at the factors that contribute to cumulative gender disadvantages, the small preferences and subtle forms of discrimination that can accumulate and create large differences in prestige, power, and position.

ADMINISTRATIVE CAREERS

While full-time faculty careers are highly defined, many administrative careers have evolved as higher education has changed. The changing nature of colleges and universities, especially the shift to being highly managed entrepreneurial organizations, has resulted in a significant increase in the need and actual numbers of administrators and staff. The National Center for Education Statistics reports that in 2003 women held approximately 48 percent of the 96,340 executive, administrative, and managerial positions in four-year colleges and universities in the United States. Describing administrative careers is complicated because of the lack of current research as well as agreement in terminology for the various groups or categories and levels of jobs. The senior-level, or top-level, refers to positions of institution-wide leadership such as presidents or chancellors (chief executive officers) along with those who are likely to report to those positions while having administrative and financial authority and responsibility for major functional areas of an institution such as provost (chief academic officer) and vice presidents such as chief financial officer and chief student affairs officer. In many colleges and universities, this level may also include deans of academic units. Mid-level positions include directors of units across the full set of organizational functions from development (institutional advancement or fund raising), campus life, athletics, campus planning, technology, and assessment. The next group of jobs are staff or professional positions that are located at various levels of the university. Some require highly specialized skills and knowledge such as legal counsel while others require more general qualities and skills such as academic advising. Thus, the prerequisite education for administrative positions is directly related to that which is expected in a particular functional area.

Careers advance through job changes and with the help of opportunity structures, networks, sponsoring, and mentoring. Recruitment for mid-level and professional positions is from an internal labor market (inside the organization), a local labor market, and, at times, the national labor market. The search is likely to be national for executive positions and those requiring highly specific advanced skills and/or extensive experience.

More women of color, White women, and men of color than White men depend upon opportunity structures and internal institutional job changes to build their career (Johnsrud & Rosser, 2000). Although there is little systematic information about opportunity structures because they differ from one institution to another, university reports by women's commissions and diversity committees are likely to be reliable sources about campus climates and opportunity structures. With the exception of senior-level positions, it is common practice that internal candidates are considered for job vacancies before undertaking an external search.

Sagaria and Johnsrud (1992) found that in a public research university policies intended to benefit women and men of color and White women had unintended adversarial consequences for them because White senior male administrators were likely to hire individuals like themselves. Describing the experiences of a small group of female provosts, Lively (2000) observed that women can benefit from internal hiring for senior-level positions when a university has racial, ethnic, and gender diversity among administrators and staff and when senior administrators are willing to take risks with hiring decisions.

Networks, sponsors, and mentors are particularly important when there is not a definable career path to a position and competencies must be extrapolated from one job to another, such as in new positions like director of diversity. Sponsors and mentors have also been important by creating new positions for protégés. In particular, this strategy has advanced the careers of women who have taken on additional and/or new responsibilities in order to meet changing institutional priorities and needs (Miner & Estler, 1985).

Search committee chairs and hiring officials are the gatekeepers of administrative advancement. Individuals in those roles are more likely to exclude someone unknown to them than someone whom they know and do not perceive as likely to be a risk, threat, or embarrassment to them. Also, because search committees rely heavily on known sources to make personal judgments based upon personal preferences and biases, Black and White women and Black men without an advocate who is known by a White male search committee member are more likely to be screened out of competition for positions than White men (Sagaria, 2002). Furthermore, fit, a philosophy and style compatible with those of search chairs and the ability to work well with others, is an important criterion for being offered a job. However, White men are less likely to perceive women and men of color and White women as a "good fit." Therefore, a sponsor or mentor may be able to reduce or eliminate concerns that White men may have that a female's assertiveness is perceived as too aggressive or argumentative, which can prevent women candidates from being hired (Sagaria, 2002).

Search firms are increasingly becoming gatekeepers for advancement to senior administrative positions. In half of the presidential searches reported to the American Council on Education, search firms were involved in the process. These firms rely on referrals and informal networks throughout the country to identify and recommend candidates.

Until more women gain senior administrative positions, this may be more of a disadvantage for women than for White men because White women and women and men of color tend to have different networks than White men, who occupy the majority of senior-level positions (Sagaria, 2002).

The growth of new managerialism (Pritchard & Deem, 1999) has resulted in an increase in the number of women in higher education administration. For example, institutional support systems positions at the University of California system increased by 104 percent between 1966 and 1991, nearly two and a half times faster than instructional positions (Gumport and Pusser, 1995). Administrative and nonteaching professional positions have been the fastest growing group of positions. This trend has continued to the present with the creation of a new administrative sector. As universities have attempted to become more entrepreneurial, to drive down costs, and to increase the rate of return from faculty members, there has been a feminization of the lower tiers of administration. In these positions, with their focus on accountability, external relations, and client services, women are expected to challenge opposition to management practices and to monitor faculty activities (Pritchard & Deem, 1999).

Women are continuing to make their way into senior-level positions. Most notable is the increase in women university presidents. Women now account for 17.8 percent of institutional leaders. This is an increase of approximately 7 percent from 1986, but it falls short of the female representation among the administrative cohort. Equally important as their numeric representation is the fact that women now lead several of the major research universities including Brown, Michigan, Michigan State, Ohio State, Pennsylvania, and Princeton. Although there are multiple career paths to the presidency, the majority of the women leading Research I universities, unlike their male counterparts, have stayed close to the (supposed) traditional presidential career path of faculty member, department chair, dean, provost, and president. Many women on this path have been able to use their provost position to convince boards of trustees of their potential as a president.

As more women assume senior leadership positions, leadership stereotypes are being challenged to open up new ways to consider how to lead higher education. These female leaders also are opening more gates through creating networks (Lively, 2000) and providing sponsorship and mentoring that have great potential to create more career opportunities for current and future female faculty, administrators, and staff.

REFERENCES AND FURTHER READINGS

Beutel, A.M., & Nelson, D.K. (2006). The gender and race-ethnicity of faculty in top social science research departments. *The Social Science Journal, 43*(1), 111–125.

Ginther, D., & Kahn, S. (2006). Does science promote women? Evidence from academia 1973–2001 (NBER SEWP Working Paper). Cambridge, MA: National Bureau of Economics Research. Retrieved October 24, 2006, from http://www.nber.org/~sewp/GintherKahn_Sciences_promo_NBER.pdf

Gumport, P., & Pusser, B. (1995). A case of bureaucratic accretion: Contests and consequences. *Journal of Higher Education, 66*(5), 493–520.

Johnsrud, L.K., & Rosser, V.J. (2000). *Understanding the work and career paths of mid-level administrators.* San Francisco: Jossey-Bass.

Lively, K. (2000). Women in charge. *Chronicle of Higher Education, 46*(41), A33–35.

Miner, A.S., & Estler, S.E. (1985). Accrual mobility: Job mobility in higher education through responsibility accrual. *Journal of Higher Education, 56*(2), 121–143.

National Academy of Sciences. (2006). *Beyond bias and barriers: Fulfilling the potential of women in academic science and engineering.* (Report of the Committee on Maximizing the Potential of

Women in Academic Science and Engineering, National Academy of Sciences, National Academy of Engineering, and Institute of Medicine). Washington, DC: National Academies Press. Retrieved October 25, 2005, from http://www.nap.edu/catalog/11741.html

Nelson, D.K. (2005). *A national analysis of diversity in science and engineering faculties at research universities.* Retrieved October 25, 2006, from http://cheminfo.chem.ou.edu/~djn/diversity/briefings/Diversity%20Report%20Final.pdf

Pritchard, C., & Deem, R. (1999). Wo-managing further education: Gender and construction of the manager in the corporate colleges of England. *Gender and Education, 11*(3), 323–342.

Rosser, V.J. (2004). Faculty members' intentions to leave: A national study on their work life and satisfaction. *Research in Higher Education, 45*(3), 285–309.

Sagaria, M.D. (2002). An exploratory model of filtering in administrative searches. *Journal of Higher Education, 73*(6), 677–710.

Sagaria, M.D. (Ed.). (2007). *Women, universities, and change: Gender equality in the European Union and the United States.* New York: Palgrave Macmillan.

Sagaria, M.D., & Agans, L.J. (2006). Gender equality in U.S. higher education: Inter/national framing and institutional realities. In K. Yokoyama (Ed.), *Gender and higher education: Australia, Japan, the U.K. and USA* (pp. 47–68). Hiroshima, Japan: Higher Education Institute Press.

Sagaria, M.D., & Johnsrud, L.K. (1992). Administrative promotion: The structuring of opportunity within a university. *Review of Higher Education, 15*(2), 191–212.

Volk, C.S., Slaughter, S., & Thomas, S.L. (2001). Models of institutional resource allocation: Mission, market, gender. *Journal of Higher Education, 72*(4), 387–413.

Mary Ann Danowitz Sagaria

Lyndsay J. Agans

Career Patterns in Schools

Career patterns refer to the regularities and differences that occur among the positions typically held by men, women, and people of color employed in PreK–12 schools and districts. For the past century, three marked patterns have endured in the United States. First, women are disproportionately represented in teaching, men in administrative leadership. Second, educators of color, whether teachers or administrators, are predominantly found in schools or districts with high numbers of students of color. Third, overall, most teachers and administrators are White. African Americans, Latinos, Asian Americans, and other people of color are significantly underrepresented, both in relation to the demographics of the U.S. population generally and to PreK–12 student enrollment more specifically.

The gender difference between teachers and administrators is one example of a broader sexual division of labor and, like most such examples, the division of labor in PreK–12 is usually seen as inequitable. Even when women move from teaching into school administration, they tend to occupy positions with less prestige and power than those of their male colleagues. The reasons for these gender differences are complex and include individual, institutional, and cultural influences on the career patterns of men and women. Complexities also surround the future career patterns of men and women in PreK–12 schools and districts. While it is possible that current trends toward more women in school administration are the harbingers of a movement toward genuine gender integration, past history suggests that it is more likely that either gender resegregation or a return to traditional sex stratification will occur.

SEXUAL DIVISIONS OF LABOR

Career patterns in schools can be understood as part of the sexual divisions of labor that characterize work universally. That is, sexual divisions have been found to hold true in the home and paid employment, in the United States and internationally, and in education as well as other fields.

Although the essence of the distinction is that there are two kinds of work—men's and women's—the divisions take a variety of forms. In one form, all or almost all of the entire population of paid employees in a particular industry or professional specialty consists of one sex. For example, most preschool teachers are females, and most school superintendents are males. Another form manifests itself as stratification by sex within the same work setting. For example, within PreK–12 teaching, the higher the grade level, the greater the proportion of teachers who are male.

Sexual divisions of labor are enduring, but they are not static. Historians have noted that, from the late nineteenth to early twentieth centuries, schoolteaching, bank telling, and secretarial work transformed from almost exclusively male to predominantly female occupations. More recently, women have made inroads into predominantly male occupational roles such as the principalship, but there have been concomitant internal redivisions by sex and school level: Women have integrated elementary school principalships in much higher proportions than high school principalships, in which men continue to be overrepresented. Thus, even when longitudinal changes in the division of labor occur, separation between men's and women's work persists.

Research on the reasons for women's movement into previously male-dominated occupational roles indicates that new opportunities for women have typically resulted from significant increases in job vacancies (due to occupational growth, turnover, incumbent exits, wars, major technological change, and the like) and/or from the deterioration of the job's working conditions or rewards, with subsequent loss of attractiveness to males. As illustrated in PreK–12 career patterns in schools, teaching shifted from a predominantly male to a predominantly female occupation as both the number of public schools increased and teachers' salaries and autonomy declined in comparison to other job opportunities for males. This shift illustrates the complex and dynamic nature of sexual divisions of labor.

Feminist scholars and other advocates of social justice have long been interested in gendered career patterns and sexual divisions of labor, largely because these separate spheres are often accompanied by differential treatment and unequal consequences. For women, the latter can include lower pay and status, fewer opportunities for advancement, devaluing of the labor itself, subordination to males, and exclusion from men's work realms. In schools, another problematic aspect of such gender asymmetries is the biasing messages they communicate to students about appropriate work roles for females and males. Conceptually, the problematizing of sexual "divisions" of labor is reflected in the use of terms more suggestive of inequities such as occupational sex segregation and sex stereotyping, stratification, ghettoization, or marginalization of women's work. Conceptually, these concerns with bias are reflected in the replacement of the more neutral language of "sexual divisions of labor" with terms that are more suggestive of inequities.

GENDERED PATTERNS

So where are the women and men in PreK–12 schools? What are the regularities that occur among the positions held by males and females?

The most recent data available from the National Center for Education Statistics (NCES) indicate that 75 percent of all teachers were female in 1999 to 2000, up from 72 percent in 1990 to 1991 and 67 percent in 1981. Although NCES data are not disaggregated by grade level and sex, some states provide that information. For example, in New York, 89 percent of elementary and 71 percent of secondary teachers were female in 2002 to 2003. In North Carolina, 94 percent of elementary and 63 percent of high school teachers were female in 2000. State data illustrate that, while females predominate at all grade levels of teaching, their proportional representation is highest in elementary schools.

Like nursing, social work, and elder care, the prevalence of women in schoolteaching echoes and reinforces cultural norms that value the "helping professions" as appropriate spheres for women's work. The data indicating greater proportions of males in the secondary than elementary grades may reflect commonplace assumptions about increased rigor and complexity (therefore status) at higher levels of schooling, as well as increased opportunities to coach sports, thus elevating job attractiveness to men. Lower proportions of male teachers at the elementary level may also reflect social biases and fears about men working with young children.

The historic and persistent underrepresentation of women in educational administration is accentuated by this backdrop of female overrepresentation in classroom teaching since, in most states, administrative certification requires prior teaching experience. In other words, it is clear that there have been ample numbers of women in the teaching workforce pool from which administrators are drawn.

Nationally, 44 percent of all principals were women in 1999 to 2000 compared to 35 percent in 1993 to 1994 and 25 percent in 1987 to 1988. While contemporary data for principalships show solid increases for women since the early 1980s, over half of all principals were women in the late 1920s. Consequently, many scholars recommend prudence when examining recent trend data about females' inroads into school administration.

In some ways, the demographic patterns among principals parallel the gendered stratification by grade level evident in teaching. That is, the proportion of women in the principalship decreases as grade level goes up. National data indicate that 55 percent of elementary, 31 percent of middle, and 21 percent of high school principals were female in 1999 to 2000. In North Carolina, 58 percent of elementary and 24 percent of high school principals were female in 2000. In New York, 60 percent of elementary and 30 percent of secondary principals were female in 2002 to 2003, up from 46 percent and 23 percent in 1995 to 1996. In addition to the influence of social norms already mentioned, the persistence of male dominance of the high school principalship may also be related to the history of gender bias in the United States against women controlling large organizations, given that high schools typically serve greater numbers of students than elementary schools. Historians and occupational sex segregation theorists trace the roots of this bias to nineteenth-century struggles of men and women to define their work roles in a newly industrialized society. As much larger, systematized, and hierarchical organizations proliferated (e.g., factories, schools, and hospitals), it became socially unacceptable for women to assume the expanded authority associated with the leadership of these more complex structures, especially those employing men as well as women. Hence, even when new types of work developed, the belief persisted that there should be separate spheres of work for men and women. Other national data indicate that, in the year 2000, approximately 13 percent of superintendents were female, up from 6 percent in 1992, and 1 percent in 1982. In 1998 (the most recent national data available), 33 percent of assistant/associate/deputy/area superintendents were female. In New York State in 2002 to 2003, 21 percent of superintendents and 46 percent of assistant/associate/deputy superintendents were female compared to 13 percent and 32 percent, respectively, in 1995 to 1996. Especially in the superintendency, but in all counts of educational administrators, experts advise caution when considering summary data. Historically and today, it has been difficult to systematically and accurately track career patterns and position occupancy by sex and virtually impossible by sex and race/ethnicity together. Often, years of data collection, job definitions, and grade-level aggregates are not consistent across studies. In the case of superintendents, for example, all manner and types may be mixed together, including county, state, vocational school district, PreK–8 systems, PreK–12 systems, and intermediate unit superintendencies. Also, some counts collapse superintendent and assistant superintendent data together, exacerbating the challenges of longitudinal or cross-state comparisons. Overall, however, the superintendency has clearly been the slowest of all school leadership positions to integrate women.

In general, women administrators are found in greater proportions in "staff" rather than "line" leadership roles in schools. The former include positions such as program coordinators, directors, district wide supervisors, and administrative assistants of various sorts. In contrast, line positions are typically defined as those with direct authority over others, often with formal evaluative responsibilities for subordinates (e.g., principals and superintendents). Since job titles for central office and other administrative staff positions vary widely and national data are scarce, state data are typically relied upon.

For example, 2002 to 2003 New York data indicate that 74 percent of assistant directors/coordinators, 61 percent of supervisors, 55 percent of directors/coordinators, 46 percent of deputy/associate/assistant superintendents, 41 percent of business managers, and 21 percent of superintendents were women. (Women's representation in school administration in New York has tended to be higher than national averages, perhaps because the state is generally considered one of the more liberal or progressive politically.) These staff data may be interpreted to illustrate the persistent pattern, in both education and other careers, that, as the formal power, status, or authority of the leadership position increases, the percentage of women occupying that role decreases.

Taken together, these patterns of position occupancy by sex in PreK–12 schools illustrate continuing gender stratification and sexual divisions of labor. More specifically, regularities and differences include: the relative scarcity of males and preponderance of females in teaching; the persistence of men managing and women teaching in schools nationally; the pattern of women administrators being more likely to occupy staff rather than line and elementary rather than secondary leadership positions; and the increasing percentages of men in administration as the scope of authority, status, and salaries of particular leadership roles rise (e.g., from elementary to secondary school principalships, and, at the central administration levels, from coordinator to assistant superintendent to superintendent).

The reasons for these patterns are multiple and complex. Contributing factors cited in relevant literatures include ideologies and social pressures about appropriate sex roles, stereotypes about women as child rearers and nurturers of the young, perceptions of a need for "tougher" management as students grow older, cultural biases about who looks and acts like a leader, the bureaucratization of schooling that was built on separate spheres for women (teaching) and men (leadership), the conceptualization of schooling and its leadership in ways that emphasize competition and authority (stereotypically masculine strengths) rather than collaboration and service, and educational employment practices that perpetuate gender bias.

Scholars provide helpful conceptual handles for these and other contributing factors by underscoring three different levels of influence on career patterns: the individual, the institutional, and the cultural. For example, from an individual perspective, it is possible to theorize the underrepresentation of females in educational administration by looking to person-centered explanations. This perspective considers factors such as parental background, family's academic and career expectations, and the individual's education, work experience, and initiative. Individual-oriented hypotheses center on inherent differences between men and women, on sex-typed psychological traits and personal characteristics, or on dissimilar job aspirations. That is, for example, perhaps women are simply unattracted by, or ill suited for, upper management positions. On the one hand, such reasoning emphasizes individual agency, choice, and self-responsibility for career outcomes. On the other, exclusively person-centered rationales have been criticized for ignoring the many additional factors that impact employment opportunities and decisions. At worst, such explanations have been accused of illustrating a "blame the victim" perspective on the differential outcomes associated with gender, class, or color that characterize many aspects of our social worlds.

In contrast, cultural explanations for gendered career patterns center on broader sociopolitical influences on individuals, groups, and organizations. They look to society as a whole, underscoring, for example, the different ways that boys and girls are socialized as well as American traditions and norms about who occupies the highest-level leadership positions, whether in government, religious, corporate, or educational sectors. The ideological and ethical climate of the times is also considered to have an effect on the composition of educational occupations by sex (e.g., Are these friendly times for acting affirmatively? Should men or women have priority in employment during economic recessions?). From this perspective, what happens in PreK–12 school careers is but one small piece of a larger culture in which gender equity is not universally valued or attained.

Closely related to the cultural are institutional perspectives. When applied to schooling, institution-centered explanations for gendered career patterns look to the education system and its structures, policies, practices, and professional norms that contribute to stratification by sex. For example, some barriers to women's advancement in educational leadership are overt, such as prejudicial or illegal application or employment interview questions (e.g., Do you think she could handle burly adolescent boys?). Others are subtler, such as the presence or absence of same-sex role models in particular occupational roles in schools. Also included in this domain is the influence of structures of opportunity for visibility within the school or district (e.g., coaching a high-profile interscholastic sport, leading the teachers' union) and power structures (e.g., networks and alliances of influentials). Policies and practices concerning recruitment and promotion provide both overt and subtle forms of institutional stratification by sex (see below).

Of course, these three levels of influence are overlapping and interactive, mutually shaping the dynamics at the other levels to jointly affect who occupies which career position. For example, cultural norms about responsibilities in the home and parenting differentially influence females' and males' personal contexts and individual actions for career pursuits. So do access to informal networks of influential others and whether or not there is a critical mass of female or male incumbents in a particular occupational stratum.

Overall, studies of gendered labor patterns conclude that the positive effects of personal and socialization factors such as aspirations, qualifications, and experience do not assure women equity with men in career development, given the powerful gender-stereotyped contextual, structural, and social forces that serve to counterinfluence individual action for employment and advancement. This conclusion holds true for PreK–12 educational administration as well as other historically male-dominated leadership roles. Some particularly relevant structural and contextual forces are illustrated in employment recruitment and promotion practices in schools.

RECRUITMENT AND PROMOTION

Recruitment refers to both formal and informal processes aimed at eliciting applicants for position vacancies. The history of PreK–12 schooling includes deep-seated traditions of informal recruitment leading to administrative hiring. That is, employment in educational leadership has not relied exclusively on unsolicited applications submitted in response to publicly announced job openings. Instead, experienced administrators (and, frequently, college professors) have always played active, influential roles in targeting, supporting, and paving the way for selected associates' entry into, and career advancement within, the field. The essence of these employment practice traditions is reliance on incumbent administrators to encourage, make contacts on behalf of, vouch for, and promote the career advancement of known prospects.

Informal recruitment often involves publicly invisible processes such as veteran educational leaders selectively communicating job opportunity information to friends, acquaintances, and other preferred potential candidates; advocating for protégés for particular position vacancies; networking with others who share common interests, affiliations, or backgrounds; seeking referrals from others in positions of power and influence in education; and grooming favored successors by providing special counsel, coaching, or opportunities to enhance leadership skills. Such practices are often referred to as "sponsorship" or sponsored mobility.

It is worth noting that the popular and professional literature about successful teacher development frequently underscores the term "mentoring," with its connotations of guidance, tutoring, advice, and support by those more experienced and knowledgeable. Parallel literatures about administrator development are much more likely to emphasize both mentoring and sponsorship as critical to initial and continued success. While sponsorship shares many of the same educative and counseling connotations as mentoring, it also includes elements of advocacy (e.g., proposing a new law; providing funding for an artist or athlete; accepting responsibility for the development of a godchild) and persuasion toward particular ends (e.g., commercial advertisement by sponsors). Additionally, the notions of sponsorship for acceptance into particular social groups (e.g., sororities, fraternal organizations) or admittance into elite organizations (e.g., country clubs, honorary societies) suggest a kind of exclusivity not associated with the more benign concept of mentorship.

Because of sponsored mobility traditions in educational leadership, commonplace recruitment and promotion practices have been criticized for being more closed than open and for contributing to the persistent overrepresentation of men in school administration. In the vernacular, these processes are sometimes referred to as a self-perpetuating "good old boys" system at work, since most of the people doing the sponsoring (incumbent superintendents, other administrators, consultants who assist school boards with administrative hiring, leaders of state and national professional organizations, and college professors) are White males.

Research on superintendent search and selection practices further illustrates how professional norms, institutionalized routines, and cultural biases can combine to impede women's access to, and advancement within, the most elevated strata of administrative careers. Prior studies reveal a mix of unwritten selection criteria that influence superintendent recruitment and hiring. These criteria do not appear in either advertisements of desired qualifications or public forums typically associated with employing a new superintendent. Instead, they manifest themselves behind the scenes in the private conversations and interviews critical to prospective candidates' advancement. These unwritten rules involve search consultants' (who are typically either veteran administrators or college professors) and school board members' stereotyping by sex, defining "best qualified" in terms of hierarchies of particular job titles, and hypervaluing "good chemistry" in determining interview success.

Examples of prejudicial gender stereotyping in this context include questioning whether a district or community is ready for a woman superintendent (a concern not raised for male candidates) or assuming strong disciplinary and other noninstructional technical abilities of males, but doubting them for females (Can she be tough enough? What does she know about construction projects and school bus maintenance?).

Moreover, the experiential backgrounds routinely described by these same key decision makers as best or strongest reflect career patterns much more likely to be followed by males than by females. The favoring of positions infrequently occupied by women (that is, previous superintendencies, assistant superintendencies, and high school principalships) diminishes women's chances of advancing through the final selection gates in superintendent search processes. Thus, narrow definitions of quality as specific positions —rather than broader leadership skills, regardless of the educational role or grade level where acquired—disproportionately benefit men and contribute to perpetuating gender stratification in school administration.

Similarly, the extraordinary influence of recruits' and applicants' interpersonal "chemistry," as judged by school board members and search consultants, can be prejudicial to the superintendent hiring process. These key decision makers describe the fuzzy nature of value filters having to do with feelings of "being on the same wavelength," where "things really clicked," and interviewers "just felt so comfortable with" particular candidates. How is it that the hypervaluing of connecting with and feeling "good in the gut" about some candidates is more likely to disadvantage females than male applicants?

Prior studies of employment decision making suggest that reliance on an interpersonal sense of connection and ease fosters the introduction of subconscious preferences for affiliations with those most like ourselves. This phenomenon is captured in similarity-attraction theory and may be expressed in the vernacular as "the comfort syndrome" in recruitment, hiring, and promotions. The concept refers to a proclivity to bond with people similar to those we are most accustomed to working with. Taken together, the demographics of school board members, search consultants, and incumbent school leaders (mostly White male), what is known about similarity-attractiveness, and the predominance of gut feelings, chemistry, and intuition in critical interview interactions (i.e., factors that foster the introduction of subconscious bias) have combined to favor male rather than female prospects for the superintendency.

HISTORY AND PROSPECTS

It remains true that, in PreK–12 schools, the prevailing career pattern is that women teach and men lead. It is also true that women's proportional representation in several administrative leadership positions has increased considerably during the past 35 years, following the rise of the modern women's movement of the 1970s.

Historians note that there had also been a decades-long increase in women's representation in PreK–12 administration between 1910 and 1930, in connection with the first women's (suffrage) movement. That earlier time period was referred to as a "golden age of women administrators," and some expected continued integration of females to eventually lead to a more gender-balanced profession. Subsequent to that golden age, however, multiple social, political, and economic factors contributed to a resegregation of the field, with women's representation in administration declining significantly over the next four decades (1930 to 1970).

The question of whether the recent upswing in women's occupancy of principalships and superintendencies will be temporary or enduring is a difficult one. Feminist researchers generally concur in recommending caution about drawing overly optimistic projections from recent gains. The accumulated scholarship points out that women have not yet attained, or ever sustained over time, equitable representation in school administration; that affirmative action legislation, Title IX protections, and other policies prohibiting sex discrimination in employment have been enforced weakly and intermittently; that sex stereotypes and bias against women in leadership persist; and that, accordingly, continued vigilance is warranted if occupational integration by sex is to be achieved.

If contemporary trends mimic history, a peak in women's proportional representation followed by a period of significant decline may be expected. That scenario would be one form of career resegregation, that is, a return to overwhelming male dominance, with women occupying small or minimal percentages of line administrative positions.

Another form of resegregation could also occur. Women's inroads into superintendencies or principalships could accelerate and endure so persistently that, over time, the positions would take 180-degree demographic turns, from predominantly male to predominantly female. Women would essentially "take over" these administrative roles, much like they did schoolteaching at the turn of the twentieth century. As with other occupations that became completely feminized, factors such as labor shortages, work quality depreciation in the view of men and society, and "male flight" from the occupation all contribute to increasing access for women.

But resegregation is just one of three possibilities that gendered career pattern experts theorize. Another scenario—genuine integration—is also possible. That is, perhaps school administration will become gender balanced with men and women represented equitably. This scenario assumes that talent and leadership potential are distributed equally among the sexes. It presumes that the work conditions and benefits of administrative work will be attractive to both males and females in the labor market. It also presumes that sponsors, other informal gatekeepers, and employers will rank male and female prospective administrators at similar levels of attractiveness. This scenario would likely be associated with a significant ideological shift culturally, with leadership viewed as the shared domain of females and males rather than primarily as "manly work." Research and theory suggest this is unlikely to occur, however, given the persistence of sexual divisions of labor to date.

A third possibility for administrative leadership career patterns is what was referred to earlier in this essay as stratification and what some theorists call ghettoization. In this scenario, women's gains in proportional representation will either be short-lived or marginalized. An example of ghettoization as marginalization would be if women completely overtook smaller, lower-paid elementary principalships but remained underrepresented in higher-status, larger, or better-paid elementary and high schools. Another example comes from studies of superintendents in the 1970s, 1980s, and early 1990s, which found that women disproportionately occupied superintendencies in the smallest, most rural, or least desirable school districts.

Of course, it is impossible to say how contemporary gendered career patterns will change in the future. Familiarity with these three theoretical possibilities, however, may provide conceptual grounding for the kinds of research and disaggregated data needed to recognize and analyze future shifts. Also, awareness of how individual plans and aspirations are mediated by institutional and cultural factors can lead to deeper understanding of trends and patterns yet to appear.

REFERENCES AND FURTHER READINGS

Blount, J.M. (1998). *Destined to rule the schools: Women and the superintendency, 1873–1995.* Albany: State University of New York Press.

Ortiz, F.I. (1982). *Career patterns in educational administration: Women, men, and minorities.* New York: Praeger.

Ortiz, F.I., & Marshall, C. (1988). Women in educational administration. In N. Boyan (Ed.), *Handbook of research on educational administration* (pp. 123–142). New York: Longman.

Riehl, C., & Byrd, M. (1997). Gender differences among new recruits to educational administration: Cautionary notes to an optimistic tale. *Educational Evaluation and Policy Analysis, 19*(1), 45–64.

Shakeshaft, C. (1999). The struggle to create a more gender-inclusive profession. In J. Murphy & K. Seashore Louis (Eds.), *Handbook of research on educational administration* (2nd ed., pp. 99–118). San Francisco: Jossey-Bass.

Tallerico, M., & Blount, J.M. (2004). Women and the superintendency: Insights from theory and history. *Educational Administration Quarterly, 40*(5), 633–662.

Tyack, D., & Hansot, E. (1982). *Managers of virtue: Public school leadership in America, 1820–1980.* New York: Basic Books.

Marilyn Tallerico

Faculty Workloads in Higher Education

The story of gender equity and education is, at all levels, one of progress and bottlenecks. In higher education, for example, women are now the majority of college and graduate school enrollees and degree recipients, but they have made fewer inroads as faculty, especially in the natural sciences and engineering (Jacobs, 1996). One important element of this story is the high level of career commitment expected from faculty. Although the public often does not fully understand the nature and rhythm of faculty life, faculty positions are, in fact, highly demanding. The demands of these jobs are pervasive. Moreover, the requirements of faculty positions are often more intensive during the childbearing and child-rearing periods of young faculty's lives.

The data discussed in this essay were drawn from the 1998 National Study of Postsecondary Faculty (NSOPF) administered by the National Center for Education Statistics of the U.S. Department of Education (U.S. Department of Education, 2001). The survey, designed to collect information on faculty and other instructional staff in institutions of higher education, is currently the most comprehensive study of postsecondary faculty. This cross-sectional survey has been administered three times: during the 1987 to 1988, 1992 to 1993, and 1998 to 1999 academic years. For the present analysis, the sample was restricted to those faculty members at four-year institutions who considered their academic appointment to be their primary job and who did not spend the majority of their time in administrative activities. This resulted in a final sample size of 11,162 faculty members of which 10,092 were full time. Selective reports from the 1992 administration of the same survey are also presented. Because the NSOPF did not solicit information on spouses of faculty members, information about those married couples in the 1990 Census in which either spouse reported her or his occupation as "postsecondary teacher" were rearranged to fill this gap.

THE FACULTY WORKWEEK

Time is a valuable—yet finite—resource about which individuals have to make allocation decisions. Juliet Schor brought this issue into the spotlight in her 1991 book, *The*

Overworked American, arguing that, after a century-long decline, working time began to increase in the 1980s. The lengthening of the average workweek, Schor contended, is the principal source of time pressure faced by individuals. Jacobs and Gerson (2004) find that a diversifying workforce has been accompanied by a bifurcation in working time, with more jobs requiring either very long or short workweeks. This time divide among jobs tends to mirror the class divide as well, with long working hours concentrated among managerial and professional workers and shorter working hours for workers with more modest educational and occupational credentials.

Working time among academic faculty reflects this larger pattern. Professors put in very long hours. Full-time male faculty report working 54.8 hours per week on average; their female counterparts report working almost as many hours (52.8 hours per week). Although a sizable minority of male (34.4 percent) and female (27.0 percent) full-time faculty do some paid consulting work, the amount of time they spend doing such work is minimal (approximately 5 hours per week). Thus, the majority of faculty working time is devoted to their main position, with outside consulting representing a minor fraction of total work effort.

Faculty work more hours per week than do those in most other occupations, even those in comparable professional positions. In 2000, the average employed man worked 43.1 hours per week, while the average male professional or manager worked 46.0 hours per week, a full nine-hour day less than professors (Jacobs & Gerson, 2004). Female professors exceed their same-sex counterparts in paid working time by an even larger margin. The average employed woman worked 37.1 hours in 2000, and female professionals and managers worked 39.5 hours on average.

Moreover, extremely long workweeks are pervasive in academia. The averages detailed above clearly indicate that a 50-hour workweek is normative, with roughly two-thirds of faculty reporting working such long hours. But a 60-hour workweek is also common; among full-time faculty, 38.1 percent of men and 32.5 percent of women report working at least 60 hours per week.

Long hours are pervasive across institutional types and academic rank. While faculty in research institutions report working the longest hours (an average of 55.8 for men and 54.0 for women), the average workweeks of full-time faculty in other institution types are quite similar. For example, male full-time faculty in liberal arts colleges work 54.0 hours per week, and their female counterparts put in 53.4 hours per week. Both male and female full-time faculty at all institutional groups average above 50 hours per week. Similarly, faculty at all ranks put in over 50 hours per week. Assistant professors work long hours but so too do tenured associate and full professors. Male assistant professors put in slightly longer hours than do their female counterparts (55.8 hours per week for the men versus 53.5 hours for the women). For men, there is a slight post-tenure slump with the length of the workweek declining by two hours, only to rise again for full professors. For women, the workweek actually grows steadily as they advance from the ranks of assistant to associate to full professor. The gender gap in working time for assistant professors is a bit sharper among those working 60 plus hours per week—43.2 percent of men and 33.5 percent of women put in these long workweeks. But long hours are not restricted to those on the tenure track. Even lecturers and instructors put in over 50 hours per week.

WORKING TIME FROM THE PERSPECTIVE OF FAMILIES

Individual workweeks are only one part of the time crunch facing faculty members. American family structure has changed dramatically in recent decades, and this has profound implications for analyses of work-family conflict. Whereas just over half of married couples fit the breadwinner-homemaker model in 1970, by 2000 three in five were dual-earner couples. Census data indicate that dual-earner couples are common in academia, particularly among female faculty. Just over half (56.2 percent) of married male faculty and nearly all (88.5 percent) of married female faculty have spouses working full time. Moreover, a sizable minority is married to other faculty members and most have spouses in a managerial or professional occupation. Women faculty are more likely to be married to male faculty (18.2 percent versus 12.5 percent), but the partners of both groups are typically professionals or managers (69.5 percent for female faculty, 70.7 percent for male faculty).

What does this mean for the work-family conflicts facing academic faculty? In earlier work, Jacobs and Gerson (2004) argued that, in order to fully understand the time crunch facing American men and women, researchers must examine working time from the perspective of families. The family workweeks of married faculty are long: 84.1 hours per week on average for male faculty and 89.3 hours per week for female faculty. A sizable minority are in couples devoting 100 plus hours per week to paid employment (17.3 percent for men versus 25.4 percent for women). Thus, the pressure generated by the long faculty workweeks discussed above are compounded by the fact that most faculty, especially most women faculty, have spouses who themselves are putting in long hours. Are academic careers family friendly? On the one hand, one might argue that the answer is yes. Faculty members do not have to punch a time clock and are not closely monitored on an hourly basis, as is the case in many occupations. The measure of control and flexibility inherent in academic work allows faculty, especially those who are parents, to be available when children are sick or when breakdowns in child care inevitably occur. However, much of this compatibility rests on the implicit assumption that faculty members are able to wait until after receiving tenure to have children.

The strategy of delaying childbearing until after receiving tenure is quite appealing in that the most demanding phase of child care would occur after the pressure and risk associated with being an untenured assistant professor is completed. But clearly this strategy depends on getting tenure relatively early in life. In other words, the "tenure first, kids later" approach relies on a certain ordered, uninterrupted life-course sequencing in which one receives his or her PhD at age 27 or 28 (which itself relies on the assumption of beginning graduate school immediately or soon after receiving one's undergraduate degree and completing the degree in five or six years) and receives tenure at roughly the age of 34. This poses an important empirical question: How old are assistant professors? If this ordered life-course sequencing is occurring, we would expect assistant professors to be in their early 30s. Is that the case?

The average age for male assistant professors is 42.4; for women, it is slightly older at 43.7. The average age of assistant professors is higher in some fields, such as education and nursing, than others, such as the physical sciences. But the average exceeds 37 years of age in all of the academic specialties. Thus, the dilemma of whether to wait until tenure to have children is a daunting one in all areas of academia with the data suggesting that most assistant professors are too old to wait until receiving tenure to start their families.

Why is it that assistant professors are older than the ordered life-course sequencing perspective would lead us to expect? One reason is that faculty members are not receiving their degrees until after their 30th birthdays. The average age at degree is 33.4 for men and 35.5 for women. Again, there is variation across specialties between fields with faculty in some fields, such as education, obtaining their degrees much later in life than in other fields, such as architecture and engineering. Nonetheless, in all fields the average

age for doctoral degree recipients is at least 30. As a result, questions about getting married and having children before achieving tenure, whether that is when one is in graduate school, holding postdoctoral fellowships or other temporary positions, or is an assistant professor, arise in all fields of academic specialization.

Another possible explanation for an age profile that does not support the "tenure first, kids later" pattern might be that faculty members are starting families before receiving their PhDs. While the cross-sectional data available to us do not allow for exact pinpointing of these events, one may make some life-course inferences about these data. For example, women obtaining PhDs in the physical sciences are slightly younger than their male counterparts (average age of 30.2 for women versus 31.4 for men). Thus, it is likely that few women in this area are having children in advance of receiving their PhD since there is no evidence of a slowdown relative to their male counterparts. In other fields, such as the arts and humanities, education, and biological sciences, women are obtaining their doctoral degrees two or more years after their male counterparts. Childbearing in advance of the degree may well be the explanation for these differences.

Finally, it may be the case that academics do not progress directly from degree receipt to a tenure-track faculty position. The data indicate that assistant professors have been at their current institution for an average of just over three years. This figure is exactly what one would expect given a six- or seven-year tenure clock, but it leaves several years unaccounted for. In other words, age at degree plus years at current institution does not add up to the respondent's current age. What explains this gap? In some fields, like biology, respondents typically worked five or more years at another institution, presumably as a postdoctoral fellow, before starting as an assistant professor. The number of years elapsed before starting as an assistant professor is much lower in other fields, including business and the social sciences. Thus, the fact that assistant professors are often in their late 30s or early 40s is due to a combination of obtaining the doctoral degree in their early 30s and spending several years in postdoctoral fellowships or temporary positions after the receipt of the degree. Taken together, these results indicate that the "tenure first, kids later" strategy is not a viable option for many in academia. For many faculty members, the most demanding years of child rearing likely coincide with the demands and uncertainty of the pretenure years.

WORKLOAD, PRODUCTIVITY, AND SATISFACTION

How can we make sense of the long workweeks put in by faculty members, particularly in light of the fact that, for many, they are combined with a spouse's lengthy employment hours and the demands of raising children? Are these hours self-imposed or are they rooted in institutional and professional expectations?

An optimistic view might hold that academia is a context in which devotion to work is self-imposed. Professors do not punch a time clock and, even at the most teaching-intensive institutions, classroom time rarely exceeds 15 hours. The time demands experienced by faculty are, thus, in some sense discretionary. Moreover, this argument holds that faculty members love their work and deeply identify with their professional role. In this sense, academia represents a secular "calling" with faculty embracing the "work devotion" schema outlined by Blair-Loy (2003). That faculty do not relinquish their professional titles or affiliations upon retirement (i.e., "Professor" simply becomes "Emeritus Professor") suggests that many professors keep working diligently into retirement as long as their strength and stamina allow. All of this might logically lead to the conclusion that, if the faculty workweek seems excessive to some, it certainly does not to faculty because it is what they chose to do.

In contrast to the view that faculty work time is self-imposed, an alternative view is that professors often find themselves caught in a set of institutional and professional expectations. In other words, normative expectations about what it means to be a good or successful academic drive many faculty members to put in excessive hours. While the institutional demands perspective would acknowledge the many attractions of academia, such a view stresses the practical challenges that large numbers of faculty confront at both elite and less selective colleges and universities.

If professors' long workweeks are due to "structural constraints," what are these structures and what are the sources of these constraints? There are four main sources of growing time pressures on faculty. First, the rising cost of higher education has brought renewed public scrutiny and, with it, calls for more emphasis on teaching. While the source of the scrutiny may differ across institution type (with public institutions often responding to budget cuts and private institutions justifying rising tuition by focusing on how much faculty attention students receive), the pressure to increase the quantity and quality of time devoted to teaching has been evident in public and private institutions of higher education. Second, the increased emphasis on teaching has been accompanied by rising expectations for research productivity. Both the form and the content of the tenure review system, formerly most developed in the elite schools, have been adopted by colleges and universities at all levels of higher education. Third, technological changes associated with the information economy have paradoxically increased the time demands and intensity of faculty jobs. Although this claim cannot be assessed with NSOPF data, anecdotal evidence strongly suggests that faculty spend countless hours reading and responding to e-mail and are often assumed by students to be available 24 hours per day. Moreover, the adoption of computers was also accompanied by a decline in secretarial support for faculty.

Finally, the rise of part-time employment in academia increases the pressures on full-time faculty members. Part-time employment in academia has risen sharply over the past 30 years as extremely low-paid part-time faculty are available to teach for a small fraction of the cost of full-time members of the standing faculty. In 1999, more than two in five (42.5 percent) postsecondary faculty were employed part time, a substantial increase from 21.9 percent found in 1970 (U.S. Department of Education, 2002). The growth in the number of part timers increases pressures on full timers in two ways. First, the reduction in the number of full-time positions makes entry into the ranks of full-time faculty that much more competitive. Furthermore, since part timers are rarely asked to serve on committees and take on other administrative roles, the growth of part-time employment means that a smaller fraction of faculty are saddled with a growing amount of administrative responsibilities. In sum, a perspective emphasizing structural constraints and normative expectations suggests that multiple course preparations, endless committee meetings, seemingly limitless productivity standards, and a relentless stream of e-mails make today's faculty work experience less than the idealized world of academia suggested by the self-imposed viewpoint outlined above.

Which of these views fits the data more closely? While it is clear that faculty overwhelmingly report being satisfied with their jobs (84.8 percent of men and 81.8 percent of full-time women report being somewhat or very satisfied with their jobs), they do voice complaints about salary, benefits, and their workload. By focusing on whether faculty report dissatisfaction with their workload, we can assess the extent to which the length of the faculty workweek is self-imposed and willingly chosen. If the self-imposed perspective is correct, then we would expect that those who put in the longest hours express few if any complaints about their workload since these faculty love teaching and research and cannot get enough of it. On the other hand, if one's workload is largely driven by institutional and professional demands such as increasing course loads and expectations for publishing, then we may find a significant number of professors who are not satisfied with their jobs. A key question, then, is whether satisfaction with workload increases with time on the job. If so, then those working the longest may not be doing so completely voluntarily. Instead, work patterns may be the result of many pressures, some stemming from the institution, others from normative expectations set by other faculty. A related question concerns the connection between working time and research productivity: Do long workweeks play a key role in contributing to success in publishing? If so, this relationship may provide insights into the reasons for the amount of time faculty spend on the job.

Faculty dissatisfaction with workload increases with hours on the job. For example, one in three (30.3 percent) female faculty working less than 50 hours per week report being dissatisfied with their workload, compared with more than two in five (44.1 percent) of those working more than 60 hours per week. The idea that greater hours are associated with more complaints about an excessive workload may seem simple, but it runs counter to the notion that people working the longest hours are all doing so simply out of a love of their jobs. So what explains the excessive workweeks that are so pervasive in academia? Our data clearly indicate that those who put in the longest workweeks are likely to publish more books and articles. The differences between those putting in over 50 hours per week versus those putting in less than 50 hours per week are substantial. However, the impact of working over 60 hours per week is even more dramatic and seems especially critical for women. If research productivity is indispensable for success in academia and if a 60-hour workweek is key for success in publishing, then working 60 or more hours per week essentially becomes a requirement of academic jobs.

Academic positions are highly sought after and very satisfying, but they are also very demanding and pose significant challenges to those striving to maintain a fulfilling family life. This remains particularly true for married women faculty whose husbands are typically very busy professionals themselves. The risk of maintaining the current systems is the loss of talent, both in terms of faculty lost through the "leaky pipeline" as well as those deterred from pursing careers in this profession. The first step in addressing these concerns is to understand that there is a problem that needs to be addressed. Policies designed to manage the demands of faculty jobs can be devised (see Jacobs, 2004) but only after recognizing that some limits need to be set on the demands posed by academic positions.

REFERENCES AND FURTHER READINGS

Blair-Loy, M. (2003). *Competing devotions: Career and family among women executives.* Cambridge, MA: Harvard University Press.

Jacobs, J.A. (1996). Gender inequality and higher education. *Annual Review of Sociology, 22,* 153–185.

Jacobs, J.A. (2004). The faculty time divide. *Sociological Forum, 19*(1), 3–27.

Jacobs, J.A., & Gerson, K. (2004). *The time divide: Work, family and gender inequality.* Cambridge, MA: Harvard University Press.

Jacobs, J.A., & Winslow, S. (2004a). Overworked faculty: Job stresses and family demands. *Annals of the American Academy of Political and Social Science, 596*(1), 104–129.

Jacobs, J.A., & Winslow, S. (2004b). Understanding the academic life course, time pressures and gender inequality. *Community, Work, and Family, 7*(2), 143–161.

Schor, J. (1991). *The overworked American: The unexpected decline of leisure.* New York: Basic Books.

U.S. Department of Education, National Center for Education Statistics. (2001). *Background characteristics, work activities and compensation of faculty and instructional staff in postsecondary institutions* (NCES 2001-152). Washington, DC: U.S. Government Printing Office.

U.S. Department of Education. (2002). *Digest of education statistics.* Washington, DC: U.S. Government Printing Office. Accessed April 5, 2004, at http://nces.ed.gov/programs/digest/

Winslow, S. (2005). Work-family conflict, gender, and parenthood, 1977–1997. *Journal of Family Issues, 26*(6), 727–755.

Winslow-Bowe, S.E. (2006). *Husbands' and wives' relative income: Persistence, variation, and outcomes.* Unpublished doctoral dissertation, University of Pennsylvania, Philadelphia.

Sarah E. Winslow-Bowe

Jerry A. Jacobs

Feminization of Teaching

Some occupations are dominated numerically by one sex. An occupation that is predominantly made up of women is said to be "feminized." Although it is easy to find examples of occupations that are feminized, either historically or in the contemporary United States, relatively few occupations have undergone a substantial change in gender composition over time. One example is clerical work in the late nineteenth and early twentieth centuries. Another is teaching.

"Teaching" is a highly diverse occupation. Some teachers teach young children; others teach young (or older) adults. Some teachers specialize in a single subject, while others teach many subjects. This essay is not about teaching in all of its diversity but rather focuses primarily on individuals employed in elementary and secondary education—that is, grade school and high school. It is useful to begin with some figures from the federal population census. Taken every 10 years, the census provides a (mostly) representative "snapshot" of the American population. Since 1860, the censuses have recorded the occupations of men and women who had an occupation to report. Although there are many issues involved in the interpretation of the census beyond the scope of this essay, for our purposes the data shown in Table IX.1 are sufficiently accurate to establish two major points.

Throughout the twentieth century, including up to the very present, the overwhelming majority of teachers have been women. At the turn of the twentieth century, the proportion of teachers who were female was 74 percent. The proportion climbed to a high of 84 percent shortly after World War I and then slipped back down to 71 percent just after World War II. From 1950 to the present, the female share held steady in the range of 71 percent to 76 percent. In 2000, the most recent year for which census data are available, the proportion of females among teachers was 76 percent.

Fluctuations aside, teaching in the United States was feminized throughout the twentieth century. The twentieth century witnessed an enormous expansion in the range of occupations held by women, particularly in professions such as law, medicine, and business management. An obvious question, which we return to later in the essay, is why this expansion evidently did not siphon more women from teaching.

Table IX.1 Percent of Females in Teaching: United States, 1860–1900

Census year	Percent of female teachers
1860	59.9 (N = 1,134)
1870	66.8 (N = 1,320)
1880	67.6 (N = 2,310)
1900	74.0 (N = 2,088)
1910	80.4 (N = 2,474)
1920	83.8 (N = 7,321)
1930	80.2 (N = 1,888)
1940	74.8 (N = 10,786)
1950	71.3 (N = 10,627)
1960	76.7 (N = 21,944)
1970	73.8 (N = 36,403)
1980	71.6 (N = 44,471)
1990	74.0 (N = 53,695)
2000	75.5 (N = 58,560)

Source: All years, integrated public use microdata samples of the U.S. census; see www.ipums.umn.edu. To be included in the calculations, individuals had to be between the ages of 15 and 79 and report their occupation as "teaching" (occupation code #93). For further details, contact the authors.

The twentieth-century pattern also invites a second query. Was teaching similarly feminized in the nineteenth century? Perhaps women have always dominated instruction in the "lower" subjects from the earliest days of the Republic, if not before.

The census data in Table IX.1 give a mixed response to this question. It is clear that the percent female was rising from 1860 to 1900. Did the upward trend begin in 1860 or predate it? This is an important question because the 1860s was no ordinary decade—it was the decade of the American Civil War and reconstruction efforts that followed.

The experience of the twentieth century suggests that wars can bring about changes in the gender composition of occupations. The economic rationale is simple: Men who would be performing certain jobs during peacetime are otherwise occupied during war and the jobs are too valuable to be left undone. During World War II, women took on numerous occupations formerly held by men, particularly in durable goods manufacturing, as the imagery of "Rosie the Riveter" attests. We know that some of the occupational gains experienced by women in the 1940s were sustained for older women (Goldin, 1990).

The figures in Table IX.1 are suggestive of a Civil War effect, because the percent female rose sharply in the 1860s but not in the 1870s. However, this is only suggestive because we do not have an estimate for 1850; it is possible that the percent female rose as strongly in the 1850s as in the 1860s. In addition, the percent female rose during the 1890s almost as much as during the 1860s—and the 1890s increase cannot be attributed to the Civil War, for obvious reasons.

Fortunately, it is possible to roughly estimate the magnitude of the Civil War effect on the percentage of females in teaching. The census is the only nationally representative source on the gender composition of teaching in the nineteenth century, but it is hardly the only source. Various states published annual education reports, and these sometimes included the gender breakdown of the teaching force. The state data are not fully comparable to the federal data nor are all states covered, but we believe the data are sufficiently reliable and the coverage sufficiently broad to provide some insight into the impact of the Civil War.

A statistical analysis, conducted by the authors, of the available data for 13 states over the period 1840 to 1915 suggests that, during the War itself, the percent female, on average, was elevated by nearly 12 percentage points above what it would have been otherwise. Although some of this effect eventually eroded (as similarly happened for women's work in general during the two World Wars), slightly more than half (approximately seven percentage points) appears to have been a long run or permanent effect. The permanent impact equals approximately the increase in feminization that would have occurred over about a decade and a half in the absence of the Civil War.

Why did the wartime substitution of female for male teachers persist after the end of the conflict? The commentary of school boards prior to the War suggests that many school officials harbored reservations against employing female teachers, especially in the winter sessions when the student population included teenage boys. Female teachers, according to this view, were less capable of disciplining older boys than male teachers. This prejudice appears to have eroded, however, during the War when the practical experience of female teachers proved otherwise. The practical experience also validated a fundamental economic advantage that female teachers had over male teachers: They were cheaper to employ. A school board could staff its schools entirely with female teachers and save money. But cost considerations were decisive only if school boards—and, ultimately, taxpayers and parents—could be persuaded that female teachers could deliver the same quality of teaching services as male teachers.

This had long been the belief in New England. During the colonial period, women taught very young children in so-called "dame schools," an organizational form that migrated from England along with the colonists. The argument, familiar to a modern audience, was that women were the "natural" caretakers of young children and hence their natural teachers.

From the early beginning of the dame school, the school year in New England evolved into a two-tier system divided into winter and summer sessions. Women quickly dominated teaching in the summer sessions but lagged behind in the winter term when older boys attended and the subjects taught, such as Latin, required a high degree of preparation. But gradually, as institutional structures and attitudes changed in ways that facilitated girls' continued learning beyond some rudimentary level, the pool of females qualified to teach more advanced subjects expanded. Women eventually came to dominate the winter sessions, as well, most likely because of these improvements in their educational qualifications. In Massachusetts in 1842, 95 percent of the teachers during the summer session were women, whereas only 33 percent during the winter session were women. By 1860, the overall percent female among Massachusetts teachers was 78 percent compared with 62 percent in 1842. This increase cannot be explained by increases in the percent female during the summer session (since this was already close to 100 percent) nor by increases in the summer session's proportion of the total teaching force; rather, the increase can only be explained by a rise in the proportion of female teachers during the winter term.

The Northeast was in the forefront of early feminization. Elsewhere a distinctive regional pattern was apparent, perhaps nowhere more prominent than below the Mason-Dixon Line where men, not women, dominated in teaching. Even right up to the eve of the Civil War, only 65 percent of teachers in urban areas and 36 percent of those in rural areas of the South were female. By comparison, females comprised 81 percent and 84 percent of the teaching force in New England for urban and rural areas, respectively. Many factors may have contributed to the stark regional divide. To take one example, economic historians have documented that the wages of women relative to men outside of teaching were higher in the South than in the North before the Civil War; other things equal, a higher relative wage would mean fewer women hired relative to men. While there is some evidence in favor of this economic explanation for the lag in feminization in the South as well as elsewhere, detailed statistical analysis suggests that the primary factors involve institutions and culture. The South, unlike the North, did not develop dame schools nor did it develop a two-tier system. These institutions, it seems, provided the necessary experience with female teachers to overcome prevailing stereotypes.

The role of culture and institutions in shaping attitudes toward female teachers is also evident in regional variation in the North. Analysis of the geographic variation in the prevalence of female teachers on the eve of the Civil War reveals the potent effect of settlers' origins. Illinois offers an instructive case study. In Illinois counties that were predominantly settled by Yankees, female teachers were quite common; but where settlement was dominated by Southerners, male teachers predominated. This pattern remains after a detailed statistical analysis that takes account of a myriad of other factors that might have affected the relative use of female teachers.

Table IX.1 demonstrates that the proportion of females in teaching continued to rise in the late nineteenth and early twentieth centuries before peaking shortly after World War I. By 1870, slightly more than 80 percent of teachers in New England were female, and, thus, there was relatively little scope for further change. However, elsewhere in the country, particularly in the South where only 33 percent of teachers were women in 1870, there was considerable room for further increase.

We should note that aggregate data for Southern states after the Civil War obscure the fact that two separate school systems existed, one for African American students and another for Whites. Although prior to the Civil War the proportion of African Americans in teaching was negligible, perhaps 1 percent in both Northern and Southern regions, by the 1880s African Americans comprised about 20 percent of the teaching force in the South. Despite sharp differences in other respects between the two types of schools, the extent of feminization was similar. In 1880, 52 percent of African American teachers and 56 percent of White teachers in the South were female. In 1910, these figures were 77 percent and 76 percent, respectively.

We have already touched upon the effect of experimenting with female teachers during the Civil War and the evidence that this experimentation had a permanent impact. But the size of this effect cannot account for all the feminization that took place over the half century after the War.

Another important factor was the spread of graded schools. In a graded school, students were segregated in classrooms according to their educational level (grade), which, for the most part, meant that they were segregated by age. Older children, including older boys, could be taught by men while younger children could be taught by women; there was, in other words, the possibility of "division of labor." Grading depended on population density and, especially for a given population of school age, on the enrollment rate. A small town or village could "afford" a graded school only if a sufficient number of persons of school age were enrolled in school. There is abundant evidence that grading was associated with a higher proportion of female teachers. For example, in Michigan in 1880, the proportion of female teachers in graded schools was close to 80 percent, 11 percentage points higher than in schools lacking grades. The share of graded schools in total enrollments increased rapidly after the Civil War, except in the South where the growth occurred somewhat later in the late nineteenth and early twentieth centuries. As graded schools expanded relative to ungraded schools, the proportion of female teachers increased.

Yet it would be a mistake to attribute all, or even most, of the increased use of female teachers after the Civil War to the spread of graded schools. Detailed individual-level data on teachers and their locations from the federal censuses of 1860, 1880, and 1910 reveal that the majority of the feminization of the teaching force between 1860 and 1910 occurred in purely rural areas where the expansion of graded schools could not have been the driving force. The Michigan data just noted are telling on this point because they identify graded and ungraded schools. Between 1880 and 1910, the proportion of female teachers rose from 69 percent to 84 percent in Michigan's ungraded schools. While the proportion of female teachers in graded schools in Michigan in 1910 was higher than this—88 percent—the gap is small relative to the change over time. The conclusion is clear: A significant shift toward female teachers took place before World War II in ungraded schools and, therefore, cannot be attributed to changes in school organization. This shift, it seems, reflected a diffusion of ideas that originated elsewhere—that women could be employed successfully as teachers even if it were uneconomical to grade the schools. By the late nineteenth century, boys and girls were mastering the same basic curriculum, and objections to female inability to discipline older children seemed to have eroded. When female teachers were seen as capable of supplying the same "bundle" of educational services as male teachers, school boards hired them in increasing numbers. The boards also realized that, in hiring female teachers, it was possible to shift expenditures on teachers (as long as class sizes did not decline) to other, worthwhile endeavors like increasing the length of the school year. The increased demand for female teachers bid up their wages relative to men but not by so much as to eliminate the economic incentive for hiring them.

Although women came to dominate teaching by the late nineteenth and early twentieth centuries, this does not mean that teaching was "gender neutral" with respect to economic rewards. Analysis of personnel records of school systems reveals that, early in the century, women were far less likely than men to "manage"—that is, become a principal or another type of administrator—even if their qualifications on paper (education and experience) were similar.

This gender gap in administrative positions effectively widened the gender gap in teacher's pay, both directly and indirectly. Because administrators were paid much better than teachers, had the gender gap in administrative positions been smaller, the gender gap in teacher's pay would have been smaller. Also, administrators set policies on issues such as salary schedules and hiring policies (for example, the marriage bars discussed below). The absence of women in this decision-making process likely perpetuated the creation of gender-specific opportunities for higher pay. Indeed, data from four cities where extensive annual personnel files were available indicate that up to 58 percent of the gender gap in promotion was due to gender discrimination.

A gender gap in teacher's pay existed long before the twentieth century—indeed, we emphasized earlier that the gap was a financial incentive to employ female teachers. But, while some of the gap in the early part of the century can be attributed to gender differences in education and experience, much of the gap is a pure difference with no explanation other than that it was possible to pay women less and get away with it. Analysis of the personnel files just mentioned indicate that between 63 percent and 84 percent of the observed gap in female/male wages was unaccounted for by differences in education or experience and, thus, attributed to wage discrimination. Indeed, school systems throughout the country were more than willing to embody such differentials in formal salary schedules—one for women, the other for men. Women's progress in teaching was also affected by marriage bars; a school board with such a bar either refused to hire a married woman (a hire bar) or fired a woman upon marriage (a retain bar). These policies reinforced the gender gap in wages since female teachers who were likely to ever marry had fewer incentives to acquire training or experience that would increase their pay status. Marriage bars were extremely common in teaching during the first half of the twentieth century but eventually gave way during World War II.

For much of American history, teaching was one of a few occupations that were readily open to educated, intellectually talented young women. In recent decades, however, women have entered many professions formerly dominated by men, notably law and medicine. The labor force participation rate of married women especially has risen over the twentieth century. A common index of gender representation, the percent female in the occupation divided by the percent female of the entire labor force, illustrates this gender desegregation well. In the 1960s, within the field of medicine, for example, this index ranged from 0.20 to 0.33; for law it was nearly zero (0.08). By 1990, the proportion of women in these professions was much more representative and the index was 0.79 for medicine and 0.94 for law (Corcoran, Evans, & Schwab, 2002). Regional differences existed in the timing and magnitude of gender desegregation, with the most rapid and extensive changes occurring in the Northeast region. Also, increases in the proportion of college-educated women in professional occupations were slightly smaller for Black women than their White counterparts. For example, the share of White college-educated women in medicine, law, and engineering increased by 33 percentage points between 1960 and 1990, while the share increased by 29 percentage points for Black women. Despite these differences, the overall trend of expanding opportunities for females during the twentieth century was undeniable.

Has the expansion of job opportunities for women outside of teaching in recent decades made teaching less feminized? At present, the answer appears to be no. The percent female in teaching has shown no sustained downward trend since 1960, the period over which educated women entered occupations other than teaching (see Table IX.1).

However, while the percent female in teaching has remained stable in the face of expanding job opportunities, there is some evidence that the most able women are increasingly opting out of teaching. The strongest evidence of such "opting-out" concerns trends in standardized test scores. For example, bringing together several sources of data, Bacolod (forthcoming) finds that the percent of female teachers who scored below the twentieth percentile on various standardized tests increased from 8 percent of female teachers born in the 1940s to 19 percent of those born in the 1960s. The fraction of those scoring above the 80th percentile fell from 41 percent to 19 percent across these same cohorts. These trends are important because, if teaching commands a smaller share of highly able women than in the past, the aggregate rate of growth of human capital in the economy and therefore the overall rate of economic growth may slow.

While important for other reasons, concerns about the quality of teachers may have few implications for overall gender composition. In particular, the supply of college graduates has grown much more rapidly among women than men in recent decades, thereby ensuring a ready potential source of female teachers. While other occupations have opened up, teaching still remains an attractive option for many women. Thus, it seems likely that teaching in the United States will remain feminized for the foreseeable future.

REFERENCES AND FURTHER READINGS

Bacolod, M.P. (forthcoming). Do alternative opportunities matter? The role of female labor markets in the decline of teacher quality, 1960–1990. *Review of Economics and Statistics.*

Corcoran, S., Evans, W., & Schwab, R. (2002). *Changing labor market opportunities for women and the quality of teachers 1957–1992* (Working Paper No. 9180). Cambridge, MA: National Bureau of Economic Research.

Goldin, C. (1990). *Understanding the gender gap: An economic history of American women.* New York: Oxford University Press.

Murnane, R.J., Singer, J.D., Willet, J.B., Kemple, J.J., & Olsen, R.J. (1991). *Who will teach? Policies that matter.* Cambridge, MA: Harvard University Press.

Perlmann, J., & Margo, R.A. (2001). *Women's work? American schoolteachers, 1850–1920.* Chicago: University of Chicago Press.

Podgursky, M., Monroe, R., & Watson, D. (2004). The academic quality of public school teachers: An analysis of entry and exit behavior. *Economics of Education Review, 23*(5), 507–518.

Linda K. Carter

Robert A. Margo

Leadership Styles

In education, as in other types of organizations, gender and situational characteristics interact to construct patterns of gender differences that vary with circumstances. When gender differences are evident, they tend to be characterized by agentic and communal behavior. Agentic leadership is task oriented, assertive, and directive; communal leadership focuses on interpersonal relationships, supporting others, and not seeking attention. When gender differences are evident, men display more agentic behavior and women more communal behavior. The extent of gender differences in leadership style depends on characteristics of schools, such as the prevalence of gender stereotypes and discrimination, proportions of women and men in leadership and subordinate roles, hierarchical organization, emphasis on stereotypically masculine tasks, and historical reliance on masculine leadership models that stress coercive power and competition. In educational settings, women prefer leadership styles that focus on organizational and social transformation, collaboration, and empowerment of others. Even in educational settings that have the characteristics that promote masculinized leadership patterns, women have developed coping strategies that allow them to be successful leaders, contributing to a larger proportion of women leaders at all levels of education and to transforming both institutions and the definition of leadership.

GENDER DIFFERENCES IN LEADERSHIP

Are there gender differences in leadership styles in educational contexts? While there is considerable scholarly research on gender in educational literature, little addresses this question, and what does is generally anecdotal or qualitative and relies on very small samples. Research on gender and leadership in broader managerial contexts is helpful, in that it demonstrates quite clearly that leadership behavior is strongly influenced by social context, that is, gender differences exist in some social situations, but not in others. Social scientists can make equally plausible cases to support both the absence and existence of gender differences in leadership styles. The key to this apparent contradiction is understanding the context in which leadership occurs. Hence, rather than dwelling on the extent of differences, it is more productive to discuss situational characteristics that are correlated with gendered stylistic patterns.

What are those stylistic patterns? Alice H. Eagly and her colleagues use the distinction between agentic and communal attributes to describe these differences. Agentic leadership behavior includes focus on tasks and problems, assertive speech, influence attempts, and calling attention to oneself; communal behaviors include focus on relationship and interpersonal problems, tentative speech, supporting others, taking direction from others, and not seeking attention (Eagly & Johannesen-Schmidt, 2001). Popular and academic literature that purports to describe gendered leadership styles generally proposes a distinction along the lines of agentic and communal behavior, using terms such as task-oriented and interpersonally oriented style, participative and directive, or democratic and autocratic. A review of multiple studies on leadership behavior by Carli and Eagly (2001) found that women display more positive social behavior and agreement than men, whereas men are more task oriented and disagree more than women.

However, this distinction is not a dichotomous dimension, but rather agentic behavior is defined more by the status of participants in an interaction regardless of their gender. In contrast, communal behavior is related to gender, with women engaging it more, often especially when interacting with other women. Research looking at the interaction of gender roles and organizational roles implies that women and men in the same leadership role behave more similarly than not, so some gender variations may be the result of gender differences in the roles occupied by women and men. Informal actions that are not functional aspects of a given leadership role may be the most discretionary and most likely to vary with gender, such as the topics of casual office conversation.

An important element of gendered leadership patterns is the influence of stereotypic expectations of women's and men's behavior. Female and male leaders are evaluated differently in experimental studies where behaviors are equated; women using direct language, disagreement, and autocratic behavior are regarded more negatively than men exhibiting the same behavior. Women leaders appear to be more constrained by gender stereotypes than men. Thus, women may learn that they are more effective when they employ communal leadership strategies, possibly to the extent that they internalize gender-stereotypic expectations and leadership styles. These kinds of factors lead to the argument that congruity of leader roles and gender roles is a critical factor in people's choice of leadership behavior, evaluations of that behavior by others, and effectiveness as leaders. Therefore, the question of whether women and men lead differently is meaningless without concurrent analysis of relevant contextual variables.

Furthermore, emphasis on the question of whether women and men have different leadership styles encourages analyses that overgeneralize, or essentialize, female and male differences. As with most gender differences, women's and men's behavior overlaps greatly, and there is much more variability within each gender than between them. Focusing solely on gender differences legitimizes a dualistic view of gender that can be seen in much of the literature on leadership in education, greatly oversimplifying the role of gender and exaggerating differences out of context.

THE CONTEXT OF EDUCATION

What are characteristics of the educational context that influence the extent that gender interacts with leadership style preferences? While there is little controlled experimental evidence about these interactions, much of the literature on leadership in education implicitly discusses context variables that promote or mitigate gender differences. Although many of the resources for this section concern higher education in the United States, authors writing about elementary and secondary school principals and superintendents and about educational systems in other English-speaking countries describe similar characteristics.

As in most areas of human endeavor, historically men have been leaders in education at all levels. Women leaders in higher education emerged at women's colleges or as deans of women in early coeducational schools at the beginning of the twentieth century. Interviews with women leaders from different generations demonstrate that leadership styles vary with changing sociohistorical contexts. For example, in one study, those who came of age during the Depression and World War II emphasized the value of education for achieving equality for women and often adopted male models of leadership. Those who came of age during the 1960s, with the civil rights, anti-Vietnam war, and feminist movements, focused on concerns about equal opportunity in education and other work settings and the inclusion of women in scholarly and curricular concerns. Those who were ascending to leadership positions in the 1990s extended those values to creating alternative modes of leadership.

Also, like other areas of human behavior, education is heavily influenced by gender discrimination and stereotyping. Work on the nature of gender stereotypes is instructive for understanding dynamics in regard to leadership. Stereotypes of out-groups often invoke the characteristics of sociability and competence, which for women take the form of the false dichotomy of sociable housewife versus competent career woman, as if sociability and competence were mutually exclusive. Such stereotypes interact with other situational factors, as when women in male-dominated businesses experience contradictory expectations more than those in gender-balanced offices. The gender imbalance in higher education, which is more pronounced in higher leadership positions and more prestigious institutions, indicates that women are under more pressure to perform competently than male peers. Countering stereotypes may be necessary to establish credibility as leaders, hence the advice frequently offered to women pursuing academic administrative careers to develop extensive expertise in finance, strategic planning, and research to overcome stereotypes of women's weaknesses. Furthermore, gender stereotypes and other stereotypes certainly interact. For example, gendered ethnic stereotypes that African American women are aggressive and hostile and Asian, Native American, and Hispanic women are deferent and passive impact perceived leadership ability. In general, women are stereotyped as less likely to demonstrate important leadership behaviors than men. The incongruity between leadership roles and female gender roles leads to prejudicial actions, such that men are more likely to have opportunities and to emerge as leaders than women.

The hierarchical organization of education is another contextual factor. Either overtly or implicitly, hierarchies assume gendered constructs. Hierarchies are endemic to education. Schools are ranked in prestige and reputation, disciplines vary in status, size of tuition is equated with value, and faculty salaries are related to institutional prestige. While it would be simplistic to argue that hierarchy and masculine values are perfectly correlated, traditional hierarchical management does mimic masculine qualities, in the extreme, a "military model" designed to control the role of emotion and caring in organizations. Feminist writers often note that organizations change to value human needs more when a critical mass of women employees is reached, particularly women leaders. While the numbers of women in education at all levels have increased, women administrators remain in the minority and are in the smallest proportion in the most prestigious colleges or positions. As schools adopt business models, hierarchical line management has replaced collegial governance in many places, perhaps undermining changes normally facilitated by increased proportions of women.

Male dominance in education has been ignored, perhaps because it seems obvious. However, ignoring male dominance has lead to failure to thoroughly analyze how deeply embedded gender constructs are in organizations. Meta-analyses of studies of leadership effectiveness corroborate the relationship between perceived effectiveness and situational expectations, as women leaders are seen as less effective when the proportion of male subordinates is greater, in highly masculinized environments like military organizations, and when a larger percentage of male raters are evaluating them. In highly masculinized organizations, men are the numerical majority, tasks are stereotypically masculine, the main goal is task completion, and hierarchy and coercive power are stressed. Leadership in masculinized contexts depends on status, self-promotion, competition, and autocratic behavior, all of which are viewed negatively when engaged in by women. Despite some evidence that education provides more opportunity than other work settings, in that women are perceived as somewhat more effective in education, government, and social services than in other kinds of organizations, education remains masculinized to some extent. For example, historical accounts of leaders in the community college arena focus on a few "great men" who have shaped the role of these colleges in higher education using frontier, pioneer, athletic, and military images. To the extent that leadership characteristics are inferred from these metaphors, the leadership styles of women and ethnic minorities are seen as deficient, limiting their access to leadership positions.

Gender is a status characteristic in our culture, giving men an edge in any situation where status matters. Women attempting to improve their own stature face a double bind because self-promotion by women can backfire. Women who are modest about their successes are recognized more than women who are moderately self-promoting. Furthermore, women must demonstrate greater competence than similar men to gain recognition, even when they have achieved high status positions. As educational management adopts corporate models, women may be further disadvantaged. Solving financial and political problems has become more prominent in the role of president. Women college presidents comment often that they feel they must work harder than male presidents to gain the confidence of their boards of trustees and are given a second chance less often after failure. Women of color believe they are especially vulnerable in this regard.

Too little is known about the interaction of gender with other cultural identities, such as ethnicity, sexual orientation, or disability, but gender and these other identity characteristics undoubtedly interact with status in complicated ways. Some educators feel that race stereotypes overpower gender expectations in treatment from others; others feel that gender is more salient; others say that gender and ethnicity are so intertwined that the debate is pointless. The role of these highly salient characteristics requires considerable further research.

GENDERED LEADERSHIP STYLES

Although readers must be mindful of these complex multivariate interactions and gaps in knowledge about leadership, analyses of leadership style do suggest patterns associated with gender that may be either the result of gender-related values or choices based on an understanding of what is effective in gendered contexts.

Women leaders often value institutional transformation explicitly, considering the ultimate reward for their persistence in academic administration creating a more congenial environment for future generations of both female and male administrators. Women leaders also report commitment to broader social transformation. For example, African American administrators frequently mention an obligation to give back to the community and mentor others. Other administrators focus on transforming the very nature of leadership by transforming the culture of one's own organization or broader societal notions of leadership. Social values go beyond focusing only on women to explicitly include work against racism, violence, and heterosexism, as well.

Another theme in writings by women administrators is the importance of understanding power relations. To succeed and transform leadership, people must understand their position and relative power in an organization. While acknowledging that women must be politically attuned to these power dynamics in their institutions, women academic leaders often say they are ambivalent about the perceived need to play power games to advance before being able to change the rules of the game. They also feel ambivalent about being pleased by their ability to use power to accomplish goals, simultaneously recognizing that it plays into the masculine definitions of leadership. In addition to finding it difficult to become assimilated while articulating a critique of male management models, feminist administrators are seldom concerned with obtaining power or establishing strong personal claims to authorship. But leaders must understand the leadership culture of their organizations, since the masculinized context so frequently found in higher education includes the assumption that effective leadership depends on status and power manifested through autocratic behavior. Understanding politics essentially means understanding the nature of formal and informal power in academe in general and in a particular institution. One way of reconciling ambivalence about playing power games is to define power as the ability to influence outcomes, rather than the ability to influence people, as one writer noted, using a metaphor of "expanding the pie" of influence, rather than a "fixed boundary" view of power (Valverde, 2003).

This ambivalence is one of many strains women leaders discuss. Organizational transformation often evokes resistance that creates stresses for women administrators, such as isolation, difficulty balancing work and personal life, self-doubt, and institutional intransigence. Fortunately, women educators also give advice about survival strategies to aspiring administrators. For instance, African American women administrators consistently describe specific tactics they use to cope with ethnic and gender discrimination, such as emphasizing the importance of self-knowledge and self-care. They counsel African American educators to develop a strong sense of their own values, beliefs, and abilities and adopt reflective leadership, attuned to long-term goals when short-term tactics require compromise.

Another prominent theme is defining situations rather than being defined by them, emphasizing that survival depends on interpretation and the meanings applied to situations, as well as on actions. If, rather than using military metaphors to describe leaders, one used metaphors of weaving, cultivating, and networking, leadership becomes a process of creating, empowering, facilitating, collaborating, and educating instead of a personality characteristic. Women often try to articulate how they lead with the express purpose of educating others about alternative modes of leadership.

Avoiding simplistic dichotomies and listening to many opinions are also values reported by women leaders. But senior administrators or boards of trustees, who define leadership as making fast and firm decisions, may misunderstand inclusive discussion; those who expect administrators to "fix things" easily will not recognize the leadership needed to arrive at complex solutions. Once again, this evokes the double bind: Women who are directive and autocratic are less effective than those who are not.

Collaboration is another important element of women's leadership styles and is consistently considered a fundamental tenet of feminist leadership. Collaboration is effective because participatory decision making is satisfying for participants and produces results and plans that people feel they own. Not only do women use collaborative leadership more often than men, they are expected to and are less effective if they choose more authoritarian leadership tactics. While much of this research focuses on women leaders in general, descriptions of women's leadership styles in higher education are consistent with researchers' conclusion that women are expected to be warmer and more collaborative in their leadership styles than men, who are expected to be more task oriented. For example, in interviews, women administrators emphasized interdependence with followers, community service orientation, and ability to create conditions of trust, caring, fairness, objectivity, focus, and vision. Skills they depend upon included empowerment, team building, and facilitation, along with problem solving and risk taking. In the framework of relational psychology, authors discuss academic presidential leadership based on connectedness, rather than control and domination. Women define their identity in terms of interdependent relations, viewing the world as made up of interconnected physical and social entities governed by needs other than control.

Despite its value, collaboration is not an easy solution to leadership problems. As noted previously, it may limit women's ability to be seen as leaders. Women presidents may be misunderstood, marginalized, or trivialized when they choose strategies different from conventional views of leadership, inadvertently reinforcing the stereotype of women as nurturers. In masculinized institutional cultures, hostile members or those fearful of the consequences of outspokenness may undermine collaboration so thoroughly that a leader has no opportunity to demonstrate the benefits of collaboration.

The expectations that women will always be collaborative can also create dilemmas for women leaders. Female and male faculty of colleges with women presidents perceive their presidents to be less collaborative than the presidents believe of themselves. Women faculty who are passionate about wanting collaborative presidents may have naive expectations about situational constraints under which presidents operate. The strengths that women leaders may bring can be overshadowed by expectations that they have complete freedom or control over decision making. Women presidents are keenly aware of this paradox, reporting that they try hard to identify when collaboration is inappropriate, as one respondent said, to distinguish when the outcome of a decision is more important than the process. For example, college leaders themselves often report anecdotally that highly masculine leadership behavior is expected by boards of trustees or central system administrators, creating a situation in which some important constituency will be dissatisfied with any leadership style.

Women from ethnic backgrounds that conflict with their preferred feminist modes of leadership encounter other dilemmas. For example, Native American and Samoan educational leaders report that being respectful of elders—men in their cultures—sometimes clashes with empowering women or makes it difficult for them to supervise men. Women also sometimes report the confusion between new leadership styles and selfless giving and motherhood. Because motherly nurturance is not expected to be reciprocated, women feel their efforts are taken for granted and not seen as evidence of leadership ability. Nurturing behavior, therefore, may discourage others' kindness and reduce recognition of leadership skills.

The desire to collaborate and help others may pose career problems for women, who see service to the community and to others similar to them as important, while service in academic departments does not necessarily enhance prospects for administrative leadership positions. In higher education, for instance, scholarly work is sometimes more important than administrative experience in selection of administrators.

Negotiating paradoxical values and expectations is necessary to survive long enough to be a change agent. Women who are uncomfortable with a double standard about appropriate leadership behavior often choose to work to change either gender-based expectations about leadership or conceptions of leadership to include more facilitative and socially positive behavior.

Thus, women lean toward leadership styles that emphasize organizational and social transformation, sensitivity to power dynamics, and collaboration. Educational contexts produce paradoxes that require women to negotiate through sociohistorical and stereotypic expectations, hierarchical organizations and masculinized cultures, and interactions of status with gender and other identity characteristics. Despite these constraints, women leaders have developed strategies to cope with these expectations and are making gradual, but steady, advancement in leadership positions in education at all levels.

REFERENCES AND FURTHER READINGS

Benjamin, L. (Ed.). (1997). *Black women in the academy: Promises and perils.* Gainesville: University Press of Florida.

Blackmore, J. (1999). *Troubling women: Feminism, leadership and educational change.* Buckingham, England: Open University Press.

Carli, L.L., & Eagly, A.H. (2001). Gender, hierarchy, and leadership: An introduction. *Journal of Social Issues, 57*(4), 629–636.

Eagly, A.H., & Johannesen-Schmidt, M.C. (2001). The leadership styles of women and men. *Journal of Social Issues, 57*(4), 781–797.

Eagly, A.H., & Karau, S.J. (2002). Role congruity theory of prejudice toward female leaders. *Psychological Review, 109*(3), 573–598.

Glazer-Raymo, J. (1999). *Shattering the myths: Women in academe.* Baltimore: Johns Hopkins University Press.

Madden, M.E. (2005). Gender and leadership in higher education. *Psychology of Women Quarterly, 29*(1), 3–14.

Nidiffer, J., & Bashaw, C.T. (Eds.). (2001). *Women administrators in higher education: Historical and contemporary perspectives.* Albany: State University of New York Press.

Reynolds, C. (Ed.). (2003). *Women and school leadership: International perspectives.* Albany: State University of New York Press.

Valverde, L.A. (2003). *Leaders of color in higher education.* New York: Alta Mira.

Margaret E. Madden

Masculinity, Homophobia, and Teaching

Feminist theory and men's studies have provided important insights into the relationships between gender, sexuality, and schooling. These fields of inquiry are varied in their theoretical analyses. One of the shared grounds of these diverse approaches has been to establish the gendered nature of schooling processes. Much mainstream work on schooling tends to see it as gender neutral. This means that at a commonsense level, schooling practices, discipline and control, the formal and hidden curriculum, streaming and administrative systems are assumed to operate beyond the sphere of gender relations. This framework is highly dependent on viewing schooling practices outside of meanings. Thus, educational research within this framework has focused on teaching as a practice that is simply connected to neutral educational objectives. However, research on schooling has highlighted how men, women, gays, and lesbians have differential access to schooling processes and hierarchies within them. Thus, the teaching profession itself contains differential power relations that are circumscribed by gender and sexuality. The usefulness of this argument is that it assists in identifying the particular patterns and structures of gendered relationships that are apparent in schools.

In response, it is argued that the mapping of gender and sexuality can involve looking at teaching practices themselves. In other words, teaching and administration are not neutral practices but contain a series of gendered and sexualized meanings and understandings. Thus, masculinity, homophobia, and teaching contain gendered values, and this is crucial to understanding how power relations are distributed. Haywood and Mac an Ghaill (2003) consider this area in great detail and argue that schooling is not simply a profession that meets educational objectives; it does this through the constitution of identity, subjectivity, and desire. This is not to displace more materially orientated accounts but to consider that such accounts need to be contextualized by how schooling processes are gendered through experience, understanding, and the attribution of meaning. Work on gender has suggested that schools through these meanings offer interpretations about what it means to be "male" or "female." More specifically, schooling processes contain gendered attributes that prioritize certain gendered identities while subordinating others. As a consequence, a focus on teaching has tended to consider the effects of teaching on the formation of student gendered and sexual identities. However, it is becoming increasingly important to consider how teaching itself is gendered. Furthermore, in order to understand more fully the specific gender dynamics of teaching in schools, it is necessary to examine the interrelationship between broader themes, such as dominant conceptions of power, authority, management, and emotional commitment.

Thus, the area of masculinity, homophobia, and teaching is complex. There is no "direct effects" model that can adequately capture how teaching impacts gender and sexual identities. What can be done is a process of establishing how masculinity and homophobia constitute teaching. Central to this constitution is the changing (state-led) nature of teaching practice.

At local levels, a reconstruction of teaching has taken place, and masculinity and homophobia are relevant in that process. Schools do not stand outside other social relations, and there is much work to be done in exploring how race/ethnicity impact masculinity, homophobia, and teaching. Alongside this, a relatively hidden area of teaching concerns how gender and sexuality impact the categories of adult/child. This is important as there continues to be a conflation between student and child and we need further data on how this relationship is lived out. Finally, schools need to be understood as shaped by a broader cultural imagination. They often become the space for the living out of values, memories, myths, national identities, and traditions, all of which contain gendered and sexual significances.

MASCULINITY

During the 1980s and 1990s, research in education opened up the discussion of masculinity, arguing that masculinities should be conceptualized in terms of relationships. Moving away from the singular "role" model based on gender, it was suggested that masculinities need to be conceptualized in relation to other categories. For example, studies indicated that the social, ethnic, class, and sexual specificities of male identities within local sites of schooling influence the range of masculinities that are inhabited. As Connell (1993) has claimed, different masculinities are constituted in relation to other masculinities and to femininities through the structure of gender relations. This led to the theorizing of masculinity in terms of multiple masculinities. For example, teaching involves a number of masculine styles. As a result, there are different masculinities with differential access to power, practices of power, and differential effects of power. If we assume that the curriculum produces spaces in which masculinities are produced, it follows that as the curriculum changes, so will masculinities. It should be added that the interplay between teaching and masculinity does not work in a deterministic way; students can effectively negotiate curriculum agendas. They do, however, represent a structure, a technique, or practice of power that is relatively fixed, closing off and opening up potential masculine subjectivities. At different times, dominant institutional styles sanction acceptable and unacceptable gender and sexual identities.

TEACHING MASCULINITIES

At a time of rapid change, teachers are currently constructing their work identities within the context of selecting and combining strategic responses to contradictory workplace demands. However, teacher "choices" cannot be understood in terms of any simple commercial metaphors. In other words, they do not take place in a sociohistorical vacuum. Dominant state and occupational discourses circumscribe the "gendering" and "regendering" of these different work practices. The restructuring of state schooling has resulted in increased complexities and contradictions. A highly salient feature is the promotion of new gender-specific hierarchies of domination and subordination. There is a long history of female teachers identifying discriminatory sex-role allocation of male teachers to positions of authority and management. More recently, this has been displaced by a growing concern with the remasculinization of the whole workplace. More specifically, in England, a legacy of the restructuring of state schooling in the 1990s is the masculinization of the administrative functions that have come to predominate school life. High status has been ascribed to the "hard masculine" functions of: the accountant, the curriculum coordinator, and the information and communications technology expert. At the same time, female teachers are associated with and directed into the "soft feminine" functions of pastoral support and counseling. In short, the remasculinization of teaching is being played out within conventional cultural forms that split that of the rational and that of the emotional. This reflects a broader division in the social world where reason is defined in opposition to nature, and nature is conceptualized as emotions, feelings, and desires.

In a study of an English secondary school, Mac an Ghaill (1994) identified three teacher occupational types: the Professionals, the Old Collectivists, and the New Entrepreneurs. These constituted the teachers' microculture, which served to mediate the production of a range of contradictory and fractured masculine identities that the teachers inhabited. The school principal as an institutional moral gatekeeper sponsored and elevated a hybrid form of new masculinity, whose main contradictory themes included bureaucratic centralization of control, rationality, overt forms of career ambition, collegiality, and delegation. They could be located within the projected post-Fordist era with its emphasis on small-scale, flat hierarchies and flexible teamwork, within a differentiated marketplace, in which new school systems are helping to shape new teaching cultures. They are representative of a new "masculine" authoritarianism in which overt forms of technologies of power are being displaced by "modern" forms of technical bureaucratic knowledge. They are developed in the high-tech offices of modern administration with their dominant discursive themes of managerial efficiency and economic rationality.

The Old Collectivists, who embodied an older style of public sector masculinity, were in the descendancy within the school, with the New Entrepreneurs—including the principal—in the ascendancy as the emerging dominant mode of modern masculinity. They were the "ideal teachers," whose masculinity was developed within the political nexus of managerialism, vocationalism, and commercialization, with its values of rationalism, possessive individualism, and instrumentalism. They were key agents in the development of curricular and pedagogical changes, in which education initiatives are primarily concerned, with the quantitative "masculine" world of the technology of change rather than the qualitative world of values. Their managerialist approach produced a positivist-based, technicist response that was overly preoccupied with the "how" rather than the "why" of curriculum change. The establishment of this entrepreneurial curriculum involved the reworking of conventional "masculine" commercial and industrial images in the process of aligning schools with commerce and industry.

Importantly, these ideological positions and styles manifested themselves in working relations and, more specifically, in their responses and resistances to changes in the school organization. The potential for conflicts became heightened as teachers were not only acting out their micropolitical interests in response to curriculum changes, they were simultaneously acting out their sexual politics through the deployment of masculinities. In other words, it is the teachers' relationship to the labor process that mediates their masculinity.

By representing the teachers' labor process as embodying ideas about what it means to be a man, we have illustrated that teachers' work is a set of relations in which masculinities are worked out. Teachers' work exists as another space where gender relations are producing masculine forms. Teachers' identities, ideologies, and pedagogical styles demonstrate a particular purchase on certain masculinities. It is a purchase on what kind of men they are.

HOMOPHOBIA

Contemporary accounts of masculinity and teaching tend to leave out issues of sexuality. Where it does appear, it is added on as part of a panoply of analytic tools including gender, race, ethnicity, class, and age. With the recent emergence of safety and protection as key themes of education, teaching practice has come into sharper critical focus with a range of publicly documented incidents problematizing professional conduct in schools. More recently, debates over age of consent for gay and lesbians and a moral panic around teenage pregnancy and HIV/AIDS have publicly connected issues of gender with issues of sexuality. In these debates, schools are often discursively constructed as desexualized. However, if we see sexuality as enmeshed in a set of power relations, this serves to highlight that rather than individualizing sexuality; the deployment of sexuality works within social relations of domination and subordination. Lesbian and gay theorists have argued that sexuality is a key element in the construction of our identity, both internally as a significant dimension of the self and externally as a social category imbued with cultural expectations by others and as a primary marker of difference. There is much evidence from lesbian and gay literature of the physical, psychological, and verbal abuse that lesbian and gay people systematically experience in homophobic and heterosexist societies. However, there continues to be little work available on this form of sexual oppression within schools. Stressing that sexuality is part of a process, it is suggested that sexual oppression, violence, and discrimination are a continual everyday phenomenon and not confined to extraordinary incidents, specific aspects of the curriculum, or student cultures. Sexual power relations are an implicit part of everyday schooling experiences. The sexual harassment of subordinated groups illustrates how these experiences embody normalized hegemonic masculine (hetero)sexualities.

Sexuality in schools has been seen to evidence itself through homophobic practices. It is suggested that homophobia is made up of two elements. First, homophobia is deemed to depend upon a derogatory understanding or perception of homosexuality. This depiction, it is argued, is often constituted by a fear or hatred of homosexual acts, behaviors, and identities. This means that homosexuality is often described as unnatural, abnormal, and dangerous. In contrast, heterosexuality is seen as natural, normal, and safe. The second element of homophobia is that it is premised on interactions with the emotional response to homosexuality, represented in a number of different ways. For example, in the field of social psychology, researchers have explored how homophobia can be internalized. As a result, individuals direct their own fear and loathing of homosexuality in on themselves. Such negative perceptions often result in physical, psychological, and emotional damage. At the same time, homophobia has been considered as something that is applied and used against individuals, groups, cultures, religions, or even nations.

In educational research, there is an overwhelming tendency to associate homophobia as something that concerns male teachers with the suggestion that the fear and loathing of homosexuality is a key feature of masculinity. Thus, in order to demonstrate masculinity, male teachers and students have to perform and display homophobia. For example, homophobic abuse may be directed at boys who do not correspond to the school's ideology of what a real or proper boy should do. This may concern wearing the right clothes, participating in appropriate sporting activities, and pursuing particular relationships with girls. From this perspective, homophobic practices are deemed to operate through and support gender relations; homosexuality is viewed as a nonmasculine characteristic. Building on the previous section on masculinity, it can be suggested that hegemonic masculinities secure their dominance through the use of homophobia. Thus, it operates to consolidate particular masculine styles and is central to gendered power relations, policing what are acceptable and unacceptable attitudes and behaviors.

At the same time, the centrality of masculinity may simplify a more complex picture. By suggesting that the use of derogatory language secures masculinities, an important question emerges over the position of female teachers. Can female teachers be homophobic? Do female teachers experience it? Much educational research has overwhelmingly associated homophobia as a male experience through its interconnection of homophobia with masculinity. A concept that runs parallel with homophobia is that of lesbophobia—a hatred and fear of lesbianism. This is usually applied to those who problematize the connection between heterosexual attractiveness and desirability. Although politically important to differentiate the gendered experience of fear and loathing toward different sexual minority communities, homophobia tends to operate across gendered categories. However, sexuality and gender are not identical, and the dynamics of power articulations cannot be automatically embedded within gender relations. This means that, by definition, sexuality can be "agendered," with the sexual working through a range of dimensions such as human/animal, adult/child, or animate/nonanimate. Although not dispensing with gender (for example, sometimes the mutual constitution between gender and sexuality in these accounts becomes blurred), those working within gay and lesbian frameworks articulate a politics of desire that operates through sexualities. Therefore, homophobia should be firmly located within the schools themselves as sexualized rather than simply gendered.

TEACHING HOMOPHOBIA

At the center of recent work on gay and lesbian issues in the school arena are the interconnections between sexual visibility and invisibility. Much of this work can be divided into two key areas. First, schools can be identified through an administrative structure that supports heterosexuality. Second, there is an invisibility of homosexuality in everyday school life. Homosexual visibility can be found in places such as homophobia. In one way, the (in)visibility couplet demonstrates the local specificity and diversity of sexual difference in the school context. In another way, this couplet provides entry into a gay and lesbian phenomenology, highlighting the effects of what is often institutionally led social injustice. Contained within the notion of (in)visibility is a policy of omission. Schools often make unavailable gay and lesbian sexualities as legitimate templates for sexual practice. Rather, heterosexuality becomes the model by which other sexual practices are defined. It is important to note that heterosexuality is deemed natural and normal and, thus, at an administrative level is conflated with neutrality. This means that sexuality may be present in schooling practices and procedures even though they appear to be neutral.

Research by Mills (1996) illustrates that such neutrality is an active shaper of how sexuality can enter into the schooling arena. In a secondary school in New Zealand, a number of students attempted through the use of posters to bring the issue of homophobia to the school's attention. The school refused the students' request to display the posters. In advocating neutrality, the students were silenced. In response, a number of school staff joined the students to get the issue heard. An important impact of this was that the teachers, in joining the students, contested the teacher/pupil binary. According to Mills, the issue of homophobia became contained as administrators deployed a discourse of professionalism. This discourse incited teachers to maintain hierarchies between teachers and pupils as a matter of professionalism. Alongside this, a discourse of consensus was also invoked to force the abeyance of the administration. Finally, through a discourse of maturity, the pupils' activities were named as immature. As a result, containing this antihomophobic movement served to normalize its invisibility and to legitimize homophobic abuse. This enabled teachers to be publicly homophobic without official condemnation.

What Mills' work highlights is how gay and lesbian issues are important to sexual majorities (heterosexuals). This can involve naming gay and lesbian issues as social problems, rather than being *subject* to social problems. By reconceptualizing gay/lesbian as disruptive and marginal identities, the sexual majority can dispel the possibilities of its own dysfunction. For example, by pathologizing sexuality in schools, invariably via the formal curriculum of health or sex education, schools educate young people into appropriate and acceptable sexual practices. As a result, Quinlivan and Town (1999) note how young people in their sample expressed their discomfort when, in sex education, the only mention of homosexuality was in the context of disease. One effect of this for the young gay men was that they felt uncomfortable with their sexual identities. Other effects included preventing them from expressing their sexual feelings at a physical level due to fears of inadequacy. At the same time, institutionally led conversations about female sexuality generated different feelings for lesbian students. As schools tend to discuss female sexuality through notions of passive sexual reproduction, lesbian identities are projected as deviant. This is often because of their assumed independence from mothering. Thus, there appears a greater sense of silence surrounding lesbians in schools than for gay men. Schools' institutional cultivation and sanctioning of normative heterosexual families situates male sexuality as active. In this context, gay sexuality corresponds with masculinity. In contrast, lesbian identities contravene the passive sexual femininity. This is reinforced through sex education in schools that tends to presume heterosexuality as a natural phenomenon.

REFERENCES AND FURTHER READINGS

Connell, R.W. (1993). *Gender and power.* Cambridge, United Kingdom: Polity Press.

Haywood, C., & Mac an Ghaill, M. (2003). *Men and masculinities: Theory, research and social practice.* Buckingham, United Kingdom: Open University Press.

Mac an Ghaill, M. (1994). *The making of men: Masculinities, sexualities and schooling.* Buckingham, United Kingdom: Open University Press.

Mills, M. (1996). "Homophobia kills": A disruptive moment in the educational politics of legitimation. *British Journal of the Sociology of Education, 17*(3), 315–326.

Quinlivan, K., & Town, S. (1999). Queer as fuck? Exploring the potential of queer pedagogy in researching school experiences of lesbian and gay youth. In D. Epstein & J.T. Sears (Eds.), *A dangerous knowing: Sexuality, pedagogy and popular culture* (pp. 242–256). London: Cassell.

Mairtin Mac an Ghaill

Chris Haywood

Liviu Popiviciu

Salaries of Academics

In 1892, Sidney Webb was asked to prepare a paper that was eventually titled "The Alleged Differences in the Wages Paid to Men and to Women for Similar Work." Despite Webb's admitted reluctance to undertake the task, the study was completed. But, he noted, "The problem is apparently one of great complexity and no simple or universal solution of it can be offered" (Webb, 1892, p. 635). The accuracy of Webb's words has been borne out by 30 years of research on pay differences between men and women in academia. Female to male salary ratios for current faculty in higher education are readily available from several sources. While calculating these salary differences might appear to be a straightforward task, researchers encounter greater difficulties in uncovering the source of the gap and reasons for its persistence over time. One complication is that, historically, male and female academics have exhibited unequal levels of productive characteristics including experience, academic rank, discipline, and scholarly output. With continued methodological developments and more representative data sets, researchers seem to be making progress. Closer examination of these gaps, however, never fails to raise new issues, and the task will not be straightforward until there is more similarity in the characteristics of men and women in academia.

THE GENDER SALARY GAP IN HIGHER EDUCATION

Salary differences between male and female workers exist across all occupations, and higher education is no exception. During the academic year 2004–2005, women teaching full time at four-year public institutions earned $57,931 and men earned $71,748 (all ranks, including instructor and lecturer, combined). In private (not-for-profit) four-year institutions, the figures, across all ranks, were $59,404 for women versus $73,140 for men. The estimated female-male salary ratio, therefore, was approximately 81 percent in both types of institutions (National Center for Education Statistics, 2006). Additional information comes from the American Association of University Professors' (AAUP) recent Annual Report on the Economic Status of the Profession, 2004–05. The AAUP's salary equity index, which shows the ratio of female to male salaries (all ranks, full time, and all institutional types), is also 80 percent in 2003 to 2004. Interestingly, this salary ratio is virtually identical to the ratio of female-to-male weekly earnings of full-time workers across all U.S. occupations in 2004, which was 80.4 percent according to the Bureau of Labor Statistics. Whereas the ratio across all occupations has risen roughly 20 percentage points in as many years, the gender salary ratio for faculty has been close to 80 percent since data by gender were first collected by the AAUP in the late 1970s.

The collection of salary data by gender was largely a response to important antidiscrimination legislation that was passed in the United States during the 1960s, including the Equal Pay Act of 1963 and Title VII of the 1964 Civil Rights Act. With respect to higher education, Executive Order 11246 was amended to prohibit sex discrimination in government contracts in 1968, and in 1972 Title VII was extended to higher education institutions via the Equal Employment Opportunity Act. Similarly, in 1972, the Equal Pay Act was extended to cover faculty and administrative salaries in higher education. The legal obligation to comply with a nondiscriminatory standard was one reason for increased research on pay differentials in academia, although the statistical methodology lagged behind the legal impetus.

Economists maintain that salary discrimination exists when equally productive workers receive different salaries, and a major research question has been whether female faculty members have been systematically underpaid relative to equally productive men in the profession with productivity usually defined in terms of qualifications (degrees earned, position held), years of experience, and output (publications, teaching).

To this day, men and women in academia still differ with respect to many characteristics affecting salary. For example, female faculty members are disproportionately found in part-time positions, and women are more prevalent in lower-paid disciplines. The same AAUP report mentioned above indicates that in 2003 to 2004, the ratio of full-time female faculty to male faculty in the full professor rank (all institutions) is roughly 50 percent, and the situation is worse at doctoral universities where women are less than half as likely as men to be full professors. Across all types of institutions, the AAUP report found that women are 10 percent to 15 percent less likely than men to be in tenure-eligible positions. Female faculty members tend to publish less than their male colleagues, and women may have less experience on average. Differential access to endowed chairs and administrative positions would further widen the gender salary gap.

Such differences raise a very difficult point. If discrimination occurs when equally productive workers receive different remuneration, how do we define "equally productive?" Statistical techniques distinguish the portion of the pay gap due to "discrimination" versus differences in "legitimate," "productive" characteristics. These terms are generally defined in the context of particular statistical models. The real issue comes down to how much of the remaining gender gap in salaries is voluntary (i.e., the result of rational, informed, choices by male and female academics). To take one example, if researchers determine that a large portion of the gender gap in salaries results from women's tendency to specialize in low-paying disciplines, do those researchers conclude that there is no discrimination or do they explore further why women may choose, or be directed into, different specialty fields? Alternatively, the fact that women tend to hold lower academic rank (a "legitimate" productive characteristic) explains much of the gender difference in salary. But, are there some reasons to believe that discriminatory promotion systems contribute to the gender difference in rank? Researchers have grappled with these subtle yet undeniable issues since the first studies appeared during the 1970s.

EXPLAINING THE GENDER SALARY GAP

A large literature attempts to explain the persistent gender gap in academic salaries. Many of the early studies, which tended to focus on individual campuses, were largely done in response to the legal imperative imposed by new legislation. This was also a time when budget-conscious administrators and concerned faculty members were interested in the salary determination process, including identifying the pecuniary reward to teaching versus research activities. One benefit of a campus-wide investigation of salary differences is that certain factors affecting salary (e.g., institutional type, control, size) are held constant. The facts that campus-wide studies were not representative of higher education and that they were generally performed for only one period, such that trends over time were not discernible, decreased the usefulness of early studies. Still, they provide important documentation that women were generally underpaid relative to comparable male faculty. The studies suggested ways in which men and women were treated differently and, maybe more importantly, began to question how any inequities might be measured. Researchers' questions spawned innovation in the methodology of measuring pay gaps and even the portion of the gap that might be attributable to discrimination. In conjunction with these statistical findings, college and university administrators would also need to develop procedures to remedy existing pay gaps perceived as discriminatory.

The majority of studies conducted throughout the 1970s uncovered a statistically significant salary advantage in favor of men, with few exceptions. In some studies, the male salary premium was apparent only at particular academic ranks. In at least one case, affirmative action programs resulted in a statistically significant salary advantage in favor of women. It also became clear that estimates of the male salary advantage were very sensitive to which faculty traits were controlled by the researcher.

The simplest research studies viewed faculty salary as the outcome of numerous faculty and institutional characteristics, including the professor's sex. If the variable representing sex achieved statistical significance, meaning that it was unlikely that the result occurred by chance, the interpretation was that, holding all other characteristics constant, the salaries of men and women differed by a fixed amount. During the 1970s, it became increasingly common to estimate separate salary models for men and women. The advantage in this approach is that researchers could determine whether women and men were paid varying amounts for each particular characteristic.

As noted throughout the literature, men and women differ with respect to many characteristics that influence salary. If women had lower levels of productive characteristics, on average, then failure to consider this fact would cause researchers to overestimate salary discrimination against women. There are also possible biases in the opposite direction. Discrimination might lead to women having lower average levels of these productive characteristics. For example, discriminatory evaluation procedures might cause female academics to occupy lower ranks, making it inappropriate to control for rank when calculating salary gaps. The resulting salary gap would constitute an underestimate of the true amount of gender discrimination. Some researchers have found that, if you compare gender salary gaps for academics across all ranks, rather than faculty members in a given rank (the latter case implies "controlling" for rank), women's salary disadvantage doubles. Not surprisingly, researchers have repeatedly returned to the issue of which characteristics should be controlled when calculating salary gaps. Academic rank appears to be one of the more problematic of these characteristics.

The methodology of computing salary gaps improved during the 1970s with the publication of Oaxaca's first paper on salary decomposition techniques and the availability of national faculty survey data, including the 1968 Carnegie Commission database and the 1972–1973 American Council on Education survey. In addition to a larger sample size, national databases offered information about many faculty characteristics. Examination of repeated cross sections would become critical in establishing trends in male-female salary gaps over time.

Oaxaca's (1973) pioneering study changed how researchers viewed and defined discrimination. According to Oaxaca, discrimination exists when the relative wage of males exceeds the relative wage that would have prevailed if men and women were paid according to the same criteria. To understand how this definition is put into practice, it helps to consider an example. Suppose that Conor and Brittany work in a factory producing chairs. Conor makes 10 chairs a day, and he is paid $5 per chair. He earns, therefore, $50 a day. By contrast, Brittany makes only six chairs a day, and she is paid $4 for each chair she produces for a total salary of $24 a day. There are two sources of the $26 salary gap between these individuals. First, Brittany is less productive (i.e., she assembles fewer chairs per day). Her lower productivity might be called a legitimate source of the resulting salary gap. But, the fact that she is paid $1 less for each chair produced is discriminatory. The Oaxaca technique breaks down total salary gaps into a portion that reflects discrimination (unequal payment for each unit produced) and a portion that is legitimate (she produces fewer units). One simple way to estimate what Brittany might earn in the absence of discrimination is to assume that she would be paid $5 for each of the six chairs she produced (a total of $30). In this nondiscriminatory world, the gender salary gap would only be $20 rather than $26.

For readers interested in statistical techniques, there is a more technical language for describing how to apply the Oaxaca technique to a large number of Conors and Brittanys: In all decomposition methodologies, the researcher estimates separate salary regressions for men and women. If one multiplies the average values of the explanatory variables for women by the estimated coefficients from the men's salary regression, one can derive an average salary for women as though they were compensated as men. The difference between women's average salary and their predicted salary, when paid as men, constitutes one estimate of discrimination. By calculating the difference between men's average salary and their predicted salary, when paid as women, one can derive a second discrimination estimate, producing a range of results. The Oaxaca technique essentially allows researchers to decompose, or partition, a total salary gap into two portions: a "legitimate" part of the salary gap derived from differences in men's and women's levels of the explanatory variables and a discriminatory gap, which stems from differences in the return to given characteristics (i.e., unequal regression coefficients from the male and female salary regressions). In recent years, several additional decomposition techniques have been developed, but they all have a similar objective, differing mostly with respect to how they define the nondiscriminatory salary system.

During the 1980s, researchers conducting campus pay studies tended to find continued evidence of salary discrimination against women, although a number of published estimates were lower than comparable figures for the 1970s. By the 1990s, campus pay equity studies were commonplace and few were actually published. The real innovation in the field was researchers' growing access to national faculty survey data, particularly studies by the National Center for Education Statistics. The common Oaxaca methodology, in conjunction with large data sets containing detailed information on individual faculty members, made it easier to detect time trends in academic pay gaps.

Table IX.2 summarizes the effect of sex on faculty salaries over time in the United States. These estimates are based on numerous studies employing national faculty data.

All of these studies are examined in either Barbezat (2002) or Barbezat and Hughes (2005). These estimates show the total salary gap between male and female faculty members holding constant a large number of institutional and individual characteristics, including highest degree, experience, publications, academic discipline, and type of institutional employer. When comparing findings across studies, it is imperative to recognize differences in the characteristics of faculty members that are available, as well as how measures are constructed and how the faculty in the study were selected. Some of these differences are unavoidable and result from changes made to the actual surveys. Many analysts investigate more than one model specification, and factors such as rank and marital status may or may not be included in their models. With few exceptions, however, the samples and salary models represented in Table IX.2 have substantial commonality. Because the researchers have controlled for so many factors, the resulting salary differences are relatively small.

The salary gap estimates found in Table IX.2 are derived from single-equation regression models. In such a model, the salary advantage accruing to one group is measured, approximately, by the coefficient on a variable representing the respondent's sex. The interpretation of Table IX.2 would be that when Ashraf (1996) studied 1969 salary data, he found roughly a 12 percent salary advantage in favor of male faculty. Using a different data sample from that same year, Barbezat (1991) calculated a 16 percent salary premium in favor of men, and Ransom/Megdal found that women earned 12.5 percent less than male colleagues. Thus, all three studies found that even when female faculty had similar research output, experience, degrees, and academic employer, as well as were located in the same fields, they experienced a substantial salary disadvantage in the late 1960s.

If you continue across the table, it becomes evident that the male salary advantage fell during the 1970s and, by 1977, male faculty members earned between 2.5 percent and 7 percent more than comparable female colleagues. If we ignore Ashraf's 1984 estimate (the only estimate in the table that was not statistically significant), there was no further progress in achieving pay equity during the 1980s. In fact, women may have lost some ground. Estimates from 1984 to 1989 indicate that the salary premium in favor of men ranged from approximately 6 percent to just over 8 percent.

This lack of progress during the 1980s only heightens interest in what occurred during the 1990s. Unfortunately, only two studies are available for this period. Toutkoushian's estimate for 1993, which indicates a 7.5 percent salary disadvantage for women, falls squarely within the range of estimates for the 1970s. In this context, the Barbezat and Hughes estimate for 1999, which indicates that men earned just over 4 percent more than comparable female faculty members, might, finally, signal continued progress toward salary equity in academia.

If we control for all relevant factors influencing faculty salary, the figures in Table IX.2 might be considered good estimates of salary discrimination against female faculty members. There are more sophisticated approaches to deriving the effects of sex on salary, specifically, the decomposition techniques of Oaxaca and others. The advantage of these techniques is that they take the total salary gaps presented in Table IX.2 and identify a unique portion of the gap that can be attributed to discrimination. Barbezat (2002) summarizes these alternative techniques and presents these more precise discrimination estimates for the same 30-year period. Briefly, the results of these alternative techniques are that male faculty members earned between 23 percent and 30 percent more than similar female colleagues in 1969. A number of researchers agree that as much as half of that salary

Table IX.2 Estimated Coefficients for Sex Effects on Salaries from National Studies, 1969–1999

	1969	1972	1975	1977	1984	1988	1989	1993	1999
Ashraf (1996)									
Male coefficient	0.12 (N = 29,672)	0.07 (N = 14,780)		0.06 (N = 2,549)	0.01 (N = 3,210)		0.06 (N = 3,258)		
Barbezat (1991)									
Male coefficient	0.163 (N = 13,613)		0.095 (N = 2,202)	0.025 (N = 3,021)	0.07 (N = 1,791)		0.066 (N = 3,077)		
Barbezat (2002)									
Male coefficient						0.081 (N = 4,607)			
Ransom/ Megdal (1993)									
Female coefficient	−0.125 (N = 53,258)	−0.105 (N = 30,638)		−0.07 (N = 3,492)	−0.073 (N = 2,599)				
Toutkoushian (1998)									
Female coefficient								−0.075 (N = 9,790)	
Barbezat/ Hughes (2005)									
Male coefficient									0.042 (N = 6,905)

difference constituted discrimination (meaning it could not be explained by differences in the men's and women's productive characteristics).

Consistent with Table IX.2, total salary gaps tended to fall over the 1970s, but the trend is less clear with respect to the 1980s. So, again, estimates for the 1990s have great importance. The most recent estimate by Barbezat and Hughes (2005) suggests that the total salary gap was approximately 22 percent in 1999. The optimistic news is that when the total gap is divided, Barbezat and Hughes find that discrimination constitutes a relatively small portion of this gap (21 percent to 27 percent), and this result is confirmed by alternative statistical techniques.

In terms of evaluating this literature, it is worth noting that the part of the salary gap that researchers designate as discriminatory may reflect faculty and institutional characteristics that the researcher has failed to consider. To take another example, researchers may attempt to compare professors with similar characteristics, say, publications, but if varying quality of publications is not considered, this biases their estimate of the portion of the salary gap attributable to discrimination. In short, even the relatively sophisticated statistical techniques have shortcomings. As they await results from new national faculty surveys, many unresolved issues occupy scholars in the field. Most of these issues revolve around academic ranks and promotions.

Researchers have debated the desirability of including academic rank in faculty salary models for some 30 years. Again, the argument against including rank is that gender discrimination may influence rank assignment, so when researchers control for rank, they underestimate the extent of salary discrimination. Although several researchers have investigated gender differences in rank attainment, few of them go on to estimate how gender differences in rank attainment contribute to the gender gap in academic salaries. Another related issue is that the promotion process from assistant to associate professor, which usually corresponds to the grant of tenure, has been studied more thoroughly than the promotion to full professor. All of these issues are summarized in Becker and Toutkoushian (2003). Moreover, Becker's and Toutkoushian's application of a new estimation method suggests that previous studies including rank may have produced more accurate gender salary gaps than those omitting rank. The authors also found discrimination in favor of men in the promotion process to full professor. While their findings are limited to one institution, their new methodology may be employed by other researchers.

Ginther's recent work also emphasizes the importance of investigating rank and salary differences simultaneously as well as the possibility that salary gaps and the processes generating them might differ across academic discipline. In 2001, Ginther found large salary differences across ranks for faculty in the natural sciences based on Survey of Doctorate Recipients (SDR) data. By contrast, Ginther and Hayes (2003), using the same SDR data for 1977 through 1995, concluded that, among humanities faculty members, the average gender salary differences for tenure-track assistant, associate, and full professors were not statistically different from zero. Despite this favorable finding, women in the sample were less likely to be promoted and took longer to be promoted than men. The authors conclude that promotion differences largely resulted from unequal treatment of women with respect to work experience, children, and number of employers. Trying to explain why female academics tended to fare better in the humanities than the natural sciences, the authors note women's higher representation in the humanities and the fact that, because humanities salaries may be lower than average faculty salaries, paying men and women the same in the humanities may be less costly. Many researchers would agree that we need to examine salary gaps "within the context of promotion," rather than focusing on salary differences alone.

Finally, researchers are beginning to appreciate the importance of pay structure in determining gender gaps in salary. For example, Barbezat and Hughes (2005) used the 1999 National Study of Postsecondary Faculty to show how differences in salary dispersion influence the gender pay gap across various types of higher education institutions. At liberal arts colleges, the unexplained portion of the gender salary gap was smaller than at research universities, perhaps due to a greater focus on overall pay equity at smaller campuses. Nevertheless, while female professors at research universities were at a bigger disadvantage relative to male colleagues, they still enjoyed a salary advantage over women teaching at liberal arts colleges. In short, the issue of how institutional salary structure affects gender salary gaps must be considered as well.

REFERENCES AND FURTHER READINGS

American Association of University Professors. (2005). Inequities persist for women and non-tenure track faculty. *Academe, 91*(2), 21–30.

Barbezat, D. (2002). History of pay equity studies. In R. Toutkoushian (Ed.), *Conducting salary-equity studies: Alternative approaches to research* (pp. 9–39, New Directions for Institutional Research, No. 115). San Francisco: Jossey-Bass.

Barbezat, D., & Hughes, J. (2005). Salary structure effects and the gender pay gap in academia. *Research in Higher Education, 46*(6), 593–730.

Becker, W., & Toutkoushian, R. (2003). Measuring gender bias in the salaries of tenured faculty members. In R. Toutkoushian (Ed.), *Unresolved issues in conducting salary-equity studies* (pp. 5–20, New Directions for Institutional Research, No. 117). San Francisco: Jossey-Bass.

Ginther, D., & Hayes, K. (2003). Gender differences in salary and promotion for faculty in the humanities 1977–1995. *Journal of Human Resources, 38*(1), 34–73.

National Center for Education Statistics. (2006, January). *Employees in postsecondary institutions, fall 2004, and salaries of full-time instructional faculty, 2004–05* (Table 3). Available at http://nces.ed.gov/pubsearch/pubsinfo.asp?pubid=2006187

Oaxaca, R. (1973). Male-female wage differentials in urban labor markets. *International Economic Review, 14*(3), 693–709.

Webb, S. (1892). The alleged differences in the wages paid to men and women for similar work. *The Economic Journal, 2*(5), 635.

Debra Barbezat

Teacher Burnout

The concept of "burnout" originated in a publication in the *Journal of Social Issues* by the clinical psychologist H.J. Freudenberger in 1974. For him, burnout represented a malaise frequently experienced by human service professionals, including social workers, mental health workers, nurses, and teachers, who come to see themselves as "wearing out." When their clients, patients, and students do not seem to improve, recover, or learn, the human service workers experience emotional exhaustion and lose their sense of accomplishment. They no longer perform their tasks effectively and sometimes even no longer care about the welfare of their clients. Soon after publication of Freudenberger's article, other psychologists isolated three central themes in burnout: emotional exhaustion, loss of a sense of personal accomplishment, and depersonalization or the blaming of the client, patient, or students for the malaise experienced by the human service professional (Maslach, 1993). Most psychological researchers describe burnout as an inability to cope with an array of life stressors. This approach tends to ascribe "blame" for burnout to the victims of burnout and proceeds to offer a panoply of strategies to enhance coping ability.

Alaya Pines (1993) characterized burnout as an existential crisis linked to a sense of meaninglessness. That is, to the extent that professionals come to incorporate their work into their self-image, a frequent occurrence in industrialized and postindustrialized societies, any condition that diminishes the personal assessment of the value of that work likewise diminishes the assessment of self-worth. When this happens, Pines argues, human service professionals come to ask, "Why am I doing what I am doing?"—a question reflecting self-doubt and a crisis of existence.

Not all views of burnout focus on individual factors associated with the ability to cope with stress. The sociological view arises out of the structural construct of alienation. Here, burnout includes all of Seeman's (1975) dimensions of alienation including powerlessness, meaninglessness, normlessness, isolation, and estrangement. Alienation has organizational and social structural roots and, therefore, its redress ought not to focus on improved individual coping skills but rather on structural change. Stress can still be a precipitating factor, as it is in the psychological models, but the causal elements of burnout are seen within the structure of the school or the structure of the educational system that creates teacher expectations (Dworkin, 1987, 1997, 2001; Dworkin, Saha, & Hill, 2003; Dworkin & Townsend, 1994; and LeCompte & Dworkin, 1991).

When professionals are unable to negotiate agreements on role performances or to determine what the role expectations are within a human service organization, they develop a sense of powerlessness, which soon leads to a sense of meaninglessness. In addition, individuals withdraw from social relationships within the organization (isolation) and question whether continued participation in the organizational role is consistent with their self-conception (estrangement). The burned-out individuals also begin to blame their clients, students, or patients for failing to improve. Finally, burned-out professionals come to feel that the organizational setting is characterized by a degree of normlessness. That is, they feel that either there are no rules or that following the rules tends to be dysfunctional. Sparks and Hammond (1981) reported that burned-out professionals report that the rules of the organization are either unenforceable or uninterpretable.

SCHOOL REFORM AND TEACHER BURNOUT

School reform movements are based on the assumption that the public schools are failing to educate the nation's future labor force, thereby jeopardizing the economic future standing of the country. In their various manifestations, school reformers have frequently noted that teachers fail to do their jobs properly and competently. Many reform efforts make the assumption that teachers will not work hard unless their livelihoods are threatened. Job stress and fear of job loss are assumed to be necessary to motivate better teaching and learning. Even in a benign form, school reform implies change, and change itself can be stressful. Since job stress precipitates job burnout, it is reasonable to assume that the implementation of school reforms will lead to heightened levels of burnout among public school teachers.

In fact, there is evidence that the morale of America's teachers has been negatively impacted by the various waves of school reform implemented at least since the Reagan administration's publication of *A Nation at Risk* in 1983. Detailed analyses by Dworkin and his colleagues (Dworkin, 1997, 2001; Dworkin, Saha, & Hill, 2003; and Dworkin & Townsend, 1994) have displayed the changing effects of school reform legislation on teacher burnout. School reform activities do not, however, impact all teachers equally. Differences in burnout level exist across teaching populations demarcated by race and ethnicity, gender, and years of teaching experience.

A Nation at Risk (1983) decried the poor academic performance of American students and predicted that, unless there were monumental changes made in public education, the country would no longer be a leader in the global economy. The year following the report, the Secretary of Education observed that the nation had responded to the challenge and had produced sweeping changes in every state. The first wave of these reforms sought to impose uniformity through standardized curricula, teacher evaluations, and rigorous requirements for student performance, promotion, and graduation. The 1980s reform attempted to guarantee that only competent teachers were in the classroom and that students who graduated from high school were proficient at the skills that would make them competent employees in American industry.

By the end of the 1980s, it was apparent that student achievement had not risen to the levels promised by the legislated reforms following *A Nation at Risk*. If legislated, centralized reforms did not appear to work; state legislatures turned to mandating reforms that stressed decentralization. Localized, site-based decision making was proposed as the remedy to raise student achievement. The argument raised by state education agencies was that if decision making is focused at the site of instruction, the quality of decisions will be better and students will more likely succeed academically.

At about the same time, the administration of President George H.W. Bush called for education to "break the mold" and establish new schools that promoted "world-class standards" under the aegis of a program called *America 2000*. The standards movement, focusing on more testing, was rejuvenated and new, private-sector models under the name "New American Schools Development Corporation" (NASDC) emerged. Many of the programs developed under the aegis of the NASDC failed to achieve "comprehensive, systemic change" through the creation of "break the mold schools." The products of the NASDC often shifted their goals from world-class student achievement to feelings of satisfaction among participants. The *America 2000* reforms (and those that followed in the Clinton administration under the name *Goals 2000*) failed to achieve most of the academic results promised by their promoters. Likewise, the more locally developed site-based decision-making plans more often resulted in "turf battles" among principals, teachers, and stakeholder groups, each contending that the control of the local schools was their own within their own mandate. Dworkin and Townsend (1994) noted that such feuds over control of the schools resulted in heightened levels of teacher burnout.

The Standards Movement (establishing statewide, uniform academic standards for children), launched following *A Nation at Risk* and exacerbated following *America 2000* and *Goals 2000,* culminated in high-stakes testing in the mid- and late-1990s. High-stakes testing involves the use of standardized achievement tests (norm-referenced or criterion-referenced) to evaluate student learning and to assess the performances of teachers, school administrators, schools, and school districts. Rewards are offered by state education agencies to school personnel and schools when test scores or passing rates are high. Punishments, including termination, school reorganization and restaffing, and loss of accreditation, are threatened when scores or passing rates remain low.

Critics of high-stakes testing have contended that such practices: narrow the curriculum taught only to that which is tested; lead to cheating by teachers and other school staff; rely on single indicators to assess outcomes (in violation of good test theory); and widen the gap between groups of students while increasing the drop-out rate in schools. However, analyses by Toenjes, Dworkin, Lorence, and Hill (2002) suggested that the high-stakes testing has forced Texas schools to take more seriously the education of their poor and minority students. Nevertheless, holding teachers responsible for a single test-score performance of their students has created additional stressors in the lives of school personnel. The consequence of the high-stakes testing reform has been a continued elevation of teacher burnout scores over those found prior to the era of no reform (Dworkin, 2001).

The most recent incarnation of the Standards Movement is found in the reauthorization of P.L. 8910, the Elementary and Secondary Education Act of 1965, currently known as the No Child Left Behind Act of 2001 (NCLB). The framework for NCLB was developed from the accountability system adopted in Texas. States wishing to continue to receive federal funds, including under the federal subsidized lunch program out of the Department of Agriculture, as well as other programs, had to submit to the Secretary of Education a plan by which 95 percent of the children in the state would be 100 percent proficient on the state-selected standardized test by the academic year 2013–2014. Adequate yearly progress (AYP) has to be demonstrated by each school; the schools that fail to meet the AYP standards can face draconian measures, including loss of some Title I monies, public school choice for their students to transfer to a school meeting its AYP goals, removal of school staff, and even closure of the campus and reorganization as a charter school. (See the "Perspectives on Critical Issues" essays in the April 2005 issue of *Sociology of Education*.)

As noted above, studies by Dworkin and his colleagues have indicated that teacher morale and burnout tend to be adversely affected by the school reform policies over the past 20 years. These studies were based on data on Texas teachers drawn generally from the 54 school districts in the Houston metropolitan area. However, there is every reason to believe that the results can be generalized to at least urban schools in the state and to most urban districts in the nation. What were the changes in the burnout scores of the teachers studied by Dworkin and his colleagues during the different reform activities?

To answer this question, data from six cohorts of teachers were studied, each consisting of teachers with varying years of teaching experience. The six different samples provide information about the relationship between teacher burnout and years teaching in an era prior to the reforms (the pre-reform 1977 sample), the reforms instituted in Texas in the mid-1980s following *A Nation at Risk* (the 1986 sample), the reforms associated with site-based decision making and the *America 2000* program (the 1991 sample), the reforms involving high-stakes testing in Texas and greater teacher accountability (the 2000 sample), and finally two samples drawn in the initial year of No Child Left Behind and two years later, after the state application was accepted by the U.S. Department of Education.

The measure of teacher burnout is derived from the "Dworkin Teacher Burnout Scale," originally presented in Dworkin, Chafetz, and Dworkin (1986) and fully discussed in Dworkin (1987). The scale consists of 10 items that represent the sociological perspective on burnout as an extreme form of role-specific alienation. In order to compare teachers across different waves of reform, their responses to the scale items were recombined and scored in a manner reflecting the relative ranking in terms of burnout of each cohort of teachers compared to all other cohorts. This permits the following interpretation as to whether burnout scores have risen or fallen during different eras of school reforms.

The 1977 pre-reform cohort had the lowest level of burnout, with burnout scores lower for more senior teachers than for new teachers. A small rise in the burnout scores at three years of experience reflects the fact that at that point a decision is made to offer teachers a permanent contract (essentially, tenure) and such a time period tends to be stressful. However, when compared with all post-reform waves, even the newest teachers had relatively low levels of burnout. There were 3,165 teachers in this sample. Burnout was highest among teachers assigned to schools where the principal was not supportive and defined them as expendable. Burnout levels were also higher among inexperienced White teachers than among any other group.

The 1986 data set consisted of 1,060 teachers, who were experiencing Texas's House Bill 72 based on *A Nation at Risk,* which imposed competency testing on teachers. The test was relatively easy and approximately 95 percent of the teachers passed it, although minority teachers passed the test at lower rates. Burnout levels during this era are the highest found for any cohort. The pattern indicates that change is stressful and particularly so when most teachers had no prior experience with school reforms that assessed the performances of teachers. The highest levels of burnout in this reform wave are for teachers with 5, 10, and 15 years experience. Burnout is three times higher for teachers with 10 years of experience in this wave than similarly experienced teachers in the pre-reform wave. The legislation mandated competency tests and established a career ladder in which all teachers who passed the test were placed at the same level on the ladder. Thus, the state denied the teachers their seniority and doubted their claims to being master teachers. The denial of a teacher's claim to expertise demoralized the experienced teachers, while the competency testing resulted in higher burnout rates among minority teachers. The racial makeup of the burnout groups changed. In the pre-reform sample, burned-out teachers were more likely to be inexperienced and White. In the 1986 sample, burnout was highest among minority teachers with 10 to 15 years of experience.

There were 261 teachers in the 1991 cohort that experienced *Site Based Decision Making*. Burnout levels for these teachers are lower than for the previous groups of teachers, as the dire prophecies (such as mass firings) had not come true. Teachers were more accustomed to reform and so, while burnout levels were higher than in the pre-reform era, differences among cohorts with different years of teaching experience were not very different, except for those with 15 or more years of experience. The lower levels of burnout among the more experienced teachers might reflect that they now had a greater share in the decision-making process (although they could still have "turf battles" with the principal).

Many of the 2,961 teachers in the 2000 data set had experienced *high-stakes testing* since the state had adopted the Texas Assessment of Academic Skills, a criterion-referenced test in 1994. However, by 2000, all of the accountability mechanisms were in place, including the possibility that schools could be closed and teachers fired for continued low student performance. The state education agency maintained an "erasure report" on teachers, indicating whether their students were changing more answers on the machine scanned answer sheets than was expected. There had been cheating scandals in districts by 2000, and some school personnel had been fired. Burnout scores for teachers almost paralleled those found in 1986 during the first reform wave, with one exception. The highest burnout levels exist among the most experienced teachers. Experienced teachers, especially teachers in high-poverty, inner-city schools, have considerable difficulty raising test scores. Their students bring to school few educational resources from home and the teachers' expertise is in classroom management, not in teaching to a new standardized test (by law each year a new test was implemented). Texas has a retirement model, termed the "Eighty System," whereby when one's age plus years teaching totals 80 one is eligible to retire at full benefits. Many of the teachers were just short of the threshold and were hoping to be able to maintain their jobs for just a few more years. The performance of their students on the standardized test became the determining factor.

There are two No Child Left Behind cohorts. Data from the first cohort were collected in the fall semester of 2002, during the first year of the federal act. This was the year immediately prior to the end of social promotion in Texas schools. While the social promotion law was passed in 1999, it was not to be enforced until 2003. Third-grade children failing the reading section of the newly created Texas Assessment of Knowledge and Skills (TAKS) test, which replaced the TAAS as the high-stakes test, would be required to repeat third grade. Teachers had to cope with both a new test and the prospect of retaining students. There were 2,869 teachers in the 2002 data set.

The second wave of data from the No Child Left Behind era collected in the fall semester of 2004 consisted of 1,771 teachers. No Child Left Behind had been fully implemented in the schools. The teachers were aware that successive low performance by their students would result in their schools' failure to meet AYP goals and the possibility of the loss of some of their students to higher-performing schools, as well as the potential reorganization of their school, accompanied by job loss.

The two No Child Left Behind waves closely parallel one another. Burnout levels for teachers with up to 15 years of experience resemble the pattern first found in the era of the implementation of high-stakes testing (in the 2000 data set). Many of the teachers in the earlier data set were drawn in the 2002 and 2004 samples. However, the implementation of NCLB resulted in a shifting upward of burnout levels for each experience cohort in 2002 and 2004 over the pattern for 2000. The small spike in the 2002 data set for teachers with 10 to 15 years of experience may reflect the growing recognition that the high-stakes testing practices will have greater ramifications for schools, given that the federal government has implemented the Texas policy. Teachers with 10 to 15 years of experience, like their counterparts during the *A Nation at Risk* era in the 1980s, consider themselves to be master teachers and may resent the state and now the federal government demanding that they prove it. Additionally, NCLB had begun to implement a definition of "highly qualified teachers" based on certification and an academic degree in the specialty area in which one instructs students. However, the two NCLB waves differed from the high-stakes testing data set of 2000 in one respect. Rather than a spike upward among teachers with 20 to 30 years of experience, there was a lower pattern of burnout among the most senior teachers. This pattern resembles the pattern for all the other data sets, where the most experienced teachers tend to be the least burned out.

GENDER, TOKENISM, AND BURNOUT BEFORE AND AFTER SCHOOL REFORM

While the overwhelming majority of teachers in public schools are women, men have maintained a proportional advantage in administrative roles. Male teachers have traditionally had an easier time leaving the classroom to become administrators without leaving public education and to rise within school organizations to higher salaries and greater responsibilities and esteem than have female teachers. In turn, the attainment of greater power, prestige, and rewards mitigates burnout. According to the National Center for Education Statistics (NCES), 70.5 percent of U.S. public school teachers in grades K–12 were women during the 1980s. During this same time period, 87.6 percent of elementary school teachers and 53.0 percent of secondary school teachers were women. In contrast, during the 1980s and early 1990s, no more than 1 in 11 and 1 in 10 principals were women. By 2000, however, NCES reports that 51.8 of all public elementary school principals and 21.8 of all public secondary school principals were women.

Deployment patterns of teachers by gender have resulted in the creation of "token group" statuses for males in elementary schools and comparable statuses for females in some departments in high schools, especially during the pre-reform era of the 1970s and 1980s. Most male teachers are in high schools, where disproportionate numbers teach science, mathematics, industrial arts, and athletics. There were relatively few female teachers in those departments, particularly prior to the 1990s. Rosabeth Moss Kanter (1977a, 1977b) proposed that tokens are likely to have many negative job experiences that heighten their sense of job dissatisfaction (and burnout). Tokens are visible and subject to specialized scrutiny by their co-workers. They may find themselves in marginal situations in which they are expected to represent their social category and also to "fit in" with members of the more dominant category. Kanter (1977a) defined "token status" as conditions in which 15 percent or fewer of a group are represented in the work setting, department, or organizational unit. She noted that the high visibility of tokens create "performance pressures" because tokens are not seen as individuals but as representatives and symbols of the stereotyped category to which they belong. Their behaviors are scrutinized to degrees beyond which their dominant peers (who represent 85 percent or more of the organization) are not. Their behaviors, and especially their mistakes on the job, are generalized to their social category (e.g., women). When tokens perform exceptionally well, another stereotyping mechanism comes into play. Stereotypes serve both as "stipulative definitions" and "empirical generalizations" (Richter, 1956). That is, evidence that supports the stereotype is accepted as further proof of the correctness of the stereotype (the empirical generalization), while evidence that is counter to the stereotype leads to the conclusion that the individual does not belong to the stereotyped category or is an exception to that category (the stipulative definition).

Dworkin, Chafetz, and Dworkin (1986) examined gender tokenism of public school teachers. In their analysis, tokens included male teachers in elementary schools and female teachers in the science, mathematics, and industrial arts programs in high schools in the 1970s and 1980s. These investigators noted that tokens carry two labels that are subject to stereotype attribution: a societal level label associated with the status of one's gender and a contextual level label depicting the scarcity of one's group within the organizational and occupational context of the individual. Male teachers in primary grades, while of token status, nonetheless were accorded the higher status of males in a female-dominated organization. The opposite was true for female teachers in a predominantly male organizational setting. The male teachers were likely to be seen as leaders and received respect and even deference. The female teachers became isolated and their input disregarded. Thus, women faculty teaching in high school science and mathematics, industrial arts, and shop departments reported greater levels of burnout than did women in programs where the percentage of female colleagues was higher. The reverse was the case for male faculty. Male faculty in elementary schools and especially those in primary grades reported less of a sense of alienation and burnout than did male teachers in grades where their percentages were significantly higher.

How are these patterns of gender, tokenism, and burnout affected by school reforms? To answer this question, the same information about burnout in the cohorts described above were examined. Generally, in no wave of data were there significant differences in the average burnout scores of males and females. Differences existed only for conditions of tokenism. Only in the 1977 and 1986 data sets were there significant numbers of female teachers who were tokens in their schools. In the 1990s and 2000s data, women were not tokens even in science, engineering, and other magnet schools.

What about the male teachers? In each wave, there were sufficient numbers of male tokens to assess the effect of that status on burnout. It seemed likely that the results of that assessment would be affected by the accountability systems following *A Nation at Risk*. Because they evaluate teachers in terms of the learning outcomes of their students, the accountability systems fundamentally alter the criteria by which teachers are evaluated. The societal status of a teacher's gender group has a reduced influence on the level of esteem in which teachers are held. Rather, the test score performances of the teacher's pupils became the paramount criterion. Additionally, the gender demographics of the teaching population changed in high school departments that had previously been predominantly male. To redress the paucity of public school girls interested in careers in science, technology, engineering, and mathematics (the STEM disciplines), more women were recruited to teach in the physical sciences and even industrial arts. Furthermore, the percentage of women leaving the classrooms to assume administrative roles in school districts also increased.

Of course, these changes had not occurred in the *pre-reform period* with the result that there were no significant differences in the burnout scores of males and female teachers in 1977. However, female tokens experienced higher burnout levels and male tokens experienced significantly lower burnout levels than did nontoken female teachers as a whole. Being tokens is associated with a greater sense of role-specific alienation for women in token statuses and a lesser sense of role-specific alienation for male tokens. Male tokens acquire the societal stereotype of leadership and become central in the hierarchy of their schools. Female tokens become more marginalized due to the same stereotyping mechanisms.

As in the pre-reform era, there were no statistically significant differences in the burnout levels of men and women in 1986 after the passage of *A Nation at Risk*. However, the reliance on testing may have militated against the advantages of male tokens. They now had burnout scores that were equal to that of the nontoken male teachers. Female tokens, by contrast, had substantially higher burnout levels than nontoken females and than female tokens had in the pre-reform era. With heightened accountability, male teachers began to worry that female tokens were becoming a potential burden in opposite-sex dominated departments due to stereotypes that the specialties of these departments were beyond the scope of women's work. Further, data collected in that 1986 sampling indicated that males in male-dominated departments tended to "stick together" more in light of the pressures from the accountability movement.

By holding teachers accountable for the standardized test learning outcomes of their children, *high-stakes testing* was threatening to all teachers, evidenced by the continued elevation of the burnout scores over those of the pre-reform era. By the late 1990s, schools no longer had a few female tokens in what had previously been male-dominated departments. Consequently, there are no data on female tokens in the waves of the 1990s and beyond. In 1998, male teachers and female teachers were, again, no different in their burnout levels. Male tokens, generally in elementary schools, had burnout levels that did not differ from those of the nontoken males.

As school accountability measures focused on student achievement and standardized test scores of the student body, males and male tokens were no longer judged by the societal stereotypes of male leadership. Rather, the only criterion by which teachers were judged was the test score performances of their students. The probabilities that only the token males would produce high student test scores is minimal. In the organizational setting, the dominant group, by simple numbers, is more likely to include teachers whose classes do well on the tests (and also who do poorly). Female teachers whose students do well counter the stereotype of expertise of the male tokens and militate against male advantage in token settings. Since the 1990s, there have been no public school settings in which female teachers are tokens. Thus, only male teachers are likely to suffer from the impact of high-stakes testing on the burnout of gender tokens.

REFERENCES AND FURTHER READINGS

Dworkin, A.G. (1987). *Teacher burnout in the public schools: Structural causes and consequences for children.* Albany: State University of New York Press.

Dworkin, A.G. (1997). Coping with reform: The intermix of teacher morale, teacher burnout, and teacher accountability. In B.J. Biddle, T.L. Good, & I.F. Goodson (Eds.), *International handbook of teachers and teaching* (pp. 459–498). Dordrecht/Boston/London: Kluwer Academic Publishers.

Dworkin, A.G. (2001). Perspectives on teacher burnout and school reform. *International Education Journal, 24*(2), 69–78.

Dworkin, A.G., Chafetz, J.S., & Dworkin, R.J. (1986). The effects of tokenism on work alienation and commitment among urban public school teachers: A test of Kanter's approach. *Work and Occupations, 13*(1), 399–420.

Dworkin, A.G., Saha, L.J., & Hill, A.N. (2003). Teacher burnout and perceptions of a democratic school environment. *International Education Journal, 4*(2), 108–120.

Dworkin, A.G., & Townsend, M. (1994). Teacher burnout in the face of reform: Some caveats in breaking the mold. In B. A. Jones & K. M. Borman (Eds.), *Investing in United States schools: Directions for educational policy* (pp. 68–86). Norwood, NJ: Ablex.

Freudenberger, H.J. (1974). Staff burn-out. *Journal of Social Issues, 30,* 159–165.

Kanter, R.M. (1977a). *Men and women of the corporation.* New York: Basic Books.

Kanter, R.M. (1977b). Some effects of proportions on group life: Skewed sex ratios and responses to token women. *American Journal of Sociology, 82*(5), 965–990.

LeCompte, M.D., & Dworkin, A.G. (1991). *Giving up on school: Student dropouts and teacher burnouts.* Newbury Park, CA: Corwin Press.

Maslach, C. (1993). Burnout, a multidimensional perspective. In W. B. Schaufeli, C. Maslach, & T. Marek (Eds.), *Professional burnout: Recent developments in theory and research* (pp. 19–32). Washington, DC: Taylor & Francis.

Pines, A. (1993). Burnout: Existential perspectives. In W.B. Schaufeli, C. Maslach, & T. Marek (Eds.), *Professional burnout: Recent developments in theory and research* (pp. 33–52). Washington, DC: Taylor & Francis.

Richter, M.N., Jr. (1956). The conceptual mechanism of stereotyping. *American Sociological Review 21*(5), 568–571.

Seeman, M. (1975). Alienation studies. *Annual Review of Sociology, 1,* 91–123.

Sparks, D., & Hammond, J. (1981). *Managing teacher stress and burnout.* Washington, DC: ERIC Clearinghouse on Teacher Education.

Toenjes, L.A., Dworkin, A.G., Lorence, J., & Hill, A.N. (2002). High-stakes testing, accountability, and student achievement in Texas and Houston. In J. E. Chubb & T. Loveless (Eds.), *Bridging the achievement gap* (pp. 109–130). Washington, DC: Brookings Institution.

Anthony Gary Dworkin

Work-Family Conflicts of Educators

Work-family conflicts result from difficulties in responding satisfactorily to the competing demands of both the work role and the family role in an individual's life. Outsiders often assume that the unique working conditions of educators buffer them from significant work-family conflicts: Teachers at all levels perform some of their work from home, have summers off from active teaching duties, and (especially at the college and university level) have more flexible schedules than most workers. However, some of these very qualities lead to significant work-family conflicts among educators. Regular on-site hours are shorter than in other jobs, but both off-site grading and class preparation as well as frequent on-site evening and weekend events can encroach upon an educator's personal and family commitments.

Although the autonomy of educators means that both K–12 teachers and college professors will share some of the same sources of work-family conflict, the gendered expectations governing different levels of the educational system lead to some diverging sources of conflict. Specifically, K–12 teaching, especially at the elementary level, has traditionally been gendered as female work; in higher education, the increasing reliance on part-time and nontenure-track faculty creates a more complicated gendering of teaching work, with tenure-track faculty positions gendered "male" and marginalized teaching positions gendered "female." In part, the cultural gendering of these teaching positions leads to different sources of work-family conflicts for the individuals who hold them.

Educators often create solutions to work-family conflict at the individual or family level, but this "privatization" of the problems of achieving work-family balance ignores the possibility of creating broader cultural change through public responses to work-family conflict. Ideas about gender and gendered interpretations of specific educational work roles have important influences on the work-family conflicts experienced by educators at all levels. Although individual and family level accommodations can do much to alleviate work-family conflict, a larger reconceptualization of ideas of work and gender are necessary for fundamental and lasting change.

SOURCES OF WORK-FAMILY CONFLICT

At its most fundamental level, work-family conflict stems from conflicts between life roles as workers and life roles as family members. Whereas specific instances of conflict arise when work requirements affect family life (W|F conflict) or when family needs interfere with one's work performance (F|W conflict), work-family conflict exists as well at a psychological level, resulting from both individual and cultural ideas about gender and role balance.

As a culture, we tend to believe that individuals understand and perform their roles hierarchically and that it is impossible for women, in particular, to be equally committed to both family and work roles. Because a man's culturally endorsed family role of "breadwinner" coincides neatly with his work role, a man can avoid some of the psychological distress that a woman faces when her expected family role of "nurturer" comes into conflict with her worker role. Women are more likely to believe that, in their actions and thought, they must prioritize either work or family. For this reason, women often understand the choices they make in specific situations as reflecting a broader orientation, either "choosing family over work" or "choosing work over family," either of which can lead to distress.

The cultural idea that individuals will order and perform their roles hierarchically leads to the expectation that individuals who consciously and emphatically prioritize one role over the other will experience less work-family conflict. What this idea ignores, however, is the extent to which cultural prescriptions regarding role hierarchies and gender constrain such choices in advance. Those who consciously "choose" to opt out of either family or work commitments make these choices in the context of a culture that believes that work-family conflict will always result when a woman attempts to succeed at both work and family roles. Although women who explicitly reject either the family or the work role may experience fewer episodes of situational work-family conflict, they are not immune to such conflict at the psychological level.

Primary and Secondary Teachers

Relatively few studies have examined work-family conflicts among K–12 teachers, and this neglect stems in part from the gendering of this teaching work as female. From this gendering arise the presumptions that primary and secondary teachers are more committed to their family roles than to their work roles and that the K–12 educational workplace is uniquely accommodating to workers with family obligations. Based on these assumptions, K–12 teachers are seen as not experiencing significant work-family conflicts, but this perception is inaccurate.

Social scientists in the 1960s and 1970s conceptualized teaching and other female-dominated fields as "semi-professions," a term that suggests both a deficiency in professional expertise and limited career commitment on the part of teachers. This understanding of the status of teaching rendered research attention to work-family conflicts of K–12 teachers less likely, because researchers have tended to focus on work-family conflicts among those assumed to have strong commitments to their work roles (e.g., women in fields traditionally dominated by men).

However, research has not supported the beliefs that primary and secondary teachers have a low level of commitment to their work and that they strongly prioritize their family roles over their work roles. Numerous qualitative studies have illustrated a strong commitment to the work role among samples of teachers, and recent quantitative research by

Cinamon and Rich (2005b) found that 70 percent of a sample of 187 Israeli teachers attributed high importance to the work role.

Like all individuals with strong commitments to both work and family, especially those with young children, teachers with a dual commitment will likely experience some work-family conflict. However, some sources of work-family conflict are unique to the K–12 educational context, suggesting the importance of more research on this population. Particular conflicts may arise from the nature of the work itself, from the current political emphasis on accountability and high-stakes testing, and from the lower status accorded teaching in comparison with other professions.

As mentioned earlier, the need to perform some teaching-related work off-site makes work encroachments on family life more likely than in other fields. Additionally, the emotional work of teaching, which mirrors the kind of emotional engagement required in rearing children, can leave teachers emotionally depleted at the end of the workday, another way in which work life can affect one's home life (Claesson & Brice, 1989).

Cinamon and Rich (2005b) found significantly higher levels of W|F conflict among high school teachers than among junior high school teachers, and they hypothesized that the emphasis on testing at the high school level in Israeli schools may have contributed to this difference. In the U.S. context, the standards and accountability movements of the 1990s, followed by the testing required by the No Child Left Behind Act of 2001, have put considerable pressure on teachers, and this pressure may well have contributed to increased W|F conflict among primary and secondary teachers.

Finally, the status of teaching as a female-gendered "semi-profession" may also contribute to work-family conflict among K–12 teachers. Interactions with parents and members of the public make it all too clear to teachers that the culture does not accord them full status as professionals. Teachers may react defensively to this perception, attempting to raise the status of the profession by acting as a professional is thought to act—that is, minimizing encroachments of family upon one's work life. In fact, research has documented a tendency for teachers to meet the demands of work over those of family when the two conflict (Blase & Pajak, 1986), suggesting that at least some K–12 teachers engage in what Drago, Crouter, Wardell, and Willits (2001) describe in the higher education context as "bias avoidance," that is, behaviors intended to minimize any seeming or actual intrusions of family life on work commitments in order to be taken seriously as a professional. To the extent that teachers wish to be respected as members of a true profession, they may adopt some of the same strategies that mothers in academic positions use to minimize F|W conflicts.

College and University Faculty

Whereas K–12 teaching in general lacks a clearly hierarchical career ladder, the extreme rigidity of the career hierarchy in higher education creates significant tensions between work and family. The normative career path, gendered male, involves moving smoothly through graduate school and then to a tenure-track job, where one advances at regular intervals from assistant professor to associate professor to full professor. The assistant professor years put the most pressure on young professors, as they struggle to prove themselves worthy of tenure. For female professors, the coincidence of the pretenure years with prime childbearing years leads to problems in adapting the female life span to this male-oriented model.

Over the past several decades, increasing numbers of women have earned doctoral degrees and begun academic careers, such that percentages of male and female assistant professors are roughly equal. However, disparities in percentages of women and men holding positions at the associate professor level suggest that more women than men fail to receive tenure. Childbearing and rearing play an important role in these different rates of tenure achievement. Mason and Goulden (2002) studied the effects of "early babies" (those born either while the parent is in graduate school or within the first five years after completing the PhD) versus "late babies" (those born more than five years after completion of the PhD) on rates of tenure achievement for male and female faculty. Though the timing of initiating parenthood does not affect men's chances of earning tenure, having a baby early makes a big difference for women: Women with early babies are significantly less likely to achieve tenure than women with late babies or no children.

The rigidly hierarchical career model of professorial work leads to a work culture that is remarkably intolerant of employment interruptions. Because of this, the common practice of temporarily drawing back from full engagement in the workforce during especially demanding caregiving periods remains essentially unavailable for academics. The tight academic job market renders temporarily cutting back on one's academic work even more problematic: Graduate students feel the need to get a tenure-track job as soon as possible, knowing that a few years after graduation, their ability to land a tenure-track job will start to decline. Pretenure faculty know that if they leave a tenure-track job to care for children, they might never get another one.

Part-time and nontenure-track faculty members face different challenges. Called lecturers, instructors, or adjuncts, they are disproportionately female, and they have less job security and are paid less—usually significantly less—than professors. Many women in marginalized academic positions hold the jobs they do because of family related aspirations or commitments that conflict with the expectations of the academic career model. Such women include those without doctoral degrees for reasons related to family or those with doctoral degrees whose family work renders the demands of a professorial academic career unappealing or impossible. The decision to work for lower pay and status than are accorded to tenured and tenure-track faculty, though sometimes narrated as a free choice, is made in response to the cultural ideology that views women, but not men, as "choosing" either work or family over the other.

SOLUTIONS TO WORK-FAMILY CONFLICTS

Most people develop individual and family level responses to work-family conflict rather than envisioning a culture-wide reconceptualization of the connections between gender and work/family roles. Whether at the individual or family level, these private strategies aim either at reducing work encroachments on family life or at minimizing family intrusions into the workplace. Research on the former has focused on general populations of dual-earner couples, whereas much of the research focused on academic populations has examined the latter.

Becker and Moen (1999) report that the majority of dual-earner couples avoid at the family level the pressures of two high-pressure careers by means of strategies to scale back in order to protect the family from work encroachments. They identify three specific strategies: placing limits on work engagements, having a "one-job, one-career" marriage (most often, the man has the career and the woman the "job"), and trading off, allowing priority to both partners' work lives, but at different times in the life course.

Because of the unusually high pressure of the pretenure years for professors and the difficulty of returning to the tenure track after exiting academia for whatever reason, these strategies are less available for those in academia, and so efforts to reduce F|W conflict become salient, particularly for female assistant professors with children. Research by Finkel and Olswang (1996) quantifies female junior faculty members' sense of the necessity of limiting F|W conflict in order to achieve tenure. Of their sample of 124 female assistant professors, 30 percent had decided not to have children and a further 49 percent had chosen to postpone childbearing. Forty percent of their study participants cited "Time required by children" as a serious barrier to achieving tenure, including 82 percent of the subsample of women with at least one child under the age of six.

A female assistant professor's decision to avoid or delay childbearing, a "free choice" made in the context of a culture that requires women to choose work or family, is a clear example of bias avoidance. Female academics who do have children in the pretenure years often attempt to limit F|W conflict by making their maternal status as invisible as possible. Such efforts can begin with timing conception attempts to ensure summer childbirth, thus avoiding interruptions of the academic semester. More problematic is the underutilization of family friendly policies increasingly in place at colleges and universities, including paid parental leaves, flexible scheduling, and the option of stopping the tenure clock for a year. Although studies have repeatedly demonstrated wide support for such policies among both male and female professors, actual utilization rates suggest that the majority of eligible faculty members do not request to use them.

Researchers assume that academic parents do not fully utilize family friendly policies because of concerns that, even when institution-wide policies support them, they may still be penalized at the department level, where decisions about tenure are made. An assistant professor's colleagues, like the larger culture, may perceive work-family balance as a zero-sum game, such that an "orientation" to work or family necessarily implies a corresponding deficit of attention to the other sphere. In a workplace governed by this model, any utilization of family friendly policies will be perceived as signaling a lack of scholarly seriousness.

These private strategies to balance the demands of work and family often provide individuals with a satisfactory experience of succeeding at multiple life roles. However, the problem with private solutions to problems rooted in culture and ideology is that approaching problems with work-family balance as a series of free choices made by individuals ignores the ways in which the possible choices—and the necessity of "choosing" work or family at all—are constrained by cultural forces that remain invisible as long as they are ignored. Fundamental change—as opposed to individual and family level accommodations to the way things are—requires broader public solutions to the problem. Starting in the early 1990s and continuing to the present, college and university administrators have implemented increasing numbers of family friendly policies, including parental leave policies, stopping the tenure clock, job sharing, employment assistance for spouses, and other policies. As policies relating to parental leaves and tenure-clock stoppage become widely accepted, researchers and faculty activists interested in work-family conflict are envisioning policy changes that go even further to make academia welcoming to those who seek to balance their commitments to work and to family.

Currently, work-family theorists are pressing for policies that recognize that child rearing involves a time commitment considerably longer than the one year of a stopped tenure clock or formal policies based on a reconceptualization of gender roles and family structure. Specifically, in light of the continuing changes in family structures and women's increased participation in paid labor, colleges and universities need to commit resources to address the needs of all members of the community, including adjunct instructors and staff members, rather than creating family friendly policies in ways that benefit primarily tenured and tenure-track faculty. As a response to the lengthy time commitment involved in rearing children, Robert Drago and Joan Williams (2000) propose the creation of half-time tenure-track faculty positions, which would allow parents to work half-time for up to 12 years before coming up for tenure.

Jerry A. Jacobs (2004), however, believes that even these policy changes, by focusing attention exclusively on the work-family conflicts of faculty members with children, ignore the root problem: the ever-increasing demands on professors' time. In his view, the creation of part-time tenure tracks, which he suspects would be populated almost entirely by women, would thus serve to reinstitutionalize gender inequity; and tenure-clock stoppage, by giving parents extra time to "catch up," diverts attention from the fact that some departments' tenure requirements cannot be met by anyone with any reasonable definition of work-life balance. In Jacobs's opinion, addressing the root cause of work-family conflict requires policy changes to limit the workweeks of *all* professors, not just those with children. Before such a policy can be implemented, however, attitudes and ideas across the culture and within particular workplaces will have to change considerably. To speed such changes along, some are attempting to facilitate work-family balance by means of cultural interventions.

Policy changes alone are not enough to affect culture-wide changes in levels of work-family conflict. Low utilization rates for family friendly policies are the norm in both academia and the nonacademic world. Sweden provides a useful example of disparities between the ideal, expressed in policy, and reality: Despite egalitarian policies designed to maximize women's workforce participation and men's parental involvement, Swedish women take the majority of leaves and perform the majority of child care; men are reluctant to take family leaves for fear of being perceived as less serious workers. Until our understanding of work shifts to allow recognition of women and men with significant caregiving responsibilities as valuable and effective workers, fundamental change will be impossible.

The cultural intervention efforts of Cinamon and Rich (2005a) in the K–12 workplace could serve as models for similar interventions at both the K–12 and the college/university levels. Cinamon and Rich used a two-pronged approach in their program for alleviating work-family conflict, one focusing on school managers (e.g., school principals and administrators) and one on teachers at high risk for work-family conflict (e.g., novice teachers who are also parents of young children). For both targeted groups, intervention focused on changing both attitudes and actions; for managers, this involved sensitivity training to enhance managers' understanding of work-family conflicts of educators as well as skill-oriented work to increase managers' effectiveness in dealing with work-family conflicts from the perspective of family friendly managerial practice.

In higher education workplaces, making such cultural interventions at the department level is essential for changing the climate for parents in academia since department-level colleagues, rather than administrators, play the most important role in tenure decisions for junior faculty members. The limited use of sensitivity training initiatives such as those just described, even at universities that are leaders in family friendly policy implementation, suggests that administrators should follow up such initiatives with concrete measures to shift attitudes of the senior faculty who actually decide the fates of junior faculty members' careers.

REFERENCES AND FURTHER READINGS

Becker, P.E., & Moen, P. (1999). Scaling back: Dual-earner couples' work-family strategies. *Journal of Marriage and the Family, 61*(4), 995–1007.

Blase, J.J., & Pajak, E.F. (1986). The impact of teacher's work life on personal life: A qualitative analysis. *Alberta Journal of Educational Research, 32*(4), 307–322.

Cinamon, R.G., & Rich, Y. (2005a). Reducing teachers' work-family conflict: From theory to practice. *Journal of Career Development, 32*(1), 91–103.

Cinamon, R.G., & Rich, Y. (2005b). Work-family conflict among female teachers. *Teaching and Teacher Education, 21*(4), 365–378.

Claesson, M.A., & Brice, R.A. (1989). Teacher/mothers: Effects of a dual role. *American Educational Research Journal, 26*(1), 1–23.

Drago, R., Crouter, A.C., Wardell, M., & Willits, B.S. (2001). *Final report of the Faculty and Families Project.* University Park: Pennsylvania State University. Retrieved June 9, 2004, from http://lsir.la.psu.edu/workfam/facultyfamilies.htm

Drago, R., & Williams, J. (2000). A half-time tenure-track proposal. *Change, 32*(6), 46–51.

Finkel, S.K., & Olswang, S.G. (1996). Child rearing as a career impediment to women assistant professors. *Review of Higher Education, 19*(2), 123–139.

Jacobs, J.A. (2004). The faculty time divide. *Sociological Forum, 19*(1), 3–27.

Mason, M.A., & Goulden, M. (2002). Do babies matter? The effect of family formation on the life-long careers of academic men and women. *Academe, 88*(6), 21–27.

Rachel Hile Bassett

Part X

Gender and Educational Policies

Overview

The term *policy* is an elusive concept. It basically refers to official statements of intentions to act on certain problems. Or, for purposes of this encyclopedia, policy can be defined as official statements of intentions to act on problems surrounding gender and education. But, even this definition remains obscure until the terms *official statements, intentions to act,* and *problems of gender and education* are clarified. This can best be accomplished by reading all of the essays in this section plus related ones in other sections listed at the end of this overview. Taken together, they provide a wide-ranging, richly nuanced, and sophisticated understanding of the nature of policies concerned with gender and education. Each essay is designed to stand alone, however, and each provides valuable, expert information about the specific gender and educational policies referenced in its title.

As the essays show, *official statements* are institutionally and organizationally formulated and enacted. Although individuals and voluntary organizations can and do influence policies, they cannot issue official statements of policy unless they hold legitimate positions of authority over educational matters. Those who do have such authority include international organizations such as the United Nations and its various agencies; multinational development agencies, such as the World Bank and the International Monetary Fund; national governments; state or provincial governments; and educational officials at all levels, including the local schools. The official policy statements of these authorities can take various forms, including reports, international conventions, laws, executive orders, court decisions, governmental or agency regulations, faculty and student handbooks, and course syllabi. Some of these statements—such as Title IX of the 1972 Amendments to the U.S. Education Act, which prohibits sex discrimination in all federally aided educational programs—deal explicitly with education and gender. But, two other kinds of statements should also be considered: education and gender policies. One of these consists of general policies against gender discrimination that cover all institutions, not just education. The U.S. Civil Rights Act of 1964, the British Sex Discrimination Act of 1975, and the UN Convention on the Elimination of all Forms of Discrimination Against Women are primary examples. The second consists of policy statements specific to education that do not view gender as a major issue even though they may have important gender effects. Examples of this kind of policy include the British Education Reform Act of 1988 and the U.S. No Child Left Behind Act of 2001.

Defining official policy statements as *intentions to act,* rather than as actions, is designed to emphasize the fact that policies may or may not lead to effective action. One reason they do not is because of the enormous complexity of policy interpretation and implementation. A law, executive order, or court decision is not an unambiguous rule that everyone understands in the same way; that can, must, and will be supported and followed by everyone; and that has clear and anticipated consequences. The ambiguity of laws is nicely illustrated by the fact that, although Title IX, described above, was enacted into law in 1972, it was not until 1975 that the U.S. Congress specified how Title IX should apply to school and college athletics, and it was not until 1976 that the Department of Health, Education, and Welfare (DHEW) disseminated the guidelines and regulations for implementing the law. Nor did these guidelines clarify Title IX for all times and all people. Additional clarifications were issued by DHEW in 1979, by Congress in the form of the Civil Rights Restoration Act of 1987, and by the Office for Civil Rights of the Department of Education (DOE) in 1996.

Many of these clarifications were stimulated by Court challenges that were raised to determine whether the DHEW and, after 1980, the DOE had correctly interpreted the law; whether all programs in an educational institution were covered by the law or only those that received federal funds; whether athletic programs for men and women could be "separate but equal"; whether schools should be required to pay compensation to students whose rights under Title IX had been violated, etc. Even if the judicial opinions that resulted from these challenges had been totally unambiguous, which they were not, there still would be problems in using court decisions to define the law without Congressional or executive action. One problem results from the fact that decisions made by most federal courts are limited to the jurisdiction of that court, and even Supreme Court decisions that affect the whole country are limited to situations that are similar to the one on which the Court based its judgments. The famous *Brown v. Board of Education of Topeka, Kansas,* decision in 1954, for example, outlawed educational segregation by race but not by gender.

The policy process does not embrace only those in government whose job it is to enact, interpret, and enforce laws about gender and education. The process also involves school administrators, teachers, parents, and pupils, all of whom have their own interpretations of what gender is or should be, what gender equity means, what the intention of the law "really" is, how seriously they must take it, and what effects it will or should have on school programs and practices. Consensus about these issues among the many actors involved is unlikely to be high, particularly when the policy in question is controversial, as gender policies inevitably are.

Although the enormous complexity of policy interpretation and implementation often prevents effective action, complexities and misunderstandings can sometimes be used as excuses for inaction that are designed to cover up deliberate resistance to policies. This resistance is particularly likely when policies are designed to shift power arrangements by increasing resources of previously underprivileged groups and, thereby, reducing the relative advantage of previously dominant groups. Policies of this type include those intended to promote gender and other forms of educational equality. As demonstrated in the readings in this section, such policies have challenged and continue to threaten the relative power and advantages of White males. These policies have already produced more opportunities for girls and women and, if fully implemented, would bring about even more extensive changes in educational structures and processes. Opposition to them has come from all levels of the political and social hierarchy, and it is not surprising that the most effective resistance has come from the higher levels of those hierarchies. President Reagan and his Cabinet, for example, were famous for their decisions to simply stop funding the enforcement of laws passed by earlier sessions of Congress with which Reagan disagreed. These included civil rights laws, such as Title IX, aimed at reducing discrimination in education, and it was not surprising that by the end of his years in office Congress felt it necessary to pass the Civil Rights Restoration Act, mentioned above, over Reagan's veto. Although this Act seems to have helped Title IX survive the Reagan onslaught, a more dismal fate, documented in the penultimate essay in this encyclopedia, befell the Women's Educational Equity Act. That essay should be read by anyone who seeks evidence for official resistance to the implementation of gender equity policies in the United States.

Evidence for official resistance to gender equity policies also comes from other countries. In those with Parliamentary governments, where the sharp separation between executive and legislative branches does not exist, the more common way of undermining popular laws passed by previous Parliaments is simply to replace them with new laws. And, the authors who describe recent developments in the educational policies of Britain, Canada, and a sampling of other developed and developing countries (see "International Policies") all confirm governmental attempts to avoid or move away from a concern with gender equity.

In the United States, this attempt clearly indicates a reversal of the course established by the government in response to the efforts of the Women's Liberation Movement, now called second-wave feminism, to define the major *problems of gender and education* as problems of gender inequities in schooling, particularly the disadvantages girls were then experiencing in comparison to boys. Within this broad, major concern were such specific problems as the underperformance of girls, compared to boys, in the fields of mathematics, science, and technology; the underrepresentation of women, compared to men, in most areas of higher, graduate, and professional education; the existence of sexist teaching materials and pedagogical practices in which girls and women and their accomplishments were invisible or undervalued; and the sexual harassment and violence directed at girls and women throughout their years of schooling.

In order to provide both fairness and equivalent role models for boys and girls, second-wave feminists also fought for policies that would foster gender parity among teachers and school officials at the elementary and secondary levels and among all academics and administrators in higher education. In particular, it was argued that more women should be recruited into academic and administrative positions and into teaching subjects, such as science and mathematics, in which male teachers predominated. Like faculty members, educational administrators should be made aware of their different behaviors toward males and females and should be required to treat and to evaluate students and faculty members of both sexes in an equitable manner, free of stereotypic assumptions about gender differences.

The official policies designed to achieve these goals had barely begun to be implemented in the United States and in other countries around the world when they came under attack by those who did not agree that equity should be a primary goal of education. Over the past 30 years, the arguments against equity policies have taken a number of forms, varying somewhat over time and across countries. A major argument has been the one that pits equity against excellence. By focusing on equity, this argument contends, schools have neglected their best and brightest students, not met their responsibility to help all students achieve at the highest levels possible, and failed to produce a labor force that can compete effectively in a globalizing, capitalist economy. Educational research does not support the claim that an emphasis on equity undermines student achievement, but research evidence has not deterred those who oppose equity policies from developing alternative educational policies—based on what are called teacher accountability, high-stakes testing, and school choice—and claiming that these newly developed policies will improve student performance. Some of those who participate in the development and implementation of these policies continue to argue against the goal of equity, but others claim that the policies they are proposing will improve the performance of all children, including those, such as disadvantaged minorities, on whose behalf educational equity policies were originally formulated. Policies that promote school choice, including the choice of single-sex schooling, for example, are sold to the public as policies that will open more opportunities for girls and boys and, thereby, result in more gender equity than policies directly aimed at equity (see "School Choice and Gender Equity" for a research-based refutation of this argument).

These mixed arguments about the goal of equity can also be found in the large amount of attention that has recently been given to the "Boy Problem." In general, this problem is defined as the underachievement of boys, compared to girls, in elementary and secondary schools. The finding that boys score lower, on average, than girls on tests of verbal ability is seen as part of the problem, as is the greater tendency of boys to drop out of school. Some of the concern with this problem reflects a genuine commitment to gender equity and to making certain that boys and girls of all backgrounds are given equal educational opportunities, attention, and support and are held to the same standards in all areas of the official, extra-, and hidden curricula. But, some of this concern flows from darker motives, including a misogynous fear that girls are usurping the higher status that boys once enjoyed in educational institutions. These critics claim correctly that girls have been making more gains in academic performance than boys and that boys are subject to far more disciplinary action and alienation from school than girls. But, these research findings then lead them to the incorrect and unsupported conclusions that girls are no longer disadvantaged, that all boys (regardless of race-ethnicity and social class) suffer from similar educational disadvantages, and that the reason for boys' failures and misbehaviors is the anti-male bias of the feminist policy agenda and the presence in the schools of too many women teachers. Those who promote these latter conclusions provide another good example of the kinds of resistance to policies that arise when those policies are designed to shift the power balance by increasing the resources of previously disadvantaged groups.

A more sophisticated criticism of gender equity policies has also emerged during the past four decades. This criticism comes from people, often feminists, who strongly believe in the goal of gender equity, but who feel that policies cannot achieve these goals unless they recognize certain basic differences between the sexes, in particular the differences surrounding reproduction. Pregnancy, for example, should not be treated as if it is an illness or a condition similar to something experienced by boys and men. Nor should motherhood be treated as if it is the same as fatherhood. Some reproduction-related differences, like pregnancy, are biological, but others, like the assignment of primary child-care responsibilities to women rather than men, are deeply embedded social and historical constructions. In either case, these critics claim that gender equity policies that ignore these differences will not be successful. Only by recognizing the very real differences, and constructing policies accordingly, can pregnant and mothering students have real opportunities to continue and complete their educations (see "Pregnant and Parenting Teens"). And only if their employers adopt and implement policies of this kind will pregnant and mothering faculty and administrators be evaluated fairly and have real opportunities to develop their careers (see "Evaluation Policies for Academics" and "Work-Family Reconciliation Policies").

In addition to the official statements of intentions to act on problems surrounding gender and education that are called policies, or sometimes public or official policies, there are also relevant *policy initiatives* that are unofficial efforts to promote opportunities and empowerment for disadvantaged groups, including women. As several essays in this and earlier sections of the encyclopedia indicate, many initiatives of this type emerged from the social movement now called second-wave feminism, and some have been enacted into official policies. Other examples are the activities of nongovernmental organizations, commonly referred to as NGOs. As Karen Monkman documents, NGOs participate in policy discourse and formulation and are often crucial determiners of the effects that policies have on the people in the areas of the world in which the NGOs operate. Women-centered NGOs have been particularly important in making certain that international development policies are implemented in ways that empower women and educational policies are interpreted and implemented in ways that increase gender equity. Some of these NGOs also are proactive in promoting gender-equitable processes and goals outside of what is required by the international funding agencies responsible for official policies.

Going beyond what is official, required, and routine is also characteristic of the large number of educators around the world who are engaged in the development of feminist pedagogy. As Berenice Fisher's essay explains, this grassroots and unofficial policy initiative takes different forms, but all who advocate feminist pedagogy are united in a passionate—and sometimes dangerous—effort to transform teaching and learning processes to the greater advantage of girls and women.

For more on gender and educational policies, see "Home Schooling," "Military Colleges and Academies," and "Public Single-Sex and Coeducational Schools" in Part III; "National Curricula" in Part IV; "Curricular Tracking" in Part V; "Educator Sexual Misconduct" in Part VII; and "Salaries of Academics," "Teacher Burnout," and "Work-Family Conflicts of Educators" in Part IX.

The "Boy Problem"

An *Education Week* editorial proclaims a "Silent Gender Gap: Reading, Writing, and Other Problems for Boys." A 2006 *Newsweek* cover decries a "Boy Crisis." A headline in the *Chicago Sun-Times* warns that "Boys, Not Girls, on Worse End of Education Gap." A bestselling book by Christine Hoff Sommers appears in 2000 trumpeting *The War Against Boys.* A *USA Today* contributor complains that "Girls Get Extra School Help While Boys Get Ritalin." *U.S. News and World Report* ponders "Are Boys the Weaker Sex?" Seemingly more and more frequently, media outlets and pundits are focusing their concern on the so-called "boy problem" in schools that holds boys are not faring well in academics, in social settings, or in health concerns compared to their female peers. This debate is occurring not just in the United States but all over the world.

Indeed, from Australia to England, from the United States to Canada, and from Iceland to Germany, a noticeable panic has developed and grown around the education of boys. Grabbing newspaper headlines, taking up bookstore shelves, and even capturing major attention from the research community and practitioners, boys' educational issues have in many ways overshadowed the 1970s, 1980s, and 1990s much-needed focus on girls' education. This has elsewhere been called the "boy turn" in gender and education research and practice (Weaver-Hightower, 2003). This turn to boys, though, has not been easy or uncontested. While much panic and work has focused on the "boy problem" in education, much feminist and profeminist thought has been directed at tempering the hysteria and establishing nuance within the emotionally heated terrain of gender reform. What are the concerns that the public, educators, and policy makers have about boys? Where has this new focus on boys come from? What has been done to try to intervene in these problems? And, what are the dangers of this new focus on the problem(s) of boys in so many places?

WHAT ABOUT THE BOYS?

"What about the boys?" has become an oft-heard refrain in the debates over boys around the world. While it can be meant or taken in many ways, it has largely come to represent the position of antifeminist backlash against the gains made for girls in schools; it is, in other words, an abridgement of a sentiment that says something like "Enough has been done for girls in schools. Now what about the boys?" Rather than using it in this sense, this question can be considered in the alternative sense of trying to delineate the issues that are commonly identified as problems for boys. In general, these problems fall into two categories: (a) academic and (b) social, physical, and medical.

Within the category of academic problems for boys, concern has centered largely on literacy. Put simply, boys tend to do less well than girls on tests of school-based literacy. In the United States, the gap between the average scores of males and females in reading at all age levels on the long-term National Assessment of Educational Progress (NAEP) has been between 7 and 15 points (on a 500-point scale) throughout the 35 years of the test's administration (National Center for Education Statistics, 2000). On writing, the gap stands even wider, with boys behind girls 17 to 24 points on the 2002 NAEP writing test, this time on a 300-point scale (National Center for Education Statistics, 2003). Similar reading results to those in the United States have been found cross-nationally, as well. The Organisation for Economic Co-operation and Development (OECD, 2003), a group representing 30 "Western," industrialized countries, finds that in all its member nations, females in the fourth grade have a statistically significant advantage over boys in tested literacy. For 15 year olds, the gap stands even wider across the countries. Many other cross-national studies similarly find that girls outperform boys on nearly every measure of literacy tested.

Other indicators of academic performance have also been of concern regarding boys. In England, for example, the number of girls getting grades A through C on General Certificate of Secondary Education exams (or GCSE, the comprehensive, subject-based exams at the end of secondary education) have surpassed boys in many subjects. Some worry that boys do not receive as many academic awards as girls, while others decry the rising gap in college and university enrollment that has begun favoring females. Some even hold that the school has become a feminine environment that hurts boys' ability to succeed in schools, an argument that has recurred often through history. The main rationale for such an argument contends that boys have biological differences in brain construction or different learning styles that are not met by current modes of teaching, though some allege that feminist efforts to make boys more like girls are behind it. Some, finally, assert that teachers and boys are emotionally disconnected from one another, which hinders boys' ability to succeed in school, as well.

The second category of concern, encompassing social, physical, and medical issues, has been treated as if interconnected with academic issues. Much concern has been expressed over attention deficit disorder and hyperactivity (ADD/ADHD) in popular discussion, particularly because the majority of those diagnosed and medicated for it are males. Males are also more likely than females to be diagnosed for special education, to be diagnosed with autism and dyslexia, to have drug and alcohol problems, to engage in risk-taking behavior, to be the victims and perpetrators of violence and crime, and to complete suicide attempts. In school, boys are more likely to receive negative feedback, they and girls think teachers like boys less than girls, and boys are far more likely to be suspended or expelled (excluded) from school or to drop out. Violence, particularly, sometimes in the form of rampage school shootings in the United States, has been a central issue that propels boys and their problems to the public stage. Clearly, such physical, emotional, and medical indicators have relevance to schools and to the general state of males during school and after.

Largely, the veracity of the indicators—boys' relative advantages and disadvantages—are not in dispute. Rather, what they mean, what has caused them, and what should be done about them has been the most contentious aspect. A diversity of opinion exists on these central questions.

CONSERVATIVE AND (PRO)FEMINIST ARGUMENTS

The debates over "the boy problem" have largely been led by conservative voices, whether antifeminist scholars or right-wing religious personalities. These writers have largely painted the issue of boys' education as one in which liberal feminist forces have polluted or destroyed time-tested practices for raising and educating boys to be "real men." Blame is laid on a lack of male role models and teachers, feminist cover-ups of boys' difficulties in order to privilege those of girls, and a lack of attention to—or "forgetting" of—school structures, curriculum, and pedagogy that fit the ways boys purportedly learn.

Feminist women and profeminist men—hereafter combined in the term "(pro)feminist" since these two groups largely agree—have objected to such portrayals of the boy problem, some questioning whether a problem really exists. Some, for example, argue that many of these effects do not indicate disadvantages based on gender but rather the *costs* of male privilege in other areas. Underachievement in literacy, for instance, can be seen as a cost of the privileged status of math and science compared to the lower, sometimes feminized, status of the humanities. Other scholars suggest that the small gaps in literacy and other achievement measures are of little consequence, for it remains true that males do better in employment rates, are paid better on average for the same work, and dominate the positions of power in business, government, sports, and culture. In other words, males' relative lack of achievement during schooling does not appear to hurt them after school. There are also concerns that concentration on boys will take attention, not to mention already scarce resources, from those programs that address problems for girls in math, sciences, and technology. Some fear that the masculinist discourses of boys as victims, schools as failing boys, and boys being allowed to "be boys" will create an environment in which girls' concerns are seen as secondary or, worse, as the privileged trying to get more advantages.

Perhaps the most important intervention in the debates over the boy problem by (pro) feminists has been countering the question, "What about the boys?" with the question, "Which boys?" This question asks advocates for boys to disaggregate the category "boys" or, in other words, to break this category down by race, socioeconomic class, sexuality, disability and ability, and so on. This (pro)feminist intervention reminds us that not all boys are having problems and, perhaps more importantly, that some boys suffer more than others. African American, Aboriginal Australian, and Afro-Caribbean British males, for example, are far more likely than European American and Anglo males to be caught up in disciplinary systems in schools and criminal justice systems outside schools. African American boys are also further behind than their White counterparts in literacy scores. Gay, bisexual, and questioning boys, as another example, face a greater disconnect with the curriculum and face more harassment at school than heterosexual boys. To not break "boys" into categories of race, class, sexuality, and so on skews the indicators in deceptive ways, making it appear as if all boys were in dire straits. Seeing the data in such limited ways might lead to wasting valuable and limited resources on those who need them far less and could further compound the oppression of those boys.

Another important impact of (pro)feminist scholars has been pointing out that the problems of boys are not new. If such indicators of boys' problems have been true for many years, why all the panic and concern now? A number of social dynamics have been driving this panic (Weaver-Hightower, 2003). A large portion of the driving force has been the popular press books and newspaper headlines mentioned earlier; these have increased the visibility of such anxieties. Parent and educator interest in these topics—their need for solutions to very real problems—encourages such work to be done, of course. Other dynamics push the boy problem debates forward, too. Feminists, as well as men's rights and mythopoetic advocates of the 1990s (stereotyped as middle-age men beating drums in the woods), have contributed a language for and awareness that males have a gender, too. Liberal feminist educational measurements that have been used successfully in the past to spur legislation to help girls, particularly equal participation rates and equal test scores, have now ironically turned in ways that highlight the problems of boys. In addition, though, much of the renewed concern can be considered a backlash against feminism, with some explicitly attempting to reestablish male dominance in education and the workforce. Similarly, the predominance of conservative, rightist educational reform has, because boys' issues have also been highly conservative, increased the visibility of test score gaps for boys and altered "common sense" about education in reactionary and antifeminist ways. Too, a global "crisis of masculinity" over civic and economic participation has spurred attention on boys, as have changes away from industrialized factory-based labor (a traditionally male domain) to service labor (a traditionally female domain) in most Western nations. Finally, the interest of publishers in a hot, new, and controversial (thus, profitable) topic has driven publication toward concerns of boys.

Though debates over the boy problem can seem polarized, it should be noted, however, that the majority of those invested in the issues lie somewhere in the middle. These people do not subscribe to either camp but rather largely are worried about the everyday necessity of raising and teaching boys. Often, such groups become a political prize, and much rhetorical energy has focused on enlisting this large set of ground forces. In the current context, conservative voices have been more successful in this effort because they have been willing to take seriously the practical concerns of parents and educators.

INTERVENTIONS

A large portion of those who have attempted to solve the practical concerns of parents and educators have written in what has been called the "practice-oriented" tradition of boys' education literature, "boyswork," or, more disparagingly, "tips for teachers." The quality of such interventions has been variable, from nuanced examination of gender as socially constructed to rather simplistic and stereotypical teaching practices (like having boys "high five" a construction paper cutout of a hand when they leave class as a way to get boys to be more active). In general, though, practice-oriented work has sought to address the major problems outlined earlier in this essay, including literacy achievement, behavior, and social ills. Collections by Bleach (1998) and Browne and Fletcher (1995) provide case studies of schools' attempts to deal with boys' issues. Alloway and Gilbert (1997) and Salisbury and Jackson (1996) suggest practical strategies and lessons to examine masculinity from progressive and feminist veins as a way to deal with the problems of boys.

A particularly well-trod ground of research on practice for boys has been literacy with the general aim being to make boys more prolific and better readers. The majority of such work has concentrated on the social aspects of literacy, particularly the supposed lack of "fit" between boys' socialization and literacy habits and the literacy expected or done in classrooms. In the tradition of mythopoetic notions of males, some suggest teachers select books that feature male archetypes and traditional male interests to get boys more interested in reading. Others suggest that teachers get over their apprehensions about violent or gross books because these are materials in which boys—stereotypically—are most interested. Still others suggest that boys lack the emotional vocabulary to succeed in tasks that current English language arts pedagogy and curriculum demands, so teachers should help boys learn this vocabulary. Research from a (pro)feminist perspective has developed critical literacy approaches that encourage students to practice social critique of reading materials, to use with boys to simultaneously address literacy skills and the features of masculinity that prevent boys from full participation in literacy.

A number of programs for African American males (answering the "Which boys?" concern) provide good examples of community-based interventions into boys' education issues. Most visible of these were the court-thwarted attempts to create Afrocentric all-male schools in Detroit, Michigan, in the early 1990s. This program and others like it across the United States spawned from concerns for the lagging educational achievement of African American boys and the increasing social ills growing from this. Boys Booked on Barbershops (called B-BOB) provides another example, in this case particularly focused on literacy skills and attitudes. Started in Memphis, Tennessee, using barbershops—traditionally one of the most stable businesses in African American communities—the program seeks to provide high-interest books and have men and boys read together. Such programs and others at the community services level often provide male mentors, often particularly targeting boys without fathers at home, along with academic enrichment opportunities and (sometimes religious) counseling that are culturally relevant to the participants, are integrated into local institutions, are staffed by people who live and work in the communities and schools, and are responsive to local needs.

THE POLICY TERRAIN FOR BOYS' EDUCATION ISSUES

The local, diffuse, informal nature of the programs described above typifies the policy terrain for boys' education in the United States. The state-centered, often judicially mandated policy structure of American education has thus far limited action on "the boy problem." Instead, interventions and programs have sprouted in local schools and districts with little or no state support (with the exception of Maine) and no policy mandate whatsoever.

The same has not been true in other countries. Perhaps more than any other country, Australia has taken on the boy problem through official, state-level, and now federal-level policy on the education of boys. The Australian House Committee's report *Boys: Getting it Right,* released in 2002, identifies learning differences, social and economic changes, and pedagogical shortcomings that, the Committee contends, limit Australian boys' ability to succeed in schools. Growing from this report and interest in its findings, the Australian government has sponsored conferences, commissioned research, and spent millions of dollars on Boys' Education Lighthouse Schools and Success for Boys grant programs. These programs have given moderate-sized grants directly to schools to develop and disseminate "best practices" in educating boys.

A great deal of policy attention internationally has also focused on the low number of male teachers, a reason often given as part of boys' difficulties in schools. The issue particularly concerns the widespread lack of male teachers in the younger grades. In Australia, the report referred to above also touches on this issue, for *Boys: Getting it Right* calls for male-only teacher education scholarships, and debate has, thus, been sparked over changing sex discrimination laws to allow such scholarships. (Pro)feminist advocates have viewed the arguments for increasing the numbers of male teachers with great skepticism. First, there is little research to suggest that male teachers are more capable of teaching boys. Second, such arguments imply a criticism of female teachers as being at fault for any problems boys have. Further, some male teachers can cause more gendered problems than they solve by, for instance, being hypermasculine or being intimidating to girls. Having more *good* teachers, not necessarily *male* teachers, has been the frequent call from (pro)feminists. These scholars also predict that scholarship schemes are unlikely to alter the reasons males avoid teaching, namely low status, low salaries, the perception of teaching as "women's work," suspicions of males as gay or pedophiles if they work with children, and other working conditions that some contend are not conducive to males staying in classrooms.

Though formal policy has been limited thus far, especially in the United States, much potential for growth in programs and even for policies to address the "boy problem" exists in many countries. In the United States, specifically, the rolling back of federal women's policy infrastructure, revisions to (some say "attacks on") Title IX sex equality legislation, renewed attention on testing that might highlight boys' deficiencies, growing cultural conservatism that drives boys' education concerns, and media coverage of the topic have all created fertile ground for the growth of interventions on the boy problem. Signals from high-ranking U.S. education officials serve to confirm the existing political will to pursue this issue. One telling example is a press release for a report on *girls'* equity issued by Rod Paige, former U.S. Secretary of Education, on November 19, 2004. "The issue now," said Paige, "is that boys seem to be falling behind. We need to spend some time researching the problem so that we can give boys the support to succeed academically." Whatever policy or practice gets created, it seems likely that the "boy problem" will command attention for several years to come. While some welcome the attention on boys' education, others vigilantly watch so that these reforms do not overshadow other equity issues.

REFERENCES AND FURTHER READINGS

Alloway, N., & Gilbert, P. (Eds.). (1997). *Boys and literacy—teaching units.* Carlton, Australia: Curriculum Corporation.

Bleach, K. (Ed.). (1998). *Raising boys' achievement in schools.* Staffordshire, England: Trentham Books.

Browne, R., & Fletcher, R. (Eds.). (1995). *Boys in schools: Addressing the real issues—behaviour, values, and relationships.* Sydney, Australia: Finch.

Ferguson, A.A. (2000). *Bad boys: Public schools in the making of black masculinity.* Ann Arbor: University of Michigan Press.

Gilbert, R., & Gilbert, P. (1998). *Masculinity goes to school.* London: Routledge.

National Center for Education Statistics. (2000). *NAEP 1999 trends in academic progress: Three decades of student performance* (No. NCES 2000-469). Washington, DC: U.S. Department of Education.

National Center for Education Statistics. (2003). *The nation's report card: Writing highlights 2002* (No. NCES 2003-531). Washington, DC: U.S. Department of Education.

Organisation for Economic Co-operation and Development (OECD). (2003). *Education at a glance: OECD indicators 2003.* Paris: OECD.

Salisbury, J., & Jackson, D. (1996). *Challenging macho values: Practical ways of working with adolescent boys.* London: Falmer Press.

Weaver-Hightower, M.B. (2003). The "boy turn" in research on gender and education. *Review of Educational Research, 73*(4), 471–498.

Marcus B. Weaver-Hightower

Evaluation Policies for Academics

Merit is often invoked as the objective basis upon which recruitment, tenure, and promotion decisions are made within the academy and outside of it. In many institutions of higher education in the United States, merit is also the major criterion that is said to be used to determine appropriate annual increases in the salaries of individual faculty members. Merit, it is argued, is the fairest way to evaluate faculty because it ensures that the best and brightest will rise to the top and that evaluations will be unaffected by personal biases of evaluators in favor of or against specific individuals or certain groups of faculty. Thus, it has been claimed that basing important personnel decisions on a merit system of evaluation will diminish gender inequalities in the academy, such as the poor placement of women and racial or ethnic minorities.

The concept of merit is troublesome, however, because it is grounded in a neoclassical economic theoretical perspective that limits one's understanding of, and responses to, organizational inequality. In principle, merit-based appointments ought to provide an equitable basis for recruitment, salary, and promotion decisions yielding more equitable outcomes for women because women, and other minorities, have a chance to be judged as equally meritorious. Where structural disadvantage exists for whole groups, however, the application of the merit principle is difficult, if not impossible. Reliance on more socially embedded theoretical perspectives on inequality provides a way of explaining such structural disadvantage and calls into question the existence of an even playing field, where all players can be judged on the same merit criterion.

These theoretical challenges to the theoretical framework of neoclassical economics suggest two alternatives to the merit systems currently used in higher education. At the very least, merit ought to be defined and measured in more inclusive ways so that women have a chance to be judged as equally meritorious with their male counterparts. A more radical response would be to eliminate merit from our lexicon and look to new ways to address gender inequality in universities. What may be happening instead is that market principles of neoclassical economic theory are being adopted by universities, in combination with merit, to determine who obtains favorable evaluations.

NEOCLASSICAL ECONOMICS AND THE MERIT SYSTEM

Neoclassical economics is rooted in the work of Adam Smith (1776). According to this perspective, the market is competitive and business organizations operate best when allowed to interact in free and unfettered competition. Society is not as important as individuals, "atomized" individuals, who each make quite independent choices for, or against, some particular product or service. The idea is that such choices are made using particular criteria, like price, quality and availability, and the organization that delivers the best mix of these "wins" the support of consumers. To achieve this, business must maximize efficiency (inputs to outputs); the most efficient organization wins under free market conditions. In this way, according to this particular theoretical perspective, some producers are appropriately rewarded over others.

This perspective is based on a series of simplifying assumptions like perfect information, rational action, and free entrance into and exit from the market. It also relies on an "invisible hand" to set things right. A key tenet of this perspective is that, left alone, the market itself is efficient and will deliver the best result for society.

Moreover, this theoretical perspective marries individualism and the idea of a meritocracy to explain how society works. According to this perspective, individuals act in the market as rational, independent players and, as far as their placement in society is concerned, individuals succeed only through their own talents and hard work. Race, ethnicity, gender, and social class are irrelevant in this view of the world. Instead, an open social system is assumed, meaning that an individual's placement in society is not constrained by anything other than that person's own merits. The key idea is that anyone can move up the social hierarchy if he or she is able and willing to work hard enough.

As a theoretical perspective, neoclassical economics is optimistic, perhaps overly so. Certainly classical theorist Adam Smith expected wealth to be generated without end under free market conditions. Society as a whole would benefit from the upward spiral of economic growth delivered by the free flow of market forces as needs were met in the marketplace and efficient owners became richer and rewarded workers by sharing this wealth with them, to the greater good of all. There is an explicit judgment here that owners and workers who succeed do so through their own merits and will be rewarded in proportion to their merit.

Neoclassical economics has become the dominant paradigm promulgated by most business schools, and most of the disciplines that drive their approaches are embedded within it. It is also the dominant paradigm in the West, in general. But, this is not to suggest that this is the only, or even the best, explanation of economy and society. Alternative explanations also inform our understanding.

ALTERNATIVES TO NEOCLASSICAL ECONOMICS

In general, these alternative perspectives developed in reaction to neoclassical ideas. Karl Marx offered one of the earliest reactions to Smith's theory. Marx lived in England during the Industrial Revolution, and he did not see the upward spiral of wealth for all that Smith had so optimistically predicted. Instead, he witnessed the horrors and atrocities of life in the sweatshops and "satanic mills" of the time. Marx, philosopher, revolutionary, and, then, social scientist, set himself the task of trying to figure out what went wrong: why Smith's perfectly reasonable theory did not result in wealth for all and a universal increase in the quality of life.

In the end, Marx ([1857–1858] 1965, [1867] 1918) argued that the system of production itself, the free market or capitalism, is the problem. It sets people against one another as only some people have ownership and control of the means of production, while others have only their labor to sell. Under free market conditions, as producers try to become the most efficient and responsive in their industry, it is rational for owners/managers to try to extract as much from workers as possible and give them as little as possible in return. This would not work in the long term, according to Marx, as not only would workers become wretched in such a system, but they could no longer afford to buy the very products they produce. Without a mass consumer market, business itself would collapse. This is the key contradiction in capitalism that Marx thought would lead, ultimately, to the destruction of that system of production. Moreover, Marx argued that capitalist society is inherently unequal, by virtue of the existence of the power differential between these two groups: owners of capital and labor. A meritocracy cannot exist where whole groups in society, particularly labor in his view, begin at a disadvantage. To suggest that everyone has an equal chance to move up the social system, to accumulate wealth, is simply a deception, according to Marx.

Later theoretical development in explanations of business, economy, and society were reactions to the ideas of both Smith and Marx. These works include those of Max Weber and the critical theorists. Although Weber (1958a, [1918] 1958b, 1968) is most famous for his analyses of formal organizations, particularly bureaucracies, and for his analysis of why market capitalism developed when and where it did, he also wrote extensively about social stratification, and much of that writing is relevant to the notion of meritocracy. Weber argued that society is layered and people reside at different locations in the social stratification system depending on their economic class (similar to Marx), social honor or status, and political power. Movement up the hierarchy is possible, but it is not simply a matter of individual effort and hard work, and most people remain roughly where they started. Placement in the hierarchy depends less on individual effort than on group memberships. In other words, people are located at positions in the social stratification system as much by their race-ethnicity and social class as by their individual merits. Occupational groups were of particular interest to Weber who saw them as not only establishing relationships to capital and wealth (as did Marx) but also determining status (prestige) and power.

Another theme of Weber's work relevant to the concept of meritocracy was his concern that economic efficiency was becoming the major criterion against which all human behaviors were being judged. Because bureaucracy, with its routinized systems, files, and hierarchy of control, was technically the most efficient form of social organization, Weber was convinced that it would come to displace all other forms. He anticipated that increasingly business—and education—would be run by large bureaucracies because of the technical and economic efficiencies they permit. He was concerned that single-minded pursuit of this economic principle was propelling this criterion for action into center stage. He was most concerned that, ultimately, society would lose the ability to judge social action and organization on anything but purely economically rational grounds. In fact, he saw that society was coming to value the economic criterion of efficiency so highly that efficiency was becoming the only legitimate basis for action. Under these conditions, making decisions based on grounds like equity or justice cannot be understood to be rational. Weber's analysis led him to the pessimistic conclusion that humanity is trapped in an iron cage of a narrow and distorted economic rationality and there is no way out.

Like Marx and Weber, theorists of the so-called Critical School provide critical insights into the nature of social organization. Forerunners of this school, writing in the 1920s, tried to explain why, despite the atrocious conditions under which much of the Western world lived, workers did not revolt and usher in a new society as Marx had optimistically hoped. Lukacs ([1923] 1971) came to the view that most people were kept happy enough, through access to sufficient food and entertainment, not to seek to change the basis of society. Gramsci (1971) argued, similarly, that it had become conventional wisdom that economy and society is naturally unequal and competitive, that it is good and proper that some people are wealthier than others, and that this is merely their reward for their talent and hard work. According to these theorists, things do not change even under difficult conditions where whole groups are systematically disadvantaged as these same people fail to see how things could be otherwise. Gramsci called this taken-for-granted, conventional wisdom that dominates our thought and action a "cultural hegemony."

Critical School theorists, like Horkheimer and Adorno ([1947] 1972) and, more recently, Habermas (1984), picked up on this idea of a cultural hegemony, and Habermas, in particular, set himself the task of trying to work out how this overly economic-rational view of the world might be challenged. His solution is startling. Habermas argues that what we need is more rationality, not less. To rely only on an economically rational view of the world—precisely what neoclassical economics does—is to consider valid only one of a number of equally valid bases for social action. At the moment, we judge social action and explain the nature of organization and gender inequality using only economic principles. More particularly, we judge most social action on the basis of its economic efficiency. The more economically efficient the answer to a particular problem, the better. This is what counts. But, as Weber (1968) argued, there are other bases that we can use both to judge social action and to guide notions of the appropriateness of social organization. These other bases include truth, truthfulness, and rightness (social justice). Habermas (1984) argues that societies need more rationality, not less, and certainly not more of the narrow and, consequently, distorted rationality that only judges action using the economic criteria that are dominant in Western thinking at the present time.

Although not explicitly concerned with the merit systems, the theories of Marx, Weber, and the Critical School make it easy to understand that an objective meritocracy, where individuals are located along a social hierarchy solely on the basis of individual aptitude and action—on their own merit—is not possible. There is no level playing field. There is no objective place to stand. People are located at positions in the socioeconomic hierarchy as much by their race/ethnicity, social class, and other group membership as by their individual merits. Under such conditions, to judge on "merit" is nonsense as not all groups have a chance to be equally meritorious. To be non-White and poor is to be at a disadvantage when decisions are made on some supposedly objective, merit-based criterion.

FEMINIST THEORIES

Although Marx, Weber, and the theorists of the Critical School moved social thought away from the emphasis on competition and individual merit of neoclassical economics, their emphasis on social stratification and group disadvantage rarely extended to women. It fell to the feminists to examine the merit system through a gender lens, but when they did so, some were more likely to reject merit systems of evaluation than others.

Most likely to embrace the merit system and the neoclassical economic theory on which it is based have been advocates of *liberal feminism*. From this perspective, women have lagged behind men economically because they have been prevented from achieving the same education, training, and job experiences that men have historically enjoyed. Once the barriers holding them back are removed and an equal opportunity structure is created, women and men will be able to compete on a level playing field, and there is every reason to assume that, over time, women will become just as meritorious as men and do just as well as men economically. In support of their theory, liberal feminists point to the advances over the past 40 years that women have made, relative to men, in educational attainments, employment status, and salaries. If women have not yet achieved the same economic level as men, argue the liberals, the remedy lies in individual efforts to increase their merit by, for example, taking more math and science courses in school; choosing college majors, such as engineering, that lead to more lucrative jobs; demonstrating higher levels of job commitment; and being more assertive and competitive.

In contrast to liberal feminism, other forms of feminist theory are more likely to reject the merit system and other individualistic solutions to gender inequality. These feminists see gender as more than an individual characteristic. Instead, it is a major organizing principle in our society. To some, called *Marxist feminists* or *socialist feminists,* gender is as important or almost as important as social class in determining where people stand (rich men highest, poor women lowest) in the organizations and institutions of societies. To others, called *Black feminists* or *multicultural feminists,* gender is as important as race or ethnicity in making this same determination (White men highest, Black or minority women lowest). To still others, *radical feminists,* gender is the most enduring and most important basis for organizing societies, and the gender hierarchy as patriarchy is based on a system of male superiority and power over females.

In contrast to liberal feminism, all of these forms of feminism share in common the notion that the differences between men and women are not differences of individual characteristics, such as merit, but are categorical differences based on the hegemonic power of men to determine how people (including less powerful men, but especially all women) will be evaluated and treated. The playing field for men and women is far from level. Men control the field and the ways in which the game can be played and scored. They define what is and is not meritorious; these definitions will be used to maintain their own power; and they will not give up this power willingly. An individual academic woman might find herself accorded high status if she were able to acquire all of the credentials and accomplishments regarded (by hegemonic men) as meritorious. But, she would probably also be regarded as atypical, or even mannish. And, if increasing numbers of women began to acquire those meritorious credentials and accomplishments, they would probably find that the criteria for merit had shifted in ways that downplayed their achievements and put increasing emphasis on the achievements of their male colleagues.

Despite their greater support for the merit system, liberal feminists would join with other feminists to argue that the poor representation of women at the senior-most levels of universities and other organizations is not simply a matter of choice. There is an argument that women choose family or family/career or career, thereby making an active decision about their career trajectory. While many women choose to commit to family, the argument runs, many successful men have made a career choice, often with the help of supporting partners who take primary responsibility for the domestic domain, subjugating their own extradomestic goals in support of this choice. However, feminist and other alternative theoretical perspectives indicate that, in many cases, such "choices" are an illusion. Social structures and expectations reinforce the position of whole groups in society. In this case, women remain primarily responsible for social reproduction roles, and this severely constrains the choices women may make. While individual women may have some choice —particularly those who, through the seniority of their position, can afford to pay for child-care and domestic assistance or who do not have a family or who receive the support of a partner who elects to subjugate his/her extradomestic goals to that woman's career—general social expectations mean that most women's choices are tightly constrained. They must negotiate both social reproduction and production or work roles, taking the lead in domestic and family matters, even as they seek to measure up against supposedly objective merit-based criteria.

ALTERNATIVES TO THE MERIT SYSTEM

The difficulty of shifting away from current merit-based approaches is underscored when alternatives to the *status quo* are considered. One approach may be to fundamentally redefine "merit," perhaps even eliminating it from our lexicon, so that recruitment and promotion decisions can be made on other bases. This approach would require universities to "reality check" current recruitment/promotion criteria, involving a review of existing positions and ranks with a view to establishing what is actually required to perform these roles competently. The idea is to establish criteria for competence. This would mean challenging assumptions that, for example, the candidate with the most publications "wins" when all that is really required is evidence of some appropriate level of productivity. Moreover, continuous service may not be as important as the caliber or quality of that service. Once a pool of competent candidates has been established, recruitment, tenure, salary, and promotion decisions can be made on other, appropriate and work-related criteria. Remedying the underrepresentation of particular groups may be one such criterion. The core idea here does not involve appointing individuals who are not competent to undertake a particular role. Rather, it is about accurately specifying the role and then selecting among competent candidates on other, relevant criteria.

Another alternative is to turn this process on its head. For example, if women are underrepresented in a particular area, the approach may be to invite applications in the first round only from women (Bacchi, 1993). This latter approach constitutes the sort of direct and unapologetic affirmative action that is, in all likelihood, necessary to ensure appropriate levels of participation by women and minorities in senior positions. Whether approaches like these are best described as redefining merit or eliminating merit is open for debate. Irrespective of this labeling, such approaches are sensible only if the notion of a meritocracy aligned with the dominant hegemony of economic rationalism is dismissed. The idea that fair and objective judgments can be made and rewards allocated solely in proportion to worth, to individual merit, is, at best, naive and, at worst, a deception.

Alternative perspectives encourage a broader view of social organization and inequality that permit strategies aimed at delivering equitable outcomes. By contrast, neoclassical economic assumptions and the troublesome concept of merit, as currently conceptualized and applied, work against any improvement in the status of women and other minorities. Rather than an adoption of evaluation policies based on alternative perspectives, however, recent years have seen an increased reliance on neoclassical economic assumptions about not only individual merit but also the importance of market competition. In the United States, in particular, but to some extent internationally, market considerations now affect academic salaries to a far greater degree than they once did. Academics in fields perceived to be in "high demand" are likely to be recruited at higher salary levels than those in fields that are overcrowded, and the most certain way to gain a large salary increase at one's home university is to obtain an attractive salary offer from a comparable university elsewhere. Grantsmanship also enters the picture with large salaries being demanded by and awarded to those who are able to bring large research grants to their campus. Such market considerations have an impact on merit systems in that they promote definitions of merit that are increasingly based on financial considerations. The worth of faculty members comes increasingly to be defined by the grants and the salary offers that they can obtain. And, although advocates of the merit system would argue that there is nothing stopping women academics from getting grants, it is easy to document the fact that the larger grants and salaries are likely to be found in those academic fields that are dominated by men. Once again, the evidence suggests a clash between the merit and market values of neoclassical economic theory and the goal of improving the status of women and other minorities.

REFERENCES AND FURTHER READINGS

Bacchi, C. (1993). The brick wall: Why so few women become senior academics. *Australian Universities Review, 36*(1), 36–41.

Gramsci, A. (1971). *Selections from prison notebooks.* London: New Left Books.

Habermas, J. (1984). *The theory of communicative action: Vol. 1: Reason and the rationalisation of society* (T. McCarthy, Trans.). Boston: Bacon Press.

Harding, S.L. (2002). The troublesome concept of merit. In G. Howie & A. Tauchert (Eds.), *Gender, teaching and research in higher education: Challenges for the 21st century* (pp. 248–260). Burlington, VT: Ashgate Publishing Company.

Horkheimer, M., & Adorno, T. ([1947] 1972). *Dialectic of enlightenment.* New York: Herder.

Lukacs, G. ([1923] 1971). *History and class consciousness.* London: Merlin Books.

Marx, K. ([1857–1858] 1965). *Pre-capitalist economic formations* (Introduction by E. Hobsbawm). New York: International Publishers.

Marx, K. ([1867] 1918). *Capital.* London: William Glaisher Ltd.

Smith, A. ([1776] 1937). *The wealth of nations.* New York: Random House.

Weber, M. ([1918] 1958a). *From Max Weber* (H. H. Gerth and C. Wright Mills, Eds.). New York: Oxford University Press.

Weber, M. (1958b). *The Protestant ethic and the spirit of capitalism* (T. Parsons, Trans.). New York: Scribner.

Weber, M. (1968). *Economy and society* (Vols. 1–2) (G. Roth & C. Wittich, Eds.). Berkeley: University of California Press.

Sandra Harding

Feminist Pedagogy

Why do some teachers describe what they do as "feminist pedagogy?" What issues arise when instructors use this approach? Feminist pedagogy is the name applied by many late twentieth and early twenty-first century teachers to their ways of teaching women's studies and other courses with a feminist orientation. Writings and discussions about this topic tend to focus on college and university settings, where most of these courses are offered. Those who see themselves practicing feminist pedagogy share a commitment to social justice for women. But such teachers diverge in how they view social justice and how they hope to promote it in the classroom.

Although feminist pedagogy is often described as employing certain techniques (e.g., sitting in a circle, keeping journals that include personal reactions, engaging in action projects), these methods may be used by teachers who lack commitment to women's liberation. Feminist teachers may or may not adopt particular strategies in their version of feminist pedagogy. Thus, the differences and similarities in feminist teaching are best understood not by describing techniques but by looking at what feminist teachers hope to achieve in their classrooms. Four major goals are equality, caring, collective resistance, and deconstruction. A given teacher may adopt more than one of these goals.

THE LIBERAL VIEW OF EDUCATION: FEMINIST TEACHING FOR EQUALITY

Many teachers of women's studies and related classes are attracted to the liberal view of education for equality and freedom that dominates Western industrial societies. Drawing on these liberal values, feminists have opposed the exclusion of females from access to equal education: Like boys and men, women and girls must be offered the knowledge and intellectual tools that all individuals need to make independent decisions. Feminist teaching for equality means making sure that student development is unfettered by discrimination (e.g., barring females from certain schools or courses of study) or attitudes that discourage female talent and ambition. The curriculum, too, must be free of gender bias: Everyone should learn to identify and reject the gender stereotypes and misinformation that permeate virtually every field of study. A truly liberal education prepares female students to develop as full human beings, to participate equally in a democratic society, and to compete successfully in a capitalist world.

This approach to feminist teaching contains both strengths and weaknesses. Its strengths lie in the insistence on equal treatment and on cultivating the ability and yearning that girls and women bring to their schooling. No one calling himself or herself "feminist" is likely to dispute these principles. The weaknesses of this approach lie in its conception of teaching as a narrowly rational process and in a tendency to minimize the impact of race, class, sexuality, physical ability, nationality, and other sites of inequality. A woman may be disadvantaged by her gender but privileged in terms of class. Or she may be disadvantaged not only by gender but also by race and class. For an individual woman, equal educational opportunity may help her to escape the limits of her situation —to become what is sometimes called an "exceptional" woman. But, the liberation of some women as individuals, however rewarding, leaves unjust social structures in place.

FEMINIST PEDAGOGIES BASED ON CARING

In response to these weaknesses, feminist teachers have called into question the individualism on which the liberal view is based and proposed alternatives to it. The liberal ideal of individual achievement, critics note, applies unequally to men and women. The model for the fully developed, independent individual is male. This model ignores the fact that men are dependent on women's support. In societies based on the ideal of individual success, women tend to be held responsible for taking care of others and compensating for the damage done to them by competition. At the same time, these societies often denigrate caring. Such denigration is evident in higher education institutions, especially research universities, where academics routinely demean pedagogical ideas and practices that seem too caring by labeling them "touchy-feely," mothering, and/or therapy.

In contrast to the liberal perspective, feminist pedagogies based on caring pay special attention to relationships. Feminist researchers and scholars have pointed out that women tend to give priority to relationships and have argued that schooling should develop the caring capacities of both boys and girls. Feminists have contrasted the distanced teaching style of so many academics with a more "connected" approach in which teachers guide students into jointly constructing new ways of knowing. Rather than remaining remote, instructors share their own intellectual struggles as researchers. Teachers nurture students so that women in particular—who so often are excluded from the public world—become fully connected to it.

The need to create a culture of caring in the classroom becomes more evident as feminist teachers and their students encounter the risks entailed in teaching for social justice. Students in women's studies and other feminist-oriented courses confront research and arguments about women's oppression. Female students face the possibility that they may have been physically, intellectually, morally, and/or politically harmed. Female as well as male students have to consider how they may have profited from gender oppression. Furthermore, students are often asked to evaluate or construct alternatives. Such classroom assignments easily evoke fear, anxiety, denial, guilt, anger, and feelings of helplessness and isolation in the face of so much systemic injustice. Course requirements may raise students' fears that they cannot live up to the teacher's feminist ideals and consequently could be punished (e.g., through humiliation, low grades).

Such fears are often expressed as a concern about "safety." The more extensively a class explores injustice, the more frequently students see differences in their own situations (and differences between themselves and women discussed in the texts). Depending in part on the gender and race of the teacher and the mix of students, a White woman student may feel unsafe in expressing confusion or guilt about her lack of awareness of racism. A student of color may feel that it is not safe to describe his own experiences of racism. A White teacher's attempts to express caring toward a student of color may easily (and sometimes correctly) be seen as patronizing. A lesbian teacher who acknowledges her sexual orientation may find that this disclosure leads some heterosexual students to feel "unsafe" or to interpret her caring gestures (usually incorrectly) as sexual harassment.

As these examples suggest, no matter how sincerely feminist teachers try to foster caring in the classroom, socially structured inequalities deeply influence what students and teachers are willing to say and do. In a given educational setting, lesbian teachers may not speak personally because they fear losing their jobs or failing to be promoted. Students of color may not voice their ideas about racism because they fear being labeled as "difficult" or "troublemakers." However, constraints on full expression do not necessarily deter it. Many lesbian teachers disclose their sexual orientation, despite fears this might generate in others. Many students of color express their anger with racism, despite the fact that some White students see this as disrupting an orderly classroom procedure, making them feel "unsafe." A general commitment to care does not dissolve the tensions that arise with such confrontations. Indeed, as feminist critics have noted, a caring attitude that fails to recognize conflict resulting from inequality of power and privilege easily turns into pity or a maternalistic form of control—attitudes that perpetuate injustice.

FEMINIST PEDAGOGIES OF COLLECTIVE RESISTANCE

Unlike teaching theories that put caring at their center, feminist pedagogies of collective resistance pay special attention to how power differences affect the relation of students and their teachers to questions of gender injustice. These pedagogies were directly or indirectly inspired by social justice movements and theories that proliferated in the 1960s—including the civil rights and Black power movements, community organizing, radical student and national liberation movements, Mao Tse-tung's revolutionary thought, and Paulo Freire's Brazilian blend of socialism and Catholicism. In part because of the influence of Marxist and socialist ideas, activists often emphasized "consciousness-raising"—the process of people talking to others in similar circumstances about their common experiences of oppression. Such discussions were seen as a catalyst for resisting injustice and transforming society into a just one.

In this spirit, radical feminists developed a specifically feminist version of consciousness-raising in which women would share their experiences and feelings of gender oppression, analyze these reports, and develop actions to promote women's liberation. Socialist feminists wanted to include attention to class exploitation as part of their discussions. Black feminists drew on their community traditions of Black women talking together about their oppression by White and Black men as well as by White women. Women of color from numerous ethnic and national traditions, lesbians, disabled women, older women, and other feminist activists adapted this collective approach to their particular situations.

Moved by such social justice initiatives, many feminist teachers in higher education have sought to integrate some form of consciousness-raising into their classrooms. Such teachers place great value on building community through mutual learning and discovering shared concerns about injustice. These discussions and projects reveal both obvious and surprising commonalities that practitioners of a feminist pedagogy of collective resistance can weave into the process of creating community in the classroom.

But, as with teachers trying to practice a pedagogy of caring, there are serious obstacles. These include the priority that higher education gives to intellectual expertise over learning from everyday experience, the academic tendency to view strongly expressed emotions as irrational, reliance on bureaucratic authority as opposed to equality of participants in consciousness-raising discussions, and the liberal denial that difference continues to play an important role in feminist teaching.

Teaching that tries to incorporate consciousness raising often creates tension within teachers as they attempt to balance their own expertise with what students can learn from everyday experience. Teachers in general are more aware than students of the limits of experiential learning. At times, students cite experiences that reinforce ignorant and prejudiced thinking. Yet, student challenges based on their own experiences also have a great deal to contribute to feminist research and teaching. The very disciplines in which feminist academics have been educated are permeated with false and questionable assumptions. Feminist scholarship, too, contains misperceptions and gaps, many resulting from an insufficient understanding of differences in power and privilege among women.

For instance, students with disabilities who question the interpretation of a text or the choice of a certain course assignment because it assumes that all women are able-bodied dispute the assumptions of feminists who have not integrated disability issues into their teaching and research. Even socially privileged students who relate experiences that employ racial and/or class stereotypes pose an intellectual challenge to feminist teachers. Such experiences, as this last example especially suggests, do not have to be accepted at face value. Rather, they can be explored for their argumentative assumptions, tested for their degree of generality, and evaluated for their implications—just like any other contribution to a full and robust discussion.

Similarly, the emotional aspect of consciousness-raising can broaden collective understanding. Feelings, too, contain assumptions that can be respectfully explored without either condemning them out of hand or assuming a self-evident meaning. If a student becomes angry in response to a feminist text on the subject of battering, a feminist teacher can help both the student and class to explore the meaning of that anger. Is a female student angry because she or someone close to her has experienced battering, or because she blames battered women for their situation, or because she thinks she should not have to read about such painful things in a college course? Is a male student angry because he is afraid he will be identified with such abuse, or because he actually condones it but cannot admit this, or because he is horrified by male violence? What can be learned from these feelings?

Although attention to feelings does not fit well with the mainstream culture of higher education, feminist teachers can draw on their intellectual authority, emotional resources (including their passion for the subject matter), and position in the educational hierarchy to bolster their counterculture values. Yet, when feminist teachers attempt to use the positive aspects of their bureaucratic authority to help validate a feminist pedagogy of collective resistance, they encounter profound contradictions.

Consciousness raising emphasizes the equal authority of participants. Feminist teachers have various degrees of bureaucratic authority over students including, in particular, the power to enforce rules, to evaluate through grading and other means, and to give or withhold institutional support. The tension between this power and student awareness of its potential for harming or helping them can create an almost insuperable barrier to working together to understand and seek alternatives to gender injustice.

At the base of this tension is the question of trust: whether it is possible for students to trust teachers who have the power to do them harm. There is no simple formula for cultivating trust, but pedagogies of collective resistance stress how consciousness-raising enables students to get to know each other and the teacher. The more teachers as well as students are able to tell their stories, the more likely students are to have a realistic picture of the risks involved in sharing experiences, feelings, and ideas. For instance, during a discussion about the impact of sexism on schooling, a female student may want to bring up her own fears of intellectual inadequacy. But, she may be understandably worried that this information could be used to harm her academic standing in the class or the school. Her ability to trust the teacher and her classmates often is and should be shaped by what she knows about them—their own experiences and values.

Teachers who seek to practice a feminist pedagogy of resistance are likely to be especially aware of the kinds of harm that result from unequal power relations. Even where the student population is relatively homogeneous, differences in privilege become apparent. A class consisting mostly of students of color may be sharply divided by ethnicity, a class composed mostly of lesbians by race and/or class, and so forth. Despite important commonalities, experiences of oppression may differ greatly. Again and again, teachers committed to a feminist pedagogy of resistance struggle with this complex question: whether a diverse group of people can reach a common understanding of injustice and whether resistance to injustice can be truly collective.

Many feminist teachers and activists have argued that, rather than being a liability, differences among women can be a source of great collective strength. Some have sought to explore this potential by working with the concept of "bridging"—the intellectual and political role that women of color, often lesbians, have been able to play in showing the points of connection between the many and seemingly incompatible social locations they occupy. Another related concept is "positionality"—the notion that social positions like gender and class are not simple or fixed but consist of complex and potentially changing relationships that involve both privileges and disadvantages (a person might be advantaged by sexual preference but disadvantaged by class and both may change). Concepts like these help teachers and students to describe the complicated and shifting network of commonalities and differences entailed in any problem of gender injustice they seek to understand and solve. A more subtle understanding of difference enables teachers and their students to evaluate feminist or nonfeminist texts or policies in terms of what has been omitted—such as consideration of how age or nationality impacts opportunity—as well as what is named.

FEMINIST PEDAGOGIES OF DECONSTRUCTION

Feminist teachers of all varieties pay particular attention to how women have been excluded from mainstream definitions of knowledge. But for teachers identified with a feminist pedagogy of deconstruction, the dynamics of exclusion have more far-reaching implications. Inspired by the work of French theorists such as Foucault and Derrida and, sometimes, by the "queer" activism of the 1980s and 1990s, these feminists focus on how language (or "discourse") continually constructs the world into mutually exclusive and often hierarchically arranged opposites (or "binaries"). Gender or racial or sexual distinctions such as man/woman, White/Black, and gay/straight assume that all individuals can be categorized in one or the other group and that one in each pair must be dominant. By uncritically employing these categories, the critics argue, feminists themselves reproduce the patterns of oppressive thought they should be disrupting. Feminist teachers who value caring and connections, the critics continue, too often assume that people called women are more naturally caring than those called men. Similarly, feminist teachers trying to practice a pedagogy of collective resistance falsely assume that sharing a common identity (such as "woman") will lead to a common understanding of injustice and collective resistance to it.

The alternative offered most frequently by deconstructionists is teaching for criticism: the continuous process of taking apart any kind of text—whether an academic article or a film or an everyday conversation—to reveal how it erases and demeans certain people or events or activities. A teacher might show the students the way in which a manifesto demanding "lesbian" rights actually excludes from consideration bisexual, transgender, or pansexual people whose sexual preferences and behaviors resist such categorization. The same instructor might help the students deconstruct a text that takes for granted categories like "working class" or "women of color." This teacher might point out, instead, that "selves" are complex and fluid social constructions, dependent upon often changeable sexual histories or class positions or racial identities. From this viewpoint, nothing can be taken as "natural"—neither anatomy nor any social distinctions based upon it.

In some respects, pedagogies of deconstruction present a profound critique of pedagogies based on caring and collective resistance. Deconstruction refuses to accept any linguistically reinforced fate—whether it involves feminist teachers believing that they should be especially nurturing or students being characterized in certain ways because they are a "woman," or a "woman of color," or a "lesbian of color," or a "working-class lesbian of color." Yet, this refusal comes at a high price. In the context of such critical teaching, no room is made for the kind of compassionate connection that pedagogies of caring value and try to cultivate. Indeed, the emphasis on criticism tends to reproduce the very reason/emotion split pervading higher education.

The deconstructionist criticism of identity politics (that is, the view that political analysis and resistance grows out of sharing a common identity) also can reinforce the relations of dominance and subordination that feminist teachers are committed to challenging. Student experience, like teacher experience, no longer can serve as the basis for disputing expert knowledge because experience itself has become highly suspect. It has become material for deconstruction rather than a base on which an argument can be developed.

Imagine a lone student who identifies as a working-class lesbian of color sitting in a class in which the teacher models criticism by deconstructing these categories. The criticism may be perfectly sound—or not. But the real-life consequences for relationships in the classroom, for connections to others outside the classroom, cannot be ignored. Perhaps the student feels liberated by being freed from the constraints of these categories. Or, perhaps she becomes even more isolated, more hesitant to participate in class, and skeptical of political groups that promote collective action by women like herself. The contexts in which the student lives her life, the subtle or not-so-subtle power dynamics of the classroom as well as the structures on inequality that she encounters outside that classroom, profoundly shape the implications of the critical viewpoints she is being taught.

CONTEXTS FOR FEMINIST PEDAGOGIES

All feminist teachers continuously make ethical and political choices not only about whether to question assumptions but whose assumptions to question, and when and how to do so. Feminist teachers drawn to the liberal vision of society base their teaching choices on belief in the value of each individual. Teachers who put care at the center of their work give priority to teaching assignments and techniques that support caring and connection. Partisans of collective resistance to injustice try to create the kind of classroom community that cultivates the search for common understandings and solutions amidst difference and conflict. Deconstructionists assign texts and set requirements according to what they believe most needs criticism.

Yet, the meaning of any choice depends on its context. In choices related to feminist teaching, two factors are especially influential. First is the actual institutional and social context in which feminist teachers do their work. Whatever their preferred pedagogy, such teachers are affected by the size and mission of the school, the kind of department in which they work, the nature of the student body, and their position within the institution —or whether they do not have a regular position and must move from school to school. Given the particular combination of conditions, teachers find themselves adopting, combining, and/or rejecting aspects from the various theories of feminist teaching: stressing individual development at one point, responding in a caring mode at another, encouraging the collective spirit for a certain classroom task, and emphasizing criticism for a different one.

The other important factor influencing the practice of feminist pedagogy is the political and intellectual climate of the institutional, local, national, and global context in which a feminist teacher works. The costs and/or benefits of putting any theory of feminist pedagogy into practice influences how teaching is actually done. For instance, a teacher who gravitates toward a feminist pedagogy of resistance might find considerable support in a small liberal arts college with a history of defending feminist activists. But, if that college is located in a city or state or province that has a conservative leadership, and/or in a country where the government is actively suppressing social justice values by limiting civil liberties and withdrawing financial support, the teacher's ability to fulfill the potentials of feminist teaching may become highly problematic.

If teachers attempting to practice feminist pedagogy share a commitment to social justice for women, such teachers also share the challenge of trying to realize their commitment in the face of backlash. Feminist teachers must cope with often intense opposition to their efforts. They may be fired, penalized, or undermined by rules and reorganizations aimed at hampering their work. Yet, feminist teachers have rich resources to draw on: their transformative values, their passionate scholarship, and their continued dedication to forging connections between their classrooms and feminist activism. Through innovative writing, ongoing debates, and conferences and workshops devoted to trying to answer the question, "What is feminist pedagogy," they show that the challenge is being met and that the work of feminist teaching continues to nurture both their students and themselves.

REFERENCES AND FURTHER READINGS

Bannerji, H., Carty, L., Dehli, K., Heald, S., & McKenna, K. (Eds.). (1991). *Unsettling relations: The university as a site of feminist struggles.* Toronto, Canada: Women's Press.

Belenky, M.F., Clinchy, B.M., Goldberger, N.R., & Tarule, J.M. (1986). *Women's ways of knowing: The development of self, voice, and mind.* New York: Basic Books.

Cohee, G.E., Daumer, E., Kemp, T.D., Krebs, P.M., & Lafky, S.A. (Eds.). (1998). *The feminist teacher anthology: Pedagogies and classroom strategies.* New York: Teachers College Press.

Diller, A., Houston, B., Morgan, K.P., & Ayim, M. (Eds.). (1996). *The gender question in education: Theory, pedagogy and politics.* Boulder, CO: Westview.

Fisher, B.M. (2001). *No angel in the classroom: Teaching through feminist discourse.* Lanham, MD: Rowman & Littlefield.

Gallop, J. (Ed.). (1995). *Pedagogy: The question of impersonation.* Bloomington: Indiana University Press.

Garber, L. (Ed.). (1994). *Tilting the tower.* New York: Routledge.

hooks, b. (1994). *Teaching to transgress: Education as the practice of freedom.* New York: Routledge.

Luke, C., & Gore, J. (Eds.). (1992). *Feminisms and critical pedagogy.* New York: Routledge.

Macdonald, A.A., & Sánchez-Casal, S. (2002). *Twenty-first century feminist classrooms: Pedagogies of identity and difference.* New York: Palgrave Macmillan.

Maher, F.A., & Tetreault, M.K.T. (1994). *The feminist classroom.* New York: Basic Books.

Naples, N.A., & Bojar, K. (Eds.). (2002). *Teaching feminist activism: Strategies from the field.* New York: Routledge.

Weiler, K. (1991). Freire and a feminist pedagogy of difference. *Harvard Educational Review, 61*(4), 449–474.

Women's Studies Quarterly. (1993). [Special issue]. Feminist pedagogy: An update. *21*(3 & 4).

Berenice Malka Fisher

Gender Equality Policies in British Schooling

Gender equality policies in British schooling have played a formal part in educational policies through legislation on sexual equality introduced 30 years ago, while specific educational legislation or reforms around schooling have paid much less explicit attention to gender per se. In this essay, the origins and sociopolitical contexts of the legislation on sexual equality and the subsequent changing practices at global, national, and local levels are reviewed from the perspective of educational and social researchers. The review is located within the context of changing research practices around education and gender issues (David, 2003). It provides a reflexive account of these changing policies and practices and demonstrates that, although there have been major changes in the official and public rhetoric about gender and education, especially with respect to the balance between boys' and girls' educational (under)achievements, examination successes at school, and involvement in various forms of education and employment, these are still not fully taken into account in the public policy debates about forms and expansions of schooling nor in the wider debates about what is now called widening participation in higher education (or universities).

Consideration is also given to changing language and/or discourses about sex or gender equality, especially with respect to education and schooling, and the ways in which these notions were and still are linked to discourses about poverty, social and economic disadvantages, or social class and race and/or ethnicity, and how these have been transformed to notions of diversity and changing notions of religious diversity and affiliation, including especially the relatively recent rise of debates about faith-based education and schooling. Disabilities and sexualities or sexual orientation is also now included in the overall question of school policies for social inclusion or exclusion.

Discussion of these policy and legislative developments over the past 30 years will necessarily also have to be linked to consideration of changing policies and practices with respect to education and schooling, with regard to educational achievements, or underachievement, examination and/or academic successes, social inclusion or exclusion, and transformations in notions of teaching and learning—now sometimes referred to as pedagogies. In particular, a key shift over this period of time has been from turning invisible issues about gender matters in education into explicit debates and research questions. However, the initial focus on making explicit questions of girls' education and schooling and ensuring adequate provision for girls in a range of different types and levels of school and further or higher education has been transformed into major public policy debates about boys' education, underachievement, and "raising boys' achievement in secondary schools"—the title of a recent major educational research publication (Younger & Warrington, 2005).

Although there is considerable research evidence about the links between social class, economic or social disadvantages and family backgrounds, racial and ethnic groupings, and boys' achievements or underachievements, these are not used in the public policy debates.

Boys have become the center of attention in professional educational circles, and the question of girls' relative disadvantage across educational provisions and in forms of vocational education and employment has been relatively occluded. This is particularly the case with respect to the evidence about boys' and girls' achievements on examinations taken at the end of secondary schooling and through their performance or successes in the General Certificate of Secondary Education (GCSE). The national benchmark standard of five examination passes at grade A* to C is still not achieved by 50 percent of the age cohort of 15 to 16 year olds, but girls now do relatively better than boys at achieving this benchmark standard, with over 50 percent of girls achieving this standard while it is a little over 40 percent of boys who do so. Thus, arguments have shifted to how to deal with boys rather than girls.

In some curiously contradictory way, however, much of the education research and public policy debate about forms of secondary schools in the past five years has again focused on social class advantages or disadvantages and achievements or underachievements within schools and education without explicit attention to gender matters. For example, the current public policy debates about the New Labour government's educational reforms of secondary schools which are creating a major furore have not, however, paid any attention to whether or not the changes will have any bearing on either boys' or girls' educational successes or underachievements in examinations. Rather, the focus has been on whether the reforms will further advantage middle-class families at the expense of working-class and economically disadvantaged families, including especially Black and ethnic minority families and their children. While the Equal Opportunities Commission has remained silent in these debates, the Commission for Racial Equality has argued, in defense of these reforms, that the critics of the planned school reforms ignore the experiences of Black Britons in education and their desire for community and parental involvement in order to deliver high standards and personalized education that will address Black underachievement.

GENDER EQUALITY POLICIES: ORIGINS, ISSUES, AND LEGISLATIVE CHANGES

Gender equality policies in British schooling were formally introduced through national legislation in the 1970s, namely the Sex Discrimination Act 1975 and the linked Equal Pay Act of 1970 that came into force in 1975, although neither piece of legislation was chiefly concerned with either education or schooling. The Sex Discrimination Act (SDA) created the Equal Opportunities Commission (EOC) to be responsible for monitoring the implementation and progress of moves to achieve equal opportunities between men and women and to deal with sex discrimination and inequality relating to gender, including the definition and implementation of good practice in the fair and equal treatment of men and women. This policy covered educational provisions, but the legislation did not provide many strong measures with respect to forms of schooling, allowing for the continuation of single-sex schooling rather than requiring coeducation or mixed schooling in state or private schools, nor about forms and content of the school curricula.

Over the following 30 years, the form and workings of the EOC have changed as the social and global political contexts have changed and especially as the British involvement in Europe and the European Union has become stronger. New and relatively separate bodies for equal rights have been established for parts of the United Kingdom as Northern Ireland, Scotland, and Wales have acquired new powers of regional and domestic administration. Nevertheless, despite these administrative developments, the EOC for England has not taken up many issues with respect to education compared with other public policies such as employment and services because of its relatively limited powers with respect to education. The EOC for Scotland and Wales have been slightly more proactive with respect to particular aspects of schooling, and each has had a very directive EOC Commissioner and Director.

There has also been the establishment of relatively similar and separate bodies to deal with disability discrimination and good practice in relation to disabled people through the Disability Rights Commission (DRC), established through the Disability Discrimination Act 1995, and racial discrimination and good practice in relation to Black and minority ethnic people through the Commission for Racial Equality (CRE), which was established through the Race Relations Act 1976. Both of these bodies have acquired relatively stronger powers with respect to education and schooling—the DRC especially around school exclusions and the CRE through crucial amendments to the legislation and also through the implementation of educational policies in relation to the Race Relations Act.

Since the 1990s, the British government has created and developed special administrative and political responsibilities for women, including an administrative unit for women's equality that was initially located in the Cabinet Office of the British Prime Minister. More recently, under the New Labour government and in its second term of office, this unit was renamed the Women and Equality unit and its responsibility relocated within the Department of Trade and Industry. While there is now a governmental responsibility for women, the post has not always carried a special ministerial remuneration.

The EOC has also developed a gender equality duty that comes into force for public bodies in 2007. The terms of this gender equality duty draw upon European legislation and policies through the European Union (EU). Indeed, many of the rights British women now have flow from Europe, and British law is influenced by the EU.

There is also legislation going through the British Parliament, the Equality Bill 2006, to develop equality and fairness for all and to create a new body—the Commission for Equality and Human Rights (CEHR)—to provide oversight of a range of forms of discrimination in respect of equality and diversity, in which gender constitutes but one dimension and where there are other issues such as disabilities, ethnic and/or racial and religious groups or minorities, as well as sexuality and sexual orientation.

There have also been some critical changes in policies and practices through other forms of legislation, local or school practices, and the practices of educators, including educational and social researchers.

EDUCATIONAL POLICY REFORMS AND CHANGES

Over the past 30 years, there have also been major changes in the form and content of educational policies and the legislative framework that sets the context for such policies in the United Kingdom. The key legislative framework for education was set during the Second World War, namely the 1944 Education Act, which was established on the principle of creating equality of educational opportunity for all, especially through extending and expanding the provision of secondary schools for all children from the age of 11 until initially 15, and later to the age of 16, with primary education for all children from the ages of 5 up to 11. This remained the cornerstone for almost 50 years, although there were major controversies about how provisions should be made and what form the schools should take—whether they were to be provided by the government centrally or through local education authorities. A key question was about whether the principle of equality of opportunity covered each school in terms of social or educational mixing of children from different social class family backgrounds or in terms of their abilities or merits. Gender was not explicitly addressed, although there were many single-sex schools (for boys and girls), especially at secondary level, that were provided by the government nationally, locally, or privately.

By the late 1980s, this legislative framework was deemed to be inadequate for a globalizing and modern economy. The Conservative government, under Thatcher, aimed to transform education through the Education Reform Act 1988. This and much subsequent legislation began a process of introducing new principles of parental choice and raising educational standards, through specifying the core and compulsory elements of the curriculum and allied assessment and achievement levels, into the public policy process. Despite this principle of choice, gender was not seen as a major issue (Arnot, David, & Weiner, 1999).

CHANGING CONCEPTS

Chief among the changes over this recent 30-year period has been shifts in the language or discourses about gender and/or sex equality both at the level of public policy and debate and within social research practices. In the 1970s, public debates focused upon notions of women's position in society and the question of forms of sex or sexual discrimination in areas of public life encompassing economic and social institutions. In particular, the focus was on the question of equal opportunities, drawing on a liberal and individualistic social agenda. This focus drew from other social movements for change and from the extension of social and human rights within the polity and internationally throughout Europe and North America. In the British arena, social movements for social justice and individual rights in relation to the rise of social democracy gave rise to movements for sexual equality and women's rights. The women's movement or women's liberation movement, strongly associated with movements for sexual liberation not only in the United Kingdom but also in Europe and North America, developed campaigns and so-called demands for women's rights and equal opportunities with respect to education, employment, and pay. Other questions of women's sexuality—abortion and contraception—were also raised, and women's family responsibilities were addressed through the campaign for child care and early child care in nurseries. Equal educational opportunities were a strong focus in these campaigns. Indeed, the demands were commonly associated not only with women workers and trade unions but also with educational movements and the students' movement in particular.

Gender as a term did not feature strongly in these public policy debates and campaigns and was not a term in common parlance or in the lexicon of social science and educational research until the 1980s. Similarly, notions of feminism as a political and social movement, and subsequently as an academic and research pursuit, were only beginning to take root. However, by the end of the 1970s, the idea of the movement for women's liberation or sexual equality being dubbed "second wave feminism" had begun to take hold, and many female education and social researchers began to adopt the term feminist for their political and academic pursuits. These drew on, and compared with, the first wave women's movement and self-styled feminism at the turn of the twentieth century in Europe and North America.

Some key academic sociologists began to distinguish sex and gender, engage with, and write about them. For example, Ann Oakley, one of the foremost British feminist sociologists, recently introduced her own work from the early 1970s by noting that the paired terms "sex" and "gender" met the need felt at that time for a conceptual distinction between the bodily constraints and social oppression that were of concern to second-wave feminists in Europe and North America. Whereas "sex" signaled bodily prescriptions and proscriptions, "gender" referred to the limits set by culture, economics, and traditions (Oakley, 2005).

Since the 1970s, however, the terms sex and gender have taken on significantly different meanings in both public policy and academic arenas, and especially with respect to what became a burgeoning field of academic and feminist endeavor—namely, work on gender and education or schooling, both nationally and internationally. By the mid-1990s, the term "gender" had eclipsed the term "sex" in relation to both educational research and public policies, although notions of sex and sexuality continued to have a place within the lexicon of social and educational research, with specific reference to social norms for the "bodily prescription and proscription" to which Oakley (2005) referred. Nevertheless, debate has raged about these terms and meanings, especially with respect to connotations about sexuality and/or sexual orientation.

For example, Judith Butler, an American feminist social philosopher, has had a major impact upon social and educational research through her work on what she initially called "Gender Trouble" (Butler, 1990). More recently, she has written that the terms "gender" and "sexuality" are very problematic and yet it is important to keep them distinct for both theory and politics. Her thinking about the term "gender" has been influenced by the "New Gender Politics" that emerged in the 1990s, a combination of movements concerned with transgender, transsexuality, intersex, and their complex relations to feminist and the new so-called "queer" theory (Butler, 2004). However, she argued that it would be a mistake to subscribe to a progressive notion of history in which various frameworks are understood to succeed and supplant one another, with notions of "sexuality" replacing notions of "gender" or vice versa. She further argued that the ideas and stories constructed about "gender" and "sexuality" are continuing to happen in simultaneous and overlapping ways since they happen, in part, through the complex ways that they are taken up by each of the political movements and theoretical practices (Butler, 2004).

Indeed, it is the case that the social and political movements around gender politics in Britain have transformed the notions and meanings of sex and gender. Within public policy arenas, these terms have an even more complex set of meanings, and legislation around gender has begun to replace legislation on sex and sexual discrimination. Government bodies and agencies concerned with sexual equality and gender have mushroomed, and the terminology has shifted in complex ways.

These questions of definition are important. For example, the Gender Recognition Act of 2004 is about sexual orientation and sexuality, and gender is now used for what used to be called sex changes. However, the legislative framework for equal opportunities for women still remains the SDA, but, as noted above, there is a new equality bill going through Parliament at the time of writing which aims to establish a commission on Equality and Human Rights (CEHR). This would replace the individual commissions such as the EOC and CRE and bring together the various different practices around gender, race/ethnicity and/or diversity, including religious diversity, disabilities, sexual orientation, and sexuality.

CHANGING CONTEXTS

There have been similar complex political and social changes with respect to education legislation, policies, and reforms, as well as our understandings of these processes. Underpinning these, too, have been changing conceptions and notions about equal educational opportunities and the links to and expressions of commitment in favor of reducing social and economic disadvantages and/or advantages on grounds of family background, defined largely in terms of social class. These are challenging and contested notions about equality of educational opportunity on individual or collective, social grounds. Throughout the 30 years under review, the issue of using educational reforms to accomplish either individual or social rights to equal opportunities for education and/or employment has been a particularly vexed question. Moreover, the question of whose individual rights should be the focus of educational reforms has been highly contested around social class, poverty or social disadvantage, ethnic/racial and religious diversity, educational and/or academic merit, and examination performance and achievements, as well as in relation to difference types and forms of state, public, and private schooling.

While this debate has raged, however, gender and/or sex or sexuality has not been at the forefront of the debates. Indeed, there is a controversial debate at the time of writing about a new piece of legislation to transform secondary schooling, through the creation of new types of secondary schools such as quasi-independent trust schools. Yet, again, neither gender nor sex is raised as part of that controversy. Indeed, hitherto, the New Labour government in the late 1990s, shortly after they came to power in 1997, had raised the question of how their education policies contributed to wider questions of social inclusion or exclusion, with an emphasis on questions of poverty and social disadvantage.

The notions of social inclusion or exclusion, as Levitas (1998) argued so cogently, are linked to wider policy matters about social welfare strategies, such as economic redistributive policies, or more moral questions about the social class system and whether or not particular policies create and sustain an underclass. They also draw on notions about social policy strategies from Europe and, indeed, the ideas about social exclusion as a proxy for social disadvantage, linked to diversity questions such as ethnicity, migrant status, race, or religion, have been developed in the European context.

Although questions of gender were tangentially linked to definitions of social class through types of family, they were and are not of central importance. The only issue raised in linked fashion has been the question of sex and sexuality in relation to young people's behavior as adolescents or teenagers. Indeed, teenage pregnancy as a major public policy issue was initially raised as part of a question of social exclusion by the incoming New Labour government in 1997. This was based upon a review of research evidence from across Europe and North America, and the "teenage pregnancy strategy" emerged as a key plank of the government's new policy for dealing with social inclusion. This was a policy in which young women who were at risk of social exclusion through their sexual behavior were to be educated to transform their behavior. A major element of this strategy, therefore, became that of providing sex and relationship education in schools.

This was also part of a wider program of transforming the styles of teaching and learning in schools, with moves toward what has been called personalized education or a focus on the individual as a key element in their processes of learning. However, personal and social education has also been mandated as part of the curriculum of schools, together with citizenship education. These are all part of the wider strategy on socially inclusive policies within education and schooling, but gender is not seen as a major policy component, despite the fact that much education and social research is now focused on these questions (David, 2003).

There is also the question of recent extensions of these debates about personalized education through schooling and into further and higher education—especially the public policy debates on education for 14 to 19 year olds and also about widening participation to and in higher education—but, again, gender is barely the focus in rhetoric. It is, however, a major facet of the studies conducted by social and educational researchers.

Quite clearly, there are resistances to the incorporation of a gender perspective into the current public debates in the United States and the United Kingdom about educational reforms and specific policies. As Stambach and David (2005) have argued, in public debates there is a focus on gender as a category rather than as a concept drawn from feminist and gender research for imagining and realizing school reform. Through an examination of the histories of educational reforms and mothers' narrative accounts of choice programming, they asserted that if the debates took up the concept of gender drawn from feminist theory and gender research, it would move discussions of school choice and mothers' school involvement in new and important theoretical and practical directions (Stambach & David, 2005). They reviewed the debates around family or parental *choice* in order to demonstrate the public resistances, and yet they showed the strong evidence of insights and experiences from feminist and gender research on women's involvement in education and schooling over the past century. They argued that gender continuously underlays the history and present-day contours of parent-school relations and school choice policies in the United States and Great Britain. They also demonstrated that women and men had held different positions within the system of formal education in the past and that their supposedly separate but equal places were, in part, being reproduced in debates and research on school choice nowadays.

COMPLEXITIES

From the vantage point of the early twenty-first century, it is clear that the origins of the policies and practices around gender equality and education derive from a complex mix of public policy developments or reforms and legislation, links with movements for emancipation, social change, and human rights, and changing international contexts—in particular, the trends toward globalization. Indeed, in order to understand gender equality policies for and in education, it is important to understand not only the legislative context but also the transformations in educational policies themselves as they are deeply embedded within other forms of social and economic transformation. Understanding this complexity has been one of the tasks of social and educational researchers, especially from a feminist and social justice perspective.

REFERENCES AND FURTHER READINGS

Arnot, M., David, M.E., & Weiner, G. (1999). *Closing the gender gap: Postwar education and social change.* Cambridge, MA: Polity Press.

Butler, J. (1990). *Gender trouble: Feminism and the subversion of identity.* New York & London: Routledge.

Butler, J. (2004). *Undoing gender.* London & New York: Routledge.

David, M.E. (2003). *Personal and political: Feminisms, sociology and family lives.* Stoke on Trent, England: Trentham Books.

Levitas, R. (1998). *The inclusive society? Social exclusion and New Labour.* Basingstoke, England: Macmillan.

Oakley, A. (2005). *The Ann Oakley reader: Gender, women and social science.* Bristol, England: Policy Press.

Stambach, A., & David, M.E. (2005). Feminist theory and educational policy: How gender has been "involved" in family-school choice debates. *Signs: Journal of Women in Culture and Society, 26* (2), 485–509.

Younger, M., & Warrington, M. (2005). *Raising boys' achievement in secondary schools. Issues, dilemmas and opportunities.* Maidenhead Berkshire, England: Open University Press.

Miriam E. David

Gender Equality Policies in Canadian Schooling

Gender equality policy in Canadian schooling has been rendered almost invisible by the politics of neoliberalism and educational restructuring. Marked by a belief in the ability of competition, privatization, and the market to deliver services more effectively and efficiently than the state, the turn to neoliberalism has led to efforts to downsize government, discipline the labor force, and reduce state spending on those public services, including education, that are essential in women's lives. As the state increasingly withdraws from the provision of social services, female teachers, like all women, have been expected to assume greater personal burdens for the care of children, the sick, and the elderly. In schools, teachers meet children whose families are living in poverty, have lost important supports in the mental health or special education arenas, are homeless, or are otherwise marginalized by cuts to government services. As wages, working conditions, professional autonomy, and the right to collective bargaining have been attacked, teachers, more than 70 percent of whom are women, have been forced to protect their own positions as workers. At the same time, educators have been called on to mount a defense of the very idea and practice of public education itself. In this context, and with the exception of "the boy problem," gender equality as an explicit policy issue has struggled to survive as an identifiable element in the broader efforts to protect the goals of equality and democratic citizenship embedded in the very concept of public education.

This was not always the case. In the period between 1970 when the final report of the Royal Commission on the Status of Women appeared and the mid-1990s when the neoliberal agenda for education became dominant, considerable activity in the realm of gender equality occurred. Women's groups, operating within the constructs of what is called the Keynesian welfare state, were able to agitate for policies and practices that would improve educational opportunities for girls and women. The passage of the Charter of Rights and Freedoms in 1982 and Canada's international commitments expressed through covenants such as the United Nations Convention on the Elimination of All Forms of Discrimination Against Women provided the constitutional and legal frameworks for equality demands. While women's groups persistently lobbied for gender equity initiatives in education, committed teachers who worked individually, in small networks and through their teacher federations, were central to the implementation of gender equity policies. The efforts of women's groups and teacher organizations also received real assistance from the femocrats (i.e., feminist bureaucrats) employed in ministries of education and school boards. However, because education in Canada is, by constitutional authority, a provincial responsibility, gender equality, or gender equity as it is more commonly called, found expression in an uneven patchwork of policies and practices across the nation. Policy variance occurred not only across the ten provinces and two (later three) territories but also within them as local school boards developed and implemented gender equity initiatives with differing degrees of enthusiasm and commitment. By the mid-1990s, however, there was a real and visible presence to gender policies in the educational domain. Gender was on the agenda.

Gender equity was seen largely in terms of curricular, pedagogical, and school climate issues as they related to girls and young women. Based on theories of sex-role socialization and liberal feminist notions of equal opportunity, gender equity policies were most often manifested in efforts to promote girls' entry to science, mathematics, and computer courses, develop nonsexist teaching materials, encourage the growth of female self-esteem and empowerment, and implement antiharassment and antiviolence initiatives. Research studies of sex-role stereotyping in textbooks led to guidelines for producing nonsexist teaching and learning materials. Posters, pamphlets, and videos featuring women in nontraditional work encouraged young women to take up a skilled trade. Workshops, conferences, dramatic productions, learning kits, and lesson aids on a range of topics including women's history, body image, date rape, and employment issues were developed for female students. Speakers' bureaus and mentoring programs were staffed by successful women who volunteered their time to share their experiences with young women and encourage them to "reach for the stars" or "be all that you can be." There were even some limited programs for boys designed to encourage them to understand gender relations or develop their empathetic, caring side.

By the early 1990s, some educators began to realize that analyses of sexism in schooling that emphasized sex-role stereotyping and socialization were relying on an oversimplified understanding of complex issues and hid the ways in which the gendered nature of education is played out in the content and practices of schooling. There was a shift to talking about the systemic nature of inequalities and developing antisexist (as opposed to nonsexist) teaching practices. At the same time, teachers began to understand the need to include race, sexual orientation, ethnicity, and disability issues in their teaching. The 1994 validation draft of a gender equity support document issued by Ontario's Ministry of Education and Training provides one example of the changes in the theorizing of gender equity that were emerging. Prepared by a diverse group of educators during the tenure of a social democratic government, the document criticized the "add women and stir" approach to curriculum building and called for a more fundamental transformation that would look for the causes of and links among all forms of discrimination. The document went on to argue for antisexist approaches to learning that would name inequitable power relations between men and women and take into account the whole social context and the intersections of race, class, and sexual orientation with gender. However, in the same year and in the same province, Ontario's Royal Commission on Learning identified sex-role stereotyping, the absence of women in physics, engineering, and technology, and the lack of women's awareness about the range of career opportunities available as key gender issues. In this understanding they were not alone, and studies in a number of provinces at about the same time reached very similar conclusions. None claimed gender equality had arrived, but few saw the necessity for any radical or substantive change.

For most teachers, this was an easy and acceptable assessment. From their relatively privileged position as incorporated professionals, teachers saw education as basically fair and female students as just being in need of some small adjustments so they could enjoy the full benefits of schooling and become more like their male counterparts. In the existing political arrangements of the welfare state, educators tended to view government as a relatively unproblematic and benign institution. Teachers had close working relationships with ministries of education and were comfortable members of the state apparatus, although, of course, there had been some disagreements and public displays of resistance around workplace issues. Women teachers did have one concern—increasing the number of women in administrative positions in schools. In Ontario, this was resolved by a 1988 employment equity (affirmative action) amendment to The Education Act that established specific requirements for hiring women into leadership positions as supervisory officers, principals, and vice-principals. By 1990, eight provincial ministries of education and school boards in six provinces had some form of employment equity policy designed to improve the representation of women in school administration. Gender equity initiatives of this kind that supported women's representation, participation, or presence and enhanced what was called "the status of women" were not always easy to achieve and were often resisted, but there was a real sense among women that progress was being made toward equality in education.

By the mid-1990s, however, instruments such as the 1988 Free Trade Agreement with the United States and the 1992 North American Free Trade Agreement had codified some of the key elements of a neoliberal transformation in Canada. Predictions that the harmonization of the Canadian, American, and Mexican economies would result in decreased funding for education, limits on collective bargaining rights for teachers, and growing efforts to impose privatization and marketization on the delivery of educational services have proven prescient. And, if the ongoing negotiations for the General Agreement on Trade in Services within the World Trade Organization are successful, the ability of national governments to ameliorate the worst excesses of capitalism and provide a measure of social justice and fairness for citizens will be further restricted. Initiatives to downsize government, deregulate the economy, discredit the Keynesian welfare state, and rework existing discourses of social justice and equity are already well underway in Canada, although the actual processes of implementation have taken different forms in specific local settings, have never progressed in a linear fashion, and often have faced strong resistance.

It is clear that teachers and school systems were specifically targeted by corporate leaders and other supporters of neoliberalism for "reform" and "restructuring." Blame was laid at the school door for Canada's lack of economic competitiveness and entrepreneurial spirit. Schools were accused of failing to produce the kinds of workers Canada needed. Teachers were criticized for emphasizing equity and social justice goals at the expense of individual merit and the academic rigor that would bring outstanding results in national and international testing. Excellence was positioned against equity. On the basis of this critique, governments, driven by the demands of the new right, which emphasized the "logic" of the market, set about reconfiguring the nature, purpose, and organization of schooling.

In response, there has been an unprecedented explosion of teacher militancy as educators sought both to protect their own position as workers and to defend public education. Two events bookend the past decade of struggle by teachers. One of the most potent manifestations of militancy occurred in Ontario in the autumn of 1997 when 126,000 teachers walked out of their classrooms to engage in a two-week political protest against the educational restructuring inscribed in Bill 160, The Education Quality Improvement Act. A similar teacher revolt occurred in British Columbia in October 2005, when 38,000 public school teachers in the province left their classrooms in an act of civil disobedience to defend their collective bargaining rights and, in particular, the right to negotiate working and learning conditions in the schools. The willingness of teachers to take job actions seen as "illegal" (although it should be noted that teacher unionists reject that definition), coupled with their ongoing efforts to challenge educational restructuring, funding cutbacks, and reform measures that intensified and deprofessionalized teaching work, is part of a wider resistance of educators and their allies to the incursion of the market and corporate rule into the public sector. That some of the strongest opposition to neoliberal initiatives should come from the teaching profession, dominated as it is by women, should come as no surprise for there is a consistent gender gap in Canadian politics as women, still largely responsible for child care, housework, and elder care, continue to bear the brunt of cutbacks to social services at the personal level and understand more viscerally what the welfare state delivered and what has been lost.

An unfortunate consequence both of educational restructuring itself and of teachers' responses to it has been the disappearance of explicit and concerted work on gender equality policies in schooling. As activist feminist teachers have been confronted with rapid and relentless changes in their workplace, they have had to make difficult decisions about what to fight and what to accommodate, about where to direct their energies and organizational efforts, and what battles to concede. Perhaps for strategic reasons having to do with promoting a shared understanding of professional identity and establishing political solidarity between women and men, the gender dimensions of educational restructuring appear to have been largely ignored by teachers and teacher unions. There is also little evidence that teachers have kept explicit discourses of gender equity alive in their classrooms. Thus, despite the fact that teaching is really women's work in Canada and that cutbacks to public services disproportionately affect women, with few exceptions, neither educators nor researchers have focused their efforts on understanding educational reform as gendered or on protecting gender equity policies and practices in schools. It is sometimes even argued that equality for girls and women in education has been achieved and that if there is any problem, it is with the underachievement of boys and the absence of men in teaching, especially elementary teaching.

In fact, many gender equity policies affecting women teachers have been stripped away over the past 10 years. For example, in Ontario, a right-wing Progressive Conservative government, headed by Mike Harris as premier, was elected in 1995 and immediately repealed all employment equity legislation. The absence of legislation, coupled with the underfunding of education, meant that school boards rid themselves of equity officers, most of whom were women, and closed their employment equity programs. Educational equity programming run out of school board offices was also eliminated as a result of funding cuts. This has had a major impact on the ability of classroom teachers to sustain gender equity teaching and programs at the school level because the leadership, resources, and professional development offered through central equity offices was lost. Explicit references to sex equity in curriculum and pedagogy have often disappeared from programs of study and have been replaced with more generic statements opposing discrimination in a general sense and emphasizing individual effort and narrow notions of equality of opportunity and personal choice. Explanations of discrimination as systemic have been expunged. Indeed, educators working on the Ontario curriculum developed in the late 1990s report being told they could not even use words such as equity in provincial documents.

Even more significant have been the challenges to collective bargaining rights. Since 1982, more than 170 regulations and laws have been passed by Canadian governments to restrict collective bargaining or roll back workers' rights. Some of these legislative changes have been directed specifically at teachers because they are organized in relatively strong unions across the nation and because they have vociferously resisted changes to their terms of employment and working conditions and have opposed the privatization and commercialization of education. By targeting teachers' labor rights, governments are, in effect, attacking an important segment of the female workforce for it is unionization and collective bargaining that have made teachers the female aristocracy of labor in Canada. Through organized action, women teachers have won decent salaries, excellent pension plans, some control over working conditions and terms of employment, maternity and family leave plans, protection from sexual harassment, and other polices of direct benefit to women. Thus, moves to curtail union and collective bargaining rights are a direct challenge to women's equality in the teaching profession and to their ability to negotiate further improvements in their work lives.

Efforts to discipline teacher unions have taken a number of forms. In British Columbia, the government rescinded the closed shop legislation that required teachers to belong to the teachers' federation in order to work in publicly funded schools. In some other provinces, there were also hints that compulsory membership provisions might be threatened although, to date, no action has been taken. In British Columbia and Ontario, however, school principals and vice-principals have been removed from bargaining units. Hence, just as more women were moving into school administration, they lost the protection of their unions, and the work environment became more adversarial and hierarchical. In addition, because of the fund-raising demands now made of schools and the introduction of a wide range of accountability mechanisms, the role of principal has shifted from instructional leader to business manager. As research in Australia and elsewhere demonstrates, this shift to the new managerialism in schools exploits the emotional labor of female vice-principals and principals in handling teacher and parent stress and distress. At the same time, lip service is paid to team approaches in schools while masculinist and hierarchical models of managing are actually imposed.

Even more damaging to teachers have been the consistent attempts to engage in contract stripping and to reassert management rights at the provincial level as part of wider efforts to reduce government expenditures and impose central control while devolving responsibility to local school boards. In some cases, teachers' salaries have been arbitrarily reduced as in Ontario and Alberta. Teachers in British Columbia faced imposed salary settlements of 0 percent. In fact, a recent study from Statistics Canada, which looked at cumulative wage increases for various occupational groups from 1997 to 2006, revealed that the real salaries of teachers and professors in Canada increased during this period by 0 percent. The flexible labor market has also found its way into teaching as the number of part-time teaching positions continues to grow. A 2003 study by the Council of Ministers of Education Canada noted that between 1989 and 1999, the number of full-time teachers in the country declined slightly while the number of part-time educators in Canada grew from 30,606 to 46, 439, a change of 52 percent. Of the part-time teachers working in 1999, 8,742 were male and 37,697 were female. As school boards continue to try to do more with less, it is likely that part-time employment for teachers may well continue to increase.

Teachers' work has also intensified. A 2005 survey conducted for the Canadian Teachers' Federation by an independent polling firm revealed that 83 percent of teachers reported having a higher workload than in 2001. Taking into account assigned classroom instruction, lesson and course planning, grading and reporting, meetings, individual help to students, parent-teacher interviews, and supervision of students in cocurricular and extracurricular activities, teachers were working, on average, 55.6 hours per week. For 51percent of teachers, class sizes had grown, and 74 percent reported increases in the numbers of special needs learners in their classrooms. Teachers are also spending increasing amounts of their own money to buy resources for their classrooms. On top of this, teachers find new expectations added to already very full workloads. Ontario, for example, has just introduced a program for beginning teachers that will require experienced teachers to add the mentoring of new colleagues to their already long list of responsibilities. The intensification of work comes at the same time as teachers face increased scrutiny of their activities through mechanisms such as detailed performance evaluations. To date, however, government attempts to implement compulsory recertification policies have been unsuccessful. Finally, it should be noted that teachers, especially female teachers, report a growing number of cases of bullying and harassment in the workplace and threats of violence from students as young people react both to the harsher conditions of their lives inside and outside of schools and to the new neoliberal discourse that situates students as consumers and education as a product.

Some mention must also be made of that special, female-dominated class of educational worker, the educational assistant or teacher's aide. These women provide before and after school supervision as well as lunchroom supervision and complete other tasks assigned by teachers. Many of them work intensively with special education students, providing individual instruction, but also administering medications, toileting students, and managing behavioral outbursts, which often means risking their own safety. As a recent strike in Ontario highlighted, educational assistants often work longer hours than they are paid for because of their dedication to children and young people and they are laid off every summer, a particular hardship because their hourly wages during the school year are low. These women are also among the most likely to lose their jobs when financial cutbacks by school boards are needed to balance budgets. Like child-care workers, another female-dominated occupational category, educational assistants experience the raw gender discrimination still apparent in the Canadian labor market.

Finally, it is important to note that shifts to standardized curriculum and new regimes of student evaluation, along with the regular round of provincial and national testing that now occurs in Canada, have affected teachers' professional autonomy in the classroom. A growing number of studies in Canada and elsewhere demonstrate how these "reforms" have narrowed the curriculum, constrained pedagogical diversity, and redefined who is competent and who counts as a student. Cutbacks to funding and changes in teaching styles forced by the new curriculum and testing programs mean that many young people are, in fact, getting left behind or thrown out as schools lack the resources to support students experiencing difficulties. In fact, educational restructuring as it has occurred in Canada places the blame for failure on individual students and their "choice" to evade hard work. The neoliberal rhetoric and practices of competitive individualism seek to subvert discourses of systemic discrimination and silence analyses that insert more collective concerns about gender, race, or class into the equation. Hence, teacher federations, concerned with the wider equity implications of educational restructuring and the commercialization and privatization of public education, are again urging more attention to equality, with a particular focus on intersections of gender, race, and sexual orientation. Many classroom teachers, however, argue that it is difficult to take time away from the prescribed curriculum to focus on equality.

There is one exception. As testing programs point to gaps between girls' and boys' achievement levels, there has been a blossoming of initiatives to deal with the "boy problem" in literacy learning and, concomitantly, with the declining numbers of men in teaching. While some of the policy debates take on the hysterical tone of the antifeminist men's rights movement and assail the schools as overly feminized and a threat to "real" boys, other responses have been more measured and raise bigger questions about what kinds of boys are experiencing difficulties, how schools and popular culture gender both boys and girls, and why we need to return to looking at gender equity program development for males and females. A study by the British Columbia Teachers' Federation in 2000 also reiterated that gender is a set of social relations shaped by the wider changes in school and society. Explicit links were made between gender troubles and the socioeconomic conditions resulting from neoliberal reforms to the economy. Thus, paradoxically, the focus on boys and men has the potential to promote a new look at gender equality policy in Canadian schooling. Another hopeful trend is a resurgence of feminist activism among young women. One example is the Miss G__ Project, a group of university and high school students, that is lobbying intensively for the inclusion of a women's studies course in the secondary school curriculum.

It is also fittingly ironic that by imposing new regimes of work intensification, control, and surveillance, governments have helped create a more politically conscious teaching force, willing to confront the neoliberal agenda and make common cause with the wider trade union movement and with social movements in Canada and internationally. A growing number of teacher unions have affiliated with local labor councils, provincial labor organizations, and the Canadian Labour Congress. Teachers have taken to the streets in the tens of thousands to protest the loss of labor rights and cutbacks to funding for public education and social services. In 2001, teachers participated in the People's Summit in Quebec City to voice their opposition to the Free Trade Agreement of the Americas. Canadian teachers also have joined colleagues from the North and South to defend public education through organizations such as the Trilateral Coalition for the Defense of Public Education and Initiatives for Democratic Education in the Americas. Through Education International, Canada's teacher federations have supported efforts to build teacher unions in the South. Since unionization is the best predictor of stable incomes and decent benefits for women workers, this initiative will likely do more to assist gender equality for female teachers and students internationally than many foreign aid programs.

Women teachers continue to work with their male colleagues in teacher federations, with other women through the larger women's movement, and with parents' groups largely run by the volunteer labor of mothers in order to protect public education as a democratic right. The goal is to contest the language, ideology, and material practices of neoliberalism, offer alternative visions of citizenship and civil society, and defend gender equality as part of a larger commitment to equity and social justice.

REFERENCES AND FURTHER READINGS

Bouchard, P., Boily, I., & Proulx, M-C. (2003). *School success by gender: A catalyst for masculinist discourse.* Ottawa: Status of Women Canada.

Bourne, P., & Reynolds, C. (Eds.). (2004). Girls, boys, and schooling [Special issue]. *Orbit, 34*(1).

Coulter, R.P. (1999). "Doing gender" in Canadian schools: An overview of the policy and practice mélange. In S. Erskine & M. Wilson (Eds.), *Gender issues in international education* (pp. 113–129). New York & London: Falmer.

McCaskell, T. (2005). *Race to equity: Disrupting educational inequality.* Toronto, Canada: Between the Lines.

Schaefer, A.C. (2000). G.I. Joe meets Barbie, software engineer meets caregiver: Males and females in B.C.'s public schools and beyond. Vancouver: British Columbia Teachers' Federation. Retrieved June 26, 2007, from http://bctf.ca/uploadedFiles/Publications/Research_reports/report(2).pdf

Young, B. (2002). The "Alberta Advantage": "De-Kleining" career prospects for women educators. In C. Reynolds (Ed.), *Women and school leadership: International perspectives* (pp. 75–92). Albany: State University of New York Press.

Rebecca Priegert Coulter

Gender Equity and Students with Disabilities

The prevalence of disability in the United States population is estimated to be between 15 and 20 percent based on the U.S. Department of Education and Census Bureau figures. Legislation in the United States is designed to improve the educational experiences of people with disabilities. However, inequities appear in the rate of identification and type and provision of special education services on the basis of gender, race/ethnicity, and socioeconomic status. The disability community has experienced a shift in paradigm from a deficit model that places the problem in the individual with the disability to a sociocultural model that examines societal response to individuals with disabilities. Accompanying this shift is the emergence of a transformative research paradigm that provides a framework for understanding the complexity of the intersection of diverse dimensions of difference and leads to modifications in the environment that allow for fuller participation by people with disabilities.

LEGISLATION CONCERNING GENDER EQUITY AND STUDENTS WITH DISABILITIES

In the United States, the civil rights law that protects girls and boys from sex discrimination in education programs is Title IX of the Education Amendments of 1972. However, this law does not address the full range of diversity in terms of disability, race, ethnicity, and socioeconomic status manifest within the categories of girls and boys. Groups who brought pressure on the legislature to pass laws on civil rights issues tended to be single-issue groups. Gender-equity professionals who fought for Title IX did not press for inclusion of equity on the basis of race or ethnicity or disability. Similarly, advocates for access for students with disabilities did not press for equity in terms of gender and race/ethnicity. Thus, the strides made in the name of gender equity ignored issues related to males and females with disabilities (Lloyd, 2001).

To understand the intersection of disability and gender equity, it is necessary to consider the protections offered by disability rights laws, such as the Individuals with

Disabilities Education Act, Section 504 of the 1973 Rehabilitation Act, and the Americans with Disabilities Act. Despite the fact that these pieces of legislation were patterned, in part, on previous statutes that prohibit discrimination on other grounds in federally assisted programs or activities, such as Title VI of the Civil Rights Law of 1964 and Title IX, the disability-related legislation refers to gender in a limited way.

The Education of the Handicapped Act, passed in 1975, was changed to the Individuals with Disabilities Education Act (IDEA) in 1990 and was reauthorized in 1997 and again in 2004. IDEA (and its predecessor legislation) resulted in fewer students with disabilities being educated in separate schools or classrooms.

IDEA contains several references to gender in Section 618. Specifically, states are required to report annually to the U.S. Department of Education on the number and percentage of children with disabilities by race, ethnicity, limited English proficiency status, gender, and disability category who are either receiving services under IDEA or have experienced disciplinary actions, including suspensions of one day or more. The statute does not mention the need to disaggregate data by gender and disability in its other provisions, such as the number of children with developmental disabilities or the section on disproportionality on the basis of race and type of disability. Another part of the IDEA legislation reauthorization aims to reduce the overidentification of African Americans for special education by requiring the federal government to better monitor special education enrollment and investigate racial disparities.

Section 504 and the Americans with Disabilities Act (ADA) are both civil rights laws to prohibit discrimination on the basis of disability. ADA focuses on discrimination in employment, public services, and accommodations. Section 504 focuses on discrimination in programs and activities, public and private, which receive federal financial assistance. Unlike IDEA, Section 504 does not require the school to provide an individualized educational program that is designed to meet the child's unique needs and provides the child with educational benefits. Fewer procedural safeguards are available for children with disabilities and their parents under Section 504 than under IDEA. If the child has a disability that adversely affects educational performance, the child is eligible for special education services under IDEA. Children who are eligible for special education services under IDEA are protected under Section 504 (but the converse is not true). If the child has a disability that does not adversely affect educational performance, then the child will not be eligible for special education services under IDEA but will usually be entitled to protections under Section 504. Interestingly, the U.S. Department of Justice Title IX Legal Manual suggests that the Section 504 and Title IX Coordinators may be the same person.

Outside of the United States, the majority (80 percent) of the world's approximately 300 million women and girls with disabilities live in developing countries and face discrimination from birth (World Bank, 2004). If a baby girl is born with a disability and is allowed to live, she must contend with negative attitudes and beliefs about disability from her family and community. Often girls with disabilities are hidden within their homes, have less access to health care services, will not attend school or work, will be subject to physical abuse, sexual abuse, and higher risk for HIV infection, will not receive rehabilitation services or HIV/AIDS education, testing, or access to clinical programs, and will receive less care and food in the home than her siblings

Only 1 percent of girls in developing countries with disabilities attend school. The literacy rate for girls with disabilities is under 5 percent. Girls who do attend school attend for a shorter amount of time than boys (United Nations, 2002). Women with disabilities do not have equal access to paid employment and are twice as unlikely to find work as men. Most girls are kept at home where they care for children and relatives, cook, clean, and do daily chores.

DISABILITIES: TYPES, DEMOGRAPHIC DIVERSITY, AND EDUCATIONAL EFFECTS

Within the United States, both the ADA and the IDEA define disabilities as a consequence of impairment. The ADA does not specifically name all of the impairments that are covered, but defines an individual with a disability as a person who has a physical or mental impairment that substantially limits one or more major life activities, a person who has a history or record of such impairment, or a person who is perceived by others as having such impairment. The IDEA legislation includes 13 categories of disability: mental retardation (MR), hearing impairments, speech or language impairments, visual impairments, serious emotional disturbance (ED), orthopedic impairments, other health impairments, specific learning disabilities (LD), multiple disabilities, deafness/ blindness, autism, and traumatic brain injury. Additionally, the text includes discussion of infants and toddlers with disabilities and persons with developmental delays and those at risk.

The U.S. Department of Education is required to report annually to Congress on the implementation of IDEA. Recent reports have identified approximately 9 percent of students aged 6 though 21 as having a disability. Unfortunately, these reports do not disaggregate type of disability by gender and other background characteristics. Nevertheless, gender and other forms of diversity are important in the population with disabilities, not only diversity among the factors specifically associated with the disability, such as the age of onset, severity, identification with cultural groups, preferred communication mode, and capacity for independence, but also diversity among other demographic characteristics, including age, race/ethnicity, and socioeconomic status.

Comparisons of the gender distributions from 1987 to 2001 for people ages 3 to 21 indicate no significant change over time in the gender distribution of students with disabilities. Males were significantly overrepresented among students receiving special education relative to students in the general population in both time periods. Greater identification across the high-incidence disability categories is evident for males. The greatest gender disparity in identification rates is found in the ED category (80 percent male), followed by LD (70 percent male) and MR (60 percent male). The definitions of LD, ED, and MR may have sufficient latitude that teachers can identify boys with behavioral problems under all three categories as a means to get them help or to move them out of the classroom. A similar overrepresentation of males (61 percent) was evident even among infants and toddlers with disabilities.

Differing identification rates are also evident within the emotional disturbance category of disability by gender, ethnicity, and age. For major racial/ethnic groups, males are at over three times the risk for being classified as emotionally disturbed than are females in the same racial/ethnic group except for Asian/Pacific Islander (for whom males are still more than twice as likely). However, females experience higher rates of internalizing psychopathology, such as anxiety, eating disorders, and mood disorders, while men exhibit higher rates of externalized psychopathology, such as aggression. Rates of depression are equal for boys and girls until the onset of puberty when the ratio of females to males diagnosed with depression increases to 2:1 and remains higher throughout adult life. Females also experience a higher rate of anxiety disorders, such as panic disorder, agoraphobia, and simple phobias. In actuality, it may be that males do not suffer anxiety and depressive disorders less than females but that it is manifested differently, for example, as hyperactivity, irritability, or irrational explosiveness.

This raises an important question of the possible underidentification of girls, with the consequence being lack of needed support services for them (Wehmeyer & Schwartz, 2001). For example, researchers report that females obtained lower scores on standardized IQ tests at the time of their admission to special education and were more likely to be placed in self-contained education settings. Boys were 10 times more likely to have behavioral factors cited in their reasons for referral. Thus, it appears that girls have to manifest more significant deficits to access special education services than boys, and, upon identification, they are more likely than boys to be placed in a more restrictive setting. It seems that girls are not as likely to act out and are, therefore, less likely to be referred for help. They must experience more significant problems than boys in order to get the support they need.

In terms of developmental disabilities, boys exhibit higher rates of autism, attention deficit, hyperactivity disorder, learning disabilities, and Tourette's syndrome (Thompson, Caruso, & Ellerbeck, 2003). The ratio of male to female rates of autism is 4:1 (and 10:1 in high-functioning autism and Asperger syndrome). Reasons for this differential are not clear, perhaps because most research in developmental disabilities has paid little attention to gender differences. A review of 563 articles that contained the word "autism" published in major psychological journals between 2000 and 2002 found that only 2 percent of the studies included comparative analyses for males and females. Typically, these studies focused on prevalence, rather than on a description of how autism is manifested or treated in males and females. It may be that autism is manifested differently in girls than boys and, in milder cases, their autism is undiagnosed, delayed, or inaccurately diagnosed as, for example, anxiety disorder or anorexia nervosa.

Overrepresentation of culturally and linguistically diverse students in special education is a fact based on both legal and research findings (Mertens & McLaughlin, 2004). On the one hand, overidentification can be traced to unfair, unreliable, and invalid assessment and diagnostic practices. On the other hand, disproportionality can result from a lack of cultural competency, understanding of cultural diversity, or ability to accommodate the diverse needs and preferences of students who are culturally and linguistically diverse. The 2000 U.S. Census suggests that the number of ethnic minority group members will increase significantly in the future, and by the year 2020, the majority of school-age children in the United States will be from racial or ethnic minority groups. At the same time, the number of teachers and other service personnel who are European American comprise over 85 percent of the education workforce. The resulting imbalance may lead to inappropriate referral decisions and placements in special education.

The increase in the racial/ethnic diversity of the general student population is also evident among students with disabilities in comparisons of 1987 and 2001 data. Hispanic students exhibited the largest increase for both groups, being half again as large in 2001 as in 1987 (14 percent vs. 9 percent). In contrast, the proportions of students with disabilities who were White or Black declined by just over two percentage points. Consistent with the increase in the Hispanic population, there was more than a fourfold increase in the proportion of students with disabilities who did not use primarily English at home: the percentage grew from 3 percent to 14 percent. Schools serving students with disabilities whose first language is not English increasingly face challenges of communicating in two languages and accommodating two cultures, in addition to the challenges posed by students' disabilities.

According to the Civil Rights Project at Harvard University, Black children constitute 17 percent of the total school enrollment and 33 percent of those labeled mentally retarded—only a marginal improvement over the 30 years that the U.S. Office for Civil Rights has collected these data (Losen & Orfield, 2002). During this same period, disproportionality in the area of ED, MR, and LD grew significantly for Blacks. Minority students, specifically Black and Native American students, are significantly more likely than White students to be identified as having a disability. For example, in most states, African American children are identified at one and a half to four times the rate of White children in the disability categories of MR and ED.

U.S. Department of Education data from 2000 to 2001 reveal that in at least 13 states more than 2.75 percent of all Blacks enrolled were labeled MR. The prevalence of MR for Whites nationally was approximately 0.75 percent in 2001, and in no state did the incidence among Whites ever rise above 2.32 percent. Moreover, nearly three-quarters of the states with unusually high incidence rates (2.75 percent to 5.41 percent) for Blacks were in the South. Based on national data, Latino and Asian American children are underidentified in cognitive disability categories compared to Whites, raising questions about whether the special education needs of these children are being met. The incidence of disability reveals gross disparities between Blacks and Hispanics, and between Black boys and girls, in identification rates for the categories of MR and ED. Most disturbing was that in wealthier districts, contrary to the expected trend, Black children, especially males, were more likely to be labeled MR. Moreover, the sharp gender differences in identification within racial groups mirrors the incidence of male/female differences in the overall population.

Being identified as a student with disabilities has had and continues to have important educational consequences. Historically, female students in secondary schools for students with disabilities were enrolled more often in life skills courses, whereas more males were enrolled in vocational education. The consequence of this is that women with disabilities are less likely to be employed and, if employed, they hold lower-paying occupations in clerical, service, and helping occupations.

The number of students with disabilities quitting high school decreased by 4 percent between 1994 and 1998 (35 percent dropped out in 1994, compared to 31 percent in 1998), and the number of students with disabilities graduating from high school with a diploma increased (51.7 percent in 1994 to 55.4 percent in 1998). The U.S. Department of Education reported that high school students with disabilities drop out at twice the rate of their peers without disabilities. Parents report that 1 percent of males with disabilities drop out because of marriage or parenthood, yet 23 percent of females drop out for the same reasons.

According to the National Center for Education Statistics, women with disabilities between 18 and 34 years old have lower educational attainment than women without disabilities. Those who are not currently enrolled in school in this age group are more likely than women without disabilities *not* to be a high school graduate (26.3 percent vs. 15.3 percent) and less likely to have a bachelor's degree or greater (9.2 percent vs. 26.3 percent). Men with disabilities have even lower educational attainment, being more likely than men without disabilities *not* to be a high school graduate (30.1 percent vs. 19.1 percent) and less likely to have a bachelor's degree or greater (6.8 percent vs. 21.3 percent).

DISABILITY RIGHTS AND PARADIGM SHIFTS

The struggle for disability rights shares an extensive overlap with the rights sought under the feminist banner. Disability and feminist theorists have similar goals in that both are concerned with the elimination of the exploitation and oppression of their respective constituencies. Specifically, females with and without disabilities have less access to appropriate educational resources and evince poorer educational and employment-related outcomes than do their male peers. Thus, Rousso and Wehmeyer (2001) conclude that disparities on these indicators support the idea that girls and women with disabilities are in a state of double jeopardy. The combination of stereotypes about women and stereotypes about people with disabilities leads to double discrimination that is reflected in the home, the school, the workplace, and the larger society.

While the disability rights movement shares many of the same concerns with feminists, important differences between the feminist and disability rights agenda exist. Feminists have overlooked women with disabilities, and, on some issues, conflict exists (Lloyd, 2001). For example, a point of tension exists between feminists and women with disabilities related to issues of sexuality, reproduction, and motherhood. Women with disabilities have to fight the prejudices that exclude them from fulfilling the traditional female roles relating to childbearing, motherhood, and self-presentation as a sexual human being. A second point of tension between feminists and women with disabilities arises in the reproductive rights issue around abortion. Feminists have argued for a woman's right to choose abortion, particularly when the fetus is developing abnormally. Women with disabilities reject the assumption that there is no place in this world for people who are physically and/or intellectually "abnormal." Additionally, the views of males and females with disabilities on caring and dependence are sometimes at variance with feminist views. Rather than viewing caregiving as a burden, men and women with disabilities reframe the issue in their demands to be allowed to undertake the caring responsibilities in their personal relationships, including the right to have the practical support they may need to accomplish the tasks associated with caring.

Both similarities and differences between the feminist and disability rights movements can be seen in the contemporary perspectives used to understand women and men with disabilities. People with disabilities have been viewed from various perspectives that have shifted through time and have been summarized as paradigms in terms of the moral model, the medical model, and the sociocultural model of disability. A paradigm is a way of looking at the world with accompanying philosophical assumptions that guide and direct thinking and action. The moral model suggests that the disability is a punishment for a sin or a means of inspiring or redeeming others. The medical model sees the disability as a problem or a measurable defect located in the individual that needs a cure or alleviation that can be provided by medical experts.

The disability community experienced a paradigmatic shift from a model that viewed disability as a defect in the individual to a sociocultural model that focuses on the adequacy of the environmental response to the disability. The deficit model has been described as preparing the child to go to school, rather than preparing the school to receive and serve an increasing number of diverse children. The sociocultural paradigm is more congruent with a feminist stance in that it evolved from the efforts of people with the lived experience of having a disability. Within this paradigm, disability is framed from the perspective of a social, cultural minority group, such that disability is defined not as a defect, but rather as a dimension of human difference. Furthermore, the category of disability is recognized as being socially constructed with its meaning being derived from society's response to individuals who deviate from cultural standards. Thus, the goal for people with disabilities is not to eradicate their condition but to celebrate their distinctness, pursue their equal place in American society, and acknowledge that their differentness is not defective but valuable.

This paradigmatic shift in the disability community serves as a basis for the transformation of the ways decisions are made about the provision of services for, and research about, people with disabilities. Previously, much of special education research derived from a deficit perspective that located the problem in an individual and focused on the disability as the reason that the individual could not perform certain functions or activities. More recently, special education researchers have shifted to a transformative perspective that focuses on the dynamic interaction between the individual and environment over the life span.

A transformative paradigm for research has emerged parallel with the emergence of the sociocultural view of disability (Mertens & McLaughlin, 2004). The transformative paradigm is a philosophical framework for research that is compatible to feminist theory. While feminist theory puts central importance on gender, transformative theory explicitly addresses multiple dimensions of diversity associated with discrimination and oppression. Transformative research focuses on the strengths of the individual and ways to modify the environment to remove barriers and increase the probability of success. It is significant that the disability communities, as well as the research community, are experiencing a paradigm shift as they reexamine the underlying assumptions that guide their theory and practice. Research framed within the transformative paradigm puts social justice at the forefront with an explicit goal of furthering human rights. Such research could yield an improved basis for policy for people with disabilities by providing insights into this community with its full spectrum of diversity.

REFERENCES AND FURTHER READINGS

Lloyd, M. (2001). The politics of disability and feminism: Discord or synthesis? *Sociology, 35*(3), 715–728.

Losen, D.J., & Orfield, G. (Eds.). (2002). *Racial inequity in special education.* Boston: Harvard Educational Press.

Mertens, D.M., Wilson, A., & Mounty, J. (2007). Achieving gender equity for populations with disabilities. In S. Klein (Ed.), *Handbook for achieving gender equity through education.* Mahwah, NJ: Erlbaum.

Mertens, D.M., & McLaughlin, J. (2004). *Research and evaluation methods in special education.* Thousand Oaks, CA: Corwin Press.

Rousso, H., & Wehmeyer, M.L. (Eds.). (2001). *Double jeopardy.* Albany: State University of New York Press.

Thompson, T., Caruso, M., & Ellerbeck, K. (2003). Sex matters in autism and other developmental disabilities. *Journal of Learning Disabilities, 7*(4), 345–362.

United Nations. (2002). *Hidden sisters: Women and girls with disabilities in the Asian and Pacific region.* Retrieved January 23, 2004, from http://www.un.org/Depts/escap/decade/wwd1.htm

Wehmeyer, M.L., & Schwartz, M. (2001). Research on gender bias in special education services. In H. Rousso & M.L. Wehmeyer (Eds.), *Double jeopardy* (pp. 271–288). Albany: State University of New York Press.

World Bank. (2004). *Impact of HIV/AIDS on disabled community largely overlooked.* Retrieved January 23, 2004, from http://Web.worldbank.org

Donna M. Mertens

Amy Wilson

Judith Mounty

International Policies

Public policies are authoritative courses of action emanating from above. Gender policies can take the form of legislation, programs, regulations, administrative practices, and court decisions. In the global context, gender policies acquire forms ranging from international conventions and declarations at global forums to programs and projects.

Public policies signal the identification of governmental priorities and, while they indicate a decision to act, they remain little more than pieces of paper until they are implemented as intended. Consequently, policies should be seen as a package that comprises four inseparable elements: enactment of intentions, drafting of regulations, implementation, and assessment of impact. These components do not occur in a mechanistically linear way, as they are part of an active political process; nonetheless, they represent essential components of all policy.

GENDER FRAMING AND POLICY DYNAMICS

If policies are solutions to perceived problems, what is the problem regarding gender? There are different perceptions of what constitute problems of gender in education. Among economists, highly influential in decisions concerning national development, the view is that the women should be given access to the labor force and that society should make use of women's contribution, which otherwise would presumably go to waste. Among state officials and political representatives, who usually follow the advice of economists, the logic of women's inclusion in the labor market leads to proposals of equal opportunity measures, which in turn center on educational parity between women and men. These officials see gender problems in education, if any, as circumscribed to access to and completion of schooling, primarily of primary and secondary levels. Among other groups, which include individuals in the women's movement and feminist scholars, the gender problem in education is much more complex. Access to schooling is crucial, but also critical are changes in mentalities and in the social relations of daily life both within and outside schools (Arnot & Dillabough, 2000; Connell, 1995).

Policies should be recognized not only as initiatives that seek change but also as initiatives that generate forces that counter perceived inequities. Gender policies tend to be contested because they are situated at the intersection of democratic values and status quo (patriarchal norms). The analysis of public policy from a gender perspective needs to be extremely sensitive to those factors and actors that either promote or oppose the formulation and implementation of gender policies.

Empirical evidence identifies *five main policy entrepreneurs in the gender area:* state administrative staffs, organized religious groups, teachers' unions, organized women's groups, and international development organizations. These groups hold different positions toward the treatment of gender in education.

In the context of the economic crisis affecting many developing countries, the common response of *state administrative staff* is to give priority to the satisfaction of basic needs and the reduction of poverty levels among national populations. The tendency of administrative staff is to assign the gender perspective in educational (and other) policies the status of peripheral issue. Moreover, the majority of politicians and civil servants in ministries of education see the problems confronting women as lying within the purview of culture or economics rather than education.

Sacred beliefs and religious practices tend to be detrimental to the advancement of women. While most *organized religious groups* grant women their right to education, they also tend to define knowledge in ways that assign motherhood as women's primary responsibility. The Catholic Church in Latin America has been a major source of resistance to curriculum changes, particularly those in sex education that have attempted to depict new forms of family arrangements and less traditional expressions of sexuality.

Mostly nationwide organizations, *teachers' unions* often exert considerable pressure on governments. They have tended to focus on the protection of salary and career interests; except for a few cases in industrialized countries, they have seldom promoted new training and curriculum materials sensitive to gender.

Organized women's groups, both international and national in character, are strong advocates of women's education. They have supported efforts to secure gender parity in schools and to introduce sex education in the curriculum. In particular, these groups have promoted the education of adult women through various nonformal education programs focused primarily on such issues as health, reproductive rights, domestic violence, income generation, and political representation.

The work of *international development organizations,* such as bilateral development agencies and some UN agencies, has been crucial to the development of policies seeking to advance the education of girls and women. These organizations concentrate on issues of access, however, leaving questions of transformative and contestatory curriculum aside. Often, these organizations define gender problems as those affecting only women and mostly those in low-income or minority groups.

GLOBAL GENDER POLICIES

Since 1990, through a series of international conferences and agreements, women's education has been identified as being crucial to national development and to the emergence of a more democratic world. The Convention on the Elimination of All Forms of Discrimination Against Women, enacted in 1979 and signed by 185 nations (as of November 2006), stands as a strong example of legal obligations to advance women's conditions, including their formal schooling. Two current global policies bring gender in education to the fore: the Education for All (EFA) Framework for Action, approved by most governments in Dakar in 2000, and the UN Millennium Development Goals (MDGs), approved by all 191 countries, also in the same year (United Nations, 2000).

EFA comprises six goals covering early childhood education, primary and secondary schooling, and adult literacy. It seeks universal access to basic education for both girls and boys by 2015. It seeks *gender parity* in primary and secondary education by 2005 and *equality* in education by 2015 (World Education Forum, 2000). UNESCO recognizes equality to be a complex concept and currently defines it as equal survival to the fifth grade of primary school (UNESCO, 2003).

MDGs policy covers eight areas of social and economic action, one of which is education. In the education area, MDGs incorporate two of the EFA goals: universal access to basic education by 2015 and gender parity in primary and secondary schooling by 2005 and at all levels by 2015 (United Nations, 2000). While the MDGs continue to recognize the importance of education, they weaken the intent of the EFA goals by avoiding early childhood education, by failing to include the goal of improving the equality of educational treatment, and by limiting the efforts in favor of literacy to the population aged 15–24 only, thus missing important demographic bands among women, such as the 25–45 age group, which would seem crucial in intergenerational social and political processes. On the other hand, while the MDGs do not recognize the issue of equality, they do consider gender parity *at all levels* of education, which includes tertiary education.

The MDGs meant to constitute an endorsement of the goals expressed and approved at previous global forums. However, the MDGs reduce the measurement of basic education to the completion of four years. The attainment of gender parity in primary education is a high goal for some developing countries, primarily those in sub-Saharan Africa and South Asia, but for several others, notably some Latin America countries, the goal has been long surpassed since parity in primary education has been achieved since the mid-1960s. The enactment of the MDGs has not been accompanied by an examination of the impacts of previous policies, and there have been no studies to explain the difficulties in implementing them. This raises questions about the seriousness of global policies, which typically are unanimously agreed upon by government delegates, occasionally enacted into law, and seldom executed.

From a gender perspective, the MDGs seem responsive to women, as Goal No. 3 explicitly addresses their empowerment. It proposes four indicators to measure empowerment: the girls/boys enrollment ratio in primary schooling, the ratio of literate females to males in ages 15–24, gender parity in labor force participation, and the proportion of seats held by women in national parliaments. The tying of empowerment to education is warranted, yet it is clear that not *any* knowledge automatically empowers. Focusing on literacy acquisition of the age group 15–24 exclusively ignores the reproductive effect that the older generations may have on the younger. One needs to think of empowerment as multidimensional; it is achieved not only through an understanding of gender relations and the ways in which these can be changed, but also through the set of mechanisms and opportunities that must be put in place in order to develop a sense of self-worth among women (Stromquist, 2002).

Since the Fourth World Conference on Women (held in Beijing, 1995), the principle of gender mainstreaming has been advocated in international circles. Mainstreaming is a principle that theoretically makes profound sense: if gender cuts across all features of our social world, gender should also be present in all policy decisions. The reality, however, is more challenging. Gender mainstreaming needs people with understanding and specific training to visualize gender dimensions and plan accordingly. Otherwise, gender mainstreaming risks lack of accountability; it cannot be easily monitored if all the expenditures are combined, and yet everyone can claim it has occurred.

GENDER POLICIES IN EDUCATION AT NATIONAL LEVELS

No comprehensive account of gender policies throughout the world exists, but there are both industrialized and developing countries for which research studies have been produced.

Several European countries have educational policies with gender perspectives. Perhaps the earliest country to adopt any is Sweden, whose policies predated the women's movement and have focused on curriculum change. By 1980, Sweden was undergoing its third curriculum change to treat boys and girls equally and to challenge traditional sex roles. An evaluation done 10 years subsequently found that teacher training was still unaffected by the consideration of gender differences, gender equality, and the implication of gender roles for classroom practices with girls and boys. However, traditionally sex-typed subjects such as sports and woodwork and needlework are now taught in coeducational classes. In the 1980s, gender equality in Sweden had turned into promoting "girls to science and technology," efforts that have been followed later in other industrialized countries. In Wernersson's view (1989), this emphasis shifts the issue of fairness and inequality to a matter of educational choice.

Educational policies have included equal opportunity legislation in Australia, New Zealand, the United Kingdom, and the United States. As a result of these measures, there has been greater protection for women against negative and discriminatory environments. In the United States, in particular, women have made gains in some previously closed fields such as medicine and law and have gained access to a diverse set of sports and sports scholarships. The United States has also enacted proactive policies, seeking to foster the development of nonsexist materials and the provision of gender-aware teacher training. In general, proactive policies have been characterized by limited funding and small scale.

Recently, the United Kingdom and Australia have expressed concern about the cognitive gains made by girls, who sometimes perform better than boys in standardized tests. This has been characterized as a "boys' failure," and critics have questioned the fairness of policies seeking to advance girls' education. Arnot and Miles (2005) respond to this preoccupation by noting that school officials are drawing on outmoded socialization theories rather than on contemporary understandings of gender identities and subjectivities about the ways in which competitive school cultures aggravate gender differences and produce disaffected masculinities.

A number of developing countries have explicit policy documents, subsequently translated into national plans. Other countries rely on major initiatives that may not be necessarily part of national plans.

Among the latter is the Female Secondary School Stipend Program enacted in Bangladesh, which grants monetary support to rural girls so that they may attend secondary schooling. This program had reached over 500,000 girls by 1995. Another instance is the PROGRESA initiative in Mexico (now called *Oportunidades*) that grants stipends to rural students and offers slightly higher stipends to girls than boys in secondary schools; by 2005, the program had reached about 5 million families. In higher education, the World Bank has engaged in measures such as scholarships, creation of new residences for young women attending university, and vocational or technical education programs, reserving a small number of places for women in nonconventional fields of study, particularly engineering and agriculture. These initiatives are mostly pilot studies that receive little follow-up.

India reports having a new plan, Sarva Shiksha Abhiyan, to have all children complete fifth grade by 2007 and will invest $1 billion to that end. A nonformal education program

(Mahila Samakya), now implemented in 9,000 villages in 10 states, is aimed at rural girls' education. Some 750 residential colleges for girls, emphasizing the enrollment of girls from scheduled castes, scheduled tribes, and other minorities are now in place. India enacted a National Policy for the Empowerment of Women in 2001, which seeks to provide comprehensive services to adolescent girls. The government of India seems to be the only one in the world that has instituted a 2 percent tax to secure universal education for all children of ages 6–14. In improving access to all, girls will presumably benefit. According to its government, India has improved its gender parity index for basic education from .38 in 1950 to .85 in 2002 (India, 2005).

Data from Latin America indicate that few countries have developed comprehensive gender equity policies. These include Argentina, Paraguay, and Bolivia. Argentina has been a pioneer in gender policies in education. Its National Program for Equality Opportunity for Women in Education (PRIOM), which functioned 1991 to 1995, succeeded in training a large number of teachers, producing useful gender-sensitive materials, and making the General Education Law (approved in 1993) incorporate the principle of equal opportunity and the eradication of sexual stereotypes in educational materials. The Catholic Church opposed the national adoption of new curricular materials proposed by PRIOM on the grounds that they would destroy the family and encourage homosexuality by questioning the "natural differences between men and women." In consequence, many of the PRIOM staff members resigned; milder curricula were subsequently developed by the Church. Paraguay's gender policies in education sought curriculum reform, teacher training, and a review of textbooks. As a result of these changes, modules on gender and sexuality were produced but as supplementary, not core, materials. Bolivia's policies sought to make gender a crosscutting theme throughout the curriculum and to incorporate such issues as health, sexuality, equity, and sustainable development. By 2002, gender reformers had been able to provide training to resource teachers (i.e., those assisting classroom teachers) and to design general guidelines and curriculum content with a gender perspective for the first three years of primary schooling. In Peru, a national plan for the education of rural girls, strongly promoted by a bilateral development agency, was adopted in 2001; a particular commission of notables is in place to facilitate plan implementation, and, while resources and action are modest, some workshops with regional and local authorities on the promotion of women's leadership are taking place. In Chile, current educational policies include gender as a crosscutting theme in the curriculum, and, since 1994, a bidding process to write and publish textbooks requires a gender equality factor.

Multinational agencies such as bilateral development agencies and those in the UN family have proven essential to the promotion of educational policies from a gender perspective in developing countries. UNESCO and UNICEF are engaged in several efforts to address gender issues in both public education and nonformal education. Bilateral agencies enable the holding of international forums by financing the preparation of documents and meetings preparatory to those conferences. They also sponsor the participation of women from developing countries. Furthermore, these agencies enter the policy picture because, under the current economic and political context, many developing countries are unable to address pressing issues in their educational budgets without the support of industrialized countries.

A long-standing pledge by bilateral development agencies has been the allocation of 0.70 percent of their GNP to developing countries, though at present, they give an average of 0.25 percent. Sachs (2005) calculates that in order to reach all of the MDGs, development assistance must increase to $135 billion by 2006—or double the current assistance.

In May 2005, European Union countries committed themselves to increasing their financial contribution for development to 0.6_percent of the GNP by 2006 and to 0.7 percent by 2015. These dates seem rather late if the MDGs goals are to be reached according to schedule.

A review of various policy papers and position documents by six international organizations influential in Latin America between 1998 and 2001 was conducted by Krawczyk (2002). This author found that these organizations promote privatization, decentralization, school autonomy, higher student achievement, and better management of resources. They also promote targeted policies (i.e., those concentrating on specific groups) as these tend to "produce important redistributive effects," and to "improve the equity of the educational system without requiring greater resources." Krawczyk found educational policies in Latin America to be "fragmented, contradictory, minimalist, targeted, and aimed at privatization." From her document analysis, it can be seen that gender issues do not emerge as a priority among these organizations.

POLICY IMPLEMENTATION

A crucial stage in the policy cycle concerns implementation. It is at this moment that the proposed intentions become a reality.

The core mechanism for national implementation of EFA goals was to be the national action plan, to be developed by "2002 at the latest" (World Education Forum, 2000, p. 22). By June 2005, the UNESCO Web site for EFA listed plans of action for only 43 countries. The emerging statistical evidence indicates that gender parity in primary education was not reached in sub-Saharan Africa by the target date of 2005 (UNESCO, 2006). EFA policies have been termed "target-setting exercises," namely, centrally identified benchmarks, with little recognition of the characteristics of the problem nor any formulation of actual steps to accomplish and evaluate the benchmarks (Goldstein, 2004).

The main means by which to assess how countries comply with the MDGs is through their submission of annual reports to the United Nations Development Programme, the agency in charge of monitoring progress in implementation. A 2005 report by the United Nations Development Fund for Women found that only 55 countries had produced such annual reports by that year.

Rarely do governments establish contact with women's groups that advocate gender-sensitive education. One exception is the Forum for African Women Educationalists. In existence since 1991, this group's core membership comprises women who are or have been ministers of education, vice chancellors, or similar educational authorities. This group has succeeded in establishing effective alliances with donor agencies and in securing funds not only to advocate girls' access to schooling but also to conduct campaigns to raise public awareness of the importance of girls' education and to implement interventions that introduce gender-sensitive teaching methodologies into the classroom. There is no counterpart organization in the other developing regions.

PREDOMINANT FEATURES OF GENDER POLICIES IN EDUCATION

Synthesizing public policy efforts thus far, the following pattern emerges:

- Universal access to education is acknowledged as a human right that is also open to women. Public policies emphasize basic education over higher levels of education. They emphasize access over content and the lived experience of education. In all, these policies are minimalist.

- The average gender policy in education is based on the principle of equality of opportunity, defined as equal treatment. As Blackmore (1999) notes, this delimitation subtracts attention from the ideological context of schooling, which tends to reproduce the social relations of gender.

- Teacher training efforts are not explicitly identified in policy documents and often the regulations that follow do not consider them. In consequence, there are very few instances of sustained reforms to introduce gender-aware preservice teacher training programs. Several countries have engaged in in-service training programs from a gender perspective.

- New curriculum materials that seek to transform gender relations in society and to address sexuality issues comprehensively tend to be highly contested. In several countries, these materials have been discarded. In others, their production has been mostly on a pilot basis and their actual use confined to the status of supplementary rather than core materials.

- In developing countries, with very few exceptions, most efforts to address gender issues in education have occurred through the input of international development agencies, both in the form of policy guidelines and in financial resources to develop new programs and projects.

- Compensatory policies, seeking to provide girls with additional resources to redress substantial inequities, are limited to a few countries. Gender policies should take into account the large gaps between rural and urban areas all over the developing world, but this should not define gender as affecting only poor women.

- In many instances, policy implementation has lagged behind policy enactment, and evaluations of gender policy impacts, particularly in developing countries, are practically nonexistent.

EXPLAINING PUBLIC POLICIES IN GENDER

Discrepancies between objectives and actual practice are not unique to gender policies, but it would seem that there the disconnect is much greater. Wernersson (1989) has observed that school policy is a step behind by necessity because ideological principles must be formulated before they are incorporated in the "official" socialization of the young. Public policies, thus, may not contribute significantly to altering power structures. But how do we explain the limited compliance, even when gender policies are modestly framed? Three rival hypotheses emerge.

The first hypothesis is that detailed features of the new gender policies are unclear and civil servants, untrained in gender issues, are unable to translate the new legislation into specific guidelines and regulations.

The second hypothesis is that the states do not receive enough pressure from gender policy entrepreneurs. Women's organized groups and feminist nongovernmental organizations spend considerable energy on other urgent issues, not on formal education. Disruptive voices are necessary to promote both policy enactment and policy implementation.

The third hypothesis is that states continue to be male and patriarchal. They go through the rituals of giving to social problems. Education accords the states compensatory legitimation because it plays up the powerful symbols of legality, rationality, and democracy. Symbols are crucial for meaning making and unavoidable in social interaction. Here we are not negating the importance of symbols but underscoring the unfortunate fact that some gender policies may serve only as useful "illusions."

Because of these possibilities, gender policies "from above" (i.e., those formulated from state arenas) need to be formulated in very precise terms to avoid uncertainty in their translation into practice, and state actors have to be given proper training both to provide them with new knowledge about gender and to erode previous ideological conceptions.

Moreover, gender policies need to be promoted by "policies from below"—characterized by persistent action and supervision by women's organized groups.

REFERENCES AND FURTHER READINGS

Arnot, M., & Dillabough, J. (Eds.). (2000). *Challenging democracy: International perspectives on gender, education and citizenship.* London: RoutledgeFalmer.

Arnot, M., & Miles, P. (2005). A reconstruction of the gender agenda: The contradictory gender dimensions in New Labour's educational and economic policy. *Oxford Review of Education, 31*(1), 173–189.

Blackmore, J. (1999). *Troubling women. Feminism, leadership and educational change.* Buckingham, United Kingdom: Open University Press.

Connell, R.W. (1995). *Masculinities.* St. Leonards, Australia: Allen & Unwin.

Goldstein, H. (2004). The globalization of learning targets. *Comparative Education, 40*(1), 7–14.

India. (2005). *National plan of action.* Retrieved June 5, 2006, from http://Portal.unesco.org/education/en/file_download.php/9a2cbbbea059f70c23fd46a98ae9096bEFANPAIndia.pdf

Krawczyk, N. (2002). La reforma educativa desde la perspectiva de los organismos multilaterales. *Revista Mexicana de Investigación Educativa, 7*(16), 627–663.

Sachs, J. (2005). *Investing in development: A practical plan to achieve the MDGs.* New York: Millennium Project.

Stromquist, N.P. (2002). Education as a means for empowering women. In J. Parpart, S. Rai, & K. Staudt (Eds.), *Rethinking empowerment. Gender and development in a global/local world* (pp. 22–38). London: Routledge.

UNESCO. (2003). *EFA global monitoring report 2003/04. The leap to equality.* Paris: Author.

UNESCO. (2006). *EFA global monitoring report 2006. Literacy for life.* Paris: Author.

United Nations. (2000). *UN millennium development goals.* New York: United Nations General Assembly.

Wernersson, I. (1989). Gender equality—Ideology and reality. In S. Ball & S. Larsson (Eds.), *The struggle for democratic education. equality and participation in Sweden* (pp. 88–102). New York: Falmer Press.

World Education Forum. (2000). *Dakar framework for action.* Paris: UNESCO.

Nelly P. Stromquist

NGOs and Their Impact on Gendered Education

Education and development processes in low-income countries of the Global South should benefit everyone; yet, historically access to and quality of education have often been unevenly distributed across gender, ethnic/tribal, rural-urban, and religious dimensions of society. Despite the aims of Education for All and other initiatives designed to increase equity in educational enrollment, attainment, and quality, gender and other disparities remain. Nongovernmental organizations (NGOs) have emerged during the past several decades as crucial actors in more effectively bridging these gaps. In particular, women-centered NGOs have been the key force in framing development efforts, including those focused on education, around the actual conditions lived by women in the Global South, and in shifting the attention to the necessity of empowering women and transforming gender-biased social structures. These educational efforts beyond the scope of traditional schooling seek to create more gender-equitable communities and societies within which schooling can then better serve both boys and girls.

NGOs work alongside and in relation to governments, multilateral organizations (including United Nations agencies such as UNESCO and UNICEF), the World Bank, the International Monetary Fund, bilateral donor agencies such as the U.S. Agency for International Development (USAID) that provide development assistance to low-income countries, communities, societal and community institutions such as schools and religious groups, and, of course, families. NGOs can be international organizations, known as INGOs (such as Oxfam and Save the Children), national in scope, or local.

Many mainstream NGOs offer a necessary alternative to state-oriented development and education efforts in ways that strengthen local institutions and achieve more positive results at less cost. Many NGOs lack bureaucratic and historical constraints that hamper innovative, experimental, and flexible efforts. Historically, however, the activities and structures of mainstream NGOs are less likely to have prioritized gender equity or included strategies that are participatory and community based, which are central to feminist educational and social change perspectives. If gender equity is to be achieved, gender must be at the center of the analysis that informs policy and practice (Moser, 1993). In addition, when gender equity is defined broadly to include not just educational indicators but also the roles of education and of women in social change, it is women-centered NGOs that tend to be more active in consistently and holistically promoting gender equity (Ruiz Bravo & Monkman, 1988; Stromquist, 2006).

This chapter discusses: (a) the role of NGOs in gender and development work internationally, as this is a backdrop for understanding; (b) how NGOs are involved in education; and, in turn, (c) how education is implicated in gender equity work through NGOs. This is followed by a focus on the transnational advocacy work of NGOs and a discussion of current issues that are important to consider, as they are influential in the work NGOs do relative to gender and education. The chapter ends with acknowledgement of the role of local NGOs in empowering women and building civil society.

NGOs, GENDER, AND DEVELOPMENT

Development work relating to gender encompasses several priorities, beginning with a focus on recognizing the role of women in development, followed by an examination of the assumptions underlying various approaches to gender issues in development, and finally an internal emphasis on how gender is embedded in the work done by NGOs and other development organizations.

Boserup (1970) revealed that the exclusion of women from development initiatives hinders development. Her research also set the stage for a more focused critique of development as not just economic development but also social development, as including education, health, and family well-being as integral dimensions. Similarly, education was deemed integral to the ability of women to participate in development, as they had been denied the knowledge and skill development to engage in their usual activities (e.g., growing food, taking care of families). During the 1970s and 1980s, researchers also recognized the relationship of mothers' educational attainment to social indicators such as fertility rates (and, therefore, family size), age of first birth, family health, and likelihood of sending daughters to school. These early gender analyses of education and development focused on including women in development. The field then moved beyond this approach of "adding women" to one in which gender relations became a focal point for change, thus shaping the development agenda; this has become known as gender and development (GAD). While this work focuses primarily on development agencies, it also relates to the work of NGOs either directly or indirectly. Many NGOs are dependent on development agencies for funding, and so their work reflects the same types of trends. Often, however, it is the women-oriented NGOs that are at the forefront of promoting a more active gender agenda, thus indirectly raising issues to be addressed by the development agencies.

Moser (1993) finds, in her analysis of gender-related development initiatives, five types of approaches: welfare, equity, antipoverty, efficiency, and empowerment. The "antipoverty" approaches recognized the importance of small-scale NGOs in reaching marginalized populations due to their familiarity with local cultures and communities. Equity and empowerment approaches went beyond trying to meet immediate practical needs, such as feeding families and finding work, and shifted the focus to strategic needs. Strategic needs are those that eliminate the basis of the practical needs by, for example, eliminating barriers to agricultural resources, to credit for income-generating activities, and to schooling for women. NGOs have been the primary providers of gender-equitable programs of these types.

A third major contribution of work done in relation to GAD is gender mainstreaming in development agencies and NGOs (Moser, 1993). During the late 1980s, increased attention was focused on the internal processes of organizations and whether they were promoting or unintentionally ignoring gender equity in their projects. Many multilateral and bilateral agencies developed requirements that all project proposals include a gender analysis to examine the impact the project would have on gender equity. In education, for example, this would mean that a project designed to increase enrollment would need to specifically consider how their strategies would impact girls. Pressure to report data by gender was also increasing in this period; gender disaggregated data are now more frequently available. It is within these changes in development work that educational initiatives have also become more gender equitable. NGOs that receive funding from other development organizations are expected to comply with these changing expectations. Some NGOs are more proactive at promoting gender-equitable processes and goals outside of what is required by the funding agencies, thus leading the way for others.

NGOs AND GENDER EQUITY IN EDUCATION

NGOs are involved in gender-equity educational initiatives through formal schooling, nonformal education initiatives for girls and women, and informal learning components in social change projects. Increasingly, the boundaries between formal school, nonformal education, and learning for social change are becoming blurred, as development workers and educators recognize the complexities of confronting gender equity and education.

Studies of *formal schooling* reveal that more than 100 million of the world's children are not in schools, and about 60 percent of these children are girls. In some countries and regions, the gender disparity is significantly larger. Gender differences in enrollment rates, school attainment, retention, literacy rates, and the like reflect sociocultural, political, and economic barriers that disadvantage girls more than boys in some regions, particularly South Asia and Sub-Saharan Africa. Governments of many low-income countries undersupport formal schooling, in part, because of the structural adjustment policies that have required, particularly in the 1980s and 1990s, reduced spending on social services (education and health) and more investment in the development of market economies. At the same time, international entities such as UN agencies have promoted increasing levels of education for all children, and the inclusion of girls and other marginalized groups through such initiatives as Education for All (EFA) and the Millennium Development Goals. Because governments' education budgets have been insufficient for supporting schools for all children, NGOs have been used increasingly often to provide those services because they can do so at a lower cost and because local NGOs are thought to be more in touch with local communities and, therefore, better able to serve them.

At the same time, families in most low-income countries are often not able to pay for school expenses (direct fees, uniforms, etc.) or the opportunity costs of sending all children to school, so difficult choices must be made, and they often choose to educate sons over daughters. Cultural beliefs or social conventions that situate boys in society as primary wage earners or as the source of old age care for parents, support family preferences for educating boys. Educating parents about the advantages of educating girls is another task often undertaken by NGOs. Other barriers to girls' enrollment relate to safety concerns (e.g., the distance girls must travel to schools is too far and they are not well-supervised in that journey; male teachers or students can take advantage of unsupervised girls); lack of latrines (girls cannot use the out-of-doors like boys can); and ineffective teaching (e.g., teachers sometimes use girls for school housekeeping tasks while teaching the boys). In addition, schools can be perceived as challenging local social norms that can make parents reluctant to send children to them. In development circles, it is understood that increasing educational rates of all children, including girls, is related to better job opportunities and more access to income-generating opportunities; both are necessary for community and national development. Formal education is also implicated in socialization processes that build national character and encourage social cohesion. With education being framed increasingly as a human right, the emphasis on equity is also strengthened.

United Nations conventions such as the Convention on the Rights of the Child and the international educational initiatives such as EFA aim for gender parity in education (equal numbers of girls and boys), along with increased enrollment rates for both boys and girls. With these motivations, development agencies and NGOs have increased their attention to gender in educational participation. Save the Children, for example, promotes "community schools" as a strategy to increase access of girls, rural residents, and other marginalized populations to education. Community schools are typically supported through local community contributions, such as labor to build schools or donations of land for school sites; they are organized by NGOs and funded by the government and/or donor agencies. Typically, the government pays a teacher after a community has provided a school site. Community schools are designed to attract more community involvement (and buy-in) and achieve higher rates of enrollment for girls. They operate on lower budgets. Sometimes they outperform traditional government-run schools.

Nonformal education (NFE) includes projects that serve both children and adults. Historically, most NFE served adults as it was intended that formal schooling served school-age children and youth. With the continuing challenges to government-run schools involving funding, access, and quality, more NFE for children has been promoted. NGOs are the primary providers of NFE, particularly national and local NGOs, but they often work through INGOs or international development agencies.

BRAC, a Bangladeshi NGO, is well known for using nonformal education as an alternative to, and feeder into, formal schooling, particularly for girls. BRAC was formed in 1972 as the Bangladesh Rural Advancement Committee, a small-scale development project designed to fight poverty and empower the poor; they now are known simply as BRAC. Substantial growth beginning in the early 1980s was followed by increasing attention to gender in the late 1980s. Today, in all of their programs, BRAC employs over 97,000 people and reaches about 100 million people in their various programs. Women constitute 99 percent of those served by BRAC's microcredit division. BRAC health workers have taught oral rehydration therapy to 13 million women in all 68,000 villages, reaching virtually all poor, rural families. They have organized men and women into more than village organizations; 65 percent of their members are women. BRAC's Education Programme initiated its Non-Formal Primary Education Programme in 1985 with 22 schools and now has over 34,000, accounting for about 11 percent of the primary school population in the country. These schools provide primary education and, more recently, secondary education to out-of-school youth, 65 to 70 percent of whom are girls. In 2002, BRAC initiated nonformal education for girls in Afghanistan, and currently runs about 90 schools there.

The BRAC primary education curriculum in Bangladesh includes the same content as the formal school curriculum but is completed in four years instead of five. (This began as a three-year program equivalent to the formal schools' four-year cycle, but has been expanded.) Married women teachers are preferred in order to provide role models for the girl students. Teachers must have 10 years of education; BRAC then trains them as teachers. They commit to four years and work with a small group of students through their four-year cycle of primary education. Teachers are recruited locally in order to accommodate travel to the school site and to ensure teacher knowledge of the local community and culture. More recently, an adolescent program for primary education has been created;

these older students complete a full five years of primary education in four years. A prepri-
mary program, a postprimary program, and teacher education initiatives have also been
instituted, and BRAC has a government partnership program focused on providing community schools and improving the quality of formal schooling. Most nonformal education
initiatives worldwide have found it difficult to interface with the formal school system.
BRAC was among the first NGOs to create a program that was of sufficient quality
that the graduates could pass the government exams and transition back into the formal
system.

BRAC's successes have been impressive in increasing girls' enrollment, enabling them
to reenter the formal school system and/or continue their education beyond the primary
level, and creating jobs and providing training for local women as teachers. BRAC's focus
on the "poorest of the poor" has been challenged during the 1990s, however, as they
scaled up to serve more communities and focused on communities somewhat easier to
reach (Ebdon, 1995; Rao & Kelleher, 2000).

BRAC has also been criticized for inequities in gender relations within the organization,
failing to accommodate the needs of female staff (e.g., by enabling women to work in the
office during menstruation instead of doing field visits), favoring new college graduates
over long-term staff, and opting for strategies that achieve quick results but not necessarily
deep structural change (Rao & Kelleher, 2000). In 2001, BRAC began the Gender Quality
Action Learning Programme to improve gender relations within BRAC by raising gender
awareness and fostering a positive working environment for both male and female staff
(BRAC, 2004).

NGOs are perhaps the primary providers of NFE for women in a wide variety of program initiatives, including community development, income generation, microcredit,
health education, literacy, and basic education. Early programs focused on providing
women with opportunities from which they have historically been excluded and programs
that focused on immediate or practical needs. More recently, some NGOs, those most
influenced by feminist analyses of development processes, target patriarchal social relations in an attempt to alter the basis of social inequities based on gender.

Tostan is a Senegalese NGO whose NFE program has now been implemented in Sen-
egal, the Sudan, Mali, and Burkina Faso. Tostan's curriculum began as a literacy program
for women and has developed over more than 20 years into a participatory project focused
on village empowerment through the active participation of women. In Mali, both men
and women attend Tostan classes, and in the Sudan, men in the community have been
recruited as support to the classes that primarily serve women. With their attention to gender relations, men's involvement is critical, as they are integral to the social relations that
are expected to change. The curricular modules focus on community hygiene, human and
women's rights, reproductive health, and social change strategies, with the latter then
being implemented through grassroots associations that are formed to address locally
chosen social concerns. Initially, trash collection, hygiene at community wells, and the
like are the focus of this work; as the participants gain experience with collective social
change, their focus has shifted to more sensitive issues such as domestic violence and
female genital cutting (Easton, Monkman, & Miles, 2003). Learning, in this sense, is a
means to an end: gender equitable social change.

While much of the gender work done in education has focused on women and girls,
NGOs have been at the forefront in shifting the focus solely from girls and women to gender relations, thus, acknowledging the complex social processes that underlie inequities
based on gender. As educational initiatives move toward including men and boys in a

broader approach to gender equity, a deeper engagement in understanding social dynamics such as patriarchy will be important.

NGOs' POSITIONING IN GLOBAL DEVELOPMENT EDUCATION

NGOs have collectively become a more powerful voice in global educational and development discourse. Leading up to the Fourth International Women's Conference in Beijing in 1995, attention was focused on the women's NGO community; they proved to be a powerful coalition in bridging communication across socioeconomic, political, and cultural boundaries. Voices of poor women, through the NGOs, were heard by the UN organizations in that conference, and NGO coalitions were built across regions and countries. Numbers of women's NGOs increased in this period. Similarly, NGO activism at the World Education Forum in Dakar in April 2000 reflected the increasing power of the NGO community to influence educational policy internationally. During the 1990s and 2000s, NGO coalitions and other types of partnership initiatives have arisen in which coordinated work across organizations is intended to minimize duplication and to benefit from the strengths of the various partners. NGOs, especially local NGOs, are thought to be more in touch with local communities, their values, and traditions, and better able to implement programs. The United Nations Girls' Education Initiative is a partnership that includes UN agencies, national governments, donor countries, NGOs, civil society, the private sector, and communities and families. NGO partners in this initiative include the Campaign for Female Education International, Campaign for Popular Education Bangladesh, Forum for African Women Educationalists, Global Campaign for Education, World Vision, among others. With NGOs involved as key partners in this initiative to coordinate efforts to improve education for girls, the hope is that the local knowledge of NGOs and communities will filter up to the international organizations and the resources from the top will filter down to the local organizations.

Whether this hope is realized depends on how a number of issues will evolve in the near future, including: (a) partnerships, (b) funding, (c) continuity and sustainability, and (d) scaling up. The politics of *partnering* focuses attention on how power is shared among entities that, by their very nature, are not equal. Whose agenda takes precedence in a partnership, for example, that involves entities such as the World Bank or USAID, international NGOs and local NGOs? How are the various ideologies that inform their diverse interests played out on a global stage in which this partnering occurs? While partnering is intended to coordinate efforts, it also has the potential of silencing those not in agreement with the dominant discourse. As the power of such a coalition expands as it gains broad support, those with alternative or minority opinions can be all but ignored. The changing role of NGOs from being primarily service providers to partners with other entities, to advocates is a dimension of this political dynamic that should be watched carefully.

Because of the dependence of NGOs on donor agencies, multilateral organizations, and foundations for funding, strategies for *funding* shape the work that NGOs can do. An overemphasis on evaluation may be leading NGOs to focus on measuring their output and, therefore, choosing activities that result in quick and recognizable outcomes at the expense of activities that address deeper and more complex concerns (Smillie, Helmich, German, & Randel, 1999). In addition, many NGOs find an increasingly competitive environment in which they must attract funding. With limited staff and, particularly with local NGOs, limited ability to spend time on complicated funding applications, the smaller or newer NGOs are disadvantaged in this process.

Closely related to funding is a concern with *sustainability and coherence* over time. Funding is often short term and based on short-term goals that can be evaluated; this can discourage goals that require long-term commitment. While sustainability is an important dimension of development and educational initiatives, social programs such as education do not have money-earning possibilities as they are not economic in nature. Therefore, sustainability should be conceptualized in terms other than economic. Sustaining social change around cultural notions of gender equity is a common element of feminist-oriented projects; this is neither quick nor easy and, so, requires continued support from funding agencies if enduring change is to be achieved. In the work of Tostan, for example, evidence of success in the form of seeing communities mobilizing around locally chosen issues that relate to gender equity tends to occur six months or more after the NFE program has ended; it takes time for the participants to practice skills learned in the program, experiment with "safer" initiatives, and, finally, engage more sensitive social issues directly. To sustain this movement the Tostan villages in Mali and Sudan found that occasional support for locating resources, getting advice, and other short-term help was needed in order to fully develop self-sustaining initiatives toward gender equity. By that time, the NFE projects were no longer funded and so the NGOs either could not comply or they had to use funding from other sources.

A final issue of concern is the *scale* of NGO projects. Increasing pressure on small, successful projects to scale up (expand the numbers of those served) can create tensions that challenge the very strengths that NGOs, especially local NGOs, have brought to bear on gender and education. While reaching more people is critical, scaling up can potentially increase bureaucratization in the NGO and distance them from the communities they intend to serve, thus reducing their success.

WOMEN AND EMPOWERMENT THROUGH NGO WORK IN EDUCATION

NGOs serve communities that larger organizations are not knowledgeable about or in touch with; they are often seen by local communities as allies, whereas the state or international organizations might be perceived more suspiciously. Beyond the ways in which NGOs contribute directly to making education more gender equitable, they are also important in providing accessible opportunities for leadership development and capacity building. Locals, who would not have access to jobs or training in larger, more distantly located organizations, are key to the work in local NGOs, and, through this work, their knowledge and skills are enhanced. This, in turn, enables local women to play a more central role in the building of a gender-equitable civil society that is better positioned to address educational issues from multiple directions.

REFERENCES AND FURTHER READINGS

Bangladesh Rural Advancement Committee. (2004). *BRAC annual report*. Dhaka: Author.

Boserup, E. (1970). *Woman's role in economic development*. New York: St. Martin's Press.

Easton, P., Monkman, K., & Miles, R. (2003). Social policy from the bottom up: Abandoning FGC in Sub-Saharan Africa. *Development in Practice, 13*(5), 445–458.

Ebdon, R. (1995). NGO expansion and the fight to reach the poor: Gender implications of NGO scaling-up in Bangladesh. *IDS Bulletin, 26*(3), 49–55.

Moser, C. (1993). *Gender planning and development: Theory, practice & training*. New York: Routledge.

Rao, A., & Kelleher, D. (2000). Leadership for social transformation: Some ideas and questions on institutions and feminist leadership. *Gender and Development, 8*(3), 74–79.

Ruiz Bravo, P., & Monkman, K. (1998). Women-centered nongovernmental and grass-roots organizations. In N. P. Stromquist (Ed.), *Women in the third world: An encyclopedia of contemporary issues* (pp. 486–497). New York: Garland.

Smillie, I., Helmich, H., German, T., & Randel, J. (Eds.). (1999). *Stakeholders: Government-NGO partnerships for international development.* Paris: OECD & London: Earthscan Publications.

Stromquist, N.P. (2006). *Feminist organizations and social transformation in Latin America.* Boulder, CO: Paradigm Publishers.

Karen Monkman

Pregnant and Parenting Teens

School-based policy responses to teen pregnancy and parenthood need to be viewed in sociohistorical and political contexts. Across many highly industrialized countries, for example, schools face a crisis of consensus over inclusiveness. Those who want schools to sort and reward students who are most "productive" within a competitive economy that offers limited numbers of "knowledge-based" jobs are pitted against those who see the classroom as a public arena for challenging social injustices, that is, for countering the sorting process their opponents encourage. Despite having won the legal right of formal inclusion in many nations, pregnant and parenting teens often find themselves segregated in alternative settings; unable to participate in regular school settings, classes, or activities; or allowed to remain in a regular school but without support services such as on-site child care. These tensions—between de facto tracking (or streaming) versus meeting special needs, between formal inclusion versus informal exclusion—shape policy debates over whether or not to use pregnancy and parenthood as a basis for grouping students and the nature of the curriculum on offer to pregnant and parenting teens.

At this moment, school districts throughout North America and elsewhere—especially in urban areas—are poised to move beyond formal integration of pregnant and parenting students, are inquiring into the meaning and practice of inclusion, and are at a crossroads. Some policy researchers and pundits recommend separate schools, while others urge supported integration.

To date much of the literature on pregnant and parenting teens has largely ignored the educational policy issues that affect their decision to remain in or return to school. But, a growing number of researchers have emphasized such factors as school organization, program focus, curriculum, and pedagogy as central to providing a gender equitable education for pregnant and parenting teens.

HISTORICAL AND POLITICAL CONTEXTS OF SCHOOL RESPONSES

Throughout the first half of the twentieth century, it was common policy to exclude pregnant and mothering students from public schools on the grounds that they posed a threat to control of sexual behavior. This is still the case in various countries around the world, particularly where primary and secondary school enrollment rates are low and the exclusion of pregnant and mothering girls opens up scarce spaces to boys.

By the 1960s, attitudes had begun to shift. In the United States, various experimental "rehabilitation" projects offering a range of educational, health, and welfare services to low-income, predominantly African American, pregnant schoolgirls were established in major cities. The projects were often affiliated with public school systems but did not enroll pregnant teens or unwed mothers in regular classes.

By decade's end, the exclusion of pregnant and mothering girls from the regular school system was still prevalent, while young men were rarely if ever expelled from school based on their parental or marital status. The civil rights movement for racial equality, however, and the second wave of the women's movement were helping to set the stage for legal inclusion. Young women and their parents, supported by community action groups, began filing lawsuits to protest their exclusion based on pregnancy and marital status.

In 1971, the U.S. Supreme Court ruled in *Ordway v. Hargraves* that it was illegal for schools to expel from regular classes students who were known to be pregnant. Congress added force to this decision by passing Title IX of the Education Amendments of 1972, which took effect in 1975. Title IX expressly prohibits the exclusion of students from their "education program" or "any extracurricular activity" on the basis of pregnancy, parental status, or marital status; schools that do not comply face the loss of federal funds. Related struggles and changing public attitudes in places like Canada, the United Kingdom, and Australia led to a move from a policy of formal exclusion to formal inclusion of pregnant and mothering students in the mid-1970s. Special programs for pregnant and parenting teens began to spring up in the latter decades of the twentieth century in many urban centers.

Over the past 25 years, as school systems in Western industrialized countries have responded in various ways to address the needs of pregnant and parenting teens, the high school graduation rates of those teens have increased accordingly. Their rates still lag behind graduation rates for those who did not give birth in their teens. And, school officials—under pressure from the rise of high-stakes testing and increased high school graduation requirements—do not always want to accommodate pregnant and mothering teens in regular high school settings, classes, or activities.

As researchers in Canada, the United States, Australia, and the United Kingdom have documented, while official policies express commitment to gender equity, it is not uncommon to find pregnant and parenting students coerced into nonmainstream settings or disciplined for excused absences related to pregnancy and parenthood. School districts commonly establish special programs and day cares off-site, forcing pregnant and parenting teens to choose between needed support services and access to a core or university preparatory curriculum or apprenticeship opportunities. Some schools have discouraged pregnant and mothering students (but rarely young fathers) from holding leadership positions or have prohibited their membership in academic societies and other extracurricular activities. For example, Amanda Lemon (age 18) was excluded from the Xenia, Ohio, chapter of the National Honor Society in the late 1990s when it was discovered she was a mother.

Local school districts in both the United States and Canada wield the most control over what services, if any, will be provided to pregnant and parenting teens, mainstreamed or not. Because the provision of education is decentralized in both countries, it is difficult to know what is typically provided and how the programs are organized. Pregnant and parenting teens appear to have remained largely segregated in alternative (sometimes remedial) programs, often off-campus or otherwise self-contained. Showcased programs tend to feature education, health, counseling, and child-care components.

More commonly, pregnant girls go on home correspondence (particularly in rural areas) or attend a temporary alternative class or school, then return to their regular school after delivering their babies. Upon their return, support services, including on-site child care, are lacking. So while they are formally included in regular classes with nonparenting peers, young mothers (because they, rather than young fathers, tend to be the primary caregivers) are effectively excluded from the larger school culture.

Because such policies are comparatively rare, it is instructive to examine the case of British Columbia (B.C.), Canada, where a policy of supported integration was pursued during the 1990s and nine out of every ten programs in the province enabled young parents to attend regular classes while providing them with child care and other support services. Three factors came together to support a full integration policy. First, a B.C. school act, passed in 1989, mandated the integration of special education students (those with learning, behavioral, and physical disabilities) into neighborhood schools, and this legislation provided ideological support for integrating pregnant and parenting students more fully into regular classes. A second factor was the commitment to developing school-based day care by the B.C. Ministry of Women's Equality. Dovetailing with this "equal opportunities" feminist perspective was a third factor, namely, a shift in government policy regarding single mothers from treating women as mothers *and* wage workers to treating women as primarily wage workers. This shift has been particularly evident in the public debates about welfare reform across a number of Western, industrialized nations in the rise of welfare-to-work ideology and in the targeting of single mothers, particularly teen mothers, as welfare "problems" if they are not working for pay outside the home or preparing to do so.

STIGMA AND GENDER

For those who position themselves as reformers or streamliners of the welfare state, teen pregnancy prevention is their primary focus. Interventions designed to reduce unwanted teen pregnancy have had mixed results. One common approach, media campaigns that stress the harsh reality of single parenting, reinforces stigmas attached to pregnant teens. Those young women who do find themselves pregnant (and 40 percent of all young women in the United States become pregnant before they turn 20) are likely to feel blamed and shamed.

The current backlash against the welfare state has included some attempts to stigmatize the men who father children born to teen mothers. One common label, "deadbeat dads," reinforces the traditional equation of fatherhood with breadwinner and may discourage young men without access to the primary labor market from taking responsibility for actual child rearing. Adult men who father children born to teen mothers have been targeted in some jurisdictions as "statutory rapists." This stigma can shift attention from unequal gender relations to age differences, though age differences may be less significant, given the difficulty that women of *all* ages have in negotiating sexual relationships with men. Furthermore, it is still quite easy for men, who do not bear the visible mark of pregnancy and who are less likely than women to take primary responsibility for child rearing, to evade scrutiny and avoid stigma, making the talk about deadbeat dads and child abusers often more rhetorical than real in its consequences.

By contrast, women's sexuality—spotlighted during pregnancy—has, historically, been used as a means to devalue and exclude them from public places such as the workplace and school. Even today, there is little room in supposedly gender-neutral organizations for reproductive concerns, and students are often treated as asexual. As discussed in the previous section, although it is no longer legal in many countries to deny pregnant and mothering girls access to an education, it is still common to segregate them, sometimes coercively and in ways that are not always in their best interest.

The gendered power relations (as well as racial, sexual, and social class power relations) at play in the construction of policies help to explain why so few young men appear to participate in school-based programs for pregnant and parenting teens. (Programs targeted specifically at young fathers are an exception, of course, but even in this case, participation rates have often been problematic.) In various qualitative studies of such programs, young men are virtually absent as formal participants. There are a number of possible explanations. First, the fathers are usually older (although usually by only two or three years), out of school, or both, so school-based programs do not reach them. Second, the vast majority of teen mothers are the primary child-care givers, and when and if their relationships with their male partners end, the women almost always retain custody of the children. Third, available services are tailored to mothers as primary caregivers. Fourth, staff members working in young parent programs are typically women, which reinforces the idea that child rearing is mainly women's work. And, to the extent that programs have a therapeutic component where, for example, the issue of male violence against women is addressed, counselors and other service providers find it complicated to include men. Fifth, the ideology of fathers as breadwinners is still prevalent so that, even when fathers are school-aged, they feel more pressure to try to obtain paid work to provide for the baby rather than to learn about child rearing.

MAINSTREAM OR ALTERNATIVE SETTINGS?

Practitioners and policy makers disagree over whether pregnant and parenting teens would be best served in mainstream or alternative settings. The debate is shaped by how prevalent and accepted teenage pregnancy and parenthood is in a particular community, which, in turn, affects the cost of providing services in a centralized or decentralized manner. In rural areas, the debate may be moot because the size and geography of a rural school district may preclude any group provision of services.

In more densely populated school districts, proponents of providing services in a separate facility typically cite one or more of the following reasons: (a) the difficulty of guaranteeing the safety of pregnant students; (b) the difficulty in a large setting of controlling negative comments from peers and school staff members that can affect pregnant young women's self-image and lower their aspirations; (c) the ability to provide flexible scheduling, special curriculum, and individualized instruction; and (d) avoidance of community controversy by minimizing other students' contact with pregnant and parenting teens.

In contrast, proponents of mainstreaming argue that their approach: (a) avoids the difficult transition to and from an alternative facility; (b) allows pregnant and parenting students to remain close to established friends; (c) allows access to a more diverse, usually more academically challenging curriculum; and (d) treats young parents as full citizens and does not add stigma by shunting students off to a separate facility.

To cast this policy debate in more theoretical terms, the tension between addressing students' "special" needs and separating and stigmatizing them exemplifies what feminist scholars have termed the *dilemma of difference*. The dilemma of difference refers to the risk people run of further stigmatizing a historically subordinate group when they either focus on the group's difference or attempt to ignore it. One risk of the mainstreaming approach is that it can fail to support students adequately and risks losing them. Yet the segregation-in-a-special-program approach risks stigmatizing students. So, for example, official school district policy may allow pregnant girls to remain in their neighborhood schools thereby allowing preexisting friendship groups to provide support while not "ghettoizing" pregnant teens. But, teen pregnancies (and births) occur at higher rates in relatively impoverished neighborhoods, and the odd girl who finds herself pregnant at an upper-middle-class school with a strong university preparatory ethos might be made to feel unwelcome by staff and peers.

Once students are identified as teen parents and are provided with services based on that difference, school adults may begin to notice traits—both positive (e.g., "teen parents are more mature than other students") and negative (e.g., "teen parents use their babies as excuses")—that distill into stereotypes. Yet, were these school adults simply to ignore the differences of the teen parents from other students, then the teen parents might not receive due consideration of their heavy responsibilities and, as a result, might fail their courses or be asked to leave school due to poor attendance.

Meeting the diverse needs of pregnant and parenting teens without separation and stigma may involve reorganizing conventional schools (perhaps to an extent unforeseen by proponents of mainstreaming) so that these needs are no longer considered "special." Such a policy of supported integration might include, for example, providing a school-based health clinic, on-site child care for students as well as school adults, flexible scheduling, and a curriculum that fosters nurturance in all students, female and male.

Researchers have identified a number of strategies and practices aimed at a policy goal of supported integration for pregnant and parenting teens. These include:

- creating community buy-in through such mechanisms as joint partnerships (e.g., between schools and community-based organizations, various branches of government, or both) and advisory boards composed of "stakeholders";
- placing programs in centrally located schools and in schools that are accepting, even promoting, of diversity;
- building political support within ideologically diverse schools by managing teacher resistance and cultivating teacher acceptance, where teacher attitudes toward pregnant and parenting teens are assumed to influence how students treat one another;
- communicating realistic expectations for, and monitoring, student attendance and progress;
- providing material and emotional support and accommodation, including on-site child care;
- enabling teen parents to communicate complex realities rather than serve as examples of what not to do or what not to be; and
- advocating with and for teen parents to challenge stereotyping, showcasing individual and program-wide success (broadly and realistically defined), and lobbying for schoolwide policies that enable increased success.

Not all strategies aimed at promoting integration and inclusion are equally effective at coping with—or, in some cases, transcending—the dilemma of difference. Norm-challenging institutional practices (e.g., adopting a schoolwide policy of excusing and accommodating student absences related to sick child care) are superior to both individual adaptations and isolated, one-on-one arrangements between a teacher and her or his colleague or between a teacher and a student. These latter arrangements, while perhaps temporarily helpful to individual teen parents, aim only to fit them into structures otherwise thought to be acceptable rather than transforming an institution that excludes on a routine basis a wide number of people because they are said to have "special" needs. For example, young parents need flexibility with regard to attendance expectations, pacing of instruction, nature of assignments, and workload. But, so, too, do students living independently, those working long hours to supplement their family's income or to care for younger siblings, and those sometimes needed by immigrant parents to serve as translators in important matters affecting the family.

TOWARD A GENDER EQUITABLE CURRICULUM

Besides their parental status, school-age parents are often different in ways that mark them as "abnormal" and in need of "special" treatment. While the specifics vary by locale, region, and nation, a disproportionate number of pregnant and parenting teens live in poverty, are academically underprepared, belong to an oppressed racial minority or historically disadvantaged group, or are not proficient in the official language of school instruction.

For marginalized groups such as teen parents, gaining formal access to schools is not enough to satisfy a strong democratic imperative. Inquiring into what (whose knowledge) is being taught and how—in other words, asking questions about curricular content and pedagogy—is equally central. Students need to develop their sense of self-worth, find out what they are entitled to as citizens, and learn the full range of acceptable means of communicating their needs to others. Schools, for example, should aim to develop students not only as workers and citizens (among other worthy goals) but as members of families in all their diversity.

Few researchers have examined the curriculum on offer to pregnant and parenting teens and even fewer from a critical or feminist perspective. Based on the available evidence, two curricular visions (discussed here as ideal types) staking out opposite ends of a continuum of programmatic approaches exist. One vision is that of a *microcosm of the "real world,"* where the student and future worker identities take precedence and teen parents are expected to give birth, return to school, eventually obtain a paying job, and adjust to the status quo. The other vision is that of a *therapeutic haven,* which exists as a girls-only environment where the mother identity takes precedence and students are provided a safe space, albeit sometimes at the expense of gaining the confidence and skills they need to succeed in the wider world.

Once again, the dilemma of difference is in evidence in the curriculum, variously enacted. The haven vision rests on the idea of difference, in this case pregnancy and motherhood, associated with womanhood; this carries with it the risk of gender essentialism by reinforcing the idea that caregiving is only women's work and limiting women to the domestic sphere. By contrast, the microcosm vision rests on the idea of sameness or commonality with other students; this carries with it the risk of gender blindness or androcentrism by taking men's current life patterns (i.e., economic provider with minimal domestic responsibilities) as the norm.

Feminists have noted that the dominant construction of mother has been associated with domesticity or privacy, in contrast to the more public social identities of student, worker, and citizen, which have been forged according to unstated male norms. This gendering of identities is obscured in part when the embodied nature of study, work, and citizenship is ignored. For example, the student identity is assumed to be gender neutral and universal, whereas in actuality the traits and activities commonly associated with women—including pregnancy, breast-feeding, and caring for children—are not associated with the image of the student. Still very much at issue is who counts as a "good" mother or father, worker, and citizen within the school and hence, in the end, who counts as a good student.

The ideology of the providing father may hurt poor men (as well as women) because it associates fathering solely with being an economic provider. Yet, because many young fathers face high rates of unemployment and poverty, the path by which they would consider themselves truly to be fathers—becoming breadwinners—is blocked. Young men are not encouraged to become nurturing caregivers.

The normative (White, middle-class) view of mothering, in North America and elsewhere, holds that the good mother is someone who always puts her child's needs above all else, meaning, for example, making sacrifices in order to provide (ideally) full-time, stay-at-home caregiving. The ideology of the good mother can be just as destructive as the ideology of the good father because young women are sent conflicting and hurtful messages about how to construct their self-image. Young women are thus encouraged to neglect their own desires and purposes and, to the extent that they do not prepare themselves for above poverty-level paid work, they make themselves even more vulnerable to the risks of the labor market and the gendered politics of the family.

Even as the meanings of motherhood, fatherhood, sexuality, paid labor, marriage, family, and citizenship are politically contested outside of schools, students seldom get the opportunity to discuss and debate the relations between the school, the family, and the paid workplace. For example, educators could ask students to explore the competing images of the good parent—full-time caregivers, economic providers, people who balance multiple roles and responsibilities and want their children's lives, too, to be balanced—and discuss who benefits and who is marginalized by such images.

REFERENCES AND FURTHER READINGS

Burdell, P. (1995–1996). Teen mothers in high school: Tracking their curriculum. *Review of Research in Education, 21,* 163–208.

Dawson, N. (1997). The provision of education and opportunities for future employment for pregnant schoolgirls and schoolgirl mothers in the U.K. *Children & Society, 11*(4), 252–263.

Kaplan, E.B. (1997). *Not our kind of girl: Unraveling the myths of Black teenage motherhood.* Berkeley: University of California Press.

Kelly, D.M. (2000). *Pregnant with meaning: Teen mothers and the politics of inclusive schooling.* New York: Peter Lang.

Kelly, D.M. (2003). Practicing democracy in the margins of school: The Teen-Age Parents Program as feminist counterpublic. *American Educational Research Journal, 40*(1), 123–146.

Lane, T.S., & Clay, C.M. (2000). Meeting the service needs of young fathers. *Child and Adolescent Social Work Journal, 17*(1), 35–54.

Luker, K. (1996). *Dubious conceptions: The politics of teenage pregnancy.* Cambridge, MA: Harvard University Press.

Luttrell, W. (2003). *Pregnant bodies, fertile minds: Gender, race, and the schooling of pregnant teens.* New York: Routledge.

Milne-Home, J. (with Power, A., & Dennis, B.). (1996). *Pregnant futures: Barriers to employment, education and training amongst pregnant and parenting adolescents.* Canberra: Australian Government Publishing Service.

Pillow, W.S. (2003). *Unfit subjects: Educational policy and the teen mother, 1972–2002.* New York: Routledge.

Solinger, R. (1992). *Wake up little Susie: Single pregnancy and race before Roe v. Wade.* New York: Routledge.

Wong, J., & Checkland, D. (Eds.). (1999). *Teenage pregnancy and parenting: Social and ethical issues.* Toronto, Canada: University of Toronto Press.

Deirdre M. Kelly

School Choice and Gender Equity

Efforts to expand school choice within the public school system have been unabated over the past decade. Fueling the choice movement are conservative social and political arguments regarding the power of the free market to inspire educational innovation, improve achievement, increase accountability, and regain parental support for public schooling. Choice is a key strategy of the No Child Left Behind Act (NCLB) in improving educational outcomes for all students. Increased school choice has been pushed through various forms, including magnet schools, charter schools, and voucher programs. Charter schools, in particular, have experienced tremendous support over the past decade. The RAND Corporation reports that there are approximately one million students in 3,500 charter schools throughout the nation (Zimmer & Buddin, 2006). NCLB supports charter schools by offering financial assistance for program design, initial implementation, planning, and evaluation (NCLB Charter Schools Program, 2004).

Alongside increased support for school choice have been concerns about gender equity in schooling. Many studies over the past 25 years have documented gender bias against girls in coeducational classrooms. Girls receive less teacher attention than boys, feel less comfortable speaking out in class, and face threats of sexual harassment in school. Though the achievement gaps between boys and girls are closing in some areas, girls' achievement still lags behind boys' in math and science and most significantly in computer science and technology majors and careers.

There is also concern that gender equity solutions have reached girls of different ethnic groups unequally. For example, low teacher expectations have been shown to disadvantage African American males in public school classrooms, but African American females fare more favorably by comparison (Hubbard, 1999). Teacher expectations are typically lower for low-income and African American students than they are for middle- and upper-income White students (Diamond, Randolph, & Spillane, 2004). Similarly, Latino males and females face different social and academic pressures from each other and from their White peers, and these pressures themselves vary depending on whether the students live in urban or rural locations (Gibson, Gandara, & Koyama, 2004). Latinas perform less well than other racial and ethnic groups of girls in several key measures of educational achievement, but they have steadily increased their high school and college graduation rates over the past 20 years, placing them ahead of their male peers (Cammarota, 2004).

While gender equity has long been discussed in terms of remedies designed to raise girls' achievement, more recently, some scholars have begun to ask, "What about the boys?" Public discourse has centered on a "crisis" for boys, focusing on their lower reading and language test scores and higher rates of special education referrals as compared to girls, as well as boys' greater propensity to be involved in violent crimes. All boys are seen as at risk of these problems, but most notably boys of color. Increasing rates of dropout and higher rates of incarceration are particularly salient for African American boys and men.

Meanwhile, many feminist researchers believe that gender equity is still problematic for girls in the United States after 20 years of weak enforcement of Title IX, which prohibits discrimination on the basis of sex in public educational programs. They argue in favor of remedies for the problem of low academic performance of women in certain disciplines. As these arguments make clear, gender bias is now understood as affecting both girls and boys, as neither group is immune to social pressures and expectations. For feminist educators and researchers, achieving gender equity in schools means acknowledging that gender bias exists in both subtle and overt forms, eliminating sexist language and stereotyping regarding girls and boys, and offering a socially critical and gender inclusive curriculum. Many argue that educators must address how the social and political agenda befitting males is embedded in school structures and practices, and they must make pedagogical, organizational, and curricular changes to even the playing field. Such educational changes are believed to benefit both boys and girls and society as a whole.

CHOOSING SINGLE-SEX SCHOOLS AND CLASSES

Over the past several years, public schools in at least 15 states have addressed concerns about the achievement of boys and girls through experiments with single-sex education. Most often, these experiments have been in the form of separate math or science classes for girls. Other manifestations of public single-gender schooling include Afro-centric academies for boys in Detroit, Baltimore, and Milwaukee and the Young Women's Leadership schools in Harlem and Chicago. Some of these experiments have been found in violation of Title IX and have been forced to close or become coeducational.

Significantly, however, in May 2002, the federal government revealed its intent to draft new regulations that would provide more flexibility for, encourage, and help support single-sex public schools. The support for single-sex schooling is seen as part of an overall plan to increase school choice and provide additional opportunities for students to choose a "better" school (U.S. Department of Education, 2004). Because of the loosening of Title IX regulations, we might expect to see many more experiments with single-sex schools in the public sector over the next few years. Up to now, most instances of single-sex schooling have been in the private sector in the United States.

Why the interest in single-sex public schooling, especially given the context of what many (see Datnow & Hubbard, 2002) see as conflicting research evidence? Most studies on single-sex schools have been conducted primarily in the private sector and, therefore, results may not generalize to public schools. Because these studies have been mostly quantitative, comparative studies of student performance, teacher-student interactions, the school context, and the context of students' lives have not been examined in great detail. Moreover, because most studies of single-sex schools have failed to examine the larger social, economic, and cultural context in which students live, we lack an understanding of the relationship between school context, family background, and academic achievement.

Despite the limitations of this research, advocates of single-sex education point to studies of Catholic single-sex and coeducational schools that find academic achievement benefits for girls and low-income and minority boys attending single-sex schools. Girls who attend all-girls schools are more apt to adopt leadership roles, become engaged in traditionally male-dominated subjects like math and science, and show improvements in self-esteem. Research on gender development conducted in the 1980s, arguing that women learn differently than men, has also helped to provide justification for all-female schooling.

All-boys classes or schools are now being looked upon as ways to improve literacy achievement and discipline and are said to improve character development. Advocates of all-male Afro-centric academies in public schools argue that the presence of African American role models and a focus on multicultural curricula can be beneficial in developing leadership skills and improving achievement for African American boys. Proponents of single-sex education also argue that the separation of the sexes is the most effective way to manage classroom behavior by eliminating distractions and peer pressures for both boys and girls. Clearly, the reasons behind the recent establishment of single-sex schools are no longer simple; they represent efforts to address not only gender bias, but also racial and cultural issues as well.

Is single-sex schooling truly a panacea, or does the answer to improving social and academic outcomes for boys and girls lie in a school's ability to provide quality teachers, peer relations, special resources, and/or other factors? In a study we conducted of 12 public single-sex academies (6 boys; 6 girls) in California, we found that three important interrelated conditions contributed to the positive experiences of some low-income and minority students in the academies: the single-sex setting, financial support from the state, and the presence of caring proactive teachers. Organizationally, the arrangement provided social benefits for the students who attended them. The single-sex organizational arrangement spared students the distractions and negative aspects associated with coeducational schools. It offered the girls, for example, the freedom to make decisions about their appearance without harassment from the boys and provided them with a safe haven to concentrate on their academic work. Funding also had an enormous impact on the schools. With the grant money provided by the state, schools were given the ability to provide special resources and support for the students who attended them, benefits that were previously absent for these children before the single-gender experiment. Students benefited from small classes and, in some cases, from extra teachers, special academic tutoring, on-site health care facilities, counseling, and field trips. Several schools also provided computers with the newest and most sophisticated software.

Although the organizational arrangements and financial support were important, they were not enough to explain the success of the single-gender schools in our study. It was the influence of caring educators who worked closely with the students that was crucial. In gender-segregated classes, these teachers reported that they were able to have candid and focused discussions designed to meet the social and moral needs, as well as the academic needs, of their students.

School administrators reported that attracting and keeping good teachers at these schools with children who had tremendous academic and emotional needs was very difficult (see Hubbard and Datnow chapter in Datnow & Hubbard, 2002). Teacher and administrative turnover created dire consequences for students whose lives were already plagued by instability. Some students complained they could never be sure who the teacher might be because substitutes appeared frequently. This instability added to their feelings of confusion and anomie. Even when students had permanent teachers, they were often new, inexperienced, and frequently knew little about working with low-income and minority youth—a scenario that compromises the success of many public schools that educate predominately low-income and minority students throughout the nation.

Students' experiences were also less positive when teachers shaped curriculum, instruction, and discipline in ways that reinforced gender stereotypes. Many teachers were unwilling to challenge traditional gendered expectations concerning academic interests and student behaviors, finding it difficult to move from a biological to a social construction of gender. However, the exceptions we observed among some teachers suggested that teachers in single-sex (and coed schools) can have a positive effect on students' understandings of gender if they have a gender equity agenda, which many of the teachers who taught in the schools in our study did not have. Overall, our study revealed that students need more than school choices that allow them to be segregated by sex. If the single-sex arrangement is to be successful, we argue that it must be expanded to include a more comprehensive agenda of opportunity (Hubbard & Datnow, 2005).

TOWARD A COMPREHENSIVE AGENDA OF OPPORTUNITY

Separating students by gender is not by itself likely to achieve either equity or excellence for boys and girls. Our own prior work and review of the literature suggests that efforts to improve schooling options for girls and boys in the public sector should include adequate funding and caring teachers who understand the importance of personalizing the educational experience for children who come to school with a range of academic and social needs. Importantly, the schools need to be driven by a strong theory of gender equitable education. If we are to attract and train highly qualified teachers in these public schools, teachers need access to relevant training and administrative support in order to become aware of critical issues in students' lives, including gender and racial biases, harassment, sexuality, and homophobia. Educators need to have a strong sense of why they are implementing gender equity solutions or special programs for girls and/or boys.

There are two major obstacles to creating a strong sense of mission of gender equity in K–12 education. First, educators perceive that they have many other pressing issues to address, including strong pressures for accountability and for elimination of persistent racial inequities. Gender bias is not viewed as a serious concern and/or one for which they are responsible or prepared to tackle. Second is the fact that many educators and the public at-large believe that gender equity issues have been solved, at least with respect to girls. Recent news media reports about the number of girls exceeding the number of boys enrolling in and graduating from four-year colleges helps to fuel such beliefs. However, when we look at the achievement of women postcollege, we see that the proverbial glass ceiling still exists, with women occupying far fewer high-level positions in politics, the corporate world, the sciences, and academia. The societal conversation about gender equity is made even more complicated by media reports of a trend toward more women "choosing" to stay home to raise children. Such reports give an erroneous sense that equal opportunities exist for women in the working world and that women are simply not taking advantage of them. The lack of affordable, high-quality child care and the unwillingness of many employers to help women balance family and work are rarely considered in the equation. This larger societal conversation about gender equity and gender roles and the role of K–12 teachers in addressing the problem needs to be taken up when we consider programming for girls and boys.

Conversations deliberately designed to break down gender stereotypes need to occur in both single-sex and coeducational classrooms. As gender bias persists in society, it is incumbent upon educators to respond to this inequity by educating students about the negative impact gender bias has on both boys and girls. In addition to promoting self-esteem, gender identity, and enhanced achievement, programs for girls and boys should (arguably at a minimum) raise antisexist attitudes to a level of political awareness aimed at trying to alter socially constructed gender patterns (Kruse, 1996). Ideally, we would expect single sex *and* coeducational classrooms to actively promote an emancipatory agenda for girls and boys. In order for teachers to engage in this kind of education, however, the problem of gender bias has to move to the radar screen along with other issues of inequity. Teachers need support to construct a curriculum that will raise awareness and empower students. They need assurance from school administrators and state and federal policy makers that their efforts are important. In other words, if single-gender classrooms are going to contribute in a meaningful way to the societal discourse on gender equity and impact the negative consequences of gender bias, teachers should be held accountable for their efforts in this area as well.

Single-sex settings offer the potential to advance gender equity, but the organizational arrangement alone does not ensure it. Decisions about choosing programs specifically focused on girls or boys also need to guard against becoming a new form of tracking or resegregation. Segregation might lead to a safe or comfortable space for some populations, but it can create tensions for race and gender equity. As Kruse (1996) has warned, sex-segregated education does not guarantee a particular outcome because it can be used for emancipation or oppression. What is crucial are the intentions, the understanding of people and their gender, and the pedagogical attitudes and practices.

Consideration needs to be given to the reasons why such programs are important for students and what is gained and what is lost as a result of their implementation, both for students who leave and for those who remain in mainstream options. If schools—especially single-sex schools—pursue a gender blind approach under the guise of equal opportunity and choice, and if policies refocus attention on the plight of boys (or girls) without a careful analysis of equity, the gendered culture of schooling and society is likely to continue.

REFERENCES AND FURTHER READINGS

Cammarota, J. (2004). Gendered and racialized pathways of Latina and Latino youth: Different struggles, different resistances in the urban context. *Anthropology and Education Quarterly, 35* (1), 53–74.

Datnow, A., & Hubbard, L. (Eds.). (2002). *Gender in policy and practice: Perspectives on single-sex and coeducational schooling.* New York: RoutledgeFalmer.

Diamond, J., Randolph, A., & Spillane, J. (2004). Teachers' expectations and sense of responsibility for student learning: The importance of race, class, and organizational habitus. *Anthropology and Education Quarterly 35*(1), 75–98.

Gibson, M., Gandara, P., & Koyama, J. (Eds.). (2004). *School connections: U.S. Mexican youth, peers and school achievement.* New York: Teachers College Press.

Hubbard, L. (1999). College aspirations among low-income African American high school students: Gendered strategies for success. *Anthropology and Education Quarterly, 30*(3), 363–383.

Hubbard, L., & Datnow, A. (2005). Do single-sex schools address the needs of low income and minority students? An investigation of organizational, financial and social factors. *Anthropology and Education Quarterly, 38*(2), 115–131.

Kruse, A.M. (1996). Single sex settings: Pedagogies for girls and boys in Danish schools. In P. Murphy & G. Gipps (Eds.), *Equity in the classroom: Towards effective pedagogy for girls and boys* (pp. 173–191). London: Falmer.

No Child Left Behind Act of 2001. (2004, July). *NCLB charter schools program. Title V. Part B. Non-regulatory guidance.* Available at http://www.ed.gov/policy/elsec/guid/cspguidance03.pdf

U.S. Department of Education. (2004). *Federal register: March 9, 2004* (Vol. 69, No. 46). Retrieved June 14, 2004, from http://www.ed.gov/legislation/FedRegister/proprule/2004-1/030904a.html

Zimmer, R., & Buddin, R. (2006). *Making sense of charter schools: Evidence from California.* Santa Monica, CA: The RAND Corporation. Retrieved July 25, 2006, from http://www.rand.org/pubs/occasional_papers/2006/RAND_OP157.pdf

Amanda Datnow

Lea Hubbard

Sexual Harassment Policies and Practices

Margaret Mead once argued that a new taboo is needed in educational institutions, one that requires faculty to make new norms based on caring as a central and active value. The need to make sexual harassment a taboo continues in schools and colleges as evidenced by the high incidence of harassment reported by students. An adequate policy for getting to the heart of harassment problems in the educational system not only requires a clear definition of harassment, policy statements against the behavior, and the enactment of laws to enforce such policies but also requires the efforts and support of the school's administration at all levels and continual training of all individuals, as well as procedures that *encourage,* not just allow, complaints. Success requires action to prevent and remedy sexual harassment as well as to train the entire school/campus on legal and psychological aspects of sexual harassment. With both a policy and the procedure for carrying it out in place, not only will the school be on stronger footing in any legal action, it will find that, human relations–wise, the entire school benefits from an environment of cooperation and respect.

DEFINITIONS AND LEGISLATION

Sexual harassment is defined legally as unwelcome sexual advances, requests for sexual favors, and other verbal or physical conduct of a sexual nature when any one of three criteria is met: (a) submission to such conduct is made either explicitly or implicitly a term or condition of the individual's employment or academic standing; (b) submission to or rejection of such conduct by an individual is used as the basis for employment or academic decisions affecting the individual; and (c) such conduct has the purpose or effect of unreasonably interfering with an individual's work or learning performance or creating an intimidating, hostile,, or offensive work or learning environment.

As these criteria indicate, there are two types of sexual harassment situations that are described by this legal definition: quid pro quo sexual harassment and hostile environment sexual harassment. *Quid pro quo sexual harassment* involves an individual with organizational power who either expressly or implicitly ties an academic or employment decision or action to the response of an individual to unwelcome sexual advances. Thus, a teacher may promise a reward to a student for complying with sexual requests (e.g., a better grade, letter of recommendation for college, or a job) or threaten a student for failing to comply with the sexual requests (e.g., threatening to not give the student the grade earned). *Hostile environment sexual harassment* involves a situation in which an atmosphere or climate is created by staff or other students in the classroom or other area in the school that makes it difficult, if not impossible, for a student to study and learn because the atmosphere is perceived by the student to be intimidating, offensive, and hostile.

The legal definition identifies the conditions under which a behavior may constitute sexual harassment, but generally does not give specific examples. Empirical definitions of sexual harassment are derived from men's and women's descriptions of their experiences of sexual harassment. Examples include: *gender harassment,* which consists of generalized sexist remarks and behavior not designed to elicit sexual cooperation but to convey insulting, degrading, or sexist attitudes about women or men; and *sexual bribery,* which is the solicitation of sexual activity or other sex-linked behavior by promise of a reward (e.g., passing grade) (Fitzgerald et al., 1988).

Because U.S. courts have recognized that sexual harassment is a form of gender discrimination, it is covered by antidiscrimination legislation such as Title IX of the 1972 Education Amendments, which states that: "No person in the United States shall, on the basis of sex, be excluded from participation in, or denied the benefits of, or be subjected to discrimination under any educational program or activity receiving federal assistance."

In order to promote effective and equitable resolution of sexual harassment complaints, it is necessary for educational institutions to have an explicit antiharassment policy that complies with the provisions of Title IX. The Office for Civil Rights (OCR) has emphasized that educational institutions have an affirmative duty to issue a strong policy prohibiting sexual harassment on which students and employees are trained, to conduct a full investigation of all complaints of sexual harassment, and to administer appropriate disciplinary action toward individuals who have violated the school's/campus's policy statement.

Schools, similar to workplaces, should exercise "reasonable care" to ensure a sexual harassment-free environment and retaliatory-free environment for students. This "reasonable care," adapted from the Supreme Court ruling in *Faragher v. Boca Raton* (524 U.S. 775, 1988), includes the following at a minimum: establishment and dissemination of an effective antisexual harassment policy and an effective investigatory procedure and the provision of training in sexual harassment, in general, and in the school's policy and procedures specifically.

INCIDENCE OF SEXUAL HARASSMENT

The first scientific national study of academic sexual harassment of children and adolescents was conducted by the American Association of University Women in 1993. In this study, incidence rates of students' experiences with sexual harassment was collected from 1,632 girls and boys in Grades 8 through 11 from 79 schools across the United States. Students were asked the following question, adapted from the legal definition of sexual harassment: "During your whole school life, how often, if at all, has anyone (this includes students, teachers, other school employees, or anyone else) done the following things to you when you did not want them to?"

The list of types of sexual harassment that followed this question included: (a) made sexual comments, jokes, gestures, or looks; (b) showed, gave, or left you sexual pictures, photographs, illustrations, messages, or notes; (c) wrote sexual messages or graffiti about you on bathroom walls, in locker rooms, and so on; (d) spread sexual rumors about you; (e) said you were gay or lesbian; (f) spied on you as you dressed or showered at school; (g) flashed or "mooned" you; (h) touched, grabbed, or pinched you in a sexual way; (i) pulled at your clothing in a sexual way; (j) intentionally brushed against you in a sexual way; (k) pulled your clothing off or down; (l) blocked your way or cornered you in a sexual way; (m) forced you to kiss him or her; (n) forced you to do something sexual other than kissing.

Results indicated that four out of five students (81 percent) reported that they had been the target of some form of sexual harassment during their school lives. With respect to gender comparisons, 85 percent of girls and 76 percent of boys surveyed reported that they had experienced unwelcome sexual behavior that interfered with their ability to concentrate at school and with their personal lives. African American boys (81 percent) were more likely to have experienced sexual harassment than White boys (75 percent) and Latinos (69 percent). For girls, 87 percent of Whites reported having experienced behaviors that constitute sexual harassment, compared with 84 percent of African American girls and 82 percent of Latinas.

The AAUW study also found that adolescents' experiences with sexual harassment were most likely to occur in the middle school or junior high school years of sixth to ninth grade. Although the majority of harassment in schools is student-to-student or peer harassment, 25 percent of girls and 10 percent of boys reported they were harassed by teachers or other school employees. Comparable incidence rates have been reported in the literature subsequent to this AAUW report.

In addition, in 2001, AAUW found results similar to their earlier research. They sampled 2,064 students in public school in Grades 8 through 11. Eighty-one percent of students experienced some form of sexual harassment during their school lives, 59 percent occasionally, and 27 percent often. This study also found that girls were more likely than boys (85 percent vs. 79 percent) to experience sexual harassment ever or often (30 percent vs. 24 percent often). In addition, 32 percent of students reported being afraid of being sexually harassed, with girls more than twice as likely as boys to feel this fear (44 percent vs. 20 percent). Eighty-five percent of students reported peer sexual harassment, and 38 percent reported being harassed by a teacher or other school employee.

In the first large-scale study with college students, Fitzgerald and her colleagues (1988) investigated approximately 2,000 women at two major state universities. Half of the women respondents reported experiencing some form of sexually harassing behavior. The majority of these women reported experiencing sexist comments by faculty. The next largest category of sexually harassing behavior was seductive behavior, including being invited for drinks and a back rub by faculty, being brushed up against by their professors, and having their professors show up uninvited at their hotel rooms during out-of-town academic conferences.

More recently, Hill and Silva (2005) reported findings from their nationally representative survey of 2,036 undergraduate students (1,096 women; 940 men) commissioned by the American Association of University Women Educational Foundation. Their research found that sexual harassment is experienced by the majority of college students. Approximately one-third of the students reported physical harassment, including being touched, grabbed, or forced to do something sexual. Hill and Silva (2005) also reported that men and women are equally likely to experience sexual harassment although in different ways. For example, women were more likely to report experiencing sexual comments and gestures while men reported experiencing homophobic comments. Furthermore, Hill and Silva (2005) found that men are more likely than women to harass.

For certain student groups, the incidence of sexual harassment appears to be higher than for others. Graduate students, for example, report more harassment than undergraduates. Other groups reporting higher than average experiences of sexual harassment include women of color, especially those with "token" status; students in small colleges or small academic departments, where the number of faculty available to students is quite small; women students in male populated fields, such as engineering; students who are economically disadvantaged and work part time or full time while attending classes; lesbian women, who may be harassed as part of homophobia; physically or emotionally disabled students; women students who work in dormitories as resident assistants; women who have been sexually abused; inexperienced, unassertive, socially isolated women, who may appear more vulnerable and appealing to those who would intimidate or coerce them into an exploitive relationship.

Fitzgerald and Ormerod (1993) concluded that it is reasonable to estimate that one out of every two women will be harassed at some point during her academic or working life, a proportion indicating that sexual harassment is the most widespread of all forms of sexual victimization. This estimate has been supported by countless numbers of empirical research studies, using different methodologies to collect incidence data, in different parts of the world, including Australia, Brazil, China, Italy, Israel, Pakistan, Puerto Rico, Sweden, and Turkey (see chapter by DeSouza & Solberg in Paludi & Paludi, 2003).

IMPACT OF SEXUAL HARASSMENT ON STUDENTS

The 1993 AAUW study reported that approximately one in four students who had been sexually harassed did not want to attend school or cut a class. In addition, one in four students became silent in their classes following their experience of sexual harassment. With respect to the emotional aspects of sexual harassment, the AAUW study reported the following experiences, in rank order, among the students who were sexually harassed: embarrassment; self-consciousness; being less sure of themselves or less confident; feeling afraid or scared; doubting whether they could have a happy romantic relationship; feeling confused about who they are; and feeling less popular. In addition, 33 percent of girls who reported experiencing sexual harassment no longer wished to attend school. Thirty-two percent of girls stated that talking in class was more difficult, and 20 percent indicated they had received lower grades. Girls further reported that they altered their behavior to decrease the likelihood of sexual harassment by avoiding people or places, including avoiding school events. Twelve percent of the boys who reported experiencing sexual harassment did not want to attend school; 13 percent of the boys indicated they talked less in class following incidents of sexual harassment.

Fineran and Gruber (2004) reviewed the impact of sexual harassment on children and adolescents. They noted that the outcomes of sexual harassment can be examined from three main perspectives: learning-related, social/emotional, and health-related. Responses include depression; feeling sad, nervous, threatened and angry; loss of appetite; feelings of helplessness; nightmares or disturbed sleep; loss of interest in regular activities; isolation from friends and family; and loss of friends. Fineran and Gruber (2004) also reported long-term effects from sexual harassment: depression, loss of self-esteem, lowered grades, lost educational and job opportunities that affect students after high school graduation that may cause fewer career choices.

Similar to the research findings with children and adolescents, studies with college students have documented the high cost of sexual harassment to individuals. Research with college students indicates that there are career-related, psychological, and physiological outcomes of sexual harassment. For example, women students have reported decreased morale, decreased satisfaction with their career goals, and lowered grades. Furthermore, women students have reported feelings of helplessness and powerlessness over their academic career, strong fear reactions, and decreased motivation. College students have also reported headaches, sleep disturbances, eating disorders, and gastrointestinal disorders as common physical responses to sexual harassment (see chapter by Lundberg-Love & Marmion in Paludi & Paludi, 2003).

POLICIES AND PROCEDURES OPPOSING SEXUAL HARASSMENT

One change over eight years identified in the 2001AAUW study of sexual harassment of students was that 69 percent of students, compared to 26 percent in 1993, indicated that their schools have a sexual harassment policy statement. In addition, in the 2001AAUW study, 36 percent of students compared to 13 percent in 1993 reported that their schools distribute training/educational materials on sexual harassment.

A disturbing finding from the 2001 study, however, is that, despite more schools having policy statements and offering students educational materials on sexual harassment, students continue to engage in sexual harassment and rarely tell school administrators about being victimized. Similar findings have been reported by college students. If they do tell anyone about their experiences, it is usually a friend. Males are twice as likely as females to tell no one about being sexually harassed. Research with college students across the world indicates that, despite the fact they report experiencing behaviors that fit the legal definition of sexual harassment, they do not label their experiences as such.

Although the existence of laws and policies opposing sexual harassment are no guarantee that it will be reported, there is considerable evidence indicating that students are less likely to experience teacher/student sexual harassment and peer sexual harassment if they attend schools/colleges that have a policy prohibiting sexual harassment that is widely disseminated and enforced. A policy alone will not solve sexual harassment, but it is the foundation on which to build a strategy of prevention.

According to OCR, a comprehensive approach for eliminating harassment includes developing and disseminating strong, written policies specifically prohibiting harassment. These policies should take into account the significant legal factors relevant to determining whether unlawful harassment has occurred and should be tailored to the needs of the particular school or school district. Components of an effective policy statement that have been identified in the sexual harassment literature that accomplishes OCR's recommendations include a statement of purpose of the policy, legal definition of harassment, behavioral examples of harassment, a statement concerning the impact of sexual harassment, a statement of the school's responsibility in responding to complaints, a statement concerning confidentiality of complaint procedures, a statement concerning sanctions available, a statement prohibiting retaliation and establishing sanctions for retaliation, a statement concerning false complaints, and identification and background of individual(s) responsible for hearing complaints, including telephone numbers and office locations.

A school or campus that pays attention to each of these will be doing what is necessary to put together a program that will meet the needs of students and stand the ultimate test in courts, if that should ever become necessary. A court test of a policy probably will never happen if the policy is designed to do what it would be tested for: its ability to prevent and handle problems before they get out of control and before the level of legal liability is reached.

Once the policy is completed, it must be clearly and regularly communicated. OCR recommends that the policy statement be reissued each year by the senior administrator as well as placed prominently throughout the school/campus. In addition, the policy statement should be published in student, faculty, and employee handbooks.

The responsibility for communicating the policy statement must be made a part of the job description of anyone with authority in the school/campus. It is also recommended that students sign a sheet that they have been given a copy of the policy and that they understand their rights and responsibilities (Paludi & Paludi, 2003).

Results from the AAUW studies as well as other empirical research on students' experiences with sexual harassment suggest that procedures for investigating complaints of sexual harassment must take into account the psychological issues involved in the victimization process. These issues include individuals' feelings of powerlessness, isolation, changes in their social network patterns, and wish to gain control over their personal and career development. Research has indicated that the experience of participating in an investigative process can be as emotionally and physically stressful as the sexual harassment itself. Therefore, it is important not only to build in several support systems but also to help complainants and alleged perpetrators cope with the process of the complaint procedure. Counselors may work with the investigator for this purpose (Paludi & Barickman, 1998).

Although each school district and college typically establishes its own complaint procedure that fits with its unique needs, OCR has identified three guidelines that apply to investigations of sexual harassment. One of these is that the school has an obligation to make the environment free of sexual harassment and free of the fear of being retaliated against for filing a complaint of sexual harassment. A second guideline is that individuals should be informed that the school will not ignore any complaint of sexual harassment. And, the third guideline is that investigations of sexual harassment complaints will be completed promptly.

In addition to these guidelines, OCR offers several "practical considerations" for establishing effective grievance procedures. These considerations take the form of questions that should be answered in the document describing the procedures for grievances: How many levels will the procedure have, and what will be the time frame for each level? Who may file complaints on behalf of the injured party? Should investigations be conducted by building administrators, other building staff, or district-level officials? Should an evidentiary hearing be part of the process? Should district-level administrators review the investigator's decision in all instances or only when the decision is appealed?

TRAINING AND OTHER EDUCATIONAL PROGRAMS

Schools and campuses are required to take reasonable steps to prevent and end sexual harassment of their students as well as their faculty, administrators, and employees, including facilitating training programs on sexual harassment awareness. Training programs involve more than a recitation of individuals' rights and responsibilities and what the law and school/campus policy requires. Training also requires dealing with individuals' assumptions and misconceptions about power as well as the anxieties about the training itself. Stereotypes about females, males, sex, and power often remain unchallenged unless individuals participate in effective trainer-guided intervention programs (Paludi & Paludi, 2003).

In addition, training programs on sexual harassment must provide all individuals with a clear understanding of their rights and responsibilities with respect to sexual harassment. Training must also enable individuals to distinguish between behavior that is sexual harassment and behavior that is not sexual harassment. Training programs also provide individuals with information concerning the policy statement against sexual harassment and investigatory procedures set up by the school. Finally, training programs have as their goal to help empower individuals to use their school's procedures for resolving complaints.

There has been relatively little empirical research on the impact of training programs on individuals' attitudes and behavior with respect to sexual harassment. The available research has indicated that training increases the tendency to perceive and report sexual harassment and makes college students more sensitive to incidents of sexual harassment especially when case analyses are used. Training also assists sexual harassment contact persons with listening and helping skills and confidence, and it increases knowledge and changes attitudes (see Paludi & Paludi, 2003).

To supplement the training programs in sexual harassment awareness, there are additional educational programs that have been recommended in the literature. These suggest including information on sexual harassment in new student/employee orientation materials; facilitating a "sexual harassment awareness week" and scheduling programs that include lectures, guided video discussions, and plays; reporting annually on sexual harassment; encouraging teachers to incorporate discussions of sexual harassment in their classrooms; encouraging students to start an organization with the purpose of preventing sexual harassment; providing educational sessions for parents about sexual harassment and the school district's policy and procedures (see Sandler & Stonehill, 2005, for additional suggestions).

Interventions created to combat sexual harassment should involve students in making policies intended to alter the school climate with regard to these forms of victimization in order to promote positive interaction among students; this will serve to promote inclusion and empowerment for students. Interventions should also send a clear message that sexual harassment will not be tolerated. Teachers, administrators, parents, and all school staff should be included as well as students. It is only when the entire school community is included that successful change can occur.

REMEDIES THROUGH THE OFFICE FOR CIVIL RIGHTS

The OCR enforces Title IX of the 1972 Education Amendments. When their investigations indicate a violation of Title IX has occurred, OCR provides an opportunity to the school district/campus to voluntarily correct the problem. If the school refuses to correct the situation, OCR initiates enforcement action.

Remedies sought by OCR for harassment include corrective and preventive actions to stop the harassment and minimize the chance of its recurrence. This can take the form of counseling and/or discipline of the harasser and age-appropriate training for students and staff on how to recognize harassment and what to do if they are harassed or observe harassment. Other corrective and preventive actions include psychological or other counseling; compensatory education to make up for any time lost from the educational program as a result of the harassment; adjustment of any grades affected by the harassment and/or the opportunity to repeat a course (without additional cost at the postsecondary level). If the complainant was forced to leave the academic program due to the harassment, reimbursement for any costs that occurred as a result and/or an opportunity to reenroll should be provided. An example would be tuition reimbursement for a public high school student who was forced to leave the high school because of the harassment and enrolled in a private school instead. Another example would be an opportunity for a student who was forced by the harassment to drop out of college to reenroll.

REFERENCES AND FURTHER READINGS

American Association of University Women Educational Foundation. (1993). *Hostile hallways: The annual survey on sexual harassment in America's schools.* Washington, DC: Author.

American Association of University Women Educational Foundation. (2001). *Hostile hallways: Bullying, teasing, and sexual harassment in school.* Washington, DC: Author.

Fineran, S., & Gruber, J. (2004, July). *Research on bullying and sexual harassment in secondary schools: Incidence, interrelationships and psychological implications.* Paper presented at the Association for Gender Equity Leadership in Education, Washington, DC.

Fitzgerald, L., & Ormerod, A. (1993). Sexual harassment in academia and the workplace. In F. Denmark & M. Paludi (Eds.), *Psychology of women: A handbook of issues and theories* (pp. 553–582). Westport, CT: Greenwood.

Fitzgerald, L., Shullman, S., Bailey, N., Richards, M., Swecker, J., Gold, Y., Oermerod, M., & Weitzman, L. (1988). The incidence and dimensions of sexual harassment in academia and the workplace. *Journal of Vocational Behavior, 32*(2), 152–175.

Hill, C., & Silva, E. (2005). *Drawing the line: Sexual harassment on campus.* Washington, DC: American Association of University Women Educational Foundation.

Paludi, M., & Barickman, R. (1998). *Sexual harassment, work, and education: A resource manual for prevention.* Albany: State University of New York Press.

Paludi, M., & Paludi, C. (Eds.). (2003). *Academic and workplace sexual harassment: A handbook of cultural, social science, management and legal perspectives.* Westport, CT: Praeger.

Sandler, B.R., & Stonehill, H. (2005). *Student-to-student sexual harassment in K–12: Strategies and solutions for educators to use in the classroom, school, and community.* Lanham, MD: Rowman & Littlefield Education.

Michele Paludi

Students' Rights in U.S. Higher Education

When considering the topic of students' rights in U.S. higher education, it is important to recognize that the rights of college students at public institutions of higher education are fundamentally different from those of students attending private institutions of higher education. As the Supreme Court noted in *Tinker v. Des Moines Ind. Comm. School Dist.* (393 US 503, 1969), "It can hardly be argued that either students or teachers [at public institutions] shed their constitutional rights...at the schoolhouse gate." However, private institutions of higher education have no legal obligation to afford students the rights guaranteed by the Constitution. The courts will, instead, demand that private institutions afford students the rights promised in various institutional documents including the student handbook. Beyond constitutional rights, public institutions will also be expected to afford students those additional rights set forth in institutional documents. The courts have treated those documents as the foundation of a contractual relationship between institutions and students. Another source of students' rights in higher education is federal legislation, which typically places obligations on all institutions that are recipients of federal financial assistance.

FROM UNFETTERED AUTHORITY OF COLLEGES TO DUE PROCESS FOR STUDENTS

For the first 300 years of the history of American higher education, colleges and universities were assumed to have basically unfettered authority over college students. In 1913, the Kentucky Supreme Court formally articulated the legal theory that would continue to hold sway for another 50 years. In *Gott v. Berea* (156 Ky 376), the court ruled that colleges and universities stand *in loco parentis,* or literally in place of the parents. The court observed:

> College authorities stand *in loco parentis* concerning the physical and moral welfare, and mental training of the pupils, and we are unable to see why to that end

they may not make any rule or regulation for the government, or betterment of their pupils that a parent could for the same purpose.

The court placed few limits on the rules that colleges and universities could establish beyond those rules that were "unlawful or against public policy."

For almost five decades following this decision, the courts rejected virtually every attempt to challenge an institution's authority to discipline students in the manner the institutions considered appropriate. During this period, most institutions enforced rules that severely limited student behavior and often placed greater restrictions on women students than men. Common parietal rules during this period included curfews for women students—although less commonly for men—prohibitions against smoking in public, dress codes, and restrictions on riding in cars.

The turning point in the history of students' rights occurred in 1961 with the decision from the U.S. Court of Appeals for the Fifth Circuit in *Dixon v. Alabama State Board of Education* (294 F. 29 150). This case arose as a result of disciplinary action taken by the state of Alabama against a group of students at Alabama State College for Negroes in Montgomery (now Alabama State University). Six students filed suit against the Alabama State Board of Education after they were removed from the institution for their involvement in civil rights protests. The students participated in demonstrations at a segregated lunch counter in the basement of the Montgomery County Courthouse as well as in a demonstration on the steps of the state capitol. The day following the demonstration at the state capitol, which involved more than 600 students, Governor John Patterson convened a meeting of the State Board of Education to consider disciplinary action against 29 students whom the governor considered the "ring leaders" of these civil rights protests. The students did not attend the hearing. In fact, the students were not even informed that the Board was meeting. The State Board of Education voted, based largely upon information from the Governor, to expel nine students and to place the other students facing charges on probation. The students were notified in writing by Dr. Trenholm, president of Alabama State, of this action in letters dated March 4 or March 5.

With the support of the Legal Defense and Education Fund of the National Association for the Advancement of Colored People, including Thurgood Marshall and Jack Greenberg, six of the expelled students brought suit in federal court against the Alabama State Board of Education claiming that their constitutional rights had been violated. After the district court ruled for the state, the students appealed the decision to the United States Court of Appeals for the Fifth Circuit. That court ruled that due process requires notice and some opportunity for a hearing before students at a tax-supported college are expelled for misconduct. The court ruled that when the state takes action against an individual, the Constitution demands that due process be afforded. The court noted:

> In the disciplining of college students there are no considerations of immediate danger to the public, or of peril to the national security, which should prevent the Board from exercising at least the fundamental principles of fairness by giving the accused students notice of the charges and an opportunity to be heard in their own defense.

It is difficult to overestimate the significance of the court's ruling in *Dixon.* Although the Supreme Court did not hear the *Dixon* case, it later described the ruling as a landmark decision in the area of student discipline in public higher education. While the *Dixon* case is now more than 40 years old, the court's decision remains the foundational statement of student due process in public higher education. The rights to notice of the charges and an opportunity for a hearing at which to present a defense against the charges remain at the heart of students' due process rights in public higher education. More broadly, *Dixon* represents the federal courts' first application of the U.S. Constitution to the legal relationship between public institutions of higher education and students. This decision is grounded in the Fourteenth Amendment's due process clause.

In the years that followed, numerous courts have reinforced and expanded the rights articulated in *Dixon* and, despite some difference in legal interpretations, courts usually will accord students the right to hear the evidence against them and to present oral testimony or, at minimum, written statements from witnesses. There are, however, issues upon which various courts have reached different conclusions. Most notable is the right to counsel in student disciplinary proceedings. In *Gabrilowitz v. Newman* (582 F.2d 100 (1st Cir., 1978)), the Court of Appeals for the First Circuit concluded that, because the student was facing criminal charges resulting from the same set of facts, he was entitled to receive advice of his attorney during the disciplinary hearing. However, the U.S. Court of Appeals for the Seventh Circuit in *Osteen v. Henley* (13 F.3d 221, 223 (7th Cir., 1993)) concluded that the right to counsel was potentially even more limited.

In addition to the specific requirements of due process, the Supreme Court also requires that institutions avoid rules that are unconstitutionally vague. In *Connally v. General Const. Co.* (269 US 385, 1926), the Court noted that rules must be clear and specific enough that people are not forced to guess at their meanings and differ as to their applications. Because the Supreme Court has not directly addressed the rights enjoyed by college and university students at public institutions, the specific requirements of due process are not as clearly established as other areas of constitutional law and requirements may vary somewhat from one jurisdiction to another.

It is important to recognize, however, that not all disputes between a student and the institution demand the same level of due process. The Supreme Court has clearly distinguished between the process required when students are dismissed for academic reasons and the process required when they are dismissed for reasons related to their conduct. In *Board of Curators of the University of Missouri v. Horowitz* (435 US 78, 1978), the Supreme Court ruled that students facing suspension or dismissal for academic performance are only entitled to be informed of the faculty's dissatisfaction with their academic performance and that the faculty's decision was careful and deliberate.

OTHER CONSTITUTIONAL RIGHTS

In addition to their rights under the due process clause of the Constitution's Fourteenth Amendment, students at public colleges and universities in the United States are also granted rights under the First and Fourth Amendments and the Fourteenth Amendment's equal protection clause. While private institutions are not required to afford students constitutional rights, private institutions will also be expected to provide the rights described within the institution's contracts with students. Under the First Amendment, students at public colleges and universities are entitled to freedom of speech, freedom of the press, freedom of assembly, and freedom of association.

Many of the cases through which these rights were established took place during the student protest era of the 1960s and early 1970s. In *Healy v. James* (408 US 169, 1972), for example, the court noted that state colleges and universities are not immune from the sweep of the First Amendment and that First Amendment protections should apply with no less force on college campuses than in the community at large. The courts have granted the greatest protections under the First Amendment to expression that takes place in a public forum. While institutions cannot base restrictions on the content of student expression, institutions can place reasonable time, manner, and place restrictions on student protests. More recently, the courts have invalidated institutional policies that prohibited or punished racist or intolerant speech. In the late 1980s and early 1990s, the courts overturned hate speech codes at a number of institutions including the University of Michigan, the University of Wisconsin, and George Mason University. Hate speech codes referred to institutional policies that were developed to prohibit racist or intolerant speech, particularly when directed at women or students of color. In more recent cases, the courts have invalidated such policies even if they have never been enforced because, by their very existence, they have a "chilling effect" on freedom of speech. These cases, along with Supreme Court precedents, make it clear that public institutions are extremely limited in their ability to lawfully restrict student speech. However, institutions can constitutionally punish conduct or behavior, as distinct from speech, which is motivated by bias or intolerance.

While the First Amendment does not include a clear right of association, the Supreme Court has noted that it was implicit in rights articulated in the First Amendment. In the previously cited *Healy v. James* decision, the Supreme Court ruled that Central Connecticut State College had violated the First Amendment in refusing to recognize a student chapter of Students for Democratic Society because the college's president disagreed with the group's beliefs. However, the court did identify three forms of behavior for which an institution could justifiably refuse to recognize a student organization: refusing to follow reasonable campus rules, interrupting classes, and engaging in illegal activity or inciting imminent lawless action. In subsequent cases, the court's decision was extended to require that institutions that grant student groups access to institutional funding and the right to reserve rooms on campus must also do so without regard to the content of the group's beliefs. In *Rosenberger v. Rector and Board of Visitors of the University of Virginia* (515 U.S. 819, 1995), the Supreme Court ruled the institutions making funding decisions for student organizations must be viewpoint neutral in the decision-making process. The Supreme Court returned to the issue of funding student organizations when students at the University of Wisconsin challenged, as violating the First Amendment, the use of their mandatory student activity fees to support student organizations with which they disagreed. In *Board of Regents v. Southworth* (529 U.S. 217, 2000), the court ruled that mandatory student activity fees did not violate the First Amendment as long as the fees were distributed in a manner that was viewpoint neutral.

Students at public institutions also enjoy protections under the Fourth Amendment against unreasonable searches and seizures. However, these rights are generally less extensive than the rights enjoyed by citizens in their homes. The primary exceptions that limit students' Fourth Amendment rights are institutions' ability to conduct certain administrative searches. For example, institutions can legally engage in searches for the purpose of protecting health and safety. Violations of institutional policy discovered in the course of these searches can be used as the basis for disciplinary action or even criminal prosecution. The courts have also often allowed warrantless searches when the purpose of the search is the enforcement of institutional policies rather than criminal prosecution. Other exceptions include searches conducted with consent, items in plain view, and searches conducted in emergency circumstances. As with other areas of constitutional law, these restrictions do not apply to administrations at private institutions unless they are acting at the direction of the police.

RIGHTS AGAINST DISCRIMINATION

College and university students also enjoy two types of protection against illegal discrimination. First, students at public colleges and universities are protected in part by the Fourteenth Amendment's equal protection clause. The Fourteenth Amendment served as the foundation for the Supreme Court's decisions in both *Brown v. Board of Education* (347 US 483, 1954), which made racial segregation in public schools illegal, and *United States v. Virginia* (518 US 515, 1996), which ordered that women be admitted to Virginia Military Institute and the Citadel in South Carolina.

Second, students at colleges and universities that receive federal financial assistance are also protected under a number of pieces of federal civil rights legislation. All public universities and almost all private universities are recipients of federal financial assistance that includes not only direct federal aid to the institution but also any federal financial aid received by students. There are only a small number of private institutions of higher education that do not allow their students to participate in any federal financial aid programs. These institutions include Bob Jones University (SC), Grove City College (PA), and Hillsdale College (MI). At institutions that receive any federal funds, the relevant aspects of federal civil rights legislation to students include:

- Title VI of the Civil Rights Act of 1964 (42 U.S.C. §2000d)
  No person in the United States shall, on the ground of race, color, or national origin, be excluded from participation in, be denied the benefits of, or be subjected to discrimination under any program or activity receiving federal financial assistance.
- Title IX of Education Amendments of 1972 (20 U.S.C. §1681 *et seq.*)
  No person in the United States shall, on the basis of sex, be excluded from participation in, be denied the benefits of, or be subjected to discrimination under any program or activity receiving federal financial assistance.
- Section 504 of Rehabilitation Act of 1973 (29 U.S.C. §794)
  No otherwise qualified individual with a disability in the United States...shall, solely by reason of her or his disability, be excluded from the participation in, be denied the benefits of, or be subjected to discrimination under any program or activity receiving federal financial assistance.

Two issues related to federal civil rights legislation require additional consideration: affirmative action and sexual harassment. The Supreme Court addressed the legality of affirmative action programs in higher education in its 2003 decisions in *Gratz v. Bollinger* (539 US 244) and *Grutter v. Bollinger* (539 US 306). Justice Sandra Day O'Connor, writing the majority opinion in *Grutter,* reinforced Justice Lewis Powell's decision 25 years earlier in *Regents of Univ. of Cal. v. Bakke* (438 US 26 5, 1978). Justice O'Connor ruled that the Equal Protection Clause of the Fourteenth Amendment to the Constitution does not prohibit the narrowly tailored use of race in admissions decisions to further a compelling interest in obtaining the educational benefits that flow from a diverse student body. However, the legal issues related to affirmative action were not resolved fully by the *Gratz* and *Grutter* decisions as the court has yet to articulate the parameters of a narrowly tailored admissions process.

When considering Title IX of the Educational Amendments of 1972, the issues reach far beyond admissions. The courts have extended protections against sexual harassment in the business context to the educational field. The Supreme Court has addressed sexual harassment in education twice in recent years in *Gebser v. Lago Independent School Dist.* (524 U.S. 274, 1998) and *Davis v. Monroe County School Dist.* (526 U.S. 629, 1999).

Although both of these cases are from K–12 settings, the rulings also apply to colleges and universities. Under the *Gebser* ruling, colleges and universities can be held liable for monetary damages for sexual harassment as a violation of Title IX. In order to succeed in a sexual harassment claim against an institution for sexual harassment by an employee, a student must demonstrate that actual notice was made to officials who have authority to act and who responded with deliberate indifference. The *Davis* ruling extended *Gebser* to address student-on-student sexual harassment that creates a hostile environment in violation of Title IX. The student must demonstrate that the sexual harassment was so severe, pervasive, and objectively offensive that it can be said to deprive the victims of access to the educational opportunities or benefits provided by the school. In addition to lawsuits, students can also file a complaint with the U.S. Department of Education for violations of Title IX. While the student cannot receive monetary damages, the U.S. Department of Education has the authority to order institutions to make policy changes.

STUDENT PRIVACY RIGHTS

The Family Educational Rights and Privacy Act (FERPA) was passed by Congress as part of the Educational Amendments of 1974. FERPA was an amendment to this larger piece of legislation sponsored by Senator James Buckley. FERPA conferred upon parents, or eligible students, three primary rights related to their education records: (a) the right to inspect and review/right to access education records; (b) the right to challenge the content of education records; and (c) the right to consent to the disclosure of education records. In the context of higher education, it is important to understand that, by definition, the rights under FERPA rest with the students regardless of their age. This differs significantly from the K–12 context where the rights rest with parents until the student turns 18.

Under FERPA, the records cover what the regulations refer to as "education records" and are defined very broadly to include all records that are directly related to a student and maintained by an educational agency or institution or by a party acting for the agency or institution. There are various documents or records that are excluded from the definition of education records including: sole possession records, records of a law enforcement unit, employment records (except when a student is employed as a result of his or her student status), certain medical records, and alumni records. Students may request access to their education records, and institutions are required to provide a student access to, but not generally copies of, the education records in question.

FERPA also generally limits the release of students' education records without written consent. However, Congress has enacted numerous exceptions to the written consent requirement since FERPA's passage. These exceptions include:

- release to school officials with legitimate educational interest,
- release to the parents of dependent student as defined by the IRS,
- release in a health or safety emergency,
- release of directory information,
- release of the final results of a disciplinary proceeding to the victim of alleged crime of violence,
- release of information regarding violations of institutional alcohol policies or laws to the parents of student under the age of 21, and
- release of information regarding the final results of a disciplinary proceeding to the public when a student is found responsible of a violation that corresponds to the definitions of a crime of violence.

Congress has continued to expand the exceptions to the written consent requirement in recent years. The Supreme Court also ruled that students could not use 42 U.S.C. §1983 as the grounds for a civil lawsuit against an institution for violations of FERPA. The court placed the responsibility for enforcement of FERPA's mandates on the U.S. Department of Education (*Gonzaga Univ. v. Doe,* 536 U.S. 273, 2002).

GENDER AND STUDENTS' RIGHTS

There are inherent gender issues in any discussion of students' rights in U.S. higher education. In the era of *in loco parentis,* male and female students were subjected to disciplinary systems that severely constrained behavior and addressed violations of those rules in a manner that did not place a high value on students' rights. However, it should be acknowledged that female students faced even greater restrictions on their behavior. The decisions in *Dixon* and other student discipline cases of the 1960s and 1970s, coupled with broader societal changes, helped to remake student life on campus. While all students enjoyed new freedoms on campus, the past restrictions may have made this change more profound for female students.

In more recent years, rules governing students' rights have dealt with gender in two distinct ways. Some have explicitly focused on gender, especially on abolishing gender and other forms of discrimination. Others purport to be gender-neutral rules concerning the rights of all students, regardless of gender. Not surprisingly, the former are often more controversial than the latter. Title IX, for example, has evoked controversies on campuses, in courts, and in Congress ever since its original passage. Even today, it is viewed by some as having failed to achieve equity for women in school sports, while others see it as a law that has imposed reverse discrimination on men by eliminating some of their athletic scholarships and teams in favor of giving undeserved support to women.

Even when rules are gender neutral in formulation, they may not be so in perception or in practice. Rules of conduct, for example, may make no mention of gender but may raise important gender issues in those student discipline cases that arise from the roles of male students as perpetrators and female students as victims of violations of the code of student conduct. While not the most commonly adjudicated cases on campus by far, cases that involve students as both victims and perpetrators create a tension between the rights of the accused student and the rights of the accusing student. Under the laws and court cases summarized here, public institutions of higher education have a legal obligation to address the rights of both groups, whatever their gender composition, when dealing with student disciplinary cases, including student-on-student sexual harassment and physical assaults.

REFERENCES AND FURTHER READINGS

Dannells, M. (1997). *From discipline to development: Rethinking student conduct in higher education* (ASHE-ERIC Higher Education Report, *25*(2)). San Francisco: Jossey-Bass.

Downs, D.A. (2005). *Restoring free speech and liberty on campus.* Oakland, CA: The Independent Institute.

Kaplin, W.A., & Lee, B.A. (2006). *The law of higher education* (4th ed., Vols. 1–2). San Francisco: Jossey-Bass.

Lancaster, J. (Ed.) (2006). *Exercising power with wisdom—The bridge from legal to developmental practice.* Asheville, NC: College Administration Publications.

Paterson, B.G., & Kibler, W.L. (Eds.). (1998). *The administration of campus discipline: Student, organizational, and community issues.* Asheville, NC: College Administration Publications.

Silverglate, H.A., & Gewolb, J. (2003). *FIRE's guide to due process and fair procedure on campus.* Philadelphia: Foundation for Individual Rights in Education.

Stoner, E.N., II, & Lowery, J.W. (2004). Navigating past the "spirit of insubordination": A twenty-first century model student conduct code with a model hearing script. *Journal of College and University Law, 31*(1), 1–77.

John Wesley Lowery

Title IX and School Sports

According to figures provided by the National Women's Law Center (2002), the number of girls and women participating in school-based sport in the United States has skyrocketed over the past 35 years. During 1971 to 1972, the 300,000 girls participating in high school athletics in the United States made up only 7.4 percent of all high school athletes. By 2000 to 2001, almost three million girls were participating in high school athletics and the percent of girls among all high school athletes rose to around 42 percent. At the collegiate level, in 1971 to 1972 only 30,000 women participated in intercollegiate sport, accounting for only 15 percent of all college athletes. By 2000 to 2001, there were 150,000 women participating in college sports and 42 percent of all college athletes were women. The single factor that best explains the 800 percent increase in girls' participation in high school sports and the 400 percent increase in women's participation in intercollegiate sports is Title IX of the Education Amendments of 1972, an equal opportunity law that prohibits sex discrimination in education. Despite the progress toward gender equity within school-based sport, women still do not enjoy equal or equitable opportunities in athletics relative to men. Although there is widespread public support for Title IX and gender equity within sport, the controversy around dismantling male dominance within athletics remains.

EMERGENCE AND DEVELOPMENT OF TITLE IX LEGISLATION

Building on the successes of the civil rights movement, in the late 1960s and early 1970s women's rights activists worked on drafting legislation to address discrimination against women. Using the language of the Civil Rights Act of 1964 as a model, advocates for gender equity in education developed the federal Title IX legislation that prohibited sex discrimination within educational institutions in the United States that receive federal monies. In 1972, Congresswoman Edith Green and Senator Birch Bayh introduced the Title IX legislation to Congress, and without too much fanfare or controversy Congress passed the legislation that same year (Suggs, 2005). On June 23, 1972, President Nixon signed Title IX of the Educational Amendments into law. In part, the statute reads: "No person in the United States shall, on the basis of sex, be excluded from participation in, be denied the benefits of, or be subjected to discrimination under any educational program or activity receiving Federal financial assistance" (20 U.S.C. § 1681 et seq.).

Although Title IX applies to all types of educational programs and addresses issues such as sexual harassment, the law quickly became associated with gender equity in athletics. Partly by design, there was very little discussion during the congressional debates of how the antidiscrimination bill was to affect school-based sports. However, in 1974 when the Department of Health, Education, and Welfare (HEW) was drafting the Title IX regulations on college sports, debate over how Title IX was going to affect college sports emerged. Senator John Tower of Texas proposed an amendment to Title IX that would exempt revenue-producing sports (i.e., men's football) from being tabulated when determining Title IX compliance. Congress rejected the Tower amendment. Senator Jacob Javits of New York then put forth an alternative amendment that cleared the way for the passage of Title IX regulations for interscholastic and intercollegiate athletics. In 1975, Congress passed and President Ford signed into law the Title IX regulations.

The Title IX regulations established the following: (a) sex discrimination is prohibited in any interscholastic, intercollegiate, club, or intramural athletics; (b) separate sport teams for women and men are allowed; however, if a sport is not offered to one group, the excluded sex must be allowed to try out for the team provided that the sport is not a contact sport; and (c) equal opportunity in treatment and participation must be provided, whereas equal expenditures for female and male teams is not mandatory. Elementary schools were given one year to comply with the regulations, and secondary and postsecondary educational institutions were given three years to comply. Currently, the Office of Civil Rights (OCR) at the U.S. Department of Education oversees Title IX compliance, complaints, and violations. The OCR assesses Title IX compliance on a program-wide basis. The ultimate penalty for noncompliance is the withdrawal of federal financial assistance to the school. To date, no institution has lost federal funding because of noncompliance with Title IX regulations.

In 1979, Title IX regulations were further developed and adopted by HEW through the document "Policy Interpretation: Title IX and Intercollegiate Athletics." This document set out the basis of the Title IX three-prong test of compliance. In 1996, these compliance requirements were clarified by the OCR through the document "Clarification of Intercollegiate Athletic Policy Guidance: The Three-Part Test." These policy interpretations specify three dimensions of gender equity in athletics: *participation, scholarships,* and *other benefits of sports programming.* Postsecondary institutions have the flexibility of complying with Title IX in the area of *participation* through any one of three prongs, which has become known as the three-prong test. The first way for a school to comply with the participation requirements is to demonstrate that female and male students participate in intercollegiate athletic programs in numbers substantially proportionate to their undergraduate enrollment at the school. This prong is known as substantial proportionality and requires a comparison of the ratio of female and male athletic opportunities to female and male full-time undergraduates. The second way a school can meet the participation requirement of Title IX is to show a history and continuing practice of program expansion for the underrepresented sex. The third way an institution can comply is to demonstrate that the athletic department is fully and effectively accommodating the interests and abilities of the underrepresented sex.

The OCR has no preferred way for an institution to comply with the Title IX participation regulation; however, the first prong of substantial proportionality has been deemed a "safe harbor" for Title IX compliance (U.S. Department of Education, 2003). During the 1990s, courts repeatedly ruled that if an institution complies with the substantial proportionality prong the institution is essentially immune from lawsuits and complaints filed with the civil rights office (Suggs, 2003). Courts have cited figures of plus or minus 3 to 5 percentage points as the criterion to determine if a school is offering proportional opportunities in athletics to women and men students. According to a report by the U.S. General Accounting Office (GAO, 2000), from 1994 through 1998, the OCR reviewed 74 cases involving Title IX participation complaints. Of these, 28.4 percent (21 schools) were held in compliance under prong one and the rest of the schools complied under prongs two or three.

In the area of *scholarships,* Title IX requires that an educational institution must ensure that the athletic scholarships given to female and male student athletes are awarded in about the same ratio as the percentages of females and males participating in the athletic program. If women make up 42 percent of the athletes at the institution, then women must receive about 42 percent of the scholarship money awarded by the athletic department. In the area of *other benefits of sports programming,* an institution must ensure that female and male athletes are treated equitably in the provision of (a) equipment and supplies, (b) scheduling of games and practice times, (c) travel and daily allowance, (d) access to tutoring, (e) coaching, (f) locker rooms, (g) practice and competitive facilities, (h) medical and training facilities and services, (i) publicity and promotions, (j) recruitment of student athletes, and (k) support services.

ENFORCEMENT CONTROVERSIES AND LEGAL CHALLENGES

Since the law was enacted, there have been many rounds of heated debates and controversies about how Title IX should be enforced (Staurowsky, 1995, 1996; Suggs, 2005). As HEW was drafting the Title IX regulations for athletics in the late 1970s, the National Collegiate Athletic Association (NCAA), which offered few programs for women, rallied against the regulations. Conservative members of Congress, such as Senator Jesse Helms, also attempted to curtail Title IX enforcement. Nonetheless, the positive effect of the legislation on girls' and women's participation in athletics was immediate. Even before the three-year grace period had ended in 1978, women's sports grew by leaps and bounds. Schools hired women coaches, added girls/women's teams, and converted existing girls/women's intramural programs into varsity programs. These changes reflected and contributed to the growing women's movement in the United States during the period.

However, by the early 1980s, progress toward equal opportunities for girls and women in sports slowed. The election of President Reagan in 1980 ushered in a backlash against civil rights laws and gains. In 1980, the U.S. Department of Education was established and the OCR began to oversee Title IX. In the mid-1980s, the control of women's intercollegiate sports shifted from the women-dominated Association for Intercollegiate Athletics for Women to the male-dominated NCAA, even though the takeover was contested in a legal battle that reached the U.S. Supreme Court. Another major setback to gender equity for women in sports came with the 1984 court case of *Grove City College v. Bell* (465 US 555). In this pivotal case, the Reagan administration argued that only entities within universities and colleges that were direct recipients of federal funding should have to comply with Title IX regulations. The U.S. Supreme Court agreed and the ruling effectively exempted athletic departments from Title IX regulations. The power of Title IX in the area of athletics was immediately lost.

As the political and economic climate started to change in the late 1980s, Congress passed, over a veto by President Reagan, the Civil Rights Restoration Act of 1987, which restored the original power of Title IX in the area of athletics. The Civil Rights

Restoration Act, which passed in 1988, explicitly states that all programs supported and offered by a school that receives federal monies must comply with Title IX regulations. Athletic departments were no longer exempt from Title IX. As an indication of the political and legal shift regarding Title IX, in 1990 the OCR issued a Title IX Investigation Manual for schools to evaluate Title IX compliance. With Title IX restored, female athletes seized the moment to use the courts to force schools to comply with Title IX. In 1992, one of the most critical Title IX legal cases—*Franklin v. Gwinnett County Public Schools* (503 US 60)—came before the U.S. Supreme Court. The case involved a sexual harassment allegation from a high school student against a coach at her school. The student claimed that school officials knew about the harassment but did nothing to stop it. In their decision, the Supreme Court ruled for the first time that plaintiffs suing institutions for Title IX violations could seek monetary damages for alleged intentional sex discrimination. The decision immediately gave Title IX more enforcement teeth. Schools that ignored the law before were put on notice that financial penalties could be awarded by the courts in Title IX cases. Schools took note and athletes began demanding their rights.

In situations where schools dropped women's sport teams to deal with financial shortfalls, women athletes were particularly successful in their strategy of turning to the courts. Simply threatening a lawsuit was also an effective strategy to gain more opportunities and resources for women in athletics (Pelak, 2002). One of the most important victories for Title IX during the 1990s was the class action suit against Brown University, which was filed in 1992 and made its way to the Supreme Court in 1997. The case was initiated when Brown University dropped its varsity programs for women's gymnastics and women's volleyball. The Brown case revolved around the appropriateness of the three-prong test and particularly the issue of proportional representation of women students in athletics. Lawyers for the administration of Brown University claimed that men were more interested in sports and, thus, it is appropriate to offer men students more opportunities to participate in sports. The Supreme Court disagreed and refused to hear the Brown case. Thus, the ruling by the lower court, the First Circuit, that Brown University was in violation of all prongs of the three-part test for equitable participation held. Brown University was forced to reinstate women's gymnastics and women's volleyball (Haworth, 1997).

This was a symbolically important Title IX case because Brown University spent millions of dollars fighting the case and had a large number of groups and institutions sign onto the case on their behalf, including 60 colleges and universities, numerous collegiate coaching associations, various athletic and higher-education associations, USA Wrestling, USA Swimming, United States Water Polo, 48 U.S. Representatives, and one U.S. Senator. In the end, the administration of Brown University and the many other opponents of Title IX lost the case. The court decision made it clear that stereotypes purporting that women do not want to participate in competitive athletics was not a valid argument at the turn of the twenty-firs century.

The 1990s also brought new legislation that encouraged heightened enforcement of Title IX. In 1994, Congress passed the Equity in Athletics Disclosure Act (EADA), which requires coeducational institutions that participate in any federal student financial aid program and have an intercollegiate athletics program to disclose, with annual reports, certain information regarding their athletics program. The EADA requires athletic departments to report roster sizes of women's and men's teams, as well as budgets for recruiting, scholarships, coaches' salaries, and other expenses. These data are proving to be useful in highlighting the persistent gender inequalities in collegiate athletics and are helping in local efforts to make educational institutions more accountable. The National Women's Law Center, which has litigated many of the Title IX lawsuits and lobbied heavily in favor of strong enforcement of Title IX, has used the EADA data to file complaints against institutions with gender imbalances in their athletic departments. During the 1990s, the Clinton administration also demonstrated strong support for enforcement of Title IX. Norma Cantu was named the Assistant Secretary of Education for Civil Rights in 1993 and fought hard to improve enforcement of Title IX. As mentioned above, in 1996 the OCR issued a policy guidance document that clarified in a strict fashion the regulations around equity in participation opportunities known as the three-prong test.

With the successes of Title IX court cases and enforcement during the 1990s, a backlash emerged. Opponents of Title IX claimed that gender equity regulations were hurting men's sports and that the way the courts were applying the three-prong test was an illegal quota. Male wrestlers and their supporters, who believed that Title IX was the reason why men's wrestling programs and other nonrevenue men's sports were being cut, led the organized opposition. In 2002, the National Wrestling Coaches Association and other Title IX opponents filed a federal lawsuit against the U.S. Department of Education challenging Title IX regulations and policies. After the Supreme Court refused to hear the case, the wrestlers and others opposing Title IX regulations found a sympathetic ear in the Bush administration. During June 2002, Roderick Paige, the new Secretary of the Department of Education under President George W. Bush, convened a Commission on Opportunity in Athletics to supposedly see that athletic opportunities were expanding and to ensure fairness to all athletes. The women's rights community was outraged by the commission, which they saw as an effort to undermine Title IX enforcement and reinforce male dominance in athletics. The Commission proceedings were fraught with tensions, and observers claim that concern for the inequities that women still face in athletics was rarely expressed during commission debates (Suggs, 2005). At the end of the six months of proceedings, the commission submitted a report with recommendations to the U.S. Secretary of Education. Commission members Donna de Varona and Julie Foudy strongly disagreed with the report and submitted a minority report urging the U.S. Department of Education to step up enforcement of Title IX. One year later, the OCR issued a clarification of Title IX policy that did nothing to change existing Title IX regulations but emphasized the flexibility of the three-prong test and discouraged schools from dropping sport teams to comply with Title IX regulations.

According to the empirical evidence, blaming the decline in men's wrestling teams on Title IX regulations is simply unfounded (National Women's Law Center, 2002). Between 1984 and 1988, a time when Title IX did not apply to athletic departments because of the *Grove City* court case, the number of NCAA men's wrestling programs dropped by 55 from 289 to 234. Since Title IX was not in effect during these years, it is hard to blame the loss of the wrestling programs on the gender equity legislation. In contrast, between 1988 and 2000, a 12-year period in which Title IX applied to athletic departments, there were about the same number of men's wrestling programs dropped. If Title IX were responsible for the loss of wrestling programs, one would expect that far more programs would have been dropped during the 12-year period than the earlier four-year period. Moreover, during this same period, women's gymnastics also suffered a substantial decline. Between 1982 and 2000, 90 of the 179 women's gymnastics programs sponsored by the NCAA were dropped, representing almost of half of the existing programs.

Schools decide to drop teams for a number of reasons including decreasing interest in specific sports, liability considerations, and/or preservation of the budgetary dominance of masculine flagship sports such as football. Despite the claims by the wrestling coaches and other opponents of Title IX, the evidence shows that between 1981 and 1998 the overall number of men's sport teams increased and men's intercollegiate athletic participation rose (National Women's Law Center, 2002). While certain men's sports like wrestling have declined, other men's sports, such as baseball, crew, football, lacrosse, and soccer, have increased. Likewise, some women's sports such as field hockey and gymnastics have also declined while other women's sports such as ice hockey and soccer have increased. Blaming the loss of wrestling or other nonrevenue producing men's sports on Title IX is misplaced and contributes to an unhelpful antagonism between women's and men's sport programs (see Staurowsky, 1996). Rather than looking to needless expenditures and/or inflated participation rates within high profile men's football and basketball programs, opponents of Title IX scapegoat women athletes, who still are not enjoying equitable opportunities within school-based sport.

TITLE IX, ATHLETIC ASSOCIATIONS, AND STATES

Lawsuits and public debates around high school athletics have centered on the inferior treatment of girls rather than centering on the issue of unequal participation rates of girls and boys (Suggs, 2005). Compared to boys' teams, girls' teams are often relegated to inferior fields and gyms and often use inferior equipment and uniforms. The issues surrounding practicing and game times are also important at the high school level. In Michigan, gender differences in the seasonal sport schedules are currently being debated in a lengthy court battle. A group of parents sued the Michigan High School Athletic Association in 1998 over the atypical seasonal sport schedule that had high school girls, in contrast to boys, playing basketball in the fall and volleyball in the winter, even though in the rest of the country high school athletes play volleyball as a fall sport and basketball as a winter sport. The parents argue that the irregular schedule systematically disadvantages girls in general and in particular girls seeking college scholarships, which are typically given after playing seasons. In 2004, the U.S. Court of Appeals for the Sixth Circuit sided with the parents and ruled that the Michigan High School Athletic Association violated the constitutional rights of the girls. While an appeal in the case is still pending, the girls at Michigan high schools continue to play an off-season schedule.

An earlier case with important implications for the promotion of gender equity at the high school level involved the Tennessee Secondary School Athletic Association (TSSAA), which the U.S. Supreme Court heard in 2000. This case involves the question of whether the TSSAA, a nonprofit corporation that regulates interscholastic athletics in Tennessee's public and private high schools, should be considered a state actor and, thus, be required to comply with the equal protection clause of the Constitution. The Supreme Court ruled that the TSSAA was subject to the U.S. Constitution because the association operates as an arm of the state. This decision is important to Title IX because it means that state athletic associations cannot insulate themselves from liability for civil rights violations when they limit girls' opportunities to participate in interscholastic athletics.

Unlike state athletic associations at the high school level, the NCAA has not been held subject to Title IX or constitutional protections. In *National Collegiate Athletic Association v. Smith* (525 US 459, 1999), the Supreme Court held that the NCAA was not subject to Title IX simply because it receives funding from federally funded schools. Their decision, however, left open other legal arguments for coverage of national athletic associations in Title IX compliance. Although the NCAA is not currently subject to Title IX legislation, the association has an interest in encouraging member institutions to comply. In 1991, NCAA published a landmark gender equity study on its member institutions. The study found that women were only 30 percent of athletes on varsity teams and women's teams of NCAA member schools received only 23 percent of operating budgets of athletic departments.

Although the NCAA has not been a perennial supporter of Title IX, during the 1990s, their actions and statements in reference to Title IX became more positive. In response to the findings of their 1991 gender equity study, the NCAA established a Gender Equity Task Force in 1993. The task force has continued to track gender inequalities at NCAA member schools and has served as an important body to encourage institutional progress on gender equity. One process that the NCAA put into place during the 1990s is the requirement that Division I schools conduct a self-study of gender equity as part of their cyclical certification process. In addition, when the OCR issued a clarification that allows Internet surveys of undergraduate students to be used as a way to measure women's interest in athletics, the NCAA came out opposing the new policy interpretations because they believed, along with women's rights advocates, that the Internet surveys could be used to dismantle progress on Title IX compliance. These and other efforts have encouraged NCAA member schools to take positive steps toward increasing women's opportunities within athletics and demonstrate the NCAA's growing commitment to Title IX.

States have also acted, or failed to act, in terms of encouraging gender equity within school-based sports. At least 20 states have either passed legislation or have legislation pending that aims to improve gender equity in athletics. Some states have also provided monetary assistance in the form of tuition waivers for women athletes and monies for building facilities for women's athletics. In 1998, the National Organization for Women negotiated an out-of-court settlement with the whole California State University system to comply with a state law that mandates immediate progress toward gender equity in athletics. There are, however, important differences across states in terms of Title IX compliance. Research has found that schools located in southern states offer far fewer opportunities to girls and women in athletics than schools in non-Southern states. Educational institutions in the northeast and far west offer the most equitable athletic opportunities for girls and women in the country.

THE STATUS OF TITLE IX TODAY

Despite the progress made toward achieving gender equity within education-based sports, girls and women are still not receiving their fair share of opportunities, resources, and attention. As the percentage of women students increases at college campuses across the country, athletic departments are finding it increasingly difficult to reach gender proportionality within athletics. During 2003 to 2004, just over 57 percent of college students were women, but only 42 percent of college athletes were women. At the high school level, the percentage of female student athletes appears to be stalled around 42 percent. Monetary expenditures, such as scholarships and team budgets, remain woefully unequal even at the turn of the twenty-first century. Although gender relations within athletics have changed dramatically over the past 35 years, much work remains to be done. The resistance to fully dismantling male dominance within athletics and the persistence of stereotypes that purport that boys and men deserve more opportunities within athletics than girls and women suggest that equitable opportunities in education are secured only through continued struggle.

REFERENCES AND FURTHER READINGS

Haworth, K. (1997, April 4). Colleges, sporting groups, and lawmakers back Brown University's appeal in Title IX case. *The Chronicle of Higher Education,* A36.

National Women's Law Center. (2002). *The battle for gender equity in athletics: Title IX at thirty.* Washington, DC: Author. Retrieved from http://www.nwlc.org

Pelak, C.F. (2002). Women's collective identity formation in sports: A case study from women's ice hockey. *Gender and Society, 16*(1), 93–114.

Staurowsky, E. (1995). Examining the roots of a gendered division of labor in intercollegiate athletics: Insights into the gender equity debate. *Journal of Sport and Social Issues, 19*(1), 28–44.

Staurowsky, E. (1996). Blaming the victim: Resistance in the battle over gender equity in intercollegiate athletics. *Journal of Sport and Social Issues, 20*(2), 194–210.

Suggs, W. (2003). A federal commission wrestles with gender equity in sports. *The Chronicle of Higher Education, 49*(17), A41.

Suggs, W. (2005). *A place on the team: The triumph and tragedy of Title IX.* Princeton, NJ: Princeton University Press.

U.S. Department of Education. (2003). *Further clarification of intercollegiate athletics policy guidance regarding Title IX compliance.* Washington, DC: Office of Civil Rights, U.S. Department of Education. Retrieved from http://www.ed.gov/about/offices/list/ocr/title9guidanceFinal.html

U.S. General Accounting Office. (2000). *Gender equity: Men's and women's participation in higher education* (Report to the Ranking Minority Member, Subcommittee on Criminal Justice, Drug Policy and Human Resources, Committee on Government Reform, House of Representatives. Report number: GAO-01-128). Washington, DC: Author.

Cynthia Fabrizio Pelak

Women's Educational Equity Act

The Women's Educational Equity Act of 1974 reflects the historic federal role in education in the United States. Indeed, while the history of education in the United States is a history of local control, the traditional federal role in education policy and law has been a significant and powerful one for more than a century—from the establishment of land grant universities to make higher education widely available nationwide to passage of federal laws to promote equity and access to education for disenfranchised groups. The GI bill, for instance, made college possible for military veterans, including low-income men who otherwise would never have had the opportunity to gain postsecondary education. In many ways, this important federal education policy helped to create the middle class in the United States.

The 1960s and 1970s marked a new era in which the federal role in education sought to ensure equality of opportunity and overcome decades of discrimination on the basis of race, ethnicity, and—ultimately—sex. The "War on Poverty" launched by President Lyndon Johnson, for example, produced the landmark 1965 *Elementary and Secondary Education Act* and the *Higher Education Act*—to provide new federal funds to schools, colleges, and communities to address poverty which, as President Johnson said, is the "taproot" of unequal and inadequate educational opportunities. Indeed, 40 years later, it is clear education, particularly postsecondary education, remains the most sustainable route from poverty to social and economic self-sufficiency.

In the 1960s, Congress passed new civil rights statutes and put money behind them with new education funding programs. Title VI of the *Civil Rights Act of 1964* for the first time outlawed discrimination on the basis of race in all federally funded programs, including education. And, the law's Title IV established a small federal funding program to assist schools in their efforts to comply with desegregation mandates. In addition, the aptly named *Emergency School Aid Act* authorized new federal funds to help school districts end racial segregation and improve schooling for African American students and overcome two centuries of official racial discrimination the Supreme Court had overturned in *Brown v. Board of Education* (1954).

Continuing in this tradition, Congress took a bold step in 1972 to confront sex discrimination in education. The passage of Title IX of the *Education Amendments of 1972*—a new civil rights law—marked a new era in our nation's antidiscrimination law and policy. Modeled on the major civil rights legislation of the 1960s—particularly Title VI of the *Civil Rights Act of 1964*—Title IX for the first time banned discrimination on the basis of sex in federally funded education programs.

Shortly thereafter, Arlene Horowitz, a young staffer in Congresswoman Patsy Mink's [D-HI] office, suggested perhaps Congress should create a new program (similar to the Title IV funding program) to help schools, colleges, and communities implement the mandates established by Title IX. The result was the *Women's Educational Equity Act of 1974* (PL 95-561) sponsored in the House of Representatives by Congresswoman Mink and in the Senate by Senator Walter Mondale [D-MN]. The statute also created the National Advisory Council on Women's Educational Programs whose members were appointed by the President and confirmed by the U.S. Senate—a rarity among education advisory committees.

The Women's Educational Equity Act (WEEA) was, and is, the only federal education program whose sole purpose is the promotion of equal education for women and girls. Since its first funding year in 1976, the WEEA program supported model programs in every possible aspect of education—and many of these programs became permanent fixtures in the educational equity arena.

Although its funding never exceeded $10 million per year—a pittance in the context of federal education funding—WEEA targeted its resources effectively. In its early days, beginning with its first funding year (1976), WEEA supported a range of programs designed to bring educational equity into the schools and colleges. These included, for example, leadership development programs to enable women to qualify for management positions in education—as principals, superintendents, and college presidents; teacher training programs designed to enable classroom teachers to promote educational equity through both pedagogy and equitable treatment of students; and programs to promote equity for girls and women in "nontraditional" curricula and professions—math, science, and engineering, in particular. WEEA funding also supported the development of new educational materials to eliminate sex bias across the curriculum, efforts to confront sex discrimination and sexual harassment in schools and colleges and to ensure compliance with Title IX, and efforts to provide equitable educational and training programs for "reentry" women returning to higher education.

To ensure widespread dissemination of materials produced by WEEA grantees, the WEEA office (then part of the Office of Education in the U.S. Department of Health, Education, and Welfare) awarded a contract to the Education Development Center to establish the WEEA Publishing Center. The Center would review and publish the products of WEEA grants and sell them at reasonable cost, thus disseminating WEEA's successes nationwide. The WEEA office also convened annual meetings of WEEA grantees and provided a range of technical assistance services to grantees.

Beginning in 1979, the newly reauthorized WEEA program, with a new director (this author, who came to the program from the civil rights and feminist movements and from federal government service in civil rights), launched a "new WEEA" with a new set of funding priorities—based on extensive public comments on the proposed regulations for the WEEA program, which had been reauthorized by Congress. These priorities revolutionized WEEA in many ways—and perhaps contributed to the backlash to come. To begin, WEEA targeted substantial resources to projects specifically addressing educational equity for women and girls of color and to projects that focused on educational equity for women and girls with disabilities. This represented the first, and perhaps last, federal effort to support efforts to confront the impact of combined race/ethnicity and gender discrimination, bias, and stereotyping as well as combined gender and disability discrimination, bias, and stereotyping.

For many grantees, in fact, this was the first time they had received any federal education funding—and these WEEA grants helped to launch many organizations and leaders in the struggle for educational equity and women's leadership nationwide. For example, a recent front page article in the *New York Times,* "As Tribal Leaders, Women Still Fight Old Views" (February 17, 2006, A1), referred to a WEEA grantee as the source for data on the number of Native American women in tribal leadership: "In 1981, a study paid for by the Department of Education and called 'Ohoyo One Thousand' found that 69 of the more than 500 federally recognized American Indian tribes and Alaska Native villages were headed by women" (A1–A9). Under the new WEEA funding priorities, Ohoyo (which means "woman" in Choctaw) conducted national and regional conferences of Native women leaders, which built a powerful network that lasted long after the end of WEEA funding.

Asian Women United received WEEA funding for materials development (books such as *With Silk Wings,* for example) and for a program for Asian immigrant women that later became an independent organization that continues to grow and flourish. The Disability Rights Education and Defense Fund received WEEA grants for a range of curricular and training programs—and the original program staff and participants continue to be leaders in promoting equity for women and girls with disabilities. These are only three of the many institutions and programs that flourished with this newly focused WEEA funding. Further, the new WEEA funding priorities also inspired colleges and schools, as well as other organizations, to address the needs of women and girls of color and women and girls with disabilities.

The implementation of these new funding priorities marks one of WEEA's most significant accomplishments—making the response to combined sex plus race/ethnicity and disability discrimination, bias, and stereotyping a centerpiece of federal educational equity policy and practice. In addition, the new WEEA continued the program's traditional focus both on Title IX implementation and on promotion of women into educational leadership —but with a new twist in each arena. First, the new WEEA established a very specific priority designed to promote actual compliance with Title IX by schools and colleges—with funding not only targeted to school districts, colleges, and universities but also to those nonprofit organizations whose mission is promotion of educational equity for women and girls.

Second, rather than focus on further training of women for educational leadership—the regulations responded to the fact that exceptionally well-trained women still were being passed over for senior management positions in education. The new WEEA, therefore, established a funding priority to provide real nondiscrimination and equity training for those educational decision makers—members of school boards and boards of trustees, for instance—who are responsible for hiring educational leaders and whose bias—though often unconscious—excluded many women from positions as principals, superintendents, and college presidents.

Finally, the new WEEA regulations required all applicants, regardless of their proposed program, to demonstrate that their activities would promote educational equity for women and girls of color and for women and girls with disabilities—thus transforming the focus of the WEEA program across the board.

Despite—or perhaps because of—these successes, the Reagan Administration in the early 1980s rejected educational equity as a primary function of federal education policy. A hallmark of this policy change was the assault on the Women's Educational Equity Act. Although the full story has not yet been told, both Susan Faludi (1991) and Myra and David Sadker (1994) discuss the attacks on WEEA as emblematic of the backlash against women's equality and the assault by the New Right on federal support for educational equity.

Indeed, *Mandate for Leadership,* the Heritage Foundation's 1981 blueprint for the incoming Reagan administration on strategies to implement its agenda, specifically targeted the WEEA program for elimination—describing WEEA as "an important resource for the practice of feminist policies and politics." In 1982, an anonymous article in the magazine *Conservative Digest* attacked the WEEA Director as a "monarch in a feudal Washington bureaucracy" and recommended her "swift dethronement" because she was "twisting the grant approval process" and turning WEEA into "a money machine for a network of openly radical feminist groups."

The Reagan administration proposed substantial cuts to the WEEA appropriation, which a bipartisan coalition on Capitol Hill attempted to reverse. Then, in 1982, the WEEA Director was transferred to a nonexistent task force and the expert proposal field readers were fired and replaced with conservatives who neither understood nor supported educational equity, as Faludi has noted. Finally, in 1983, the WEEA Director was fired as the WEEA program office was demoted from its perch in the immediate office of the Assistant Secretary to a "section" at the lowest bureaucratic level.

The attack continues to this day—now formulated to suggest that promoting educational equity is no longer necessary because the "problems" WEEA was designed to solve no longer exist and women and girls are doing well, or "better than boys," in school. Clearly, a visionary WEEA program would evolve to respond to these allegations. Indeed, such a WEEA program would develop new funding priorities that would address the educational equity issues of the twenty-first century—which continue to plague our schools and workplaces. However, while WEEA continues to be reauthorized by Congress and funded at a minimal level (less than $3 million per year) despite administration requests for zero funding, the essence of the forward-thinking WEEA program has not survived. WEEA no longer is a voice for systemic change in education, its grants program is small and limited to more "traditional" educational activities, and its WEEA Publishing Center (later called the WEEA Equity Resource Center) no longer distributes WEEA products (as of early 2003)—its long-standing contract with the Education Department having ended.

The WEEA mission—to ensure truly equal education for all women and girls—has yet to be fulfilled. It is a transformational mission, as it requires that schools and colleges not only change their curricula and pedagogy but also work with other organizations and institutions to eliminate the patriarchal structures of U.S. society and to replace them with more egalitarian structures. In 1885, Lucy Stone declared that: "In education, in marriage, in everything, disappointment is the lot of woman. It shall be the business of my life to deepen that disappointment in every woman's heart until she bows down to it no longer." Today, supporters of educational equality for women and girls understand that their transformational mission must continue to be the business of their lives, for the benefit of generations yet to come.

REFERENCES AND FURTHER READINGS

Faludi, S. (1991). *Backlash: The undeclared war against American women.* New York: Crown.

Sadker, M., & Sadker, D. (1994). *Failing at fairness: How America's schools cheat girls.* New York: Charles Scribner's Sons.

Leslie R. Wolfe

Work-Family Reconciliation Policies

Work-family reconciliation policies are institutional and organizational arrangements designed to secure adequate care for children and to help adults cope with the conflicting demands of employment and family life. The need for such policies has grown along with women's increased participation in the labor force and the concomitant reduction in the time and energy they have to spend on unpaid care work, not only for children, but also for their partners, their home, and their extended families. Although the traditional model of the male breadwinner and female homemaker has become increasingly rare, men continue to invest their time primarily in the workplace while women struggle to combine employment with unpaid work in the home. As a result, work-family policies are often seen as women-oriented policies rather than as policies designed to increase gender equality.

Like most workers, educators often face competing demands in their roles as employees and caregivers in the home. However, unlike most workers, some educators, especially female teachers, have often chosen their occupation in the hope that it will help reduce work-family conflict. Their reasoning is that teachers' work/school hours, holidays, and vacations will correspond more closely to those of their own children than will the work schedules of nonteachers. Such reasoning as a basis for choosing teaching over other jobs is a good example of the kinds of private solutions to the problems of work-family conflict that are common in the United States. Although such private solutions can be adaptive for individual women and their families, they also exacerbate long-standing problems of gender inequality at home and in the labor market. Women who choose a job because it may be compatible with caregiving in the family are likely to settle for lower incomes. These choices can also render them more economically dependent and more at risk in the event of family dissolution than their male counterparts who are likely to have both higher status and higher paying jobs.

To overcome gender inequalities while at the same time providing high-quality care for children and solutions to work-family conflicts, Janet Gornick and Marcia Meyers (2003, 2004, 2005) have recently proposed a set of policies designed to achieve what British sociologist Rosemary Crompton (1999) has labeled a "dual-earner/dual-carer society." This is a society that recognizes the rights and obligations of women and men to engage in both employment and caregiving and is committed to meeting children's needs for intensive care and nurturance. According to Gornick and Meyers, achieving a dual-earner/dual-carer society in the United States would require the expansion of government policies that socialize the costs of rearing children and help both women and men to blend employment with care work. They argue that forcing parents to rely on personal solutions, such as cutting back on paid working hours or placing their children in substitute child care for long hours, exacerbates gender inequalities and places many children at developmental risk.

Employers can help to solve these problems through, for example, voluntarily granting flexibility in work schedules or paid leaves. Employers' efforts provide helpful but insufficient support for parents. Because these workplace accommodations are targeted primarily on women in high-status jobs, they can also contribute to inequalities among women and across families. Public policies that use the redistributive and regulatory powers of government have the potential to help parents manage the competing demands of employment and caregiving while promoting gender equality and reducing inequalities among children from different social class backgrounds. There are two critical areas for government intervention: policies that support shared earning and caregiving by both mothers and fathers through the regulation of working time and family leave policies, and policies that provide high-quality, affordable substitute care through public early childhood education and care programs.

The good news is that the United States does not have to develop such policies and programs in a vacuum. Many Western industrialized, democratic nations provide existing models for how government can help families resolve the conflict between caring and employment responsibilities and how children can be treated as national resources. Although none of these countries has yet achieved a fully egalitarian, dual-earner/dual-carer society, they do provide many good examples of ways in which government can support men and women in their efforts to share earning and caring work and to provide quality early childhood education and care.

POLICIES THAT SUPPORT SHARED EARNING AND CARING

In the absence of public policies that support dual-earner/dual-carer arrangements, parents in the United States craft a variety of private solutions for managing competing demands. One of the most significant is adjustments to working hours and schedules. Although adaptive in the short term, these adjustments often exacerbate gender inequalities and impose substantial costs on parents, particularly mothers.

One common adjustment to working hours and schedules by American parents consists of a reduction in the labor force attachment of only one parent, and it is overwhelmingly the mothers who take this action. Unfortunately, this solution turns out to be costly for women as they suffer what some social scientists refer to as the "mommy tax" for reductions in employment and consequent losses in earnings throughout their working years. By one estimate, the "mommy tax" is as much as $600,000 to $1,000,000. Other mothers manage child-care demands through part-time employment compatible with their household duties. They, too, pay a penalty. This penalty is particularly great in the United States because policies to protect part-time workers lag those in much of the industrialized world. American labor laws provide very little protection against employers paying part-time workers less (per hour) than their full-time counterparts, or denying them benefits such as health insurance. Some estimates show that women who work part time in the

United States earn 20 percent less per hour than comparable full-time workers, and they often forgo employment benefits as well as opportunities for advancement.

These private solutions are costly for women. They also exacerbate gender inequalities by devaluing caregiving work as "women's work." Men rarely incur the financial costs associated with parenthood because their employment rates and hours of work are generally insensitive to the presence or ages of their children. These arrangements do penalize men in another important respect, however, by marginalizing their participation in the home and in the care of their children.

Government policies that currently exist in many European countries support parents' decisions to limit their labor force engagement by providing national health insurance programs that cover all citizens and by prohibiting discrimination against workers who choose part-time work. The European Union Directive on Part-Time Work encourages member states to eliminate obstacles to part-time work and requires pay and benefit parity. Without such discrimination measures, a woman who chooses to work part time instead of full time may be forced to sacrifice substantial compensation and career opportunities. The European approach also serves to improve the quality of part-time work by reducing the segregation of part-time workers into a limited range of occupations and industries. Many of these policies are not new. Since 1978, for example, Sweden has offered parents the right to work six hours a day at prorated pay until their children reach the age of eight.

Other parents in the United States solve their child-care needs by adjusting their work schedules, for example, with couples working opposite shifts and engaging in "split-shift parenting." One-third of all parents in the United States and one-half of single parents work nonstandard hours. Split-shift parenting has the advantage of engaging fathers in caregiving and providing parental care for children. It is also problematic. Research indicates that couples who rely on one parent working nonstandard hours report more health problems, lower marital quality, and a higher likelihood of divorce. Children in these families have also been found to fare worse on developmental and school outcomes than other children.

To improve the lives of these children and their families, certain societal shifts are necessary. For instance, in the United States, men still face gendered expectations in the job market that limit their caregiving choices. Despite the existence of the Family and Medical Leave Act (FMLA) of 1993, employer surveys report that the majority of managers believe that parental leaves are inappropriate for men. A dual-earner/dual-carer society would require crucial changes in attitudes, as men and women would engage symmetrically in both paid work and unpaid domestic labor. That outcome would involve men shifting a substantial number of hours from the labor market to the home while women would shift a more modest number of hours from the home to the labor market. Families, however, will not be able to bring about these societal shifts on their own. Instead, employer cooperation and public policy provisions are necessary.

One crucial government policy is paid family leave. Paid family leave policies encompass: programs such as maternity leave (granted to mothers around the time of childbirth), paternity leave (granted to fathers around the time of childbirth), parental leaves (granted to both mothers and fathers for extended periods of time, generally following maternity or paternity leaves), and leave for family reasons (provided to attend to children's unpredictable needs throughout childhood). Many Western nations provide various forms of leaves, helping to ensure job security for mothers and wage replacement for several months as well. In addition, securing fathers' rights and benefits—and encouraging their usage—is essential for the establishment of a dual-earner/dual-carer society. The Nordic countries stand out among other Western nations for their commitment to encouraging fathers to take up their benefits. These countries have established what are known as "daddy-quotas" in which leave periods not taken by the father are not transferable to the mother. Instead, if the father does not use his leave, it is lost to the family. Such policies help establish a cultural norm where paternity leave is encouraged.

In the United States, in contrast, while the FMLA grants some new parents the right to *unpaid* leave—usually up to 12 weeks per year—paid leave is much more limited. The lack of paid leave deprives parents of caregiving time, strains families' finances, and exacerbates gender inequality. Fewer than half of employed women and the great majority of employed men have no paid leave rights at all, forcing many to either leave employment following childbirth or adoption or return to work after only a short break. In the United States, the absence of paid leave leads to the result that nearly 80 percent of employees fail to take advantage of their FMLA-provided leave when needed due to their inability to afford unpaid leave. As it stands, the FMLA contributes to gender inequality despite the fact that men and women have exactly the same rights under the law. The gender earnings gap results in couples being more likely to decide that the mother should take the leave (and forgo her pay) since her income is likely to be the lower one. Like the mother who works part time, those who take unpaid family leaves often incur a "mommy tax" and may face a lifetime of economic penalties for their decision. In many European countries, gender inequalities in employment and care are ameliorated by family leave provisions that provide leave rights and benefits for both mothers and fathers. While family leave varies substantially across countries, the common denominator for many countries other than the United States is wage replacement, whether partial or full.

Beyond family leave provisions, a dual-earner/dual-carer society requires some overall adjustments in working time regulations. Throughout Europe, for instance, the standard workweek has been shortened for a variety of reasons, often related to helping employees meet their family's caregiving needs. In the United States, the standard workweek has not been reduced in over six decades, and average annual work hours have actually risen in recent years, hindering American families' abilities to provide adequate child care. While in the United States the Fair Labor Standards Act (FLSA) of 1938 set the standard workweek at 40 hours, it is notable for what is *not* addressed. The FLSA does not prohibit mandatory overtime; its regulations do not apply to salaried professionals, nor does it mandate maximum weekly work hours as labor laws in many European countries do. Additionally, the FLSA provides no protections for part-time workers (other than the minimum wage), or annual vacation rights, or extra compensation for individuals working nonstandard shifts—all of which are provided in most other Western nations. A growing share of the United States labor force, primarily salaried professionals, is exempt from overtime requirements as well. Thus, many employees in the United States receive inadequate protections under the FLSA.

In contrast, throughout the rest of the Western world, numerous working time policies have been established to help families—for example, by decreasing weekly work hours (usually to the range of 35 to 39 hours), by making high-quality part-time work available, and, finally, by ensuring levels of vacation time that allow parents to spend substantial periods of time with their families. France, for instance, has reduced its workweek to 35 hours, in part, to support families. Additionally, the law applies to virtually all workers, including many salaried executives who would be exempt from FLSA—and it is enforced. While workers in the United States have no rights to vacation time, European countries offer generous vacation time to workers, generally starting at a minimum of four weeks per year. This can, of course, be used by families to provide care for their children during the summer break from school.

A dual-earner/dual-carer society also must necessarily take into consideration school schedules, particularly the length of the school day versus the length of the average work-day, and the care needs of older children during summers and other school holidays. In order to avoid having millions of unsupervised children due to such incompatible sched-ules, more flexible working arrangements and extended family leave arrangements could be solutions to the current incompatibility between the work schedules of most parents and the school schedules of their children. Throughout the rest of the Western world, vari-ous solutions have been crafted to address this dilemma such as longer school years, lon-ger school days, and flexible working arrangements. Although changes in school calendars are much discussed in the United States, this discussion usually focuses on how best to improve student achievements. Little attention has been given to the ways in which such changes might help parents solve some of their work-family conflicts or affect the recruit-ment of men and women into teaching.

EARLY CHILDHOOD EDUCATION AND CARE POLICIES

In addition to time for caregiving, parents need safe, high-quality, and affordable alterna-tives to direct parental care. The largely private child-care system in the United States is widely regarded as a system in crisis. In part, the crisis results from the high cost of non-parental child care. These costs average about 9 percent of family earnings per month, roughly equal to or higher than tuition at public colleges in most states. In addition to cost concerns, however, there are quality concerns involved with privatized child-care solu-tions. In the United States, child care is regulated primarily for health and safety issues. There is little regulation of caregiver qualifications or wages outside of public early edu-cation programs. Ironically, although child-care costs are prohibitive for many families, child-care professionals, overwhelmingly women, are among the most poorly paid of all workers in the United States and most lack employment benefits. One result, clearly, is the impoverishment of many women who work as child-care professionals. A second is compromises in child-care quality. Women who work as child-care providers have gener-ally low educational levels, little or no specialized training in the field, and very high rates of turnover. Given that adult-child interactions are the primary factor in child-care quality, it is not surprising that the overall quality of care provided by these workers is mediocre, on average, and poor in many settings. It is America's most vulnerable children, those from impoverished or otherwise disadvantaged families, who suffer the greatest conse-quences from poor-quality care, low-income families who bear the heaviest cost burden for purchasing private care, and women who pay the "gender penalty" for working in the largely female, poorly paid child-care workforce.

Early childhood education and care in a number of other industrialized countries resolves many of these problems and inequalities by ensuring access to affordable, high-quality care for children. Care is provided for all children above the age of three in most of the countries in Western Europe, with government assuming 80 to 100 percent of costs. In several, public child care is also widely available for children under three. These national governments also set standards for program quality and the education and com-pensation of child-care and early education professionals. Early childhood educators in other industrialized countries are typically highly educated and earn wages that are at or even above the average for other workers. As a result, care is widely available to families, regardless of income; overall quality is high; and women are not impoverished by their commitment to caregiving and early education professions.

For the United States to support dual-earner/dual-carer arrangements, transforming child care from a market-based to a largely public system is essential. Most fundamentally, access to care must be an entitlement and a much larger share of the costs of providing high-quality care must be assumed by government. The government currently pays an estimated one-third or less of these costs; the remainder are paid out-of-pocket by parents or through the "donated" labor of other family members who care for children without compensation. A more equitable distribution of 80 percent of costs to government and 20 percent to parents, the average in many European countries, would ensure access to care for all families, equalize labor market opportunities for men and women, and reduce the gender inequalities that result from low wages for child-care professionals. In addition to sharing the costs, the government has a critical responsibility to set and enforce standards for program quality, professional qualifications, and compensation.

In their call for an expansion of public child care and early education options, Gornick and Meyers (2003, 2004, 2005) differ from many feminists who advocate for extensive reliance on substitute care in order to reduce gender inequalities by freeing women to work as much as men. The dual-earner/dual-carer perspective emphasizes the role of child care as a mechanism to support employment opportunities for both mothers and fathers and to enhance child development. It also emphasizes the importance of parental care, by both mothers and fathers, and particularly for very young children.

The benefits of this combination of policies could be substantial for children who would have both time with their parents and high-quality care outside the home. These benefits are documented in a growing body of research that links high-quality child care to children's cognitive development and school readiness, a particularly crucial measure from an educator's perspective. Children from low-income and otherwise disadvantaged homes appear to show the most benefit from high-quality child care and suffer the most from poor-quality care. The disproportionate impact on low-income children has particularly important implications in the United States, where working families are far more likely to be poor or near-poor than are those in other Western countries. As of 2000, almost 20 percent of children in the United States were living in families classified as officially poor and as many as 40 percent to be in "near-poor" families that have incomes below 200 percent of the official poverty line.

PROSPECTS FOR WORK-FAMILY POLICIES IN THE UNITED STATES

There are many obstacles to the adoption of work-family policies in the United States and even more obstacles to implementation of the entire package of work-family policies proposed by Gornick and Meyers (2003, 2004, 2005). A primary obstacle is cost or the perception of what the cost of such policies might be. In the rest of the Western world, most of these policies are funded through payroll taxes and/or general revenues. In the Western nations that provide the most generous benefits, such as Denmark and Finland, expenditures on family leave and early childhood care and education programs constitute less than 2 percent of Gross Domestic Product. The United States currently spends about one-tenth that amount, but it seems unlikely that even this minuscule amount will be increased unless there is considerable demand, mobilized and communicated to government. Private dilemmas for American families will need to be translated into political demands.

Hewlett, Rankin, and West (2002) make a similar argument calling for "taking parenting public" and the necessity of building a new social movement composed of parents. They argue that a cultural shift is necessary, primarily a transformation in attitudes that gives a higher priority to parenting and places it on the public agenda. While Americans continue to embrace market solutions to their work-family dilemmas, the current failure of those privatized solutions may well present an opportunity for conversations about engaging more government support for parenting modeled after our Western counterparts.

It seems likely that women will embrace both the effort to take parenting public and the vision of the dual-earner/dual-carer society to a greater extent than men. Many women are already trying to combine earning and caring, and they are likely to welcome policies that would help them to stay connected with the labor market while still bearing and rearing children. It is less certain whether men will welcome the opportunity to take paternity leaves, even well-paid ones, so that they can play a more active role in parenting. Despite the availability of various programs in other countries that offer leaves to fathers, men's take-up of these benefits remains well below that of women everywhere. Employer resistance, workers' perceptions of employer resistance, and the continuing gender wage gap all contribute to fathers' lower take-up. Despite the fact that such public programs and expanded workplace supports exist and enable couples to choose more egalitarian parenting and work arrangements, low take-up of these benefits by fathers is telling. Thus, there is still some obvious resistance to gender equality throughout the Western world when it comes to work and family obligations. Beyond that, however, there is the added push toward gender parity in that, as family issues become politicized, they move out of the marginalized "women's domain." Family issues can begin to garner attention in the public sphere and, particularly, on political agendas.

When it comes to government-funded child care, Americans may be able to look to their own country for some inspiration. Since the United States was historically the world leader in its extension of public education to all children, one way to develop support for government-regulated and financed child-care programs might be to present them as simply an extension of existing school systems. Many school districts already provide some preschool education, although most avoid providing care for children under the age of three. Also, a child-care system tied to public schools runs the risk of extending to younger children the inequities in funding and quality for which the American locally based school system has become infamous. A better model might be a federal program like Head Start that has a demonstrated record of success and could be extended to children of all socioeconomic backgrounds and of even younger ages.

To move toward a national child-care system and other policies that support earner-carer families will require major changes in the role of the American government. Many parents in the United States are struggling with enormous problems as they try to meet the responsibilities of involved parenting and allocate work and care in ways that are fair and economically feasible. But, they are also being told by the media and some governmental officials that these are problems of their own making and, therefore, they are personally responsible for solving them. People need a broader perspective from which to assess what many regard as their personal problems or shortcomings. Educators can help people develop this broader perspective by providing valuable information about the widespread nature of these problems, the already existing policies and programs in other countries that can help to alleviate them, and alternatives to American competitive individualism such as the dual-earner/dual-carer society in which governmental policies are truly designed to help families and promote gender equality.

REFERENCES AND FURTHER READINGS

Crompton, R. (Ed.). (1999). *Restructuring gender relations and employment: The decline of the male breadwinner.* Oxford, England: Oxford University Press.

Gornick, J., & Meyers, M.K. (2003). *Families that work: Policies for reconciling parenthood and employment.* New York: Russell Sage Foundation.

Gornick, J., & Meyers, M.K. (2004). Welfare regimes in relation to paid work and care. In J. Zollinger Giele & E. Holst (Eds.), *Changing life patterns in Western industrial society* (pp. 45–67). Amsterdam, Netherlands: Elsevier Science Press.

Gornick, J., & Meyers, M.K. (2005). Supporting a dual-earner/dual-career society. In J. Heymann & C. Beem (Eds.). *Unfinished work: Building equality and democracy in an era of working families* (pp. 371–408). New York: New Press.

Hewlett, S.A., Rankin, N., & West, C. (2002). *Taking parenting public: The case for a new social movement.* New York: Rowman & Littlefield.

Kathleen J. Fitzgerald

Janet C. Gornick

Marcia K. Meyers

Name Index

Subject Index

Numbers in **boldface** refer to the main entry on or overview of the subject.

About the Editors and Contributors

Barbara J. Bank is Professor Emerita of Sociology and of Women Studies at the University of Missouri–Columbia. She has been honored with a Fulbright Senior Scholar Award, visiting fellowships at the Australian National University, and three awards for outstanding teaching. Her scholarly presentations and publications, including *Contradictions in Women's Education: Traditionalism, Careerism, and Community at a Single-Sex College* (2003), reflect her interests in the areas of social psychology, gender studies, and the sociology of youth and education.

Sara Delamont is Reader in Sociology at Cardiff University, Wales, U.K. She was elected an Academician of the U.K. Academy of Social Sciences in 2000. In 1984, she was the first woman President of the British Educational Research Association, and she was also the first woman Dean of Social Sciences at Cardiff University. She is currently editing two journals, *Teaching and Teacher Education* and *Qualitative Research,* and her most recent single-authored book is *Feminist Sociology* (2003). Her ongoing research interests include an ethnography of how the Brazilian martial art capoeira is taught in the United Kingdom.

Catherine Marshall is Professor of Educational Administration and Policy at the University of North Carolina, Chapel Hill. Her gender studies focus on leadership and policy in education. She has also studied gender policy internationally. Her *Feminist Critical Policy Analysis* (1997) demands policy attention to a range of gender issues. Marshall also conducts research on state education politics and gender issues in education careers. She initiated the formation of Leadership for Social Justice, an international network for equity advocacy. Her books, *Reframing Educational Politics for Social Justice* (2005) and *Leadership for Social Justice* (2006), are used to shift the educational administration field away from managerial assumptions to equity advocacy leadership.

Sandra Acker is Professor in the Department of Sociology and Equity Studies, Ontario Institute for Studies in Education of the University of Toronto in Canada where she has recently served as Associate Dean (Social Sciences), School of Graduate Studies. She has worked in the United States, Britain, and Canada as a sociologist of education, with interests in gender and education, teachers' work, and higher education. Her current research is focused on university tenure practices, women academics in leadership positions, graduate student experiences, and transitions in teacher education institutions. She is the author of *Gendered Education* (1994) and *The Realities of Teachers' Work: Never a Dull Moment* (1999).

Lyndsay J. Agans is a doctoral student and research assistant in Higher Education at the University of Denver. Her scholarship focuses on organization and governance as it relates to change and reform for equality in higher education.

Debra Barbezat is Professor of Economics at Colby College in Waterville, Maine. She received her PhD from the University of Michigan with an emphasis on labor economics. Her research has focused specifically on academic labor markets including male-female pay gaps, the effects of collective bargaining, and the influence of seniority, job mobility, and salary structure on academic salaries.

Rachel Hile Bassett is Assistant Professor of English at Indiana University–Purdue University at Fort Wayne. Her research focuses on early modern English literature, and she is the editor of *Parenting and Professing: Balancing Family Work with an Academic Career* (2005).

Karen Bojar is Professor of English and Coordinator of Women's Studies at Community College of Philadelphia where she has taught for the past 30 years. She has published extensively on feminist pedagogy and the relationship between women's studies, service learning, and feminist activism. She has had a long history in grassroots feminist politics. Currently, she serves as President of Philadelphia NOW, chairs its Political Action Committee, and is on the board of the Pennsylvania NOW-PAC. She is also a board member of NARAL-PA Foundation.

Linda K. Carter is a graduate student in Economics at Vanderbilt University in Nashville, Tennessee. Her research interests include the economic history of education in the United States and the use of innovative strategies to improve educational outcomes in less-developed countries. She is the author of *A Hard Day's Night: Evening Schools and Child Labor in Early 20th Century New Jersey,* a study of the factors determining attendance at night school among New Jersey child workers that is part of her dissertation.

Rebecca Priegert Coulter is Associate Professor in the Faculty of Education, University of Western Ontario, Canada. She has published several articles and chapters on gender equity policies and practices in Canada and coedited *History Is Hers: Women Educators in Twentieth-Century Ontario* (2005). In recognition of her contributions to the education of girls and women, she won the 2005 Achievement Award from the Canadian Association for the Study of Women and Education.

Amanda Datnow is Associate Professor at the Rossier School of Education at the University of Southern California. Her research focuses on the politics and policies of school reform, with a particular focus on educators' professional lives and issues of equity. She is the author of *Integrating Educational Systems for Successful Reform in Diverse Contexts* (2006) and numerous other books and articles.

Miriam E. David is Professor of Policy Studies in Education and Associate Director for Higher Education of the Teaching and Learning Research Programme based at the Institute of Education, University of London, U.K. She has an international reputation for her research and scholarly publications on education, family, gender, and policy sociology.

Miriam Hernandez Dimmler is a PhD candidate in the Clinical Science Program at the University of California, Berkeley. Her research focuses on family socialization processes in ethnic minority and low-income families, school-based interventions for family, urban education, and minority mental health.

Anthony Gary Dworkin is Professor of Sociology at the University of Houston, Texas; cofounder of that university's Sociology of Education Research Group; and editor of *The New Inequality Series* at SUNY Press. Additionally, he serves on the council of Research Committee 04 (Sociology of Education) of the International Sociological Association. His publications include works on teacher burnout and student dropout behavior; minority-majority relations and racial and ethnic stereotyping; gender roles; the impact of accountability systems on student learning outcomes; and, most recently, accountability and high-stakes testing under No Child Left Behind. He is currently coediting *The International Handbook on Research on Teachers and Teaching.*

Janet Enke is Chair of the Social Science Department at Metropolitan State University in St. Paul, Minnesota. She has written on young women's experiences in high school varsity athletics and has been recognized four times for her excellence in teaching.

Berenice Malka Fisher is Professor Emerita of Educational Philosophy at New York University. Her articles and chapters address topics as diverse as women role models, the impact of disability on women's friendships, and feminism and political theater. Her book, *No Angel in the Classroom: Teaching Through Feminist Discourse,* won the 2002 Distinguished Publication Award of the Association for Women in Psychology. Her current interests include feminist education, political discourse, and the peaceful resolution of political conflict.

Kathleen J. Fitzgerald is Assistant Professor of Sociology at Columbia College in Columbia, Missouri. Her research and teaching interests include gender, race, education, family, and social policy.

Elizabeth Glennie is a Research Scientist at Duke University's Center for Child and Family Policy and Director of the North Carolina Education Research Data Center. Much of her research has focused on the American educational system with an emphasis on school engagement and educational achievement. In particular, she analyzes factors that influence student engagement with school and those affecting teacher job satisfaction and turnover rates.

Janet C. Gornick is Professor of Political Science and Sociology at The Graduate Center, City University of New York (CUNY), and Professor of Political Science at Baruch

College, also part of CUNY. She is also Director of the Luxembourg Income Study, a cross-national research institute and data archive located in Luxembourg. She has written extensively on work-family reconciliation policies in the industrialized countries and is coauthor of *Families That Work: Policies for Reconciling Parenthood and Employment* (2003).

Linda Grant is Professor of Sociology at the University of Georgia, Adjunct Professor in the Social Foundations of Education program, and an affiliated faculty member of the Institute for Women's Studies. She recently completed a term as deputy editor of the journal *Sociology of Education.* Her research focuses on equity and inequality in education and in medical and scientific careers.

Sandra Harding is Vice-Chancellor and President of James Cook University, Queensland, Australia. She is a sociologist whose key scholarly interests revolve around the sociology of work, organization, and inequality. Her current research is focused on the conditions for enterprise development and organization survey methodology. She has a keen professional interest in education policy and management.

Chris Haywood is Programme Director of Media, Communication, and Cultural Studies at the University of Newcastle upon Tyne in the United Kingdom. He has published widely in the area of sexuality, gender, and age and is coauthor of *Men and Masculinities* (2003) and *Gender, Culture and Society: Contemporary Femininities and Masculinities* (2006).

Lea Hubbard is Associate Professor in the School of Leadership and Education Sciences at the University of San Diego, California. Her work focuses on educational inequities, as they exist across ethnicity, class, and gender. Her latest book, *Reform as Learning: When School Reform Collided with Organizational Culture and Community Politics in San Diego* (2006), combines sociocultural theories of learning with organizational life and policy adaptation.

Jerry A. Jacobs is Merriam Term Professor of Sociology at the University of Pennsylvania. He has served as editor of the *American Sociological Review* and President of the Eastern Sociological Society. His research has addressed a number of aspects of women's employment including authority, earnings, working conditions, part-time work, and entry into male-dominated occupations. He is coauthor of *The Time Divide* (2004). His research has been funded by the National Science Foundation, the Spencer Foundation, the Sloan Foundation, Atlantic Philanthropies, and the Macy Foundation. His current research projects include a study of women's entry into the medical profession, funded by the Macy Foundation, and a study of working time and work-family conflict among university faculty.

Kerri Keegan is a recent graduate of Hofstra University's School Counseling program in Hempstead, New York. She plans to obtain a position as a school counselor. Her research interest is in prevention programs for teenagers focused on self-injury and bullying.

Deirdre M. Kelly is Professor in the Department of Educational Studies at the University of British Columbia. Her research interests include alternative girlhoods, critical feminist policy analysis of schooling, and teaching for social justice. She is the author of *Last*

Chance High: How Girls and Boys Drop In and Out of Alternative Schools (1993) and *Pregnant with Meaning: Teen Mothers and the Politics of Inclusive Schooling* (2000), which won a 2003 American Educational Studies Association Critic's Choice Award.

Kimberly Kelly is a doctoral candidate in sociology at the University of Georgia. Her research focuses on gender, women's activism, inequality, and interaction. She is currently studying grassroots abortion activism.

Charlotte A. Kunkel is Associate Professor of Sociology at Luther College in Decorah, Iowa. She specializes in gender studies and has taught widely in sociology and women's studies. She actively pursues research and scholarship that promotes equality for all. Her current interests include diversity education and women's transnational identities and immigration.

John Wesley Lowery is Associate Professor of Educational Studies in the College of Education at Oklahoma State University in Stillwater. He has written extensively on topics related to student affairs and higher education, particularly legal and legislative issues.

Mairtin Mac an Ghaill is Professor of Sociology at the University of Birmingham in the United Kingdom. His current research involves exploration of the figure of the male migrant among the Irish diaspora in England. He is the author of *The Making of Men: Masculinities, Sexualities and Schooling* (1994) and *Contemporary Racisms and Ethnicities* (1999).

Margaret E. Madden is Provost and Vice-President of Academic Affairs at the State University of New York at Potsdam. A social psychologist, she specializes in the psychology of gender and was President of the Society for the Psychology of Women (Division 35 of the American Psychological Association) in 2004. Recent publications focus on enhancing the representation of gender and ethnicity in the psychology curriculum and analyses of women's and gender issues in higher education administration.

Laurie Mandel is founder of The GET.A.VOICE™ Project (www.getavoice.net), an organization that proactively addresses name-calling and gender-based verbal violence in schools through awareness, empowerment, and leadership. She is an American Association of University Women fellow and is an educator at Murphy Junior High School, Three Village Schools, New York. In 2004, she was the recipient of the Myra Sadker Curriculum Award from American University for her work on gender issues at the middle school level.

Robert A. Margo is Professor of Economics and African-American Studies at Boston University in Massachusetts and a Research Associate of the National Bureau of Economic Research. A specialist in the economic history of the American economy, his books include *Race and Schooling in the South (1990), 1880–1950: An Economic History* (2000), and *Women's Work: American Schoolteachers, 1650–1920* (2001).

Donna M. Mertens is Professor in the Department of Educational Foundations and Research at Gallaudet University in Washington, DC. She writes extensively about the merger of the disability community and the transformative approach to research in such books as *Research and Evaluation Methods in Education and Psychology: Integrating Diversity with Quantitative, Qualitative, and Mixed Methods* (2005).

Marcia K. Meyers is Professor of Social Work and Public Affairs and Director of the West Coast Poverty Center at the University of Washington. She has published extensively on issues of poverty and social welfare policy in the United States and in a comparative context. She has coauthored *Families That Work: Policies for Reconciling Parenthood and Employment* (2003).

Karen Monkman is Associate Professor of Comparative Education, Social and Cultural Foundations of Education, and Educational Policy Studies at DePaul University in Chicago, Illinois. Her educational research relates to gender, immigration, nonformal education, and social change.

Judith Mounty is Director of the Center for American Sign Language Literacy at Gallaudet University in Washington, DC. She focuses her work in the area of psychological health in the deaf community and coedited *Assessment of Deaf and Hard of Hearing Adults: Critical Issues in Testing and Evaluation* (2005), which addresses measurement issues specific to the deaf population.

Keith B. O'Neill is a doctoral student in the Higher Education Administration program at Bowling Green State University in Ohio. He has been active in the National Association of Student Personnel Administrators, the Ohio Association of Student Personnel Administrators, and Sigma Pi fraternity.

Michele Paludi is President of Human Resources Management Solutions and Participating Full Professor of Management at Union Graduate College. She has published several texts on sexual harassment, including *Ivory Power: Sexual Harassment on Campus* (1990), which received the Myers Center Award for an Outstanding Book on Human Rights in the United States.

Cynthia Fabrizio Pelak is Assistant Professor of Sociology at the University of Memphis in Tennessee. She has published articles on gender/race/class and sport in the United States and South Africa. She is currently working on a project examining the persistence of sexist naming practices of women's athletic teams at universities and colleges in the southern United States.

Liviu Popoviciu is Lecturer in Communication and Cultural Studies at the University of Newcastle upon Tyne in the United Kingdom. He has a particular interest in exploring the interconnections among globalization, nationalism, and subjectivity. He has recently completed his PhD dissertation entitled *Children and National Identity. How Children Conceptualise Identity: A Comparison of Case Studies from Romania and England.*

C. Roger Rees is Professor in the Department of Health Studies, Physical Education, and Human Performance Science at Adelphi University in Garden City, New York. He has written extensively on school sports, including *Lessons of the Locker Room: The Myth of School Sports* (1994). His research focuses on how to make interscholastic athletics a more positive influence on the lives of schoolchildren.

Joanne Roberts is a Research Scientist at the Wellesley Centers for Women at Wellesley College in Massachusetts. She conducts research in the areas of quality of early care and education, child-care voucher use, and school readiness.

Wendy Wagner Robeson is a Research Scientist at the Wellesley Centers for Women at Wellesley College in Massachusetts. Her research includes early care and education studies, school readiness, and the National Institute of Child Health and Development Study of Early Child Care and Youth Development.

Mary Ann Danowitz Sagaria is Professor of Higher Education at the University of Denver and a 2007 Fulbright Scholar at the Vienna University of Economics and Business Administration. Her research focuses on leadership, academic careers, governance and administration, and gender and racial equality.

Nilofar Sami is a PhD student in the Clinical Science Program at the University of California, Berkeley. Her research focuses on risk and resilience in children and adolescents, especially from impoverished backgrounds including immigrants and refugees, and research-based community interventions that promote academic achievement and well-being.

Daniel Sciarra is Associate Professor of Counselor Education and Chairperson of the Department of Counseling, Rehabilitation, Special Education, and Research at Hofstra University in Hempstead, New York. He is both a licensed psychologist and a certified school counselor. His main research interests are in multicultural counseling and the role of the school counselor in the academic achievement of Latino students.

Charol Shakeshaft is Professor in the Department of Foundations, Leadership, and Policy Studies at Hofstra University where she teaches courses on gender, statistical analysis, evaluation methodology, and school safety. She is author of a Congressionally mandated study on educator sexual misconduct and is currently examining the ways in which states collect information on school violence, as well as the extent of sexual abuse of special education students.

Randall G. Shelden is Professor of Criminal Justice at the University of Nevada–Las Vegas. He is the author of several books and articles on the subject of crime and delinquency, including *Youth Gangs in American Society* (2004) and *Delinquency and Juvenile Justice in America* (2006). His Web site is www.sheldensays.com.

Bridget Sledz is a recent graduate of Hofstra University's School Counseling program in Hempstead, New York. She is currently working as an academic adviser at Polytechnic University in Brooklyn, New York. Her research interest is in factors affecting retention rates in higher education.

Elizabeth Stearns is Assistant Professor of Sociology at the University of North Carolina at Charlotte. Research interests include sociology of education, interracial friendships, and inequality in the contemporary United States. Her recent research efforts have focused on the interplay of individual and school-level characteristics on students' probability of dropping out of high school and student engagement with formal education. She is a contributing author to *Race in the Schools: Perpetuating White Dominance?* (2003).

Nan Stein has been a Senior Research Scientist at the Center for Research on Women at Wellesley College since 1992 where she directs national research projects on sexual harassment, gender violence, teen dating violence, and bullying in schools. She has written several curricula for schools on these issues and has published dozens of articles in the popular press as well as in educational and legal journals. She has also served as an expert witness in lawsuits about sexual harassment and gender violence in schools.

Nelly P. Stromquist is Professor of Comparative and International Education in the Rossier School of Education at the University of Southern California. She is interested in issues of gender equity, state policy, and social change. Two of her most recent books are *Feminist Organizations and Social Transformation in Latin America* (2006) and *Education in a Globalized World: The Connectivity of Economic Power, Technology, and Knowledge* (2002). She is former President of the Comparative and International Education Society and a 2005–2006 Fulbright New Century Scholar.

Marilyn Tallerico is Professor of Education at Binghamton University in Binghamton, New York. Her research interests include gender and politics in public school educational leadership; women and the superintendency; promoting diversity, equity, and excellence in educational administration; and superintendent–school board relationships.

Robert Vitelli is Director of Development at Long Island Gay and Lesbian Youth where he has worked extensively with gay, lesbian, bisexual, and transgender youth to develop the organization's Safe Schools Initiative into one of the largest and most comprehensive programs of its kind in the United States. He is also an instructor of human sexuality at Nassau Community College.

Marcus B. Weaver-Hightower is Assistant Professor of Educational Foundations and Research at the University of North Dakota. He was a Fulbright scholar to Australia who has written extensively on masculinity and the education of boys.

Rhona S. Weinstein is Professor of Psychology at the University of California, Berkeley. She has written extensively on the multilayered dynamics of academic expectations and self-fulfilling prophecies, with implications for school culture change. She is the author of *Reaching Higher: The Power of Expectations in Schooling* (2002), which won the American Educational Research Association Division K Book Award and the Virginia and Warren Stone Prize from Harvard University Press.

Amy E. Wells is Faculty Research Fellow and Associate Professor of Higher Education in the Department of Leadership and Counselor Education at the University of Mississippi in Oxford. She has written on the history and development of education in the South, Rockefeller philanthropy, and multicultural Greek organizations.

Edward G. Whipple is Vice-President for Student Affairs and Adjunct Associate Professor of Higher Education and Student Affairs at Bowling Green State University in Ohio. He has served in a variety of administrative roles in Greek life and student affairs and has published a number of articles on topics related to these areas. He has served in leadership positions at the national level with the National Association of Student Personnel Administrators, the National Association of State Universities and Land-Grant Colleges, the Association of Fraternity Advisors, and Phi Delta Theta International Fraternity.

Barbara Morrow Williams, JD, PhD, is an education organizational consultant living in Columbia, Missouri. She has authored articles on African American mothers and cultural capital and coauthored articles on school leadership. Her research and writing interests include women, aging in leadership roles, schools as organizations, and First and Fourth Amendment issues in organizations. She was a David L. Clark Seminar Scholar in 2005, and her dissertation case study of a female, African American superintendent was nominated for the Politics of Education Dissertation Award for 2006.

Amy Wilson is Assistant Professor in the Department of Educational Foundations and Research at Gallaudet University in Washington, DC. She is Director of the International Development for People with Disabilities Program.

Sarah Winslow-Bowe is Assistant Professor of Sociology at Clemson University in South Carolina. Her research interests focus on gender inequality, the intersections of work and family, and the life course. In addition to her publications on gender inequality and work-family issues in academia, she has written about trends in work-family conflict from the 1970s through the 1990s and the relationship between welfare reform and women's enrollment in postsecondary education. Her current research examines persistence and variation in wives' income advantage and its relationship to reported levels of marital conflict. This research has been supported by the Woodrow Wilson Foundation and recognized by the Sociologists for Women in Society and the Family Sections of the American Sociological Association and the Society for the Study of Social Problems.

Leslie R. Wolfe is President of the Center for Women Policy Studies, a multiethnic feminist think tank in Washington, DC, founded in 1972. She was Director of the Women's Educational Equity Act Program in the U.S. Department of Education from 1979 to 1983; her previous federal government career began at the U.S. Commission on Civil Rights, where she was Deputy Director of the Women's Rights Program. After leaving government service, Wolfe served as Director of the Project on Equal Education Rights of the NOW Legal Defense and Education Fund before joining the Center for Women Policy Studies in 1988.

Deborah Worley is a doctoral student and graduate assistant in Higher Education in the Department of Leadership and Counselor Education at the University of Mississippi in Oxford. She has extensive experience in student affairs, including career services, experiential education, and student leadership development. Her research emphases include student assessment and learning outcomes for master's students.